Bronze Statue of Buddha at Kamakura

ACROSS

AMERICA AND ASIA

NOTES OF A FIVE YEARS' JOURNEY

AROUND THE WORLD

AND OF RESIDENCE IN

ARIZONA, JAPAN

AND

CHINA

BY

RAPHAEL PUMPELLY
Professor in Harvard University, and sometime Mining Engineer in the service of the Chinese and Japanese Governments

NEW YORK
LEYPOLDT & HOLT
1870

STEREOTYPED BY
DENNIS BRO'S & THORNE,
AUBURN, N. Y.

PRINTED BY
THE TROW & SMITH BOOK M'F'G CO.,
50 & 52 GREEN STREET, N. Y.

As so many of the following pages relate to experiences illustrating the wisdom of that diplomatic policy which, in bringing China into the circle of interdependent nations, promises good to the whole world, I dedicate them to the chief author of that policy—

TO

ANSON BURLINGAME.

MERCATOR CHART, SHOWING THE AUTHOR'S ROUTE.

PREFACE.

After preparing the volume of "Geological Researches in China, Mongolia, and Japan," for publication by the Smithsonian Institution, I was induced to write a simple narration of a journey which encircled the earth in the Northern temperate zone, at a time of unusual interest in several of the countries visited.

The social disorganization in Arizona presented a phase of border life of the worst type indeed, but most valuable as showing the effect of the absence of the usual restraints upon society.

Extensive travel in the interior of Japan and China under commission from the native governments, and the long journey from China over the table land of Central Asia, and through Siberia to Europe, brought me face to face with the inhabitants of these interesting countries, and with the influences which Nature has used in moulding them to their present forms.

I have tried to present in a continued series of sketches these important regions, which are being brought, by the reaction of the spirit of the age upon their natural capacities, into the circle of interdependent nations.

The incidents and adventures of an eventful journey are used freely, as forming some of the best illustrations of the social condition of the races in the midst of which they occurred.

During a residence of several months at Mr. Burlingame's house in Peking, in the most interesting period of diplomacy in China, I was enabled to gain an insight into many questions affecting the foreign and internal policy of the empire. The knowledge thus acquired I have sought to embody in the chapter on Western Policy in China.

The MS. was finished early in 1868; the policy, therefore, which is recommended in reference to our Indian question was arrived at before the adoption of substantially the same means by the present administration.

Those of my readers who are interested in Japanese Art will feel as much indebted to Mr. John La Farge as I am, for kindly writing the chapter on that subject.

The cuts facing pages 175 and 180, and the maps of Yesso and of the Yang Ho district, are taken from the Geological Researches in China, Mongolia, and Japan, by permission of the Smithsonian Institution.

The wood-cuts are engraved by Messrs. W. J. and H. D. Linton. The lithographic maps and illustrations were executed under the supervision of Mr. J. Bien. I would express sincere thanks to both Mr. W. J. Linton and Mr. Bien for the especial interest they have taken in furthering the execution of the illustrations.

Finally, I would acknowledge the deep obligation I am under to the many friends abroad and at home who, by hospitality and a thousand kind actions, have smoothed the route of travel and the difficulties of publication.

R. P.

LIST OF ILLUSTRATIONS.

MAPS.

* From the author's "GEOLOGICAL RESEARCHES IN CHINA, MONGOLIA AND JAPAN." (Smithson. Inst. 1868.)

CONTENTS.

CHAPTER I.

THE OVERLAND COACH.

CHAPTER II.

THE SANTA RITA VALLEY.

CHAPTER III.

THE FRONTIER AND THE DESERT.

CHAPTER IV.

CLOSING SCENES.

CHAPTER V.

PACIFIC OCEAN.

CHAPTER VI.

YOKOHAMA.

CHAPTER VII.

YOKOHAMA (CONTINUED).

CHAPTER VIII.

POLITICS.

CHAPTER IX.

EXCURSIONS.

CHAPTER X.

FIRST JOURNEY IN YESSO.

CHAPTER XI.

RELIGIONS OF JAPAN.

CHAPTER XII.

SECOND JOURNEY IN YESSO.

CHAPTER XIII.

SECOND JOURNEY IN YESSO.

CHAPTER XIV.

JAPANESE ART.

CHAPTER XV.

INTRODUCTION TO CHINA.

CHAPTER XVI.

GEOGRAPHICAL SKETCH OF CHINA.

CHAPTER XVII.

JOURNEY UP THE YANGTZ' KIANG.

CHAPTER XVIII.

BOAT-JOURNEY ON THE UPPER YANGTZ'.

CHAPTER XIX.

THE CHINESE AS EMIGRANTS AND COLONIZERS.

CHAPTER XX.

PEKING AND ITS NEIGHBORHOOD.

CHAPTER XXI.

THE CAVERN NEAR FANGSHAN

CHAPTER XXII.

VISIT TO THE COAL MINES.

CHAPTER XXIII.

JOURNEY ALONG THE GREAT WALL.

CHAPTER XXIV.

WESTERN POLICY IN CHINA.

CHAPTER XXV.

FROM PEKING TO NAGASAKI.

CHAPTER XXVI.

THE TABLE-LAND OF CENTRAL ASIA.

CHAPTER XXVII.

SIBERIA.

CHAPTER XXVIII.

SIBERIA (CONTINUED).

APPENDIX I.

APPENDIX II.

APPENDIX III.

APPENDIX IV.

APPENDIX V.

ACROSS AMERICA AND ASIA.

CHAPTER I.

ARIZONA.

In the autumn of 1860 I reached the westernmost end of the railroad in Missouri, finishing the first, and, in point of time, the shortest stage in a journey, the end of which I had not even attempted to foresee. My immediate destination was the silver mines of the Santa Rita, in Arizona, of which I was to take charge, as mining engineer, for a year, under the resident superintendent.

Having secured the right to a back seat in the overland coach as far as Tucson, I looked forward, with comparatively little dread, to sixteen days and nights of continuous travel. But the arrival of a woman and her brother, dashed, at the very outset, my hopes of an easy journey, and obliged me to take the front seat, where, with my back to the horses, I began to foresee the coming discomfort. The coach was fitted with three seats, and these were occupied by nine passengers. As the occupants of the front and middle seats faced each other, it was necessary for these six people to interlock their knees; and there being room inside for only ten of the twelve legs, each side of the coach was graced by a foot, now dangling near the wheel, now trying in vain to find a place of support. An unusually heavy mail in the boot, by weighing down the rear, kept those of us who were on the front seat constantly bent forward, thus, by taking away all support from our backs, rendering rest at all times out of the question.

My immediate neighbors were a tall Missourian, with his wife and two young daughters; and from this family arose a large part of the discomfort of the journey. The man was a border bully, armed with revolver, knife, and rifle; the woman, a very hag, ever following the disgusting habit of dipping—filling the air, and covering her clothes with snuff; the girls, for several days overcome by sea-sickness, and in this having no regard for the clothes of their neighbors; — these were circumstances which offered slight promise of comfort on a journey which, at the best, could only be tedious and difficult.

For several days our road lay through the more barren and uninteresting parts of Missouri and Arkansas; but when we entered the Indian territory, and the fertile valley of the Red river, the scenery changed, and we seemed to have come into one of the Edens of the earth. Indeed, one of the scenes, still bright in my memory, embraced the finest and most extensive of natural park.

Coming suddenly to the brow of a high bluff we found that we had been travelling over a table-land, while beneath us lay a deep and widely-eroded valley, the further limits of which were marked by distant blue hills. The broad flat bottom-land was covered with a deep-green carpet of grass, and dotted, at intervals of a few miles, with groves of richly-colored trees. As a work of Nature it was as much more beautiful than the finest English park, as Nature had spent more centuries in perfecting it than the nobleman had spent years.

The fertile country reserved for the Indians is only partially cultivated by them. Although considerable success has attended the attempts to elevate these tribes, the ultimate result of the experiment is by no means certain. The possession of negro slaves by the Indians could not but be attended by even greater evils than the use of this labor among the white population.

Before reaching Fort Smith every male passenger in the stage had lost his hat, and most of the time allowed for breakfast at that town was used in getting new head-coverings. It turned out to be a useless expense, however, for in less than two days we were all again bareheaded. As this happens to the passengers of every stage, we estimated that not less than fifteen hundred hats were lost yearly by travellers, for the benefit of the population along the road.

After passing the Arkansas river, and travelling two or three days through the cultivated region of northeastern Texas, we came gradually to the outposts of population. The rivers became fewer, and deeper below the surface; the rolling prairie-land covered with grass gave way to dry gravelly plains, on which the increasing preponderance of species of cacti, and of the yucca, warned us of our approach to the great American desert. Soon after our entrance into this region we were one morning all started from a deep sleep by the noise of a party coming up at full gallop, and ordering the driver to halt. They were a rough-looking set of men, and we took them for robbers until their leader told us that they were "regulators," and were in search of a man who had committed a murder the previous day at a town we had passed through.

"He is a tall fellow, with blue eyes, and red beard," said the leader. "So if you have got him in there, stranger, you need'nt tote him any further, for the branch of a mesquit tree is strong enough for his neck." As I was tall, and had blue eyes and a red beard, I did not feel perfectly easy until the party left us, convinced that the object of their search was not in the stage.

The monotony of the route across the desert was somewhat varied by the immense republics, as they are commonly termed, of prairie dogs. The plains inhabited by these animals were covered by the low mounds raised over the entrance to their burrows, and separated from each other by a distance only of a few yards. As we approached them the animals disappeared; but at some distance from us, ahead and on either side, thousands of the dogs were visible, each one squatting on the top of a mound, and regarding us with the most intense curiosity. As we came nearer, one after the other suddenly plunged its head into its burrow, and, after wagging its fat body for an instant, disappeared altogether. Here and there a solemn owl, perched at the mouth of the burrow, or a rattlesnake basking at the entrance in the sun, showed that these dwellings were inhabited by other occupants than their builders. One can scarcely picture a more desolate and barren region than the southern part of the Llano Estacado between the Brazos and the Pecos rivers. Lying about 4,500 feet above the sea, it is a desert incapable of supporting other plant or animal life than scattered cacti, rattlesnakes, and lizards. Our route winding along the southern border of this region, kept on the outskirts of the Camanche country.

Here we were constantly exposed to the raids of this fierce tribe, which has steadily refused to be tamed by the usual process of treaties and presents. They were committing serious depredations along the route, and had murdered the keepers at several stations. We consequently approached the stockade station-houses with considerable anxiety, not knowing whether we should find either keepers or horses. Over this part of the road no lights were used at night, and we were thus exposed to the additional danger of having our necks broken by being upset.

The fatigue of uninterrupted travelling by day and night in a crowded coach, and in the most uncomfortable positions, was beginning to tell seriously upon all the passengers, and was producing a condition bordering on insanity. This was increased by the constant anxiety caused by the danger from Camanches. Every jolt of the stage, indeed any occurrence which started a passenger out of the state of drowsiness, was instantly magnified into an attack, and the nearest fellow-passenger was as likely to be taken for an Indian as for a friend. In some persons, this temporary mania developed itself to such a degree that their own safety and that of their fellow-travellers made it necessary to leave them at the nearest station, where sleep usually restored them before the arrival of the next stage on the following week. Instances have occurred of travellers jumping in this condition from the coach, and wandering off to a death from starvation upon the desert.

Beyond the Pecos river the scenery became more varied. The route lay over broad plains, where the surface sloped gently away from castellated and cliff-bound peaks. Here, from an hundred miles away, we could see the grand outlines of the Gaudaloupe mountains, planted like the towers and walls of a great fortress, to render still more difficult the approach to the great wastes lying to the north and east.

Over the hard surface of this country, which is everywhere a natural road, we frequently travelled at great speed, with only half-broken teams. At several stations, six wild horses were hitched blind-folded into their places. When everything was ready, the blinds were removed at a signal from the driver, and the animals started off at a run-away speed, which they kept up without slackening till the next station, generally twelve miles distant. In these cases the driver had no further control over his animals than the ability to guide them; to stop, or even check them, was entirely beyond his power; the frightened horses fairly flying over the ground, and never stopping till they drew up exhausted at the next station. Nothing but the most perfect presence of mind on the part of the driver could prevent accidents. Even this was not always enough, as was proved by a stage which we met, in which every passenger had either a bandaged head or an arm in a sling.

At El Paso we had hoped to find a larger stage. Being disappointed in this, I took a place outside, between the driver and conductor. The impossibility of sleeping had made me half delirious, and we had gone but a few miles before I nearly unseated the driver by starting suddenly out of a dream.

I was told that the safety of all the passengers demanded that I should keep awake; and as the only means of effecting this, my neighbors beat a constant tatoo with their elbows upon my ribs. During the journey from the Rio Grande to Tucson my delirium increased, and the only thing I have ever remembered of that part of the route was the sight of a large number of Indian campfires at Apache pass. My first recollection after this, is of being awakened by the report of a pistol, and of starting up to find myself in a crowded room, where a score or more of people were quarrelling at a gaming table. I had reached Tucson, and had thrown myself on the floor of the first room I could enter. A sound sleep of twelve hours had fully restored me, both in mind and body.

My first thought was to make the necessary preparations for the journey to Tubac and the Santa Rita. Having soon succeeded in securing a place in a wagon which was to start in a day or two, I gave up the interval to see the little of interest in the town and neighborhood.

It was here that I first saw the effect of an extremely dry and transparent atmosphere. All the ravines and rocks of the Santa Rita mountains are distinctly visible from Tucson, a distance of more than thirty miles; and in the very dry season, as at the time of my visit, the tall pines on the summit could be clearly distinguished standing out against the sky.

Accustomed to judge of heights and distances in the atmosphere of the Eastern States and Europe, I did not hesitate, on being first asked to guess at the distance, to place it at less than ten miles.

The most interesting objects of curiosity in the town were the two great masses of meteoric iron which have been mentioned by the various travellers who have passed through this region.* These had long lain in a blacksmith shop, serving as anvils, and nothing but the impossibility of cutting them had saved them from being manufactured into spurs, knives, etc. The largest mass, half buried in the ground, had the appearance of resting on two legs; but when removed, in 1860, it was found to be a ring of iron, varying from 38 to 49 inches in its external, and from 23 to 26½ inches in its internal diameter, and weighing about 1,600 pounds. It lies now in the middle of the great hall of the Smithsonian Institution at Washington, bearing the name of the Ainsa Meteorite, having been brought, in 1735, from the Sierra de la Madera by Don Juan Bautista Ainsa, and forwarded to Washington by his descendants. The other, shaped like a slab, about 4 feet long, 18 inches broad, and 2 to 5 inches thick, weighs 632 pounds, and is now in San Francisco, having been sent thither in 1862 by General Carleton.†

Leaving Tucson early in the morning, we ascended the valley of the Santa Cruz by a sandy road. At first we passed a few patches of land cultivated by irrigation, but soon these were succeeded by the broad sandy plains of this region, relieved from absolute barrenness only by a great number of acacia trees, and a still greater abundance of cacti, of many and large varieties.

The valley of the Santa Cruz, after bending around the Santa Rita mountains, widens out north of Tubac into a broad plain, rising gently toward the Santa Rita mountains on the east, and the Tinajita mountains on the west. The material forming this plain is part of an extensive marine deposit, probably of the Quaternary age, which has filled all the valleys of the western parts of Arizona and Sonora south of the Gila river. Its depth and the loose character of its sand and gravel material causes the almost immediate disappearance of the water that falls in the rainy season, and this is only brought to or near the surface where the rocks underlying the plain-deposit rise. Thus we find only those plants growing on these plains which require the least amount of water for their sustenance.

* See "Bartlett's Explorations," Vol. II, p. 297.

† An analysis of this mass by Prof. G. J. Brush, and description of both pieces, has been given by Prof. J. D. Whitney in the proceedings of the California Academy of Sciences, Vol. III, pages 30 and 48, from which papers the above details are extracted.

A few miles brought us to San Xavier del Bac, an ancient mission founded by the Jesuits for the conversion of the Papago Indians. The mission building is still in tolerable preservation, with all the interior ornamentation and objects of worship of the chapel. The successors of the zealous founders have long since disappeared, but the Indians, with a feeling of mixed pride and superstitious reverence, guard it according to their ability as a sacred legacy.

We passed several stock ranches, situated on the river at points where water could be obtained. The houses have generally only one room, are built of sun-dried mud, and roofed with branches of the mesquit, covered with a layer of mud.

Late at night we camped about ten miles north of Tubac. Early the next morning we were startled from sleep by the approach of a wagon, which turned out to contain the Superintendent of the Santa Rita mines, Mr. H. C. Grosvenor, and a friend, who had come out to meet me.

As we continued our journey southward, the character of the country gradually changed.

For a short distance the bed of the Santa Cruz was filled with running water, and its banks supported a grove of large cottonwood trees, giving a welcome shade from the hot rays of the sun, while a heavy growth of grass covered the flat.

On our left rose the high, double-peaked Santa Rita, the highest of the mountains of Arizona south of the Gila river. A bold, precipitous spur, the Picacho del Diabolo, juts out into the valley, a promontory of naked rock, and a favorite post from which the Apache watches for the opportunity to make a raid.

Crossing the Santa Cruz, we passed the Canoa, a stockade house used as an inn, a place destined to see in the following year an awful massacre. A further ride of fourteen miles brought us to the old Spanish military post of Tubac. The restored ruins of the old village were occupied by a small mixed population of Americans and Mexicans, while near by a hundred or more Papago Indians had raised a temporary camp of well-built reed lodges.

After breakfasting we left Tubac, and travelling eastward about ten miles, now ascending the dry bed of a stream, now crossing the gravelly mesa, we reached the hacienda of the Santa Rita mines, my destination.

Arizona, at the time of my visit, comprised simply the tract of country known as the Gadsden Purchase, having been bought of the Mexican Government, through our Minister, Mr. Gadsden, for $10,000,000, to serve as a southern route for a railroad to the Pacific. Taken from the States of Chihuahua and Sonora, it was bounded by these on the south, by the Gila river on the north, the Colorado river on the west, and the Rio Grande on the east. It thus formed a long narrow strip lying between 31 and 33 degrees N., and containing about 30,000 square miles. The present boundaries of Arizona are Utah and Nevada on the north, New Mexico on the east, Sonora on the south, and California on the west.

Western Arizona* and northwestern Sonora, of which I have more particularly to speak, lie between the watershed of the Rocky Mountains and the depression occupied by the Gulf of California and the Colorado river.

This region is crossed by parallel granite ridges, running generally north or northwest, and rarely more than sixty miles long and ten to thirty miles apart. The intervals between the mountains are occupied by plains rising gently from the centre to the ridges on either side, and extending around the ends of these. Thus the whole country is a great plain, out of which rise the many outlying sierras of the Rocky range, as islands from the sea. Of these peaks probably none reach a height of 10,000 feet above the ocean, while the elevation of the plains increases gently from the level of the Gulf of California to about 6,000 feet at the watershed between the Gila and the Rio Grande.

The greater number of the mountain ridges, especially those having a northerly and northwesterly trend, are of granite, flanked near the base with crystalline schists; and to this structure is due the regularity of their sierra outlines. Districts of hilly land of much less elevation than the sierras are made up of porphyritic rocks, limestones, and metamorphic strata, of undetermined age, which give to the hills rounded outlines, broken here and there by cliffs and jagged dykes of intrusive rocks, or by metalliferous veins.

Large areas of the country were once covered by a sheet of

* Now Arizona, south of the Gila.

volcanic rock, which now remains, capping many summits left by erosion, and forming the picturesque sombrero, or hat-hills.

The valleys, as was said above, are occupied by a thick deposit, chiefly of loose sand and angular gravel, which has filled up the inequalities of the surface.

In western Arizona and northwestern Sonora, over a belt reaching nearly one hundred miles from the coast, the fall of rain is very small, and has not been sufficient to cut even the smallest of water-courses in the loose deposit of the plains. But further east, as we approach the higher land and the Santa Rita mountains, the annual precipitation is greater, and broad valleys with cañons are everywhere cut deep into the plains, leaving these last to be represented only by the mesas or terraces remaining between the valley and the sierras on either side.

Properly speaking, the whole region in question has no rivers excepting the Gila, the bed of which above its junction with the Salinas river is often, and below that point sometimes, dry. Bartlett supposes the Gila river to be navigable as far as the Salinas with small flat-bottom boats, during the season of high water. The little rain that falls over a vast region fills the water-courses for only a few hours, after which what is not evaporated sinks, to follow its under-ground course through the loose sand of the stream bed.

Where the water collects during the rainy season in natural rock tanks, or in clayey depressions in the soil, it quickly evaporates, leaving a crust of soda, lime, and potash-salts, which, spread as they often are over large areas of the desert region, aid in heightening the effect of the mirage.

Climatic influences have given a marked and peculiar character to the vegetation of this part of the continent. Toward the coast of the Gulf of California the plains are barren and arid deserts, where the traveller may ride hundreds of miles without seeing other plants than dry and thorny cacti. Granite mountains bordering these deserts are even more awful in their barrenness; neither tree nor cactus, nor even a handful of earth, can be seen on their sides; they tower high above the plains, great masses of white rock reflecting the rays of the sun with dazzling brilliancy.

The only supplies of water to be found over an area of many

thousand miles, are at a few points in the mountains, where the rains leave in natural tanks enough to last for a few months. During the rainy season, which sometimes fails, shallow pools are formed in slight depressions on the surface, to be exhausted after a few days' exposure to the fierce rays of the sun.

Further from the coast, the plains begin to show more vegetation; gradually appear the palo-verde, the mesquit, and a greater variety of cacti, and on the hills scattered saguaras (the giant Cereus). Still further east appears a denser growth of mesquit and palo-verde, out of which rises a perfect forest of the gigantic columns of the saguaras, covering the lowlands and foot-slopes of the Baboquiveri range. Between these mountains and the peaks of the Santa Rita, the character of the country changes; the plains are cut in the direction of the longer axis by the deep valleys, which receive tributary cañons from the mountains on either side. All that here remains of the original plains are the mesas or table-lands lying between the river and the sierras.

These mesas, consisting of loose gravel and sand, retain much of the desert appearance, but they are clothed with a hardy grass, and stunted acacias. In many of the valleys the bottom-lands have an extensive growth of the bean-bearing mesquit; and large cottonwood trees, and in some places fine groves of ash, shade the beds of streams in the neighborhood of hidden or running water.

On the hill-sides, above the level of the mesas, are scattered the dwarf live-oaks of the country, the trees varying from twelve to twenty-five feet in height, and presenting the appearance of old apple-orchards. Higher up the mountain-sides the oaks are mingled with cedars, and at an elevation of about 6,000 feet above the sea begin the few pine forests of this part of the Rocky Mountains.

The abundant growth of grass, and the mildness of the winters, render central Arizona a country well adapted to grazing. But away from the Gila river, excepting at a few scattered points, there is no land suitable for cultivation, owing to the absence of water for irrigation. On the extensive bottom-lands of the Gila, the ruins of long-fallen towns and of large aqueducts, and widely distributed fragments of pottery, indicate the former occupation of this region by an ancient and industrious population, related probably to the scattered remnants of the Moqui race, who are fast dying out in their strongholds on the high table-lands of the Colorado river, their last refuge from the more savage tribes by which they are now surrounded. The widely-spread traces of their arts, and the ruins of their many-storied buildings, sometimes built of stone, prove that this race once cultivated great areas of country which are now desert wastes.

CHAPTER II.

LIFE AT THE SANTA RITA.

THE hacienda of the Santa Rita mines, which was to be my home, lay in a broad and picturesque valley, shut in on the north by the lofty range of the Santa Rita mountains, and on the south by high and castellated cliffs of dark porphyries and white tufa. Through the open valley, toward the west, towering over fifty miles of intervening country, the horn-like peak of the Baboquiveri mountain was always visible, its outline sharply cut on the clear sky. The Santa Rita valley consists mainly of mesa-land, its outline broken by jagged rocks, rising like islands from the plain, or by the round-backed spurs from the mountains. The surface of these spur-hills is roughened by a net-work of innumerable mineral veins.

The drainage from the mountains passes through the valley in a deeply-cut cañon, containing here and there a little water, while throughout the rest of the valley, with the exception of two or three small springs, water can be had only by digging. The tree growth has the characteristics of the country given in the last chapter. A few cottonwoods occur along the water-courses, and a good growth of mesquit trees and acacias covers the bottom-land. The mesa is the home of a great variety of cacti, the yucca, and the fouquiera, a shrub sending up from the root a large number of simple stems, covered with sharp thorns, and in the season bearing beautiful flowers. Scattered live-oaks twenty to thirty feet high are peculiar to the spur hills. As we approach the summits of the higher hills the live oaks give place to small cedars, while on the Santa Rita mountains, at an elevation of about 6,000 feet, begins an invaluable but limited growth of fine pine timber.

The whole valley and its enclosing hills are covered with abundant grass of several kinds, which, while of great importance to the country, give to this a parched appearance. It is in reality a crop of hay, never being green excepting where burnt off before

THE SANTA RITA VALLEY.

the rainy season. The peculiar effect of this vegetation is heightened by the abundance of the short columnar fish-hook cactus, the yucca, the broad thorn-pointed leaves of the Spanish bayonet, and the tall lance-like stem of the century plant, bearing its gracefully-pendant flowers.

The scenery of Arizona, dependent in great part on its climate and vegetation, is unique, and might belong to another planet. No other part of the world is so strongly impressed on my memory as is this region, and especially this valley. Seen through its wonderfully clear atmosphere, with a bright sun and an azure sky, or with every detail brought out by the intense light of the moon, this valley has seemed a paradise; and again, under circumstances of intense anxiety, it has been a very prison of hell.

A few days after my arrival at the mines, in company with Mr. H. C. Grosvenor, the agent, I started on a journey to Fort Buchanan, twenty-two miles distant. Our route lay in part through a rocky and gloomy defile, along one of the war-trails of the Apaches leading into Sonora. From the countless tracks in the sand it was evident that a successful party of raiding savages had returned with a large drove of horses and mules.

A few miles before reaching the fort we stopped at the house of an Arkansas family, one of the daughters of which had escaped most remarkably a few months before from Indian captivity and death. She had been married the previous year, and had accompanied her husband to the Santa Rita mountains, where with a party of men he was cutting timber. While alone in the house one day, she was surprised and taken off by a small band of Apaches, who forced her to keep up with them in their rapid journey over the mountain ridges, pricking her with lances to prevent her falling behind. The poor woman bore up under this for about ten miles, and then gave out altogether, when the savages, finding they must leave her, lanced her through and through the body, and throwing her over a ledge of rocks, left her for dead. She was soon conscious of her condition, and stopping the wounds with rags from her dress, she began her journey homeward. Creeping over the rough country and living on roots and berries, she reached her home after several days. I was told that the first thing she asked for was tobacco, which she was in the habit of chewing.

Continuing our journey through the valley of a tributary of the Santa Cruz river, we reached our destination — Fort Buchanan. This fort, like most of our military establishments in the Rocky Mountains, consisted simply of a few adobe houses, scattered in a straggling manner over a considerable area, and without even a stockade defence. What object the Government had in prohibiting the building of either block or stockade forts, I could never learn. Certainly a more useless system of fortification than that adopted throughout the Indian countries, cannot be well imagined. In this case the Apaches could, and frequently did, prowl about the very doors of the different houses. No officer thought of going from one house to another at night without holding himself in readiness with a cocked pistol. During the subsequent troubles with the Indians, when the scattered white population of the country was being massacred on all sides for want of a protection the Government was bound to give, the commandant needed the whole force of 150 or 200 men to defend the United States property, while with a better and no more costly system of fortification this could have been accomplished with one quarter that number, and the lives of many settlers saved by the remaining force.

The next day, after riding out with Lieutenant Evans to see some springs which are forming a heavy deposit of calcareous tufa, we started on the return journey. We had passed a thicket about 500 yards from the fort, and had gone a little distance beyond this, when we met a man driving a load of hay. In a few minutes, hearing the report of a gun, we looked back, but having made a turn in the road and seeing nothing, we rode on our way. Several days afterward, I learned that the man we had met had been killed by Indians hidden in the thicket, and that the shot we heard was the one by which he fell. The Apaches were probably few in number, as they did not attack Grosvenor and myself.

The victim was a young man from the Southern States, and a letter in his pocket showed that he had been to California to free and place in safety a favorite slave. On his way home, finding himself out of money, he had stopped to earn enough to carry him through, when he died the common death of the country. Four years later, my successor, Mr. W. Wrightson, and Mr. Hopkins were killed at this same thicket by Apaches, who afterwards massacred the few soldiers left to garrison the fort.

The valley of Santa Rita had been, it is said, twice during the past two centuries the scene of mining industry; and old openings on some of the veins, as well as ruined furnaces and arastras, exist as evidence of the fact. But the fierce Apaches had long since depopulated the country, and with the destruction of the great Jesuit power, all attempt at regular mining ceased.

The object of the Santa Rita Company was to re-open the old mines, or work new veins, and extract the immense quantities of silver with which they were credited by Mexican tradition. In Mexico, where mining is the main occupation of all classes, tales and traditions of the enormous richness of some region, always inaccessible, are handed from generation to generation, and form the idle talk of the entire population. The nearer an ancient mine may be to the heart of the Apache stronghold, the more massive the columns of native silver left standing as support at the time of abandonment. It is not strange, therefore, when we consider how easily our people are swindled in mining matters, that we find them lending a willing ear to these tales, and believing that "in Arizona the hoofs of your horse throw up silver with the dust."

The capital of our company was not proportionate to the results expected to be achieved, and the work before us was correspondingly difficult. Everything had to be done with the means furnished by the country. We needed fuel, fire-proof furnace materials, machinery and power, and the supply of these furnished by nature in Arizona was of a kind to necessitate a great deal of trouble and experimenting, when taken in connection with the peculiar character of our ore. This and the work of exploration and opening of the veins kept me closely occupied through the winter.

The season was promising to pass without our hacienda being troubled by the Indians, when one morning our whole herd of forty or fifty fine horses and mules was missing. There were no animals left to follow with, and the result of a day's pursuit was only the finding of an old horse and two jackasses.

Several times during the remainder of the Winter and Spring

we were attacked by Apaches, and our mines were the scene of more fighting than any other part of the territory.

Aside from this, little of note occurred, until news came that the troops were to be recalled, leaving the country without any protection. The excitement was very great among the settlers, who were scattered over the country in such a manner as to be unable to furnish mutual assistance.

To make the matter worse, the military began an uncalled-for war with the Apaches. In the beginning of April, I believe, some Indians, of what tribe was not known, carried off a cow and a child belonging to a Mexican woman living with an American. Upon the application of the latter, the commandant at Fort Buchanan dispatched a force of seventy-five men to the nearest Apache tribe. The only interpreter attached to the expedition was the American who was directly interested in the result.

Arriving at Apache pass, the home of the tribe, the lieutenant in command raised a white flag over his tent, under the protection of which six of the principal chiefs, including Cachees, one of the leaders of the Apache nation, came to the camp and were invited into the tent.

A demand was made for the child and cow, to which the Indians replied, truly or falsely, that they knew nothing of the matter, and that they had not been stolen by their tribe.

After a long parley, during which the chiefs protested the innocence of their tribe in the matter, they were seized. One of the number in trying to escape was knocked down and pinned to the ground with a bayonet. Four others were bound, but Cachees seizing a knife from the ground, cut his way through the canvas and escaped, but not without receiving, as he afterward told, three bullets fired by the outside guard.

And this happened under a United States flag of truce. At this time three of the most powerful tribes of the nation were concentrated at Apache pass, and when Cachees arrived among them, a war of extermination was immediately declared against the whites.

The next day they killed some prisoners, and in retaliation the five chiefs were hung. Our troops, after being badly beaten, were obliged to return to the fort.

In the meantime, orders came for the abandonment of the territory by the soldiers. The country was thrown into consternation. The Apaches began to ride through it rough-shod, succeeding in all their attacks. The settlers, mostly farmers, abandoned their crops, and with their families concentrated for mutual protection at Tucson, Tubac, and at one or two ranches.

When, in addition to this, the news came of the beginning of the rebellion at the East, we decided that as it would be impossible to hold our mines, our only course was to remove the portable property of the company to Tubac. We were entirely out of money, owing a considerable force of Mexican workmen and two or three Americans, and needed means for paying for the transportation of the property, and for getting ourselves out of the country.

As the Indians had some time before stopped all working of the mines, our stock of ore was far too small to furnish the amount of silver needed to meet these demands, and our main hope lay in the possibility of collecting debts due to the company. In pursuance of this plan I started alone but well armed to visit the Heintzelman mine, one of our principal debtors. The ride of forty miles was accomplished in safety, and I reached the house of the superintendent, Mr. J. Poston, in the afternoon. Not being able to obtain money, for no one could afford to part with bullion, even to pay debts, I took payment in ore worth nearly $2,000 per ton, with a little flour and calico. This was dispatched in the course of the afternoon, in charge of two of the most fearless Mexicans of the force at the mine.

The next morning I started homeward alone, riding a horse I had bought, and driving before me the one that brought me over. I had so much trouble with the loose animal, that night found me several miles from our hacienda.

Only those who have travelled in a country of hostile Indians know what it is to journey by night. The uncertain light of the stars, or even of the moon, leaves open the widest field for the imagination to fill. Fancy gives life to the blackened yucca, and transforms the tall stem of the century plant into the lance of an Apache. The ear of the traveller listens anxiously to the breathing of his horse; and his eye, ever on the alert before and behind, must watch the motions of the horse's ears, and scrutinize the sand for tracks, and every object within fifty yards for the lurking-place of an Indian.

Still, night is the least dangerous time to travel, as one is not easily seen so far as by day. But after a few night journeys I found the mental tension so unbearable that I always chose the day-time, preferring to run a far greater risk of death to being made the prey of an overstrained imagination. Then, too, in such a state of society as then existed, the traveller in the dead of night approaches a solitary house, perhaps his own, with much anxiety, the often occurring massacres of the whites and Mexicans by Indians, and the as frequent murders of the Americans by their own Mexican workmen, rendering it uncertain whether he may not find only the dead bodies of his friends.

About three miles from the hacienda, in the most rocky part of the valley, the horse in front stopped short, and both animals began to snort and show signs of fear. There could be little doubt that Indians were in the neighborhood. Both horses started off at a run-away speed, leaving all control over either one out of the question. Fortunately, the free horse, taking the lead, made first a long circuit and then bounded off toward the hacienda, followed by my own. After a break-neck course over stony ground, leaping rocks and cacti, down and up steep hills, and tearing through thorny bushes, with clothing torn and legs pierced by the Spanish bayonet, I reached the house.

The wagon with the ore, although due that morning, had not arrived, and this was the more remarkable as I had not seen it on the road. When noon came the next day, and the ore still had not arrived, we concluded that the Mexicans, who knew well its value, had stolen it, packed it on the mules, and taken the road to Sonora.

Acting on this supposition, Grosvenor and myself mounted our horses, and, armed and provisioned for a ten days' absence, started in pursuit.

We rode about two miles, and descended to the foot of a long hill, making a short cut to avoid the bend of the wagon-road, which for lighter grade crossed the dry bed of the stream a few hundred yards higher up.

We were just crossing the arroyo to climb the opposite hill, when looking up we saw the missing wagon just coming in sight and beginning the descent. One of the Mexicans rode a wheel mule, while the other was walking ahead of the leaders. We had evidently judged our men wrongly, and when Grosvenor proposed that we should go on and come back with them, I objected, on the ground that the Mexicans, seeing us prepared for a long journey, would know at once that we had suspected them. We therefore decided to turn back, but taking another way homeward we immediately lost sight of the wagon. After riding a few hundred yards we dismounted at a spring, where we rested for a quarter of an hour, and then rode home.

As the afternoon passed away without the arrival of the wagon, we supposed it had broken down, and at twilight Grosvenor proposed that we should walk out and see what caused the delay. I took down my hat to go, but, being engaged in important work, concluded not to leave it, when my friend said he would go only to a point close by, and come back if he saw nothing. It was soon dark, and the two other Americans and myself sat down to tea. By the time we left the table, Grosvenor had been out about half an hour, and we concluded to go after him.

Accompanied by Mr. Robinson, the book-keeper, and leaving the other American to take care of the house, I walked along the Tubac road. We were both well armed; and the full moon, just rising above the horizon behind us, lighted brilliantly the whole country. We had gone about a mile and a half, and were just beginning to ascend a long, barren hill, when, hearing the mewing of our house-cat, I stopped, and, as she came running toward us, stooped and took her in my arms.

As I did so, my attention was attracted by her sniffing the air and fixing her eyes on some object ahead of us. Looking in the direction thus indicated, we saw near the roadside on the top of the hill, the crouching figure of a man, his form for a moment clearly defined against the starlit sky, and then disappearing behind a cactus. I dropped the cat, which bounded on ahead of us, and we cocked our pistols and walked briskly up the hill. But when we reached the cactus the man was gone, though a dark ravine running parallel with our road showed the direction he had probably taken. Of Grosvenor we yet saw nothing. Continuing our way at a rapid pace and full of anxiety, we began the long descent toward the arroyo, from which we had seen the wagon at noon. Turning a point of rocks about half-way down, we caught sight of the wagon drawn off from the road on the further side of the arroyo.

The deep silence that always reigns in those mountains was unbroken, and neither mules nor men were visible. Observing something very white near the wagon, we at first took it for the reflected light of a camp-fire, and concluded that the Mexicans were encamped behind some rocks, and that with them we would find our friend. But it was soon evident that what we saw was a heap of flour reflecting the moonlight. Anxiously watching this and the wagon, we had approached within about twenty yards of the latter when we both started back—we had nearly trodden on a man lying in the road. My first thought was that it was a strange place to sleep in, but he was naked and lying on his face, with his head down-hill. The first idea had barely time to flash through my mind, when another followed—it was not sleep but death.

As we stooped down and looked closer, the truth we had both instinctively felt was evident—the murdered man was Grosvenor.

It would be impossible to describe the intensity of emotion crowded into the minute that followed this discovery. For the first time I stood an actor in a scene of death; the victim a dear friend; the murderers and the deed itself buried in mystery.

The head of the murdered man lay in a pool of blood; two lance-wounds through the throat had nearly severed it from the body, which was pierced by a dozen other thrusts. A bullet-hole in the left breast had probably caused death before he was mutilated with lances. He had not moved since he fell by the shot that took his life; and as the feet were stretched out in stripping the corpse, so they remained stretched out when we found him. The body was still warm, indeed he could not have yet reached the spot when we left the house.

I have seen death since, and repeatedly under circumstances almost equally awful, but never with so intense a shock. For a minute, that seemed an age, we were so unnerved that I doubt whether we could have resisted an attack, but fortunately our own situation soon brought us to our senses. We were on foot, two miles from the house, and the murderers, whoever they might be, could not be far off, if indeed the spy we had seen had not already started them after us. Looking toward the wagon, I thought I could discover other bodies, but we knew that every instant of time was of great importance, and without venturing to examine closer we started homeward.

There was only one white man at the hacienda, and a large number of peons, and we did not yet know whether the murderers were Indians, or Mexicans who would probably be in collusion with our own workmen.

If they were Indians, we might escape by reaching the house before they could overtake us; but if they were our Mexicans, we could hardly avoid the fate the employé at the house must already have met with.

Taking each of us one side of the road, and looking out, one to the left, the other to the right, our revolvers ready, and the cat running before us, we walked quickly homeward, uncertain whether we were going away from or into danger. In this manner we went on till within a half a mile of the houses, when we reached a place where the road lay for several hundred yards through a dense thicket—the very spot for an ambush. We had now to decide whether to take this, the shorter way, or another, which by detaining us a few minutes longer would lead us over an open plain, where we could in the bright moonlight see every object within a long distance. The idea of being able to defend ourselves tempted us strongly toward the open plain, but the consciousness of the value of every minute caused us to decide quickly, and taking the shorter way we were soon in the dark, close thicket. As we came out into the open valley, the sensation of relief was like that felt on escaping untouched from a shot you have seen deliberately fired at you. Just before reaching the house, we heard Indian signals given and answered, each time nearer than before; but we gained the door safely, and found all as we had left it; the American, unaware of danger, was making bread, and the Mexicans were asleep in their quarters. We kept guard all night, but were not attacked.

Before daylight we dispatched a Mexican courier across the mountains to the fort, and another to Tubac, and then went after Grosvenor's body. We found it as we had left it, while near the wagon lay the bodies of the two Mexican teamsters.

We were now able to read the history of the whole of this murderous affair. The wagon must have been attacked within less than five minutes after we had seen it at noon, indeed while we were resting and smoking at the spring not four hundred yards from the spot. A party of Indians, fifteen in number, as we found by the tracks, had sprung upon the Mexicans, who seem unaccountably not to have used their firearms, although the sand showed the marks of a desperate hand to hand struggle. Having killed the men, the Apaches cut the mules loose, emptied the flour, threw out the ore, which was useless to them, and drove the animals to a spot a quarter of a mile distant, where they feasted on one of them and spent the day and night. A party was left behind to waylay such of us as might come out to meet the team. When Grosvenor neared the spot he was shot by an Indian, who, crouching behind a cactus about ten feet distant, had left the impression of his gunstock in the sand. Knowing well that their victim would be sought by others, they had left the spy we had seen; and had not the cat directed our attention to him at the moment when he was moving stealthily away, thereby causing us to walk rapidly to the scene of the murder, and faster back, we could hardly have escaped the fate of our friend.

During the day Lieutenant Evans arrived with a force of nineteen soldiers, having with difficulty obtained the consent of his commandant, and soon after Colonel Poston reached the mines with a party of Americans. Graves had been dug, and, after reading the burial service and throwing in the earth, we fired a volley and turned away, no one knowing how soon his time might come.

I now foresaw a long and dangerous work before us in extracting the silver from our ore. We could, indeed, have abandoned the mines, and have escaped from the God-forsaken land by accompanying the military, which was to leave in two weeks. But both Mr. Robinson and myself considered that we were in duty bound to place the movable property of the company in safety at Tubac, and to pay in bullion the money owing to men, who without it could not escape. To accomplish this would require six weeks' work at the furnace, crippled as were all operations by the loss of our horses and mules.

It was of the first importance that we should increase our force of Americans, not only for protection against the Apaches, but more especially against the possible treachery of our Mexican workmen, for at almost every mine in the country a part or all of the whites had been murdered by their peons. One of the party which had come that day from Tubac was engaged on the spot. Partly in the hope of getting a small force of soldiers who should remain till the abandonment began, and partly to persuade an American who lived on the road to the fort to join us, I resolved to accompany Lieutenant Evans, who was obliged to return the next day.

Taking with me a young Apache who had been captured while a child, and had no sympathy with his tribe, I rode away with Lieutenant Evans, intending to return the next day. The wagon-road lay for ten miles along a tributary of the Sonoita valley, then ascended the Sonoita for twelve miles to the fort, while a bridle-path across the hills shortened the distance some two or three miles by leaving the road before the junction of the two valleys. To reach the house of the American whom I wished to see, we would have to follow the wagon-road all the way; and as more than a mile of it before the junction of the valleys lay through a narrow and dangerous defile, on an Apache war-trail that was constantly frequented by the Indians, Lieutenant Evans would not assume the responsibility of risking the lives of his men in a place where they would be at such disadvantage. While I felt obliged to acknowledge that it would be imprudent to take infantry mounted on mules through the defile, it was of the first necessity that I should see Mr. Elliot Titus, the American living near the junction of the valleys. At the point where the hill-trail left the road, bidding good-bye to Lieutenant Evans, who, could he have left his men, would have accompanied me himself, I was soon alone with Juan, my Apache boy. As we neared the gorge I observed that Juan, who was galloping ahead, stopped suddenly and hesitated. As I came up he pointed to the sand, which was covered with fresh foot-tracks.

It was evident that a considerable party of Indians had been here within half an hour, and had dispersed suddenly toward the hills in different directions. Our safest course seemed to be to press forward and reach Titus's house, now about two miles off. We were on good horses, and these animals, not less alarmed than ourselves, soon brought us through the defile to the Sonoita creek. To slip our horses' bridles without dismounting, and refresh the animals with one long swallow, was the work of a minute, and we were again tearing along at a run-away speed. We had barely left the creek when we passed the full-length impression of a man's form in the sand with a pool of blood, and at the same instant an unearthly yell from the hills behind us showed that the Apaches, although not visible, were after us, and felt sure of bringing us down. Our horses, however, fearing nothing so much as an Indian, almost flew over the ground and soon brought us in sight of Titus's hacienda. This lay about two hundred yards off from the road in a broad valley shaded by magnificent live oaks.

As we rode rapidly toward the houses I was struck with the quietness of a place generally full of life, and said so to Juan.

"It's all right," he replied; "I saw three men just now near the house."

But as we passed the first building, a smith's shop, both horses shied, and as we came to the principal house, a scene of destruction met our eyes.

The doors had been forced in, and the whole contents of the house lay on the ground outside, in heaps of broken rubbish. Not far from the door stood a pile made of wool, corn, beans, and flour, and capping the whole a gold watch hung from a stick driven into the heap. Stooping from the saddle I took the watch and found it still going.

As I started to dismount, to look for the bodies of the Americans, Juan begged of me not to stop.

"They are all killed," he said, "and we shall have hardly time to reach the road before the Indians come up. Promise me," he continued, "that you will fight when the devils close with us; if not I will save myself now."

Assuring the boy, whom I knew to be brave, that I had no idea of being scalped and burned without a struggle, I put spurs to my restless horse, and we were soon on the main road, but not a moment too soon, for a large party of Apaches, fortunately for us on foot, were just coming down the hill and entered the trail close behind us. A volley of arrows flew by our heads, but our horses carried us in a few seconds beyond the reach of these missiles, and the enemy turned back. Slackening our speed we were nearing a point where the road crossed a low spur of the valley-terrace, when suddenly several heads were visible for an instant over the brow of the hill and as quickly disappeared. Guessing instantly that we were cut off by another band of Indians, and knowing that our only course was to run the gauntlet, we rode slowly to near the top of the hill to rest our animals, and then spurred the terrified horses onward, determined if possible to break the ambush. We were on the point of firing into a party of men who came in full view directly as we galloped over the brow of the hill, when a second glance assured us that instead of Apaches they were Americans and Mexicans, burying an American who had been killed that morning. It was the impression of this man's body which we had seen near the creek. He had been to the fort to give notice of the massacre of a family living further down the river, and on his return had met the same fate, about an hour before we passed the spot. An arrow, shot from above, had entered his left shoulder and penetrated to the ribs of the other side, and in pulling this shaft out a terrible feature of these weapons was illustrated. The flint-head, fastened to the shaft with a thong of deer-sinew, remains firmly attached so long as this binding is dry; but immediately it is moistened by the blood, the head becomes loose, and remains in the body after the arrow is withdrawn. The Apaches have several ways of producing terrible wounds; among others by firing bullets chipped from the half oxidized mats of old furnace heaps, containing copper and lead combined with sulphur and arsenic. But perhaps the worst at short range is produced by bullets made from the fibre of the aloe root, which are almost always fatal, since it is impossible to clear the wound.

On reaching the fort and seeing the commandant, I was told by that officer that he could not take the responsibility of weakening his force, and that the most he could do would be to give me an escort back to the Santa Rita. As the troops from Fort Breckenridge were expected in a few days, I was led to expect that after their arrival I might obtain a small number of soldiers. But when, after several days had passed without bringing these troops, the commandant told me that not only would it be impossible to give us any protection at the Santa Rita, but that he could no longer give me an escort thither, I resolved to return immediately with only the boy Juan. In the meantime a rumor reached the fort that a large body of Apaches had passed through the Santa Rita valley, had probably massacred our people, and were preparing to attack Tubac. I was certainly never under a stronger temptation than I felt then to accept the warmly-pressed invitation of the officers, to leave the country with the military, and give up all idea of returning to what they represented as certain death. But I felt constrained to go back, and Juan and myself mounted our horses. I had hardly bid the officers good-by when an old frontiersman, Mr. Robert Ward, joined us, and declared his intention of trying to reach his wife, who was in Tubac. As we left the fort a fine pointer belonging to the commandant followed us, and as he had become attached to me, we had no difficulty and few scruples in enticing him away to swell our party. We took the hill trail, it being both shorter and safer, and had reached a point within three miles of the Santa Rita without meeting any very fresh signs of Indians, when the dog, which kept always on the trail, ahead of us, after disappearing in the brush by an arroya, came back growling and with his tail between his legs. We were then two or three hundred yards from the thicket, and spurring our horses we left the trail and quickly crossed the arroya a hundred yards or more above the ambush, for such the fresh Indian tracks in the dry creek had shown it to be.

We reached our mines safely, and found that although almost constantly surrounded by Apaches, who had cut off all communication with Tubac, there had been no direct attack. Our entire Mexican force was well armed with breech-loading rifles, a fact which, while it kept off the Indians, rendered it necessary that our guard over our peons should never cease for an instant. Nor did we once during the long weeks that followed place ourselves in a position to be caught at a disadvantage. Under penalty of death no Mexican was allowed to pass certain limits, and in turn our party of four kept an unceasing guard, while our revolvers day and night were never out of our hands.

We had now to cut wood for charcoal and haul it in, stick by stick, not having enough animals to draw the six-horse wagons. This and burning the charcoal kept us nearly three weeks before we could begin to smelt. Our furnaces stood in the open air about one hundred yards from the main house, and on a tongue of high-land at the junction of two ravines. The brilliant light illuminating every object near the furnace exposed the workmen every night, and all night, to the aim of the Apache. In order to obtain timely notice of the approach of the Indians, we picketed our watch-dogs at points within a hundred yards of the works; and these faithful guards, which the enemy never succeeded in killing, more than once saved us from a general massacre. The whole Mexican force slept on their arms around the furnace, taking turns at working, sleeping, and patrolling, receiving rations of diluted alcohol, sufficient to increase their courage without making them drunk.

More than one attempt was made by the Apaches to attack us, but being always discovered in time, and failing to surprise us, they contented themselves with firing into the force at the furnace from a distance. In the condition to which we all, and especially myself, had been brought by weeks of sleepless anxiety, nothing could sound more awful than the sudden discharge of a volley of rifles, accompanied by unearthly yells, that at times broke in upon the silence of the night. Before daylight one morning our chief smelter was shot while tending the furnace; it then became necessary for me to perform this duty myself, uninterruptedly, till I could teach the art to one of the Americans and a Mexican.

I foresaw that the greatest danger from the Mexicans was to be anticipated when the silver should be refined, and made arrangements to concentrate this work into the last two or three days, and leave the mine immediately after it was finished.

Dispatching a messenger, who succeeded in reaching Tubac, I engaged a number of wagons and men, and on their arrival everything that could be spared was loaded and sent off. The train was attacked and the mules stolen, but the owner and men escaped, and bringing fresh animals, succeeded in carrying the property into Tubac.

At last the result of six weeks' smelting lay before us in a pile of lead *planchas* containing the silver, and there only remained the separating of these metals to be gone through with. During this process, which I was obliged to conduct myself, and which lasted some fifty or sixty hours, I scarcely closed my eyes; and the three other Americans, revolver in hand, kept an unceasing guard over the Mexicans, whose manner showed plainly their thoughts. Before the silver was cool, we loaded it. We had the remaining property of the company, even to the wooden machine for working the blast, in the returned wagons, and were on the way to Tubac, which we reached the same day, the 15th of June. Here, while the last wagon was being unloaded, a rifle was accidentally discharged, and the ball passing through my hair above the ear deafened me for the whole afternoon.

Thus ended my experience of eight months of mining operations in an Apache stronghold.

CHAPTER III.

THE FRONTIER AND THE DESERT.

THE social condition of Arizona from 1857 till 1862, and later, was one which could not fail to furnish much food for thought to even a superficial observer. When the country came into the possession of the United States, it was almost entirely depopulated, excepting the Indian tribes. After the conclusion of the Gadsden treaty it was entered by Colonel C. D. Poston with a party of explorers, and soon gained a reputation as a silver district from the high assays of ores discovered by that party. A considerable number of companies were soon formed to work mines in various parts of the country. In addition to the people sent out to work in different capacities at the mines, an American population, both floating and settled, was soon formed, mostly from the Southern States, and of men unaccompanied by families. Many of these were old frontiersmen, many more were refugees from the slackly-administered justice of Texas, New Mexico, and California; and when the vigilance committee cleared San Francisco of its worst social elements, a large number of the ruffians and gamblers expelled from that city made their home in Arizona. In addition to this there flowed into the country many thousands of Mexicans, who had formed the most degraded class in a land where social morality was, in every respect, at its lowest ebb.

There was hardly a pretense at a civil organization; law was unknown, and the nearest court was several hundred miles distant in New Mexico. Indeed, every man took the law into his own hands, and the life of a neighbor was valued in the inverse ratio of the impunity with which it could be taken. Thus public opinion became the only code of laws, and a citizen's popularity the measure of his safety. And popularity, in a society composed, to a great extent, of men guilty of murder and of every crime, was not likely to attach to the better class of citizens. The immediate result of the existing condition of public opinion was to blunt all ideas of right and wrong in the minds of new-comers who, suddenly freed from the legal and social restraints of the East, soon learned to justify the taking of life by the most trifling pretexts, or even to commit it for the sake of bravado. Murder was the order of the day among a total white and peon population of a few thousand souls; it was daily committed by Americans upon Americans, Mexicans, and Indians; by Mexicans upon Americans; and the hand of the Apache was, not without much reason, against both of the intruding races. The treachery of Mexican workmen went to such an extent that I believe there was hardly a mine in the country at which the manager, or in several instances all the white employés, had not been at sometime assassinated by their peons for the sake of plunder.

Such has been the condition of society in a part of our country within the past ten years: and it existed without the influence of actual war. It is true that a state of things more or less resembling that I have tried to sketch is incidental to the early history of many frontier districts, but it can hardly be said to have augured well for the future of a region in which it was claimed that an enduring civilization was springing up on the ruins of the Jesuit efforts, which were really far more successful.

That the region in question has a future that is both bright and near, there can, I think, be little doubt. Its prospects are dependent on the development of a mineral industry and the occupations subservient thereto. My own observations have convinced me that Arizona contains many rich deposits of silver, copper, and lead, and probably of gold also; but to work these profitably will require, in most if not in all instances, the overcoming of peculiar obstacles that now exist. Without at present touching upon the Indian question, the first essential to success is an improvement in the means of transportation from the mines to the coast, and between the different mining districts. During the short period when mining industry was trying to struggle into existence, supplies, including machinery, reached Tucson in central Arizona, by three different routes: from Indianola, Texas, 1087 miles; from Fort Yuma, on the Colorado river, over 250 miles; and from Guaymas, on the Gulf of California, nearly 400 miles distant.

A shorter and safer route than any of these will be necessary, ·nd when furnished with a good wagon road, or ultimately with a railway, the first essential to the development of industry of any kind will have been attained.

A reconnoissance, made for the Government by Major Fergusson, has shown that a good wagon-route exists between Tucson and Lobos Bay on the Gulf of California. The distance is 211 miles, or about 171 miles from Tubac, and by digging a limited number of wells the road would be made easily practicable at all seasons. The harbor of Libertad, on Lobos Bay, is considered by Major Fergusson to be a good one, and capable of admitting vessels of heavy draught.*

Owing to the scarcity of fuel and water, and to the character of the ores, it is probable that the mining companies will be obliged to have central reduction works, or to sell a part or all of their ores to such establishments, carried on independently. The owners of these works, by being able to mix and grade the various ores of different mines, would have it in their power to reduce them far more cheaply and with less loss of silver than could the individual mines. Low-grade ores, comparatively free from lead and zinc, and containing under $80 to $100 silver per ton, would probably be most cheaply worked by the Spanish-American amalgamation, or *patio* process; while the richer and poorer classes of silver ores, containing much copper, zinc, antimony, and arsenic, not being suitable for amalgamation, would work well in the furnace when mixed with the oxidized and unoxidized silver-lead ores of the country.

For fuel, the mines and works must, for some time to come, be dependent on the scanty mesquit and live-oak trees, as the nearest coal known is 200 to 300 miles distant. The scantiness of the growth of these trees, and their small size, will soon raise the cost of fuel. In view of this, experience might prove it to be desirable to carry the smelting only so far as the production of rich mats and argentiferous lead, and to ship both these products from the nearest port.

The troubles with the hostile tribes will disappear before the immigration that will be necessary to inaugurate successfully a mining industry and to furnish the mines with means of subsistence.

* See "Letter of the Secretary of War communicating copy of report of Major D. Fergusson on the country, its resources, and the route between Tucson and Lobos Bay. Senate, 37th Congress, Ex. Doc. No. 1."

An important obstacle to be overcome is the uncertain character of Mexican labor. The Mexicans in Arizona, freed from the restraints of peonage, which is practically a system of slavery, and working for Americans, toward whom they feel only hatred, give full play to the treachery of their character. In this connection the proximity of the boundary line is a serious evil.

Mexican labor is good when properly superintended, or better yet when employed on the *partido* plan, in which gangs working in ore are interested to the extent of a specified share.

At the Santa Rita, workmen at the furnace received $1 per day of twelve hours; able-bodied miners $15 per month; and other Mexican laborers $12. In addition to these wages, each man had weekly a ration of sixteen pounds of flour. At the same time, American workmen received from $30 to $70 per month and board.

The system of paying the Mexicans the greater part of their wages in cotton and other goods, on which the company made a profit of from one hundred to three hundred per cent., reduced the cost of labor to a minimum. This last plan, however, being foreign to American ideas, would soon disappear before the competition that would arise under the influence of a vigorous mining industry.

It seems doubtful whether Americans * can be profitably used for hard work in the climate of Arizona, but I think it not improbable that voluntary Chinese labor would be found to be highly advantageous and superior to the Mexican.

Arizona, although very inferior as an agricultural region, is capable of supplying a large mining population with the first necessities of life. The plains and valleys of the higher portion have large tracts of good grazing-land; and many now barren valleys, when skilfully irrigated, as was anciently the valley of the Gila river, would yield abundant crops of corn, wheat, and other grains.

So long as the present lack of all humane relations exists between the various Apache tribes and the whites, safety for property and person will obtain only through an ever-increasing immigration and the gradual extermination of the warlike occupants of the soil.

---

* By Americans I refer throughout to the white natives of the United States.

One cannot but look upon the history of our intercourse with the original owners of our country as a sad commentary on the Protestant civilization of the past two centuries. In the history of no other conquest, heathen or Romish, do we find such a record of long-continued atrocity and treachery on the part of the conquerors, or of utter failures of badly-conceived and dishonestly-executed plans for the elevation of the conquered race. The example of duplicity set by the early religious colonists of New England, has been followed by an ever-growing disregard for the rights of the Indian; and for nearly two hundred and fifty years the outposts of our population have been the theatres of scenes for which no centralized government would dare assume the responsibility.

So long as our population continued small, and its advance slow, the extensive reserves set aside for Indians seemed to offer a lasting home for the rapidly-vanishing race; and later, when our fast-increasing and wide-spreading numbers sought only agricultural lands, it seemed that, as a hunting people, they might find abundant area for subsistence on the table-lands of the Rocky Mountains. But this, the last hope of the remaining tribes, is being destroyed, since the continued discoveries of the precious metals have drawn our pioneers to every nook, no matter how barren, of that immense region.

While our forefathers made at least a show of paying the natives for the land taken from them, there is now not even a pretence of such compensation, at least not in the southern Rocky Mountains. The Indian country is subdivided between the various tribes, whose range is limited by more or less defined boundaries. As by far the greater number are almost solely hunters, the area necessary to their support is out of all proportion to that required for the subsistence of an equal number of agriculturists. With the influx of a mining population, the Indians, unable to encroach upon the territory of neighboring tribes, are gradually driven to the most barren parts of the mountains, and with the disappearance of game are reduced to the verge of starvation. Whether they oppose bravely at first the inroads of the whites, or submit peacefully to every outrage until forced by famine to seek the means of life among the herds of the intruder, the result is the same. Sometimes hunted from place to place in open war; sometimes their warriors enticed away under peaceful promises by one party, while a confederate band descends on the native settlements, massacring women and children, old and young; they are always fading away before the hand of violence. No treaty or flag of truce is too sacred to be disregarded, no weapons too cruel or cowardly to be used or recommended by Americans. Read the following quotation from a late work:

"There is only one way to wage war against the Apaches. A steady, persistent campaign must be made, following them to their haunts—hunting them to the 'fastnesses of the mountains.' They must be surrounded, starved into coming in, surprised or inveigled—by white flags, or any other method, human or divine—and then put to death. If these ideas shock any weak-minded philanthropist, I can only say that I pity without respecting his mistaken sympathy. A man might as well have sympathy for a rattlesnake or a tiger." *

I have quoted the above passage, because it expresses the sentiment of the larger part of those directly interested in the extermination of the Indians, who are also exercising a constant pressure on the Government, and making healthy and just legislation in the matter impracticable.

If it is said that the Indians are treacherous and cruel, scalping and torturing their prisoners, it may be answered that there is no treachery and no cruelty left unemployed by the whites. Poisoning with strychnine, the wilful dissemination of small-pox, and the possession of bridles, braided from the hair of scalped victims and decorated with teeth knocked from the jaws of living women—these are heroic facts among many of our frontiersmen.

In the territory under the control of the Hudson's Bay Company—the interests of that organization requiring a proper treatment of the Indians—very little trouble has ever been experienced during a long intercourse with the natives; and the same may, I believe, be said of the relations between the Mormons and the surrounding tribes. Throughout Spanish America the Jesuits succeeded to a high degree in their endeavor to elevate the condition of the conquered race, and the limit to their success was always determined by the cupidity of the home government, and of the mining population.

* Sylvester Mowry in "Arizona and Sonora."

Without difficulty these zealous apostles founded missions, and traversed parts of the Rocky Mountains which are now accessible to only a strong military force. Leaving our own continent, we find in Russia, China, and many other lands, a successfully pursued policy, resulting in a greater or less elevation of conquered races. The nomad Tarter tribes, brought under Russian rule, in Russia and Siberia, have been transformed, even where not christianized, into a different mode of life, forming a highly respected class, following the same occupations equally successfully with the Russians, among whom they live.

I can explain the different condition of our relations with the Indians, only by supposing that, in the presence of long-continued dishonesty in our Indian agencies, public opinion has shaped itself into conformity with the interests of the frontiersman, who is restrained by no higher law than his own grossly selfish aim. Perhaps the question has already passed beyond the control of the Government; certainly, at present, it is being worked out under more general laws—those which control animal life; it has become a struggle for existence, a contest in which the nobler moral faculties have no part.

There is, perhaps, no doubt that the aboriginal race will soon disappear from the United States; nor can it be denied, if the mere contact with us, without the use of violence, causes them to melt away, that their disappearance is for the advantage of the world at large, since the fact of a natural decrease would prove them to be lacking in ability to do their share in the world's work. But it is the duty of Government to see that their disappearance shall take place through the natural decrease in the number of births. This result can be effected only by causing the tribes to remove to reservations, where they may be protected by Government in their rights, and made to respect the rights of others. The policy at present followed toward the hostile tribes is not only unjust, but it is an unpardonable waste of men and money. Costly treaties are made with difficulty, only to be immediately broken, as well by the Indians as by the settlers, and by the very agents appointed to execute the obligations of the Government. Indian agents, appointed to represent the Government, and distribute presents among the Indians, carry on with them a profitable but shameful trade, bartering not only arms and spirits, but the very presents of Government, against horses and mules, which they know well the Apache must first steal from Mexicans and Americans. It was out of these thefts, made to fulfil the dishonest contracts entered into with Government officials, that the majority of the Indian troubles arose in Arizona.

If war between the hostile tribes and the whites is unavoidable, let its prosecution be transferred from the irresponsible settlers to the military, and waged with the definite object of concentrating the Indians upon liberal reserves, and there accomplishing all that can be effected toward their elevation by the efforts of Government, and of missionary enterprise of any religion.

When we deposited the movable property of our company at Tubac, we did so under the supposition that that village would be a point at which a large part of the white and Mexican population would concentrate for mutual defence, until the fresh troops, whose coming was rumored, should arrive. As soon as the contents of the wagons were stored away, the silver assayed, and our debts paid, I determined to make a journey for recreation into the Papagoria—the land of the friendly Papago tribe. In company with Colonel C. D. Poston and Mr. J. Washburn, I reached the Cerro Colorado or Heintzelman mine, then being worked by the first-named gentleman. Here we took a Mexican guide and laid in our provisions, consisting of pinole—powdered parched-corn—sugar and coffee.

Early the next morning we left the mine, and, following the Indian trail westward for several miles, came onto the great Baboquiveri plain. This broad stretch of wild grass-land being one of the main thoroughfares of the Apaches, we were obliged to keep a good look-out all day. But notwithstanding the great heat, and the danger from Indians, the combined effect of the grand scenery and the prospect of reaching a country where comparative safety would allow a few nights of unguarded sleep, filled me with new life, and I gave myself up again to the fascinating influence of nature in the Rocky Mountains. Twenty miles or more to the west of us, rose the sharp and lofty peak of the Baboquiveri, its eagle-head outline and every feature sharply defined, while the range out of which it towers up stretched away in long wings of glistening, barren rock, till lost in the northern and southern horizons.

As we entered the valley from our position on its eastern border, the broad plain lay before us. Descending in a gentle slope to the centre, and thence rising gradually to the same height along the base of the opposite mountain range, it was a wide expanse of grassy steppe, and forests of mesquit and cacti. Detecting us from afar, a drove of wild horses trotted off over the grassy surface, and we watched their graceful course as with streaming tails and flowing manes they disappeared in the distance.

The only other signs of life that break the monotony of these journeys, are given by the herds of bounding antelopes, or by the red or gray wolf as he trots slowly away from the traveller, stopping dog-like ever and anon to turn and watch the intruder. The tracks of the great grizzly bear, the marks of the huge paw of the no less ferocious panther, and the sudden and frequent sound of the rattlesnake, warn the traveller of other dangers than the Apache.

Taking a diagonal course over the plain, we reached the foot-hills of the Baboquiveri range at the approach to Aliza pass. It was late at night before we had wound through the rocky defile, and by the light of the full moon ascended to the spring near the top. After watering the horses from our hats, and drinking a supper of pinole in water ourselves, we took turns at watching and sleeping.

Early the next morning we reached the summit of the pass. The Baboquiveri range forms the boundary between the Papagoes and Apaches, two tribes differing widely in appearance, character, and habits, and between whom there has ever been hostility.

The Papagoes guard carefully the approaches to their country, and these passes have been the scenes of many desperate battles. But the desert character of the Papagoria is its best defence, since, in view of the great scarcity of water over an immense area, it would be almost certain death to a party of Apaches to penetrate far into it. At the summit of the pass stands a large pile of stones, literally bristling with arrows, both old and new. Whether this was a landmark or battle monument I did not learn.

A ride of twenty miles over a gravelly plain, which reflected the intense heat of the sun, brought us to Cahuabi, a Papago village on the skirt of the desert. Here two silver mines, the Cahuabi and Tajo, had been worked for a short time some years before and temporarily abandoned. Both of these veins, one containing free gold, as well as silver ore, give good promise; indeed, I consider the Cahuabi district to be one of the richest for silver in Arizona. The fact that it lies in the desert, with barely enough water to cook with, will be a serious hindrance to its development.

Most of the Papago villages on the desert are several miles from any water, and one of the chief occupations of the women is the obtaining of this necessary of life, and bringing it home. I say obtaining, for getting water is there often a labor of patience, skill, and danger. In many places it is to be had only by digging. A spot is chosen where the rock dips under a deposit of sand, and an opening like a quarry is sunk in the latter, exposing the rocky surface. The little water that trickles slowly, drop by drop, along the plane of contact between sand and stone, is collected with the greatest care and patience, till the labor, sometimes of hours, is rewarded by one or two gallons of water in the earthen vessel, which the woman then bears on her head, perhaps six or nine miles, to her home. In very dry seasons, water can be had only by extensive digging of this kind. A friend once reached one of these wells at a time when, after a succession of dry seasons, the Indians were dying from thirst. He found a large number of natives digging recklessly, far below the surface, and following down the line of contact between sand and rock, in the vain hope of finding a few drops of water. In their despair, they undermined the high face of the sand, and it fell, burying for ever a number of the unfortunate creatures.

From Cahuabi we made an excursion into the desert to visit a mine being opened by some Mexicans. At the outset, our way lay over a gravelly plain covered with small scrubby acacias, and the green, leafless palo-verde, over which towered countless columns of the saguarra (Cereus giganteus). This giant cactus, one of the wonders of the vegetable world, impresses a peculiar character on the scenery in which it occurs. Often a simple shaft, nearly as large at the top as at the base, it rises thirty and even sixty feet above the ground. Its green surface is fluted like a

THE SAGUARA.

Grecian column, and armed from base to summit with small clusters of long thorns, while a coronet of beautiful, highly-colored flowers encircles the base of the hemispherical top. In the season, these flowers are replaced by a sweetish fruit, as large as a hen's egg, which forms an important source of food among the Papagoes. This fruit is made into an agreeable syrup, which seems to be as much prized among these Indians as the sugar and syrup of the maple are among the northeastern tribes.

Beneath the soft-green exterior, the body of the shaft is a skeleton of poles, finger-thick, as long as the plant, and irregularly connected together into the form of fasces. These poles, taken from dead trunks, furnish, with the exception of the bow and arrow, the only means of reaching the fruit.

So strongly do these cacti resemble Grecian columns, that one is almost tempted to look for fallen Corinthian capitals and ruined temples. It is a curious coincidence, that the natural object which is best suited to furnish the prototypes of the fluted Grecian column and the Roman fasces, should belong to an order of plants not represented on the eastern continent, and to a species restricted to a small area on the immense deserts of the New World.

Reaching the new mine, we found the Mexicans at work in an irregular opening, from which about a wagon-load of good-looking argentiferous copper ore had been taken. This they would have to transport nearly one hundred miles before they could smelt it. In Mexico, where all the men are more or less miners, it is common, especially since the decline of the great mining industry, for a number to club together for the purpose of working some old or new mine on shares. The present laxity in the enforcement of the mining laws, the general absence of security to property, and an inherent love of gambling, are all favorable to such enterprises. While many new discoveries of value are made in this manner, the fact that they are not recorded, and the ruinous system followed by these people in robbing the pillars of old mines, render the operations of the *gambucinos* a serious evil to the country.

Returning to Cahuabi we began our homeward journey, intending to reach Arivacca by a trail crossing the mountains south of the Baboquiveri peak. We encamped for the night near the western foot-hills of the range, and from our elevated position the vast plains, stretching away toward the Pacific, were spread out before us. To this grand landscape the brilliant light of the full moon lent its enchanting power, rendering more weird the unfamiliar plant forms, silvering the distant ridges of barren granite and the surface of the boundless desert. Not a sound, nor even a breath of air, broke the silence of the night; and as I yielded to the influence of the scene, I seemed to be a wanderer in dreamland.

Soon there came the doleful bark of the red wolf, growing louder and nearer as these animals approached and hovered about the camp.

In the morning I found that the rawhide thongs had been gnawed off from my saddle, although it had served me for a pillow all night.

Before night we reached Fresnal, a Papago village. Near this we encamped by a spring of good water, surrounded by fine ash and mesquit trees, and lying in a ravine descending from the Baboquiveri peak. Our intention was to leave Fresnal on the following afternoon, but while preparing to break camp an accident occurred by which all our plans were changed. While we were eating our pinole, a sand-storm was seen whirling rapidly toward us from the desert, and we all hastened to wrap our fire-arms in the blankets, to protect them from the penetrating dust. In doing this Mr. Washburn let his revolver fall. It instantly went off, and discharged a ball into the inner side of his right thigh. An examination showed that the ball had not come out, and it seemed almost certain that it had entered the abdomen, and that death must soon follow. A hasty consultation resulted in sending a Papago on Mr. Washburn's horse to Tucson, about 80 miles distant, for a doctor, while Colonel Poston, with the guide, started for Arivacca, about 40 miles off, by the trail over the mountain, to bring an ambulance, and I remained to nurse our wounded companion. During the afternoon we found that the ball had glanced around the outside of the pelvis, and following the spine had lodged itself between the muscle and bone, near the shoulder blades. Being entirely ignorant of everything relating to surgery, I did not venture to cut it out, but decided to wait for the doctor's arrival, keeping the wound constantly washed in the meantime. After an absence of less than two days and a half, the Papago returned, having nearly killed the fine horse he rode, and bringing a letter, in which the doctor regretted the impossibility of undertaking a journey in the existing condition of the country.

Five days passed without bringing any news from Colonel Poston, and concluding that another friend had swelled the long list of victims to the Apaches, I made preparations to await the time when I should either help my companion into his saddle or dig his grave. Recovery seemed almost impossible, with the thermometer ranging from 116 to 126 degrees in the shade, and when night brought only a parching desert-wind.

Day after day passed by without bringing any change in our prospects, or in the condition of the wounded man. The Papagoes of the neighboring village, from whom I bought milk and boiled wheat, were at first friendly: their frequent visits to our camp relieved the tedious monotony of the long days, and I occupied my time in learning their language. But gradually these visits became rarer, and finally ceased altogether. The old chief raised the price of milk from one string of beads per quart, to two strings, and the smallness of my supply of this currency rendering it necessary to raise their value in the same proportion, our relations became daily less and less friendly. Our isolated position thus grew every day more unpleasant, surrounded as we were by Indians who were nominally friendly, but who had murdered more than one helpless traveller.

Nearly two weeks had passed since the accident, when a Mexican arrived from Colonel Poston bringing provisions, and a letter, from which we learned that after leaving us they had lost their way at night on the Baboquiveri plain, and after wandering about for three days without food or water, the guide became insane and strayed away toward the south. Poston, finding water the next day, had regained sufficient strength to retrace his steps toward the Baboquiveri peak, till coming into the trail he reached Arivacca, delirious and half dead, on the fifth day. When his reason returned he learned that the Apaches had made a descent on the place a few days before, killing several men and driving off all the animals. He advised us to hire a party of Papagoes to bring Washburn in on a litter. I immediately made the proposition to the chief, beginning by offering a horse, and ending with the offer of horses and arms by the dozen. It was useless. The old man was tempted; but most of the warriors being away for the summer, he would not venture to expose the village to a raid from the Apaches by sending the young men with us.

The Mexican left the welcome provisions and returned to Arivacca, and again the same tedious routine of watching and waiting was resumed. Nearly all my time during the day, and much of the night, was occupied in keeping water on Washburn's wound. By this means, together with the dryness of the climate, it was kept free from gangrene, and the condition of my patient was apparently improving.

One day the unexpected but welcome sound of a creaking wheel was followed by the appearance of a wagon drawn by oxen, and escorted by eleven Mexicans. It was a party who had gone from Sonora, over the desert, to open a mine, and were now returning with a load of ore. The scarcity of water on the desert had caused them to take the route along the foot of the mountains, and, fortunately for us, the first wagon that had ever passed this way came in time to give us relief. A bargain was immediately made—the Mexicans, who were on foot, agreeing to take Washburn to Saric, in Sonora, for five dollars. Making as comfortable a bed for the wounded man as was possible, over the rough load of ore, we began this new stage of our journey.

The oxen made slow progress, rarely over ten or twelve miles a day, and now and then losing a day altogether; still it was a great relief to be again on horseback. At Poso-Verde we reached the border of the Papagoria. Here the Indians had taken advantage of the existence of a spring, and abundant grass, and we found a well-stocked ranch of horses and cattle. The spring was a small pool, in which stood, during the heat of the day, all the cattle that could find room, and in it the Indians bathed every morning. Already from a distance we smelt the water, and when we reached it, it seemed more like a barn-yard pool than a reservoir of drinkable water. Still we were forced to use it there, and to lay in a supply.

Leaving Poso-Verde we turned from the mountains unto a broad plain, bearing scarcely any other vegetation than scattered tufts of grass. As we were now exposed to the Apaches, we were obliged to keep a constant look-out. The Mexicans had no amunition, and ours was useless to them. In two or three days it was suddenly discovered that we were out of provisions and tobacco. A Mexican was instantly sent ahead on our extra horse to get supplies at the nearest village in Sonora, and it was hoped he might meet us on the second or third day, at least in time to prevent any deaths from starvation.

But when the third day passed without his return, it was evident that hunger was telling fearfully on us. The Mexicans became, all of them, more or less deranged, as much from want of tobacco as from hunger; we could make but little progress, as our companions wandered away from our course, and my time was divided between guiding the oxen and keeping the men near the wagon. I was entirely ignorant of the route, and, not being able to rely on the random talk of the crazy guides, could only keep a southerly course, and trust to accident for finding water.

The Mexicans tore open my saddle-bags in search of tobacco, an action I had neither the strength nor the heart to resist. I began to feel that my own reason was leaving me, and that only a speedy relief could save us from death.

Fortunately, before night overtook us, we reached a low range of hills, and my heart beat fast as I saw a number of *petalhya* cacti growing from the rocks. It was the season for their fruit, and enough of this was found to supply a scanty meal all around.

The next day, fearing to go on, we remained quiet, and I stood guard with drawn pistol, till the following morning, to prevent the starving men from killing one of the oxen, knowing well that it must inevitably cause the death of Washburn. Toward noon of the fifth day a horseman was seen coming from the north, who proved to be our Mexican bringing provisions. He had passed us in the night, and had gone a long day's journey beyond us, before cutting our trail. Our deliverer was torn from his horse by the men, in their impatience to get at the supplies, but, before taking a mouthful of food, we all quickly rolled cigarettes, and each inhaled one long draught of delicious smoke, and then fell to eating. Fortunately, the man had been wise enough to hide most of his load, to prevent the effects of over-eating in our condition. By the next morning we were nearly recovered from the effects of starvation, as was shown by the returned sanity and straightened forms of all of us. Thus ended one of the most awful episodes of my journey.

Two or three days more brought us to Saric, where the sympathies of the entire female population were immediately enlisted in behalf of Mr. Washburn, and we were soon furnished with as comfortable quarters as the poor frontier village could supply. This was not much, however, consisting of a room, in which we spread our blankets on some fresh cornstalks.

The Apaches had made a raid on the place that day, and the village was in a state of excitement. An old Spaniard was found whom we both knew, and who, having some knowledge of surgery, proceeded to cut out the ball.

This was done successfully, the lead coming out in two pieces. By careful treatment, and constant nursing on the part of the kind-hearted Mexican women, Washburn in less than two weeks was on the road to certain recovery, and I prepared to leave him, to return to Arizona. When on the point of starting I was seized with chills and fever, and for a week was the patient, in turn, of every lady in the village. But kind nursing, aided by emetics and warm water by the pailful, restored me, and, leaving a country where the men are mostly cut-throats, and the women angels, I rode toward Arizona.

CHAPTER IV.

CLOSING SCENES AND ESCAPE.

At Arivacca I found Colonel Poston impatiently awaiting the arrival of the agent of Colonel Colt, to whom he had transferred the lease of the Heintzelman mine. Being both of us anxious to leave the country, we determined on a journey together through the principal mining districts, to the city of Mexico, and thence to Acapulco, or Vera Cruz. Before beginning this we visited Tubac, where we found the population considerably increased by Americans, who had been driven in by the Apaches, from the ranches of the Santa Cruz valley.

In three days we were ready to return to the Heintzelman mine, and the morning of the fourth day was fixed for our final departure from Tubac. But a circumstance occurred in the evening which interfered with our plans. Just before dark a Mexican herdsman galloped into the *plaza*, and soon threw the whole community into a state of intense excitement. He had gone that morning with William Rhodes, an American ranchero, to Rhodes's farm, to bring in some horses which had been left on the abandoned place. The farm lay about eighteen miles from Tubac, on the road to Tucson, and to reach it they passed first through the Reventon, a fortified ranch ten miles distant, and then through the Canoa, a stockade inn, fourteen miles from Tubac. At the inn they found the two Americans who had charge of the place, cooking dinner; and telling them they would return in an hour to dine, they rode on. Having found the horses, they returned, and, before riding up to the house, secured the loose animals in the corral, and then turned toward the inn. Their attention was immediately drawn to a shirt, drenched in blood, hanging on the gate, and, approaching this, a scene of destruction confronted them. The Apaches had evidently been at work during the short hour that had passed. Just as they were on the point of dismounting, they discovered a large party of Indians, lying low on their horses, among the bushes a few hundred yards off the road. At the same instant that they put spurs to their horses, to escape toward the Reventon, the Apaches broke cover, and reached the road about one hundred yards behind the fugitives.

There were not less than a hundred mounted warriors, and a large number on foot. About a mile from the inn, Rhodes's horse seemed to be giving out, and he struck off from the road toward the mountains, followed by all the mounted Indians. The Mexican had escaped to the Reventon, and thence to Tubac, but he said that Rhodes must have been killed soon after they parted company.

It being too late to accomplish anything by going out that night, we determined to look up the bodies and bury them the following day. Early the next morning I rode out with Colonel Poston and three others, to visit the Canoa. To our great surprise the first man we met, as we rode into the Reventon, was Rhodes, with his arm in a sling. He corroborated the story of the Mexican, and told us the history of his own remarkable escape. Finding his horse failing, and having an arrow through his left arm, he left the road, hoping to reach a thicket he remembered having seen. He had about two hundred yards advantage over the nearest pursuers, and as he passed the thicket he threw himself from the horse, which ran on while he entered the bush. The thicket was very dense, with a narrow entrance leading to a small *charco* or dry mud-hole in the centre. Lying down in this he spread his revolver cartridges and caps before him, broke off and drew out the arrow, and feeling the loss of blood buried his wounded elbow in the earth. All this was the work of a minute, and before he had finished it the Indians had formed a cordon around his hiding-place and found the entrance. The steady aim of the old frontiersman brought from his horse the first Apache who charged into the opening. Each succeeding brave met the same fate as he tried the entrance, till six shots had been fired from Rhodes's revolver, and then the Indians, believing the weapon empty, charged bodily with a loud yell. But the cool ranger had loaded after each shot, and a seventh ball brought down the foremost of the attacking party, and the eighth the one behind him. During all this time the Indians fired volley after volley of balls and arrows into the thicket, in the hope of killing their hidden opponent. After the twelfth shot there came another whoop, another charge, and one more warrior fell. Then the Indians, who knew him well by name, and from many former fights, called out: "Don Guiglelmo! Don Guiglelmo!—Come and join us; you're a brave man, and we'll make you a chief." "Oh, you devils, you! I know what you'll do with me if you get me," he answered. After this Rhodes heard a loud shout: "Sopori! Sopori!"—the name of the ranch of a neighboring mine—and the whole attacking party galloped away.

After a few minutes, finding the Indians all gone, Rhodes left the thicket and found his way to the Reventon. Thus happened one of the most remarkable defences and escapes, and one that could have been carried out only by a cool courage, such as few men even with a long frontier experience can command.

Leaving the Reventon we rode toward the Canoa. As we approached it the tracks of a large drove of horses and cattle and of many Indians filled the road. Soon we came in sight of the inn, and two dogs came running from it toward us. With low, incessant whining they repeatedly came up to us, and then turned toward the inn, as if beseeching our attention to something there. When we entered the gate a scene of destruction indeed met us. The sides of the house were broken in and the court was filled with broken tables and doors, while fragments of crockery and iron-ware lay mixed in heaps with grain and the contents of mattrasses. Through the open door of a small house, on one side of the court, we saw a body, which proved to be the remains of young Tarbox, who coming from Maine a short time before had been put in charge of the inn. Like many of the settlers, the first Apaches he had seen were his murderers. Under a tree, beyond a fence that divided the court, we found the bodies of the other American and a Papago Indian, who, probably driven in by the Apaches, had joined in the desperate struggle that had evidently taken place. These bodies were pierced by hundreds of lance wounds, and were already in a terrible condition.

Our small party of five took turns in keeping watch and digging the graves. Burying the Papago in one grave, and the two Americans in the other, we wrote on a board—"Tarbox;" and under, this: "White man, unknown, killed by Apaches." How often does that word "unknown" mask the history of some long-mourned wanderer from the circle at home.

We had just finished the burial, when a party of Americans, escorting two wagons, rode in sight. They were on their way to Fort Buchanan, where they hoped to discover the *caches* in which commissary stores had been hidden on the abandonment of the conntry. Happening to ask them whether Mr. Richmond Jones, superintendent of the Sopori Company's property, was still in Tucson, I was told that he had left that town for the Sopori early on the previous day.

Knowing that he had not yet reached home, we instantly suspected that he was killed. As the party had met with no signs of Indians till near the Canoa, we began a search for his body in the neighborhood, and before long a call from one of our number brought us to the spot where it lay. A bullet entering the breast, two large lances piercing the body from side to side, and a pitchfork driven as far as the very forking of the prongs into the back, told the manner of his death. Wrapping the body in a blanket, we laid it in one of the wagons and turned toward Tubac. Finding the spot where Rhodes had left the road in his flight from the Indians, Poston and myself followed the tracks till we reached the scene of his desperate fight. The place was exactly as Rhodes had described it, and the *charco* was covered with the branches cut loose by the Apache bullets, while the ground at the entrance was still soaked with blood.

At Tubac a grave was dug, and in it we buried Richmond Jones, of Providence, R. I. Like Grosvenor, a true friend of the Indians, he fell by them a victim to vengeance, for the treachery of the white man. The cry of Sopori, raised by the Indians when they left Rhodes, was now explained; they knew that in Jones they had killed the superintendent of that ranch, and they were impatient to reach the place and drive off its large drove of horses and cattle before the arrival of any force large enough to resist them. This they effected by killing the herdsmen.

The next morning, bidding good-bye to Tubac, Poston and myself returned to the Heintzelman mine. I was to pass a week here, for the purpose of examining and reporting on the property; but hearing that a wagon-load of watermelons had arrived at Arivacca, and having lived on only jerked beef and beans for nearly a year, I determined to go on with Poston and pass a day at the reduction works. It was arranged that two of the Americans should come to Arivacca the next day, to carry the mail through to Tucson. They came; but, the letters not being ready, their departure was postponed till the following morning.

About an hour and a half after these two men had left Arivacca, they galloped back, showing in their faces that something awful had happened.

"What is the matter?" asked Poston

"There has been an accident at the mine, sir."

"Nothing serious, I hope?"

"Well! yes, sir; it's very serious."

"Is any one injured—is my brother hurt?"

"Yes, sir, they're all hurt; and I am afraid your brother wont recover,"

My friend dared to put no more questions; the men told me the whole story in two words—"all murdered."

Mounting my horse, which had already been saddled to carry me to the mine, I returned quickly with the two men. We found the bodies of Mr. John Poston and the two German employés, while the absence of the Mexicans showed plainly who were the murderers. I heard the history of the affair afterward in Sonora. A party of seven Mexicans had come from Sonora for the purpose of inciting the peons, at Arivacca and the mine, to kill the Americans and rob the two places. They reached Arivacca the same day that Poston and myself arrived, and finding the white force there too strong, had gone on to the mine. Here they found no difficulty in gaining over the entire Mexican force, including a favorite servant of Mr. Poston. This boy, acting as a spy, gave notice to the Mexicans when the white men were taking their siesta. Without giving their victims a chance to resist, they murdered them in cold blood, robbed the place, and left for Sonora. Laying the bodies in a wagon just arrived from Arivacca, we returned to that place. I found that during my absence the peons had attempted the same thing at the reduction works, but being detected in time by the negro cook, they were put down. That evening we had another burial, the saddest of all, for we committed to the earth of that accursed country the remains not only of a friend, but of the brother of one of our party.

I will add here that the accident which so nearly proved fatal to Washburn on the desert, in all probability saved his life, since by delaying his return to the Heintzelman mine, where he made his home, it saved him from the general assassination.

After this occurrence we both abandoned our proposed journey, and determined to leave the country by the nearest open route. The events of the past week, added to all that had gone before, began to tell on my nerves, and I felt unequal to the task of making a dangerous summer journey of over one thousand miles through Mexico.

The arrival of a Spaniard whom we knew well, decided our route. He brought the news that a vessel was to arrive at Lobos Bay, on the Gulf of California, to take in a cargo of copper ore. So we determined to leave with him for Caborca, on our way to Lobos Bay. Indeed, the only route open to us lay through Sonora, as it was out of the question for two men to think of taking the ordinary routes through Arizona.

The day after the funeral we put our baggage into the returning wagons, and following these, on horseback, left Arivacca. Our own party consisted of Poston, myself, and the colored cook. Crossing the Baboquiveri plain we passed around the southern end of the Baboquiveri range. Here I entered again upon the great steppe, which, stretching northward through the Papagoria, and southwestward to the Altar river, had so lately been the scene of our eventful journey. On the skirt of this plain we encamped for the night.

The effect of the grand scenery and wonderfully clear atmosphere of this strange land, is to intensify the feelings of pain or pleasure which at the time sway the traveller's mind. Thus, while under ordinary circumstances, the surroundings of this our first encampment would have been engraved on the memory with all the shading and coloring of a sublime and beautiful night-scene, the events of the past week formed a background on which the picture of that night remains impressed with all the weird gloom of the darkest conceptions of Breughel or Doré. The bright moon-lighted heavens were suddenly overcast, in the north-east, by the first thunder-cloud I had seen in the territory. Above us the sky was clear, but over the mountains we had left all was dark and gloomy. As the thunder rolled in peal after peal, and lightning broke in great columns, its sudden light impressing on the eye the weird rock-forms and frowning cliffs of the Arizona mountains, it seemed a fitting end to the scenes we had left behind, and as though that region were realizing its name, and were in reality the "Gate of Hell."

Our route lay for two or three days, as far as the Altar river, over hard, gravelly plains, generally bearing grass and scattered mesquit trees and cacti. The Altar river is a mere rivulet at nearly all seasons, but along its course are many places which might become flourishing ranches, were not all attempts at industry rendered hopeless by the raids of the Apache. Following the river we reached Altar, a village built of adobes, and containing a population of about 1,900 souls, including the ranches of the inmediate neighborhood.

The productions of this part of Sonora are chiefly maize, wheat, barley, beans, and some sugar and tobacco.* Watermelons are raised in large numbers. A solitary date-palm, standing near Altar, is evidence of the attempts of the early missionaries to introduce fruits which seemed suited to the climate.

On the fourth day of our journey we reached Caborca, a village containing about 800 inhabitants, chiefly agriculturists and miners. It was in the fine old mission-church at this place that the filibustering party under Crabbe met their fate.

Here we were welcomed by an acquaintance, Don Marino Molino, who offered us the hospitality of his house. Much to our disappointment, we learned that the coming of the expected vessel to Lobos Bay had been postponed for several months, and it became necessary to choose another way out of the country. Our choice of routes was limited to two: the one leading to Guaymas, about 200 miles distant, and the other to Fort Yuma, nearly as far to the northwest, on the Colorado river.

While we were in Caborca, some of the former peons of the

---

* "The prices of wheat and barley are about the same at all the pueblos, viz, wheat at harvest time $1.50 per fanega, (150 lbs.); wheat at seed time $3.00 per fanega, (150 lbs); barley at harvest time $1,00 (120 lbs.); at seed time $2,50-$3,00; beans cost from $3.00 to $8,00 (average $5.00) per fanega; corn the same as wheat, but the fanega weight 200 lbs. Beef cattle and all kinds of stock are scarce. I estimate that about 4,000 head of cattle belong to Caborca, and perhaps 5,000 to 6,000 are on the Galera rancho; six miles from there they sell steers for $5,00 to 12,00. Animals are generally fattened for slaughter in the towns, where they sell for about $20,00; heavy fat oxen from $40,00 to 60,00; tallow brings a high price.

"At Pitiquito, about six and one-half miles from Caborca, there is raised annually: of wheat about 8,000 fanegas; of corn say 2,000 fanegas. Cotton thrives well."—*Report of Major D. Fergusson, to the Secretary of War.*

Heintzelman mine, who had been of the assassinating party, were seen walking in conscious security through the streets. We heard that they not only boasted openly of their part in the murder, but that they had formed a party of twelve desperadoes to follow and waylay Poston and myself, for the sake of the large quantity of silver we were supposed to have in our baggage. Our friends warned us of the danger, and advised us to increase our force before continuing the journey. At the same time a report was brought in by a Mexican coming from California, that Fort Yuma was to have been already abandoned, and that owing to two successive rainless seasons, many of the usual watering-places on the desert route to the Colorado were dry. There was one distance, he said, of one hundred and twenty miles, without water, and on this some of the party to which he belonged had died from thirst.

We decided, however, on this route, as, besides leading directly to California, it exposed us mainly to the dangers of the desert. One thing caused us much uneasiness: this was the question as to how we should cross the Colorado river, supposing the Fort were really abandoned. That river is deep, and broad, and the current rapid; and the abandonment of the fort would, considering the hostile character of the Yuma Indians, necessarily cause the abandonment of the ferry also.

There was in Caborca an American, named Williams, who had been found some weeks before dying from hunger and thirst, on the shore at Lobos Bay. Brought into Caborca, and kindly treated by an old lady of that place, he had already recovered, and was seeking an opportunity to leave the country. According to Williams's story, he had formed one of a party of three who had built a boat on the Colorado river, intending to coast along the Gulf of California to Cedros island, on a "prospecting" expedition. Arriving at Lobos Bay, he said, they had been wrecked, but he was unable to account for the subsequent movements of his companions. We believed his story, and liking the appearance of the man, engaged him to go with us to California, giving him as compensation an outfit consisting of a horse, saddle, rifle, and revolver. As soon as we had engaged a Mexican, with several pack-mules, we were ready for our journey. Our party now consisted of four well-armed men, not counting the Mexican muleteer.

Several friends escorted us as far as our first encampment, which we reached in the night, and left us the following morning, but not without repeatedly warning us to keep an unceasing watch for the party that was sure to follow us.

The first inhabited place we passed was the Coyote gold-placer, near which are the ancient Sales and Tajitos gold and silver mines, and, in the neighboring Vazura mountains, the Coyote copper mine. The ore of the latter is a rich, brilliant black sulphuret. The Sales and Tajitos were worked with profit till the insurrection of the Indians.

The next settlement in which we encamped was Quitovac, a place which had some celebrity for its gold placers before the discovery of that metal in California. It had been our intention to take the route to the Colorado river, leading through the Sonoita gold district, in preference to that passing through San Domingo. These routes, diverging at a point a few miles beyond Quitovac, continue parallel to each other, but separated by mountains, till their reunion on the Gila river. When asked at Quitovac which route we proposed taking, we had given that by Sonoita as our choice. But as soon as we took the road in the morning it became evident that a party of horsemen had passed through Quitovac during the night, stopping for only a short time. The tracks showed them to be twelve in number, and when on reaching the fork of the trails we found that, after evident hesitation, they had taken the Sonoita route, we changed our plan and turned into that leading to San Domingo, which place we reached in a few hours. In this settlement, containing two or three houses, the last habitations before reaching the Gila river, we found Don Remigo Rivera, a revolutionary Sonoranian general. Don Remigo had withdrawn with his small force to the United States boundary, where he was awaiting a favorable opportunity for action. Leaving his men at Sonoita, he had come to pass a few days at San Domingo. As this gentleman had frequently been a guest at the Santa Rita, and at Colonel Poston's house, we received from him a cordial reception, and dismounted to breakfast on pinole and watermelons. While thus engaged, a courier rode up at full speed, and was closeted for a few minutes with our host. This man, Don Remigo informed us, brought news of the arrival, in the neighborhood of Sonoita, of twelve men, whose names he gave. It was supposed by his friends that they had come to assassinate the general.

"That is not likely to be their object," said Don Renrigo, "since, though they are cut-throats, they belong to my party, and have served under me. It is more probable," he continued, "that they are following you, as I have heard of a plot to waylay you."

Our suspicions of the morning were thus confirmed, and the necessity of being prepared for an attack became more apparent.

San Domingo lies on the boundary, and the trail leaving the ranch keeps for a few miles south of the line, and then enters the United States territory. To this point Don Remigo accompanied us, to show us the last watering-place before entering upon the desert. As we returned from this spring to the road, two men were seen, who, having passed us unnoticed, were travelling north. They proved to be two Americans, on their way to Fort Yuma, and they readily joined us. Our party now numbered six well-armed men, and we felt ourselves able to cope with fifty Mexicans. The size of our force now rendered it possible to keep a watch without much fatigue to any member of the party; but our greatest danger lay in the exposure of our animals, and consequently of ourselves, to death from thirst. Soon we would have to enter upon the broad waterless region, and the bones of animals already bordering our trail warned us of the sufferings of past years.

One night, as we were skirting the desert along the base of a barren sierra, Williams and myself had fallen behind the caravan, when my companion, from over-use of our Spanish brandy, began to talk freely to himself. We were just approaching a bold, high spur of the sierra, while immediately before us the trail wound between immense fragments of rock fallen from the mountains above. Williams stopped his horse, and looking at the rocks, said, half aloud:

"Here's where the d—d greasers * overtook us, and we whipped them."

As the man had said that he had never been over the road before, I thought it at first only the talk of a drunken man.

"I thought you had never been this way before, Williams," I said to him.

"Maybe I haven't; maybe I dreamt it; but when you get by

* A name applied to Mexicans by frontiersmen.

that spur you'll see two tall rocks, like columns, on the top of the sierra; them's the 'two sisters.'"

We soon passed the point of the spur, when, looking toward the top of the mountain, I saw two tall rocks, like columns, rising from the crest. My interest in this man was now excited, indeed I had already had a suspicion that he was not what we had taken him to be. Determined to learn more, I passed him my flask; we rode on together, talking about Sonora, though not very coherently on Williams's part. After riding a few miles we entered a scanty forest of mesquit and palo-verde trees, and I observed that my companion had become attentive to the surroundings. In answer to my questions he replied:

"I am looking for an opening on the left side of the trail. There's a square opening with a large mesquit at each corner, and a long branch goes from one corner across to the other; under the branch there's a mound, I guess."

He rode ahead, and soon turned out of the trail.

Following him, I entered by a narrow path and found myself with him in a square opening; there, indeed, was a mesquit at each corner, a long branch crossing the space diagonally, and under the branch a mound. The clear moon-light shone into the spot and cast our shadows over the mound, as if to hide a mystery.

"He's rotten now, I reckon;" my companion muttered. "I told him I'd spit more than once on his grave, and by G—d I've done it."

"What was his name, Williams?" I asked, passing the flask again.

"Charley Johnson."

"What did you kill the poor devil for, in this out-of-the-way place?"

"An old grudge, about a Mexican woman, when we were with Fremont. I told him I'd spit on his grave, and I've done it; ha! ha! ha! I've done it. We had a split here about a scarf—and I got the scarf, that's all."

"Who kept the priest's robes?" I asked, looking him full in the face.

At these words, Williams started and made a motion toward his pistol; but seeing that I had the advantage, inasmuch as my hand rested on my revolver, he simply exclaimed:

"What the devil do *you* know about the priest's robes?"

"Only that you were one of Bell's band," I answered, quietly.

The suspicions I had formed as soon as Williams had betrayed a knowledge of the route, were fully confirmed; our quiet-looking companion had been one of the band of cut-throats which, under the notorious Bell, had been the terror of California, soon after the discovery of gold. This party had gone to Sonora, about eight years before the time of our journey, under the pretext of wishing to buy horses. Stopping at a celebrated gold placer near Caborca, they were hospitably entertained at the neighboring mission by the old priest and his sister, who were living alone. In return for this kind reception they had hung the priest, outraged the lady, and robbed the rich church of several thousand dollars in gold. The inhabitants of Caborca had told me of this occurrence, still fresh in their minds, and of the bravado of the party in riding through Caborca, using the priestly robes as saddle blankets. Before a sufficiently strong party could be raised to follow them, they had escaped to the desert, and when finally overtaken, were found too strong for their pursuers, who were driven back.

My experience on the border with men of the class to which Williams belonged, had shown me that to manage them, or, when it becomes necessary, to associate with them, one must assume, to a certain extent, their tone; this I had done with my companion, and by this means and the aid of the brandy-flask I obtained his confidence. He acknowledged that he had been one of Bell's men, and had been on the expedition into Sonora. When he was recently brought into Caborca nearly dead, he was taken care of by the sister of the priest whom they had hung, and Williams lived in constant fear that the lady would recognize him. Not only had he escaped recognition, but he told me, as an excellent joke, that the Senora had given him a letter to her two daughters, who were living in California.

He was, at the time of our journey, a refugee from California, having murdered a man in San Francisco. The history he gave me of his life, while with Bell's band, was a combination of awful crimes and ludicrous incidents, that would swell a volume. I never knew but one ruffian who more surely deserved hanging than this companion, whom we had taken with us to increase our

DAYBREAK ON THE DESERT.

safety. That other man was one who had been a blacksmith at the Santa Rita mine, and had been discharged for trying to stab Mr. Grosvenor. Soon after this he killed a man at Tubac, and, as the sympathies of the inhabitants were with the victim, Rodgers found it necessary to leave the country to avoid lynch law. Before going, he took one of the employés of the Santa Rita to his trunk, and showing him a string of eighteen pairs of human ears, told him he had sworn to increase the number to twenty-five. From Arizona he went to Chihuahua, near which city he killed his travelling companion; and some months later we heard that, having brutally murdered a family of four persons at El Paso, for the sake of a few dollars, he had been caught and hung by his heels over a slow fire. Thus his own ears made the twenty-fifth pair.

One cannot come much in contact with such men without feeling how little human nature has been affected by the march of society, and how subject to conventional influences are even the passions of man. The workings of conscience come to seem a refinement of civilization, but so artificial that they are absent in the absence of the restraints of the civilization in which they originate. An eminent clergyman has said that colonization is essentially barbarous: certainly, from the time when the pioneer first enters a new country, until, with increasing population, the growing interests of individuals and society necessitate the bridling of crime, the standard of right and wrong is far below that even of many peoples whom we class as savages. And, other things being equal, it is by the lesser or greater rapidity of this transformation process, that we may measure the superiority or inferiority of the parent civilization.

In a few days we approached the worst part of the desert; the watering-places became more separated and the supply smaller. Our route lay over broad gravelly plains, bearing only cacti, with here and there the leafless palo-verde tree, and the never-failing greasewood bush. In the distance, on either side, arise high granite mountains, to which the eye turns in vain for relief; they are barren and dazzling masses of rock. Night brought only parching winds, while during the day we sought in vain for shelter from the fierce sun-rays. The thermometer ranged by day between 118 and 126 degrees in the shade, rising to 160 degrees in the sun. On these vast deserts the sluggish rattlesnake meets the traveller at every turn; the most powerful inhabitant, his sway is undisputed by the scorpions and the lizards, on which he feeds. The routes over these wastes are marked by countless skeletons of cattle, horses, and sheep, and the traveller passes thousands of the carcasses of these animals wholly preserved in the intensely dry air. Many of them dead, perhaps, for years, had been placed upright on their feet by previous travellers. As we wound, in places, through groups of these mummies, they seemed sentinels guarding the valley of death.

With feelings of much anxiety we encamped on the border of the *pleyas*, a depressed region, once probably a large lake, now a surface of dried mud, crossed by ridges of shifting sand. From that camp on, there lay before us a continuous ride of nearly thirty hours, before we could hope to find the nearest water on the Gila river, and it was not probable that all our animals could bear up under the fatigue and thirst.

But during the night the sky was overcast with black clouds, and there came the first rain that had fallen on this desert for more than two years. Never was storm more welcome; both we and our animals enjoyed heartily its drenching torrent. Before day-break the sky had cleared, and with the rising sun began the heat of another day. A broad sheet of water, only a few inches deep, covered the *pleya* for miles before us, and banished from our minds all fear of suffering. Across the centre of this great plain there stretches, from north to south, a mass of lava about one mile wide, and extending southward as far as the eye can reach. On this lava-wall there stand two parallel rows of extinct volcanic cones, 100 to 300 feet high, with craters. In crossing this remarkable remnant of recent volcanic action, I could look down the long and perfect vista of regular cones, till they faded away in the perspective and behind the curvature of the earth.

On the second day after the rain, the water had almost everywhere disappeared, having been evaporated by the heat and dryness of the air. Leaving the plain, we sought water in a ravine of the neighboring mountain. Finding here cavities worn in the face of the granite cliff, we each entered one and made our noon camp for once in the shade. Here I found a large pair of horns of the Rocky Mountain sheep, or "big-horn:" they weighed at least thirty pounds.

Our next camp was made at the Tinaje alta or high tanks. Here, at the head of a long ravine in the mountains, there is a series of five or six large holes, one above the other, worked in the granite bed of the gorge. After a rain these are all filled, but as the season advances, the lower ones become empty, and the traveller is obliged to climb to the higher tanks and bail water into the one below him, and from this into the next, and so on till there is enough in the lowest to quench the thirst of his animals. The higher tanks are accessible only at great risk to life. After a succession of dry seasons it sometimes happens that travellers arrive here already dying from thirst. Finding no water in the lower holes, they climb in vain to the higher ones, where, perhaps, losing strength with the death of hope, they fall from the narrow ledge, and the tanks, in which they seek for life, become their graves.

A ride of one day from the Tinaje alta brought us to the Gila river, at one of the stations of the abandoned overland stage route. Here a piece cut from a newspaper and fastened to the door of the house, first informed us of the defeat of the North at Bull Run. Indeed, almost the last news we had received before this from the East, was of the firing on Fort Sumter.

Our route now lay along the Gila river. Stopping in the afternoon, we sought relief from the heat by taking a bath in the stream; but the water which we had found pleasant in the morning was now unpleasantly warm, and on trying it with the thermometer, the mercury sank from 117 degrees in the air, only to 100 degrees in the water, which was thus two degrees above blood-heat. During the night we were travelling by the bright light of the full moon, when, looking south, I saw a black wall rising like a mountain of darkness, and rapidly hiding the sky as it moved steadily toward us. In a few minutes we were in intense obscurity, and in the heart of a sand-storm which rendered all progress impossible. Dismounting, we held the terrified animals by the lassos, and sat down with our backs to the wind. We had repeatedly to rise to prevent being buried altogether by the deluge of sand. When the storm was over the moon had set, obliging us to unload our half-buried animals and camp for the night.

The next morning we reached Colorado city (opposite Fort Yuma), on the Colorado river. This place, consisting of one house, had a curious origin, which was told me by a friend, who was also the founder. Soon after the purchase of Arizona, my friend had organized a party and explored the new region. Wishing to raise capital in California to work a valuable mine, he was returning thither with his party, when they reached the Colorado river at this point. The ferry belonged to a German, whose fare for the party would have amounted to about $25. Having no money, they encamped near the ferry to hold a council over this unexpected turn of affairs, when my friend, with the ready wit of an explorer, hit upon the expedient of paying the ferriage in city lots. Setting the engineer of the party, and under him the whole force, at work with the instruments, amid a great display of signal-staffs, they soon had the city laid out in squares and streets, and represented in due form on an elaborate map, not forgetting water lots, and a steam ferry. Attracted by the unusual proceeding, the owner of the ferry crossed the river, and began to interrogate the busy surveyors, by whom he was referred to my friend. On learning from that gentleman that a city was being founded so near to his own land, the German became interested, and, as the great future of the place was unfolded in glowing terms, and the necessity of a steam ferry for the increasing trade dwelt upon, he became enthusiastic and began negotiations for several lots. The result was the sale of a small part of the embryo city, and the transportation of the whole party over in part payment for one lot. I must do my friend the justice to say that he afterward did all that could be done to forward the growth of the place.

Making our quarters at the ferry-house, our party separated, the colored cook going, with the muleteer, back to his Mexican wife, in Sonora. The two Americans who had joined us on the road lived near the fort; with their departure, our number was reduced to three.

During our stay of several days, we saw a good deal of the Yuma Indians, a tribe which, till within a few years, was celebrated for the beauty of its women. But this quality was already causing the destruction of the tribe, and while we were there we saw the funeral ceremonies of the last of the beautiful women. Unlike most of the Indians, the Yumas burn their dead. In this instance, a pile of wood about eight feet long, and four or five feet wide, left hollow in the centre to receive the body, formed the funeral pile. The body, wrapt in the clothing of the deceased, and borne by relatives, was placed in the pile, which was then lighted. As the flames increased, friends approached the spot, with low and mournful wailing, to feed the fire with some article of dress, or ornament. One after another, the young Yuma women were disappearing, victims to disease brought by the troops, and which, it seems, the military physicians did little to prevent the spread of.

Both the men and women of this tribe are large and well built. The women wear a short skirt, made of strings of bark, fastened to a girdle around the waist, and reaching to above the knees. The most important weapon of the warriors is a short club, an unusual implement among our aborigines.

The Colorado river is about five hundred yards broad at Fort Yuma, and its yellowish waters represent the drainage of the greater part of Arizona, New Mexico, Utah, and Colorado. Navigable for steamboats to the mouth of the Virgin river, five hundred miles from the Gulf of California, it presents the means of reaching Utah with the least land travel.

Above this point it comes in from the east, and southeast, and in this part of its course, the Grand Cañon is one of the greatest of natural wonders, if, indeed, it be not the most remarkable. For a distance of nearly five hundred miles the river flows through a gorge, whose vertical, and, in places, overhanging walls, rise on either side to a height of from four to six thousand feet. Indeed, the explorations of Ives and Newberry have shown that throughout this immense area, which forms a table-land between the Rocky Mountains and the Sierra Nevada, the whole river system of the Colorado and its tributaries is sunk thousands of feet perpendicularly into the crust of the earth.

Through this almost inaccessible region are scattered the remnants of the Pueblo Indians, a disappearing race which has left, over an immense area, the ruins of large dwellings, and of extensive canals for irrigation.

After resting a few days we made preparations to continue our journey to California. An emigrant who, with his wife, had been forced by the secessionists to leave Texas, agreed to carry our baggage in his wagon. He left the ferry in the morning, while we were to start in the evening, and overtake him at the first encampment on the desert. During the day there arrived a man whom I knew to be a notorious cut-throat. This fellow, a tall one-eyed villain, who was known as "one-eyed Jack," I knew must have just come from Arizona. He wore trowsers of which one leg was white, and the other brown. It was soon evident that the new arrival and Williams were old cronies, and they passed most of the day together. Before we left in the evening I asked Williams the name of his friend, and received for answer that he was called Jack, that he had just come from California, and was going to Arizona.

We left the ferry about dusk, but before we had gone half a mile Williams had disappeared. Our route lay for several miles along the west side of the Colorado, and Poston and myself rode to the point where the road leaves the river to turn westward. Here we descended the bank to water the horses, and dismounting, waited nearly an hour for our missing companion. We finally started without him, and leaving the river, began to cross the wooded bottom-land toward the desert. We had ridden a short distance when a bush, freshly fallen across the road, seemed to be a warning that the route was impracticable further on. Poston remained by the signal, while I looked in vain for another way through the underbrush; it was evident that the bush had been cut since the passage of the wagon that morning. I had started through the open wood to strike the road some distance beyond, when my attention was drawn, by my horse's uneasiness, to a mule tied in the woods, and to a man stretched out on the ground. At a glance I saw from a distance, by the different-colored legs of the man's trousers, that "one-eyed Jack" was near me. Without stopping, I went to the road, and following this back, came upon Williams's horse fastened to a tree, and near him his owner apparently asleep. On being asked what the bush meant, he replied that he had put it there that we might not pass him while he slept. That was the last place where we would find grass, and as there would be no water for thirty miles, he said we must camp there for the night. In the mean time Poston rode up. The truth had already entered my mind but dismounting, while

I pretended to unbuckle my saddle-girth, I asked Williams where he had been.

"I went back to the river for my canteen."

This I knew was a lie, for I had seen him drink from it as we left the ferry.

"When is your one-eyed friend going to Arizona?" I asked.

"He's gone already; I saw him across the river;" was the cool reply.

The villain's coolness was admirable, but the whole plot was clear. Jumping into the saddle, and making a sign to Poston, I declared my intention of riding on to the emigrant's camp. As Williams swore he would go no further that night, we left him and soon entered the desert. We both decided that Williams and his friend had conspired to kill us while we slept, and then to murder the emigrant and his wife, and get possession of the silver which had attracted the Mexican bandits.*

Leaving the woods, which form a narrow strip along the Colorado, we passed a belt of shifting sand several miles broad, which is gradually approaching the river and burying the trees.

We reached the camp of the emigrant at about 3 A. M., and entering the abandoned station of the Overland Stage Company, slept soundly till roused by the noise of the preparation for breakfast. After we had eaten and begun to saddle our animals, Williams rode up, and entering the house rather roughly told the lady-like wife of the emigrant to make him a breakfast. Some sharp words passed between us, and Williams left the house with an oath and a muttered threat. Poston beckoned to me, and we went out. Our companion stood a few yards from the door, with his back toward us, and did not notice our approach. Poston drawing his revolver, called Williams by name. Taken by surprise he whirled around, and catching sight of the revolver, made a motion toward his own; but he was too old a hand to draw a pistol against one already pointed at him.

"Williams," continued Poston, in the coolest tone, "Pumpelly and I have concluded that it wouldn't be safe for you to go to California. The last man you killed has not been dead long

* Colonel Poston on a subsequent journey learned in Sonora, that the twelve Mexicans had followed us for more than 200 miles, but finding us always on the watch, had not dared attack us.

enough, and they have a way there of hanging men like you. We don't wish to shoot you, for we hav'nt the time to bury you. You may keep the outfit, but you had better go back and join your friend, one-eyed Jack, down there by the river; you and he can't kill us, and you can't get our silver."

With a hearty laugh, Williams held out his hand.

"Give us your hand; you're sharper by a d—d sight than I thought you was; you'll do for the border; good morning!" and jumping into the saddle, he put spurs to his horse and rode away by the road he had come. We watched him as he rode off, and could not help laughing at the fellow's cool impudence. After riding a short distance he turned, and, waving his hat, shouted: "Good-bye; bully for you!—you'll do for the border." I have given this scene in full, as an illustration of the character of a representative of one type of the frontiersman.

The desert we were now crossing begins in Lower California, and stretches several hundred miles northward, between the Sierra Nevada and the Colorado river. Portions of this great area are depressed below the level of the sea. Where we crossed it, partly in Lower California and partly in California, it was the worst of deserts. Its centre, along our route, was a broad plain of fine, sandy clay, strewn with fresh-water shells, and appeared to be the dry bed of a fresh-water lake, which was once, probably, supplied from the Colorado river. Away from this plain the surface is covered with ridges of shifting sand. The wells dug by the Overland Stage Company yield a sulphurous and alkaline water, so fetid as to be undrinkable, excepting when the traveller is driven to it by fear of death from thirst. Indeed, it often induces a disease which sometimes prove fatal. On no desert have I seen the mirage so beautiful as here.

Riding one night, we saw before us a camp fire, by which we found an American and one Mexican. As meeting a traveller on a desert is always an event, we dismounted and smoked while the others were eating. The American was on his way to Sonora, and the Mexican was his guide. We told him how dangerous it then was to travel through the intermediate country, and in Sonora.

"Well, I guess I'm pretty much proof against bullets and lances, stranger; just feel here;" he replied, putting his hand on his breast.

We felt his shirt, and found it double, and lined all round with discs of something heavy.

"Those are all twenty-dollar gold pieces; I'm pretty much proof," he continued. It was useless to give further warning to a man who published the fact that he was encased in gold, so we left him to his fate. We heard afterward, all the way to Los Angeles, that he had everywhere boasted of his golden armor; and, later still, that he had been murdered by his guide. This man was the associate of Palmer, with whom he had caused an excitement in San Francisco about a rich silver mine they pretended to have discovered in a volcano in the Sierra Nevada. After raising a large sum of money they decamped. The body of Palmer was discovered some time afterward in Tulare county.

Finally, in the beginning of September, we approached the western edge of the Colorado desert. Travelling by moonlight, we entered the valley of Carisso creek, by which the desert sends an arm, like an estuary, into the mountains which limit it. As though fearful that the traveller may forget the horrors of a thousand miles of journey over its awful wastes, the desert, as a last farewell, unfolds in this dismal recess a scene never to be forgotten.

Already from the plain, through the clear moonlight, we saw the lofty range bordering the waste, a barren wilderness of dark rock rising high above the gray terraces of sand that fringe its base, great towering domes and lowering cliffs rent to the bottom, and clasping deep abysses of darkness.

As all night long we forced our way through the deep sand of the gorge, winding among countless skeletons, glittering in the moonlight, scorched by hot blasts ever rushing up from the deserts behind us, we seemed wandering through the valley of the shadow of death, and flying from the very gates of hell.

The next day we reached the summit of the Sierra Nevada, and felt the breeze from the ocean. In an instant both horse and rider raised their drooping heads, and, quickened as with a new life, dropped the accumulated languor of months of travel.

As we descended the western declivity of the mountains, our eyes greeted everywhere by herds of cattle and magnificent live-oaks, it seemed impossible that the cheerful land we were traversing should be a frame to the scene of desolation we had left the day before.

Our route to Los Angeles lay through the stock ranches which form, with the vineyards, the principal industrial feature of the southern part of California. Almost the entire population consisted of emigrants from the Southern States, and so strong was the hatred felt toward the North, since the news of the rebel victories, that a Northerner was in as great danger as he would have been in the worst parts of the South.

With our arrival at Los Angeles ended our journey on horseback; a coasting steamer took us to San Francisco. Colonel Poston returned by the Isthmus to the Eastern States, and I passed two or three months in visiting some of the principal mining districts, preparatory to beginning the practice of my profession.

California is well known, of late, to all the inhabitants of the Eastern States, and is perhaps more widely known throughout the world, through books of travel and family letters, in every language, than any other part of the globe. Therefore I shall not stop to dwell upon it, intensely interesting though it be, not more from its great and varied natural resources than from its wonderful history. Twenty years ago an almost uninhabited and unknown region, California had every prospect of having to await the gradual westward-bound progress of population. As if by magic, the discovery of gold transformed it into a land teeming with the energy, enterprise, and daring of every people, while at the same time it became the place of refuge of all the criminals and ruffians who could escape from justice, and buy or work a passage thither. Thus arose on the instant a state of society in which justice had little voice, and in which the revolver enforced the law of might.

Such was its birth. The California of to-day is a monument of the manner in which not merely Americans, but men of every political education, once inoculated with the spirit of self-government, have evolved order and stability out of a state of dissolution. And even thus, California is but the embryo of a giant, whose future growth will be, perhaps, less dependent on the nations of the Atlantic, than on those which are destined, in the next centuries, to encircle the Pacific with the homes of future civilization.

Shortly before my arrival in San Francisco, the Japanese Government had instructed Mr. C. W. Brooks, their commercial agent, to engage two geologists and mining engineers, for the purpose of exploring a part of the Japanese Empire. Through a misunderstanding, a copy of the correspondence, which passed through our minister at Yeddo, having been sent to Washington, our own Government proceeded to make the appointments. By a pure coincidence I was chosen as one of the two men, both at Washington and at San Francisco, my colleague appointed from the former place being Dr. J. P. Kimball, and from the latter, Mr. W. P. Blake.

In preparing for this journey I became indebted to many kind friends, especially to Professor J. D. Whitney, of the State Geological Survey, and to his Assistants, Messrs. Brewer and Ashburner, as well as to Messrs. Louis Janin and Henry Janin, of the Enrequita mines.

CHAPTER V.

PACIFIC OCEAN.

On the 23d of November, 1861, Mr. Blake and myself went aboard the clipper-ship "Carrington," which was bound to Yokohama, by way of Honolulu. Among the passengers were Lady Franklin, and her niece, Miss Craycroft. At midnight, the friends who had come to see us off left the ship. With the hoisting of the anchor we cut loose from the New World, and, drifting through the Golden Gate, began the long voyage over the great ocean. The rising sun found us still in sight of the Farellones, and rocking in the long swell of a calm and glassy sea. Another clipper, also calm-bound, lay a mile or two from us; while in the distance, the white sails of pilot boats and fishing smacks seemed to fan the horizon as they rolled with the monotonous motion of the swell. The day was nearly gone without bringing a breath of air, when it became evident that the neighboring clipper and our ship were slowly but surely approaching each other. It was a large vessel, bearing only ballast, while our smaller craft was heavily loaded. Every roll of the long swell brought us nearer together, until it seemed as though every minute must bring the sharp bow of the immense ship crashing through the frail side of the "Carrington."

Captain Mather sent for the passengers to be ready for escape, and ordered the crew on deck with axes in hand. Already the black hull of the other ship towered high above us, as she rose on the top of a roll, threatening to crush us in her descent. The captains held a hurried council from their quarter-decks. As a last hope for their vessels, they decided that the "Carrington," being the heavier laden, should drop anchor. This was done, for we were still over the bar, and almost at the same instant a faint breath of air, barely perceptible to a landsman, moved our neighbor slowly off.

The "Carrington" had just made the shortest trip on record,

from Yokohama to San Francisco, having been less than twenty-seven days on the way, and we hoped that the present voyage would be correspondingly short, or less than fifty days. But we were doomed to make the longest time between the two ports.

The first part of the voyage was marked by delightful weather, in the region of refreshing trade winds. I improved the opportunity for practicing navigation, and, between this occupation and the usual amusements on shipboard the days passed quickly by.

On the 17th of December a peak of the island of Maui, and soon after the island of Molokai, and the next morning three peaks of Oahu, were visible. As we approached the last named island, the small but well-defined crater near "Coco head," and

CRATER NEAR HONOLULU.

later, that at Diamond point, rose from the surf, outposts of the great volcanic group we were entering. The following morning, having taken a pilot, we steered for the entrance to Honolulu. As we approached the island the scene was truly enchanting. A dense carpet of delicate green, like that of a newly-opened leaf, mantled the island, and descending from the tops of the high hills, disappeared behind the long tufty walls of snowy-white surf-foam. Groves of cocoanut trees and bananas, and taro-terraces, formed the foreground, above which arose the green and densely-wooded hills of the interior.

As we were to remain only a day or two at Honolulu, we hastened on shore. Having letters to Dr. Judd, one of the original cabinet members instrumental in framing the Hawaiian Government, Mr. Blake and myself received a cordial reception from that gentleman and Mr. Carter, and an invitation to make our stay at their houses. The day was spent in a pleasant ride to the Paré, a mountain pass, celebrated alike for its magnificent view and for a desperate battle fought during the war which ended in the union of all the Islands under one King. The road leading to this place winds up a broad valley, of which the sides sweep with a gentle curve, on either side, up to the foot of the high cliffs which wall it in.

The valley is cultivated, while the ravines are filled with dense foliage, and every nook and ledge on the cliffs give root-hold to luxuriant over-hanging masses of delicate green.

At last we stood on the pass. The view before us was one of which the Hawaiians might well be proud. We stood on the top of a high cliff, with a large and nearly circular valley beneath us. Away to the right and left stretched the lofty walls, curving gradually around as if to enclose the valley on all sides, and draped in rich tropical green, relieved here and there by the red and brown cliffs, and towers of rock.

Away in the distance, the green of the valley-carpet gave place to the blue of the ocean-background; the narrow belt of surf, dashed to foam over the white coral bottom, forming a line of harmony between the two colors.

While we were at the Paré, an incident occurred which illustrates a curious superstition still prevalent among the people. In examining the volcanic rock, of which the hills consist, my attention was attracted to what I took to be a wax-like mineral, known as palagonite. Detaching it without much trouble, I was surprised at finding a hole behind it, apparently containing more of the same substance.

Hoping to increase my supply of a rare mineral from a new locality, I stowed away in my pocket, without a closer examination, the piece I had obtained, and proceeded carefully to dig out the rest with my knife. Much to our astonishment, the prize produced from the hole was a half-decayed rag. A closer examination of the supposed mineral, so carefully treasured in my pocket, showed that it belonged decidedly to the animal kingdom. Mr. Carter asked an explanation from some passing natives. They explained that the substance found was the navel of some infant, it being an ancient custom, at the birth of a child, for the parents to hide this part of the infant to whom alone the place of concealment is afterward shown. Should an enemy, by any chance, discover the sacred repository, it would be in his power to "prey" to death the unsuspecting owner.

The Sandwich Islands, lying in the middle of the Pacific, between 19 and 23 degrees N. latitude, and in the track of all vessels bound from our western ports to eastern Asia, hold the most important position among the groups in the great ocean. They are the chief rendezvous for whalers; and before the decline of that branch of industry, nearly the entire commerce of the Islands centred in the necessities of these roving fleets, and the transshipment of whale oil and bone. The decrease of this external source of wealth is now being compensated by the development of the resources, chiefly agricultural, of the Islands.

With a temperature averaging 75 degrees through the year, and ranging between the extremes of 60 and 88 degrees, and always fanned by the northeast trade-winds, the climate is exceedingly healthy, and may make of the group the sanitarium of the Pacific.

When discovered by Cook, in 1778, the Islands were under the rule of separate chiefs; but about the beginning of the present century, after a desperate war, they were all subjugated by Kamehameha I. and united into one kingdom under him. In 1820 the first missionaries arrived from the United States. According to Dr. Anderson, they found property, life—everything, in fact—in the hands of the King and irresponsible chiefs—the nation composed of thieves, drunkards, and debauchees, and the people slaves to the sovereign. The labors of the missionaries began immediately, and met with the approval of the King, Kamehameha II.

In 1822 the Hawaiian language was reduced to writing, and schools were established. Under the influence of the missionaries the machinery of a liberal government with a code of laws was introduced; public works were undertaken; general education was fostered; and in 1840 a liberal constitution was granted by the King, Kamehameha IV. At present there are more than 400 schools, and one college. More than one-third of the population can read, and nearly all the children attend the schools. Several hundred works, representing a considerable range of science, literature, and religious instruction, have been translated into Hawaiian.

Increasing intelligence has increased the wants of the people. While during their condition as savages nearly all the demands of life were supplied by the voluntary gifts of a tropical nature, the requisites of civilized life are obtainable only through labor. Under this stimulus the natives have mainly, through oral instruction, attained to considerable skill in agriculture, and in manufacturing simple products, as sugar, molasses, salt, arrow-root, etc., as well as in working in iron and other metals. In 1858 the exported domestic produce, mostly agricultural, amounted to about $530,000, and the total commerce to $1,089,661 imports, and $787,082 exports, yielding $116,138 to the customs revenue. The imports have since risen to $1,800,000, and the exports to $1,330,000. The receipts of the treasury for the two years ending March 31, 1860, were $656,216, the expenditures $643,088, and the national debt $108,777. No standing army is kept beyond the royal body-guard of eighty men.

The above sketch of the history and commerce of these islands, taken mainly from the "American Encyclopedia," speaks for itself, as an illustration of the rapid change effected in the condition of the natives through the well-directed labors of an intelligent body of missionaries.

The history of our intercourse with the Sandwich Islands, presents perhaps the best standard by which we may judge of the effect of the engrafting of European civilization on the widely-spread Polynesian and Malay races.

Before the arrival of Cook on their shores, the inhabitants of these Islands were a race of savages, possessed of health and robustness to a degree equalled only among the kindred New Zealanders, and enjoying fully the indolence almost forced upon them by the abundance of the voluntary gifts of the earth. On the other hand, they were oppressed by the terrors of a dark and bloody religion, which was able at any moment to drag individuals or families to the altar as sacrifices to the caprice of a chief or a priest.

As is generally the case in new regions, European civilization has been there represented by its extremes of good and evil. For many years the Government of these Islands has been virtually in the hands of a body of zealous and intelligent missionaries, who, as we have seen, have succeeded in forming a constitutional monarchy with a liberal code of laws.

The Christian religion has taken the place of the terrible rites of human sacrifice, and with the introduction of a written language, and the establishment of numerous schools, education became open to all, and its advantages are availed of by the entire population.

In no part of the extra-Caucasian world has modern missionary enterprise effected so much social and political good as among the Polynesians, and especially in the Sandwich Islands, and it has indeed been a great good. But it would seem that those very characteristics of the Polynesian race which rendered the effecting of this possible, facilitated in even a more easy ratio the introduction of the seeds of destruction.

It is easy to understand, when viewing them as a people possessing no civilization of a higher degree than was theirs, and therefore governed by traditional customs, morally, socially, and politically, of a very low order, the offspring of the animal rather than of the intellectual faculties, that among them the influence of the debauching sailor should be as potent for evil as that of the missionary for good.

The immense difference between the results of these opposing influences may be measured by the fact that the population of the group diminished from 140,000 in 1823, to 73,000 in 1843—a loss of nearly one-half in thirty years, owing mainly to the introduction of foreign vices and foreign disease. Whether this decrease will continue till the extinction of the aborigines is perhaps not certain; but it is hardly probable that the Polynesians, as a pure race, will play any very important part in the great future that is dawning upon the Pacific world.

The costume introduced by the missionaries, nearly fifty years ago, is still the dress of the native women. It consists of long skirts, high waists, immense coal-scuttle bonnets, and, apparently, no underclothing. The effect was laughable, as we met troops of pretty girls mounted astride of ponies, and dressed in the costume of our grandmothers' portraits, chattering and laughing gayly as they cantered along, their bright-colored dresses fluttering in the wind, and scarcely concealing their well-rounded forms.

It was not without much difficulty that the missionaries succeeded in making these children of nature adopt any dress whatever, even for decent attendance at church. Even now, I have been told, on some of the islands, the people bring on Sunday all their clothing in a bundle to the door of the church, where they dress, and after service doffing their costume, carry it homeward under their arms.

Honolulu, with its pleasant society, delightful climate and tropical fruits, as well as its beautiful scenery, is destined to become a favorite resort for visitors from California and the neighboring States. Until within a few years the group enjoyed an absolute freedom from the disagreeable insects and reptiles common to the tropics, but at present mosquitoes abound, the legacy of a ship which stopped there some years ago on its way from Oregon to Asia with a cargo of lumber.

After a delightful visit of two days we left Honolulu, and again settled down to the routine of life at sea. Hoping to find more favorable winds we ran several degrees south, till brought to a standstill by a calm. Here, for days, our ship lay apparently motionless, on a perfectly smooth sea, though our observations showed that the great equatorial current was carrying us on our way at the rate of about fifty miles a day. A large shark hovered around our stern, his companion, a pilot-fish, almost always visible, swimming near the dorsal fin of the monster. A large hook, baited with beef, was thrown overboard. The shark turned on his back, and quickly swallowing the bait, turned again and was caught. The home-end of the rope was passed through a block, and soon the great monster was being raised to the quarter-deck. While in this position a violent blow from his tail against the stern of the ship shook the latter through its whole length, showering into the sea nearly our entire stock of bananas, which had been hung over the stern to ripen.

During the calm, the smooth surface of the ocean bore myriads of zoophytes, mostly Physales (Portugese man-of-war) and Velellae, with here and there an Ianthina and a Rhysostoma. The Velellae, a flat oval disc about an inch long, with an upright membrane like a sail crossing it obliquely, floated leisurely on the surface. Many dead ones were found having small mollusks attached to them, these pirates using their victims at the same time for food and means of locomotion.

The rhysostoma and physales lived for several hours in a bowl of sea water, and both of them emitted a phosphorescent light, when stirred in the dark. Many were the sharp stings we received from the long arms of the latter, when they chanced to touch the back of the hand or the face.

In violation of all sailing directions, our captain now decided to run north and then west to Japan, and with the first favorable wind we steered northwest till the calms of Cancer brought us again to a standstill, excepting the slow westwardly movement due to the current. The next wind permitted at first a northwesterly course, but soon bringing us into the region of westerly winds, our course slanted off to the north, and finally into east of north, and we ran again south into the calms of Cancer. During more than sixty days we were continually repeating this zigzag course, making some progress by casual breezes and the current in the calms of Cancer, and then running north in the vain hope of finding favorable winds. This was owing to the mismanagement of the captain, for it is an established fact, that from the 27th degree north latitude north, the prevailing winds are from the west, while from the 23d degree north latitude to the equator, they are the trades blowing from the north-east, the two regions being separated by the belt of the calms of Cancer.

At the end of a month we had not made half the distance between Honolulu and Japan. About this time it was discovered that the great iron tank on which we relied for water had sprung a leak. As it was surrounded by the cargo, it was both impossible to get at the leak to stop it, or to find out how far it was from the bottom. The deck-casks were empty, the water sinking several inches daily in the tank, and it was impossible to say when we might reach land. The passengers and crew were immediately put on rations of water, each person receiving about a quart daily.

During the greater part of the remaining distance we were tossed about by almost constant head winds and violent storms; the three new sets of sails with which the ship had begun the voyage were reduced to one set made up of patches; and the loss of the nut from a rudder-bolt threatened to leave us without the means of steering. In addition to this, a disagreement between the chronometers left us in doubt as to our exact position; for we had seen no land since leaving the Sandwich Islands, although our course crossed repeatedly the long line of low reefs and rocks stretching thence to the northeast.

On the evening of the 18th of February, the cry of "land!" brought us all on deck. A cone, so regular in shape as to leave no doubt of its being the Japanese volcano Fuziyama, was visible near the setting sun. The day and night were calm, and as we were now within the influence of the Kurosiwo—the gulf-stream of the Pacific—we were drifted northward, and in the morning were opposite Cape King. Hundreds of Japanese fishing boats were visible all day, and toward evening a favorable breeze brought us in sight of the volcano Oosima, from which arose a column of vapor.

The next morning found us off the entrance to the bay of Yeddo. Fuziyama was very distinct, its elegant cone completely mantled with snow, and rising high into the air above the intervening wooded hills. Far away, long before we had seen other land, the first glimpse we had caught of Asia and the Japanese Empire was the snow-clad cone of this graceful mountain. This beautiful volcano, rising 12,400 feet above the sea, is perhaps the first object associated with Japan in the minds of all who have seen the decorated wares of that country. It was, therefore, fitting that this only familiar object, like a solitary friend, should welcome us as strangers to a land where all else was new to us.

The entrance to the bay of Yeddo does not make itself apparent till one is nearly in it; and, owing to a misunderstanding of the sailing directions, we very nearly ran aground in taking a wrong course, which would have brought us ashore in Susaki bay. When we discovered the mistake the wind was gone, and we passed the day lazily and impatiently, watching the glassy surface of the sea for the "cat's-paw" forerunner of a breeze. The arrival of a boat, from which we bought some fish, was a welcome excitement, as our cabin stores were entirely gone, and without the fish we would have been reduced to very bad junk and hard-tack.

During the afternoon I amused myself in examining some of the many kinds of zoophytes with which these waters abound. One of these, a beroe, I believe, a small transparent bell-shaped animal, was marked with ciliated lines, radiating from the top, and continuing to the rim. Kept in a bowl of sea-water, and stirred in the dark, this animal emitted a beautiful phosphorescent light along all the ciliated lines, rendering these, and only these, distinct in every detail.

Early the next morning we beat into the Uraga channel, the entrance to the bay. On both sides the shore was formed by high hills, with numerous valleys and ravines. Rich foliage covered the declivities, while small villages or isolated houses occupied the foreground in the valleys, the terraced sides and bottoms of which last were green with young grain. Fishing boats, and nets of many kinds, lay along the shore, while hundreds of junks were taking advantage of the fair wind to leave the bay. Boats with fishermen were constantly coming off to us and offering fish. In their long dresses, it was impossible for us to distinguish between the men and women. All were anxious to get empty bottles; one of these, corked and thrown astern, would cause an exciting race between a score of boats.

Soon we passed the long tongue of land known as Treaty point, and the bay of Yeddo opened before us so large that, in the northeast, no land was visible. Here Mr. Benson, U. S. Consul, and Mr. Brower, agent of Messrs. Olyphant & Co., came on board and invited Mr. Blake and myself to make our stay at their house.

CHAPTER VI.

YOKOHAMA.

The scene which met us on landing, and through which we walked to Mr. Brower's house, was no less novel than busy. At the head of the quay we passed a long low building with black walls and paper windows. This was the custom-house, and a large number of men bearing two swords, and shuffling in sandals in and out at the doors, were the officials of this service. The broad streets, leading through the foreign quarter, were crowded with Japanese porters, bearing merchandise to and from the quay, each pair with their burden between them on a pole, and marking time independently of the others, with a loud monotonous cry—whang hai! whang hai!

We immediately reported ourselves by letters to the Governor of Kanagawa, and receiving an answer from that officer that he would communicate with the Government at Yeddo, we settled down to await further orders.

Yokohama is one of the three ports opened to foreign trade. The treaty called for the opening of Kanagawa, a large town on the opposite side of the harbor; but the native Government wishing, in accordance with its policy, to keep foreigners distinct from Japanese, built an island in a shallow harbor, separating it from the main land by broad canals. On this they erected storehouses, and built a quay. With the day appointed for opening the port arrived the foreigners, eager to reap the first fruits of trade, and these earliest comers, finding conveniences prepared for them which did not exist in Kanagawa, accepted readily the position assigned them by the cunning Government. Yokohama is infinitely better adapted to trade than Kanagawa, so far as the harbor facilities are concerned, and is far more easily defended against the attack of the assassinating Ronins. Both reasons undoubtedly entered into the plans of the Government; but other equally important motives influenced it in building this isolated town. In the first place the Yeddo Government could say to the anti-foreign party that no aliens had been allowed a dwelling-place on the island of Nippon. By this means the letter of the unrepealed law against admission of "barbarians" was evaded. In the second place, by the isolation of foreigners and all who were permitted to trade with them, it was possible to keep a thorough control over commerce.

Soon after our arrival we started on an excursion to visit the Daibutz, a colossal image of Budda. The road thither lay across the country intervening between the bays of Yeddo and Wodowara. This region is a plateau, which, facing the former bay with a bluff about 100 feet high, extends inland about twenty-five miles to the Oyama mountains. This plain is cut up by innumerable ravines and valleys which are cultivated, while the narrow intervening ridges are generally covered with forest trees. The ravines are terraced to the hill-tops, the upper half being devoted generally to wheat and other crops, while the lower half, as well as the valleys into which the ravines open, are given up to rice-culture. The water for this crop, in the ravines, is supplied by the outflow from a horizontal bed of gravel which everywhere crops out about half-way up the hill-sides. Our road, rarely wide enough for two horsemen riding abreast, lay partly over the hills, while during much of the distance it wound among the rice plantations along the tops of the narrow partitions by which the irrigating water is confined to the fields, and where a misstep of the horse would have left both him and his rider floundering in deep mud.

The highly-cultivated valleys unmarred by fences, the sober-looking farm-houses and cottages showing well-preserved age, shaded by handsome trees, and surrounded by neat hedges of growing bamboo, all united to form a landscape in which there was nothing harsh, and where the work of man seemed to harmonize with that of nature.

Our way wound through several villages where the people, especially the children, turned out to see us go by, the latter greeting us with the morning salutation: "ohaio!" "ohaio!" Several times we passed large temple enclosures with imposing gateways of granite, from which broad stone walks led through groves of magnificent trees to wide flights of stone steps, leading up the hill-side to the shrine at the top.

About noon we reached Kamakura, and leaving our horses at an inn, started on foot to visit the Daibutz. A half-hour's walk along a comparatively broad road, leading under peculiar archways placed at short intervals, brought us to the shore of Wodowara bay, and near this to our destination. Passing through an enclosing grove of evergreens, we came into a large open space paved with flagstones. In the centre of this is the image. It represents Budda sitting, in the Oriental manner, on a lotus. It is of bronze, fifty feet high, and ninety-six feet in circumference at the base, and is raised on a pedestal five or six feet from the ground.

We had all come expecting to see some grotesque idol, and we were therefore pleasantly surprised, when, instead of this, we found ourselves admiring a work of high art. It is Budda in Nirvana. The sculptor has succeeded in impressing upon the cold metal the essence of the promise given by Sakyamuni to his followers, a promise which has been during more than twenty centuries the guiding hope of countless millions of souls. This is the doctrine of the final attainment of Nirvana—the state of utter annihilation of external consciousness—after ages of purification by transmigration.

Both the face, which is of the Hindoo type, and the attitude are in perfect harmony with the idea intended to be expressed. I felt that I saw for the first time, and where I least expected it, a realization, in art, of a religious idea. No Madonna on canvas, or Christ in marble, had ever been other to me than suggestive, through the aid of an acquaintance with the subjects treated. The Budda of Kamakura is a successful rendering of a profound religious abstraction.

The head is covered with small knobs, representing the snails which tradition says came to protect Budda from the heat of the burning sun.

This image, which was made about 600 years ago, was cast in sections of a few square feet of surface each, and an inch or more thick, and when put together, the joints were fitted so closely that now, after the lapse of centuries, they can be detected only where the weather has made them visible in the discoloration.

The statue is hollow, and has in the interior a temple with many small images of the Buddist pantheon. Many of these without the lotus, would, in a Romish church, have passed readily for representations of the Virgin.

It is said that a large temple once enclosed the Daibutz, but was destroyed by an earthquake-wave from the sea.

Returning to Kamakura, we ate a hearty lunch, which had been brought and prepared by the servants of Mr. Keswick, and then started to visit the great temple grounds at this place.

Passing under a large granite gateway and crossing a stone bridge, we entered the grounds by a broad flagged walk nearly a mile long. At short intervals, we crossed paved avenues leading through the open grove of trees which bore the marks of many centuries, and ascending by broad flights of steps to elevated shrines commanding long vistas over the surrounding land. On large terraces perfectly graded and paved and surrounded by carved stone balustrades, are built the great temples which render Kamakura famous. The buildings are of imposing size, and are raised a few feet from the ground. They are built of wood, the immense beams which appear under the widely-projecting roof being richly carved with the heads of dragons and storks. Every end of a timber is capped with copper, and large quantities of this metal are used inside and out of these edifices. On some of the temples great labor had been expended in very rich and elegant carving of the woodwork, and on some of the terraces we saw several large and graceful bronze vases.

In one part of the grounds, sacredly guarded by an enclosure, there is a priapus, if one may so style a representation of the opposite sex, in a black stone, said to have fallen from heaven. It is worshipped by barren women.

At the time of our visit the temples were closed, and we were told they had not been opened for several years. On a subsequent visit I found that a runner gave notice to the priests of the approach of foreigners, in time to close the buildings. This was a recent restriction, arising out of the shameful acts of some European visitors.

Leaving Kamakura, we ascended a valley bordered by many temple grounds, and commanded by small shrines, perched at the tops of long flights of moss-grown steps of stone. Through a deep artificial cut we passed from this valley over the water-shed, and descended to the fishing village of the Kanesawa, on the bay of Yeddo, whence we reached Yokohama by boat.

Finding the Government was not likely to forward us to our destination for some time to come, I engaged a teacher and began the study of the language. The young Japanese who undertook to teach me this most difficult tongue, though naturally bright, had not only no philosophical knowledge of its structure, but he did not know one word in any other language. The instruction was obtained through the medium of an English-Chinese dictionary, the teacher taking the place of a Chinese-Japanese pronouncing lexicon. Progress thus made, though slow, was not always sure, and many were the words treasured up for use which had to be dropped when found to mean the very opposite of what I had supposed. After having carefully learned to read and write the Katakana alphabet of forty-nine letters, I was quite taken aback on finding that no books were printed in that character, and that there remained still the more difficult Hirakana alphabet, and the endless study of the Chinese character to be gone through with before I could hope to read anything beyond love-letters and novelettes.

In the beginning of March there was to be a festival at the temple of Daishi (great teacher), in honor of the inventor of the Japanese alphabet. Mr. Benson and myself, on the day appointed, entered the boat of the Consulate, and crossing the harbor, followed the shore of the bay to the mouth of a small river, the sediment from which has produced a long delta. Notwithstanding the high tide, our boatmen had a hard pull up stream, till throwing off all their clothing they worked with a will at the long sculls, marking time with the monotonous "hwang ho! hwang ho!" or the quicker "hwai hi! hwai hi!"

These boatmen, and indeed most of the men of the lower orders, are as a class the best built men I have seen. The muscles of the arm, leg, and back are equally well developed by the varying routine of their labors. The habit of being naked, with the exception of the breech-clout while at work, renders their skin much darker than that of the middle and upper classes.

After grounding several times we reached the landing nearest the temple.

Passing through the village of Kawasaki, we ordered a dinner at one of the many inns, to be ready on our return. After leaving the village, our path lay part of the way between beautiful and well-kept hedges of evergreens and narrow avenues of tall trees, and partly through extensive pear-orchards. These pear-trees have the appearance of being very old, and at about ten feet from the ground are all cut off and trained on horizontal frames, thus exposing the fruit to the sun. All the pears I tried in Japan were tasteless things, and I believe it is not yet certain whether they are pears or apples.

We soon entered the enclosure of the temple and were surrounded by the crowd of visitors dressed in gala costume.

An imposing building fronted us, approached by a broad flight of a dozen or more steps leading to a wide verandah, which went entirely around the temple. The massive overhanging roof, the great size of all the timbers used in the structure, and the gloom which seemed to pervade the interior as seen from without, all gave to the place an impressive appearance. I never approached a Japanese temple without an indescribable sensation, such as I imagine one would have felt in ascending the steps of the teocalli of Mexico during a sacrifice.

The woodwork of the temple, outside and in, is richly carved. Over the high portal there is fastened a peculiar bell, shaped like a double gong, over the front of which hangs a thick silken-rope, reaching to the verandah. As we watch the motions of the worshippers an officer of some rank arrives, and stepping from his chair washes his hands in the fountain in the middle of the court.

Slowly he mounts the steps, and giving a snake-like motion to the silken-rope, the bell gives out a clear but peculiar sound, the reverberations of which are lost in the sombre interior of the temple. Throwing himself on his knees and face, the worshipper now utters a short prayer, and rising, enters the building.

Here a large number of priests, attending apparently the chief bonze, are performing the ritual, while others are engaged in telling fortunes, or selling illustrated guides to the temple. The air is loaded with burning incense rising from swinging censers and from countless vases.

The fortune-teller holds in his hand a tube containing a large number of sticks like crochet-needles, while before him is a case containing one hundred or more drawers. With a few coins we buy the right to try our luck in reading the future. The old man shakes the box and we each pull out a stick with a number on it, which we find corresponds to a numbered box from which the priest hands us a printed paper; this being in a mixture of Chinese and Japanese, and badly printed at that, is if anything a little harder to read than futurity itself. The result of some hours of study with my teacher over this paper, was the finding that it contained a good deal about clouds and water, an old man sitting under a cherry tree—that part was obscure, but the words, kané, money, and kami, lord, evidently pointed to wealth and promotion, but as I found out later that kané also means metal and crab, and kami means head and paper and other things, I do not consider that the record of my destiny is yet unravelled.

On the wall of the temple hangs a large bronze tablet with the two alphabets, beautifully executed in high relief. The man who receives these honors can hardly be called the inventor of these alphabets, since the Katakana is made up from the Chinese radical characters, while the Hirakana is taken from characters of the Chinese adapted to a running hand. Still the application of these signs to the writing of the forty-nine sounds of the language was the beginning of a new era for Japan.

Even here, where there are crowds of visitors, everything is extremely neat, from the matted floor and waxed and polished verandah and steps of the temple to the smooth flags of the paved court and the great cluster of dustless bronze-work in its middle. With all this, the rich silk dresses and fresh faces of pretty girls and the more sober costumes of men and matrons are in keeping.

When we reached the inn the landlady showed us to a room, and soon two neatly-dressed waitresses appeared with our dinner of soup, fish, rice, seaweed, eggs, mushrooms, and beche de mer, with warm saki or rice wine. If I had previously had any prejudice against Oriental cooking, it vanished with that dinner and never returned, not even in the heart of China. The two really pretty and graceful girls waited on us as though we had been Japanese officers, even to lighting for us the tiny pipes of fragrant tobacco. I began to think that travelling in Japan was likely to be accompanied with fewer hardships than I had been led to expect. It required some exertion to leave the gayly-decked village in time to float our boat out with the tide on our way homeward.

CHAPTER VII.

YOKOHAMA.

THE name Japan, by which we know that empire, is an European corruption of *Ji pun quo* (*ji*—sun; *pun*—root, or origin; *quo*—land or country), the name by which it is called in the Peking dialect in China, and in which we see the origin of Marco Polo's Zipanga. This is the Chinese pronunciation of the Chinese characters with which the Japanese write the name of their empire, and which they pronounce Nipon, or Dai Nipon (Great Sun origin); or, as it is usually rendered, Land of the Rising Sun. The imperial banner is a red sun on a white ground. *Awa-dji-sima* (*awa*—foam; *dji*—earth; *sima*—island,) is said to have been the original name. A very ancient name seems to have been Yamato (*Yama*—mountain; *to*—east), east of the mountains, by which a province is still designated. The pure Japanese language is still called *Yamato-no kotoba.*

The Japanese empire forms the chief part of the long barrier chain of islands which, stretching along the eastern coast of Asia, separate the Great ocean from the Great continent. This chain, a mountain range partially submerged, rising above the surface of the ocean in the island of Formosa, trends northeast, through the Liukiu group, Kiusiu, Nipon, and Yesso, and, forking in the latter, sends off, due north, a geologically distinct branch in the island of Sagalien or Krafto, while the main range continues in its northeasterly course, through the long line of the Kuriles and the continental mountains of Kamschatka, to Behring's Straits.

This outlying chain is the easternmost member of an extensive system of parallel ranges, which, reaching from Birmah to the Arctic ocean, determine nearly all the details in the configuration of eastern Asia in the same manner as the Appalachian system determines the outlines and details of eastern North America. In another work,* after giving reasons for uniting most of the moun-

* "Geological Researches in China, Mongolia, and Japan." Smithsonian Institute, 1866.

tains of eastern Asia under one system, I have shown the remarkable analogies which exist between this and the Appalachians. I have there proposed to unite all the mountains of the northeast and southwest system under one name—the Sinians.

Excepting Formosa, all the large islands of this chain belong to Japan. The greatest breadth across the middle of Nipon is about 200 miles, and the average width of the empire is less than 100 miles. But its narrowness is compensated for by its length, the principal islands ranging from N. L. 31 degrees to about 50 degrees in the island of Sagalien, a length, following the axis, of over 1,600 miles.

Its backbone of older granite and metamorphic rocks is overlaid by younger formations, among which are at least coal-bearing deposits of one age, and Tertiary and Post-tertiary beds, while strata of the Cretaceous or Jurassic age exist on Yesso and Sagalien. Throughout its whole length this range is pierced by countless volcanic vents, and the lavas and tufas ejected from these sources, and in great part deposited originally under the sea, now form terraces and plains around the islands, and cover much of the interior. It is essentially a mountainous country; and though the height of the interior is not known, it seems improbable that the mountains, excepting some volcanic peaks, rise to a greater elevation than 4,000 to 6,000 feet, while even on Nipon the crest-line probably averages less than 3,000 feet. The volcano Fuziyama is said to be over 12,000 feet high, and other peaks of similar character may rise above 10,000 feet.

The rivers, although very short, being merely coast streams, are often deep and navigable for small craft; they are, however, frequently broken by falls and rapids. The bold and rock-bound coast is indented with bays and countless fiords, forming many harbors where whole fleets could ride in safety.

With such a wide extent in latitude there of course exists a corresponding range in climate. In Hakodade, according to the observations of Dr. Albrecht, the mean annual temperature (from an average of the four years 1859-62) is $48^{\cdot 22}$ degrees in 1862, the minimum being, in January, 10 degrees F., and the maximum, in August, $87^{\cdot 3}$ degrees. The fall of rain in 1862 was 47 inches; the maximum fall in one month being ten inches, in July.

Notwithstanding its insular position, the mean annual temperature of Japan, in common with that of all eastern Asia, is below that of corresponding points on the eastern coast of America, which is at least partially explained by the fact that the prevailing winter winds are from the west, blowing from the cold steppes of Tartary.

A marked difference is said by the Japanese to exist between the climates of the eastern and western coasts of Nipon, the latter being much colder and receiving a greater fall of snow than the former. The eastern coast, as far as the northern part of Nipon, is washed by the Kurosiwo, which, branching off from the equatorial current in the tropics, flows as a broad belt of warm water to the northeast, the counterpart in the Pacific ocean of the Atlantic gulf-stream. On the other hand, in the Japan Sea there seems to be a cold current, setting south from the Sea of Ochotsk. A branch from this reaches eastward, through the Straits of Tsungara, passing Hakodade with a velocity of four or five miles per hour. On a voyage in H.I.R.M. Steamer Bogartyr, from Hakodade to Nagasaki, through the Japan Sea, it was found that the current set us every day thirty to forty miles south of the position indicated by dead reckoning.

At the change in the monsoons, especially in September, the coast is visited by fearful hurricanes, called typhoons, carrying destruction in their track. Although these cyclones are felt in the waters of Yesso, their centres follow the curve of the warm Kurosiwo, which does not wash the shores of that island.

Abounding in forests from the extreme south to the northernmost islands, Japan is exceedingly rich in the variety of its trees. The moisture of an insular climate, together with the fertility of soils formed by the decay of volcanic rocks, produce an exuberant vegetation in every latitude of the empire. On the highlands of Nipon the prevailing forms are European. The valleys of southern Nipon and the forests of Kiusiu contain many tropical plants, while the investigations, especially of Gray and Maximowitch, have shown that the flora of Yesso is generically almost identical with that of the northeastern United States.

The animal kingdom does not seem to be so well represented as one might expect, when we consider that the islands must have communicated with the continent at some period since the appearance in Asia of the animals now living wild in the Japanese mountains. The list of wild quadrupeds known to foreign naturalists, seems to be confined to a species of hare, a deer, an antelope, a bear, a wild hog, fox, red and black badger, otter, mole, marten, and squirrel.

"The animals of Japan have a strong analogy with those of Europe; many are identical, or slightly varied, as the badger, otter, mole, common fox, marten, and squirrel. On the other hand, a large species of bear in the island of Yesso resembles the grizzly bear in the Rocky Mountains of North America. A chamois in other parts of Japan is nearly allied to the Antelope montana of the same mountains; and other animals, natives of Japan, are the same with those in Sumatra; so that its fauna is a combination of those of very distant regions." *

The list of domesticated animals is very small, and confined to the oxen necessary in agriculture, horses, two kinds of dogs, the small pug-nosed variety like the King Charles, and the wolfish Tartar variety, with erect ears and bristling hair. Besides the common house-cat, with a long tail, there is a variety having by nature either no tail, or one an inch or two long, and ending with a knot. The sheep, goat, and ass, seem to be unknown throughout the group.

The number of islands composing the Japanese empire is variously estimated at from 1,000 to 3,800, and the aggregate area at 170,000 square miles; Nipon, 900 miles long by about 100 miles broad, containing about 95,000 square miles; Kiusiu about 16,000, Sikok about 10,000, and Yesso about 30,000.

The population of Japan is generally placed at between thirty and forty millions. All estimates for the present must be merely arbitrary, as, although the population is probably known to the Government, it has never been ascertained by foreigners; and we are yet too ignorant of the extent of cultivable land on Nipon and Kiusiu, and, indeed, of all the other data necessary to form a rough estimate. The Japanese, not being a meat-eating people, are able to cultivate land which with us would be devoted to pasture. In no other country does as large a portion of the population support itself and supply the interior with the products of the sea. These, ranging from sea-weed to marine mammals, contribute perhaps as largely to the subsistence of the nation as

* Mrs. Somerville's "Physical Geography," p. 457. Murray, London, 1858.

do the products of the land. Both these facts form important elements in estimating the ability of the country to support life; they might seem to favor the supposition, other things being equal, of a larger population to the square mile than we find in Europe. But the feudal state of the empire, together with the mountainous character of the islands, both of them conditions opposed to expansion; the laws requiring the maintenance of a fixed forest area, which have a tendency to restrict increase; and the system of licensed prostitution without medical control, which, by producing barrenness among a large number of women, and spreading disease through all classes, acts both directly and indirectly against increase; all these and some other facts seem to weigh against the arguments for an overflowing population.

There is a strong reason for believing that the population of Nipon and Kiusiu is far below the maximum which those countries and their coasts can support. This is found in the fact that Yesso, separated from Nipon by only a strait fourteen miles broad, and having an area of 30,000 square miles, and a climate like that of Illinois and New England, with a more fertile soil than in the latter, has no population beyond fishing villages on the coast, and a few scattered aborigines in the interior.

Japanese literature, so far as known to us, gives no clue to the origin of the people. The native chronologies and histories represent the inhabitants of the islands as sprung from a race of gods through demi-gods, who, during more than a million years, occupied Japan. The authentic dates of their history begin about 670 B.C., and the apparent absence of traditions relating to a foreign origin would seem to indicate that the time of their arrival was very remote indeed.

At present the empire is inhabited by two distinct races, the Japanese and the Aino. The latter people, exclusively hunters and fishermen, and now found only in parts of Yesso, Sagalien, and the Kurile islands, as late as the sixth century occupied a large part of northern Nipon, whence they were dislodged. After a long series of bloody wars on Yesso they were brought to complete subjection in the twelfth century, by Yoshitzune, brother of Yoritomo, the first Siogun. The Ainos probably inhabited a large part if not all of the present empire before the arrival of the Japanese. It is impossible to suppose that the Ainos, with their dark skins, heavy-flowing beards and hairy bodies, should be the parent stock of the Japanese, who differ from them as much as they do from the Caucasian. If there was ever any considerable admixture of the two peoples, the traces of Aino blood seem to have entirely disappeared.

By some writers the Japanese have been derived from the Mongol family, while others see in them proof of a Malay origin. Grammatical analogies in language, and some points of resemblance physically, point to a relationship with the Mongol family. It is not impossible that the wide-spread Malay and Mongol races may have met in southern Japan, and in their union produced the present population, in the character of which many of the distinguishing features of both are combined. We cannot hope for even a proximate solution of the ethnological questions of eastern Asia until the data shall be supplied by a more thorough knowledge of the languages, early religions, myths and popular traditions than we yet possess.

The first fixed date in Japanese chronology seems to be 667 B.C. In that year the Mikado Jinmu made an expedition from Yamato against Kiusiu. In 663 B.C. a great battle was fought in Hiunga (Kiusiu) between Jinmu and Osatehico, and the following year found all Nipon and Kiusiu subject to Jinmu, who founded the throne of the Mikados. In the person of the Mikado he vested the office of high priest, representative of heaven, and emperor. He is represented as civilizing the nation, reforming the existing laws and government, and dividing time into months and years. Jinmu, to whom is given the title *ten-no* of heaven, may have been a foreigner who introduced an alien civilization, or to him may have been ascribed the founding of arts which existed previously. The succeeding Mikados conferred the command of the army upon near relatives or members of high families.

Little is recorded beyond the names of Emperors and Empresses, the occurrence of earthquakes, volcanic eruptions, and astronomical and meteorological phenomena, until the accession of Su-jin-tenno, B.C. 97. This Emperor built a Sintu temple in Isse, created four generalissimos Sioguns) for the east, west, north, and south, ordered the first census of Nipon and Kiusiu, levied taxes to build large ships, and ordered the draining of lakes for irrigation. Under his reign, Corea, divided into the kingdoms of Hakusai, Shinra, and Nin, is mentioned for the first time.

Under the next Mikado, Sui-nin-tenno, A.D. 6, the terrible custom was abolished which required that, on the death of the Emperor, the Empress and all the retinue of near attendants should commit suicide by hara-kiru.

At the death of the Empress, the highest of her ladies killed themselves by cutting their throats. This also was abolished on the death of Hiwassu-hime, Empress of Sui-nin-tenno, earthen images being substituted for the ladies of rank.

Suinin ordered the forming of ponds and canals for irrigation, and more than 800 were built in different parts of Japan.

The next Emperor, Keko-tenno, A.D. 71 to 130, after quelling obstinate rebellions in Kiusiu and northeastern Nipon, commanded the arable lands of the empire to be surveyed, and granaries to be built in all the towns, to guard against famine —a proceeding which would seem to indicate a large population. Sen-mu-tenno, A.D. 131 to 190, created the office of Daijin, the second dignity in the realm.

His successor Chin-ai-tenno, A.D. 192 to 200, dying of chagrin, caused by being defeated in an expedition which he had undertaken in person against Kumaoso, prince of Tskushi, he is succeeded by his widow, Jingo Kongo, A.D. 201 to 269. This female Mikado, who seems to have had a brilliant reign, at the beginning of her rule commanded in person an expedition to Shinra, in Corea, in which she conquered that kingdom. After three years of widowhood she gave birth to a son who was destined to become the most renowned of the Mikados. After her death, Jingo Kongo was ranked among the gods of the empire, and her life and deeds are widely commemorated in the popular literature and drama of the country.

Her son ascended the throne under the name of Ojin-tenno, A.D. 270 to 310. In the second year of his reign the islands of Yesso (Yesso and Sagalien) submitted voluntarily to the Japanese rule; thus the boundaries of the empire seem to have been at that time the same as at present, while the three kingdoms of Corea were also tributary. In A.D. 283 a woman was brought from Hakusai (Corea) to teach the art of sewing (working in ?) silk. In the following year an improved breed of horses was brought over from the same country. In A.D. 285, Wani, a philosopher, introduced the works of Confucius and the Senji-man ("thousand character book"). This last was one of the most important events in the history of the country, as the works of Confucius have undoubtedly had much to do with moulding the philosophy of Japan, and the "thousand character book" still forms the basis of primary education in the Chinese written language. The first musical instrument made in Japan, the koto of to-day, is said to have been formed in A.D. 300, from the wood of an old man-of-war.

In A.D. 306 Ojin-tenno sent an embassy to the Go country (Nanking?) in China to import into Japan the means of producing and manufacturing silk.

It is related of this Mikado, that having been advised by the brother of his prime minister that the latter was conspiring against the throne, he caused them both to plunge their arms into boiling water, when, the ordeal proving favorable to the minister, the informer was executed.

Ojin-tenno, after his death, became god of war, and his reign is looked upon with national pride.

Under Jintoku-tenno, A.D. 313 to 399, extensive inundations led to the construction of dykes along the rivers; and ice-houses and mills for cleaning rice were for the first time built.

In A.D. 367 Tamits was sent to crush a rebellion in Yesso.

Lichu-tenno, A.D. 400 to 405, appointed two scholars to write the history of the empire.

Under Yuriyaku-tenno, A.D. 457 to 479, mulberry trees were planted throughout the empire.

In A.D. 488 skilful carpenters were induced to immigrate from Corea.

In A.D. 509 the Coreans, who had begun to settle in Japan, were sent back to Corea by Government. Three years later an embassy was dispatched to Hakusai (Corea) to collect the Chinese classical literature.

Buddism entered Japan about the middle of the sixth century, apparently from Corea. With it came the zealous missionaries, who soon succeeded in spreading their faith. Toward the end of the eighth century the empire was invaded by foreigners "who were not Chinese, but natives of some more distant land," who, being continually re-enforced, were not finally repulsed till eighteen years after their arrival. These people have been referred by some to the Malays, and by others to the inhabitants of Siberia or of Kamschatka.

The reign of the Emperor Itsisio, 987 to 1012, was marked by two terrible epidemics or plagues. An important rebellion in Oshiou, the northernmost province of Nipon, has rendered the reign of Go-rei-sen famous.

Down to the end of the twelfth century Japanese history clusters around the person and deeds of the Mikados. The outline given above is mainly a direct translation from a native manual of chronology, and gives the most important features alluded to in that book. The names, dates of birth, accession and death of the Mikados, and dates of great earthquakes, volcanic eruptions, embassies to and from China and Corea, together with rebellions, make up a meager thread of historical occurrences. It is mainly interesting as showing the gradual introduction of some of the most important elements of civilization from Corea and China, whence probably nearly all of the arts were derived, to be subsequently improved upon.

Down to this period the executive power centred in the Mikado. Descended from a long line of sovereigns of one family, the representative of heaven, and himself a deity of high rank, in him centred also the glory and veneration of the nation. The character of the Mikado's office is one of the most remarkable features in the organization of Japan. He is one of the best conceived types of the Vicar of Heaven, to whom all religious and temporal power is delegated. It is probable that the idea was derived from China. But it would seem that this type of ruler, of which the Pope of Rome is the latest expression, is of great antiquity; and not only does it now exist in the Mikado, the Emperor of China, and the Dalai Lama of Thibet, but, at the time of the conquests, this idea was perhaps even more fully carried out in the Inca of Peru.

Too holy to be seen by other than the very highest of his attendants, the Sun, although himself a deity, not worthy of shining on his head, the Mikado may not touch the ground with his feet, nor even cut his nails and hair, so sacred is his body. This last duty is performed while he sleeps, and being considered a theft of these parts, the loss is not supposed to detract from his sanctity. It is said that the pots in which the food of the Mikado is cooked, and the dishes from which he eats, are used but once and then destroyed, lest they should fall into the hands of some one else on whom the use of them would bring serious consequences.

Toward the end of the twelfth century, during a period of civil commotion, when the princes had begun to grow remiss in their allegiance, Yoritomo, a prince of the imperial blood, was entrusted with extraordinary power as generalissimo. Being a man of great ability and ambition, he not only usurped nearly all secular power, but succeeded in transmitting it to his successors.

This act gave the death-blow to the real sovereignty of the Mikado. The nominal power, and all the honors and reverence due to him as Son of Heaven and Emperor, remained, indeed, and his sanction was considered necessary to all measures of great importance; but the executive passed into the hands of the Siogun, who, while ruling almost absolutely, has never claimed a higher nominal rank than the fourth deputy in the realm. The Mikado thus became a mere shadow—a tool, alternately in the hands of the Siogun, the Council of Daimios, or of contending factions, often an important instrument, but a tool still. Unable to endure the seclusion and tedium inseparable from their rank, many Emperors have abdicated in favor of their sons—sometimes successively in favor of several children—both in order to relieve themselves from the monotonous life, and to give the mothers the pleasure of seeing their children seated on the throne. The dignity has been held repeatedly by women—the widows or daughters of the preceding Mikados.

One would think that the allowance of twelve wives to the Emperor would secure a direct succession; but a large part of the Mikados have been cousins or nephews of their predecessors, the nearest of kin, whether male or female, being chosen.

Many of the Mikados have devoted their lives to literature, and Miako has become the centre of learning for the empire, while the spirit of war and military science find their home at Yeddo.

During the taikoonate of Yoritomo a long-continued rebellion on the islands of Yesso was crushed by Yoshitzune, the brother of Yoritomo. Yoshitzune, having been disgraced, is said to have travelled into northern Yesso (Sagalien), whence he crossed to the continent, where the Japanese claim that he reappeared as Gengis Khan. After the death of Yoritomo his widow entered a convent, but soon returning, ruled during the minority of her son till her death, with all the power, political and military, belonging to the rank of Siogun.

From the middle to the end of the thirteenth century the attention of the empire was anxiously turned to the movements of the Mongols under Kublai Khan. The great wave of revolution which, sweeping over the length and breadth of Asia, subjected the great continent as far as Germany to the rule of one family, threatened to overwhelm Japan—the outpost of Asia on the Pacific—at the same time that it menaced the foundations of the terrified nations of Europe.

Two powerful expeditions, worthy of the might and pride of the terrible Khan, were sent against Japan, but each time a brave resistance, aided by the stormy sea and rock-bound coast of the empire, proved its salvation, and the invaders met the fate of the fleet of Xerxes and the Spanish Armada. To another and more peaceful expedition, sailing two centuries later from the opposite extremity of the great continent, and having Japan for its destination, we owe the discovery of America. Incited by Marco Polo's account of Zipanga, given from information received at the court of Kublai, Columbus, believing in the spherical form of the earth, hoped to reach these islands or the Indies by sailing westward.

Kublai Khan, in his letter to the Japanese emperor demanding his submission, asserted that it was already the hope of philosophers to see all mankind united in one family, and declared his intention to accomplish this result by force of arms if necessary. The great Mongol conqueror tried the virtue of armed force in making Japan conform to this one-family programme, and failed ingloriously. Three centuries later, Europe applied, for a less exalted end, the more insinuating wedge of Jesuit proselytism, and, failing signally, was cast out after having obtained a strong foothold. Again, three centuries later, America, who owed her discovery indirectly to the correspondence between Kublai Khan and the Mikado, reviving the application of the "one family" idea to Japan, has by means of peaceful diplomacy paved the way for bringing that empire into the circle of nations.

During the reign of the Mongol dynasty in China the Japanese refused to hold any intercourse with that country; but on the accession of the Mings they again opened their ports and permitted trade to continue, though under a strict surveillance.

During the middle of the sixteenth century the feuds among the great lords of the empire threatened to throw the land into anarchy, and a strong arm was needed to restore order and hold the balance. This was found in Taikosama, the man who with reason is perhaps the most popular personage in their history, and who has been called the Napoleon of Japan. Beginning as a servant in the palace, and as a common soldier, he attracted the attention of the Siogun, who promoted him rapidly till in time he won the highest military rank. On the death of his master, Nabunanga, in 1585, Taikosama assumed the taikoonate, and taking the higher title of Koboe, which has been translated "lay Emperor," he soon usurped the little secular power that had till then been left to the Mikado. He must certainly have been a man of great ability, for the task he had to perform was one of the most difficult character. The fierce contest between the princes, and the danger of invasion by the armies of the King of Portugal, who had gained myriads of allies in the christianized Japanese, required both the breaking of the power of the feudal lords and the extermination of a religion which threatened the independence of the country.

If we may judge the means he employed to this end by the internal peace which seems to have reigned since his time, they must have been well conceived. Almost his first step was a war againt Corea, in which he engaged the most troublesome princes, many of whom never returned. His greatest stroke was, perhaps, the subdividing of each of the few principalities into several, thus weakening the power of individual princes by increasing their number.

Nearly forty years before the accession of Taikosama, the Jesuit missionaries under Xavier, the disciple and friend of Loyola, had obtained a foothold in Japan, and had begun a brilliant career of proselyting. Had this work remained in the hands of that order, Japan would probably have become a Christian country. Unfortunately for that result, there poured into the new field an army of Franciscan, Dominican and other friars, who soon quarrelled with the Jesuits and among themselves. Converts were made by thousands ; among them were princes of the highest rank, while Nabunanga, the predecessor of Taikosama, was counted as a warm friend of the cause.

In their unbridled zeal, this army of the church, carried away by almost unprecedented success, began a persecution of the existing religions at the same time that they transferred the allegiance of their converts from their rightful rulers to the Pope, and plotted for the subjection of the empire to the King of Portugal. So sure did they feel of their position that they not only gained the enmity of the powerful priesthood at Miako, by their wholesale destruction of temples, and the indignities offered to the bonzes, but they insolently refused to the great lords of the empire even the respect shown by one daimio toward another.

Already in the second year of his reign, 1587, Taikosama found it necessary to issue an edict banishing the missionaries. But though opposed on political grounds to the new religion, he abstained from violent persecution. Before his death Taiko caused his son six years old to be married to the grand-daughter of his most intimate friend. To this same friend he entrusted the regency. This man proved faithless to the trust, and, usurping the taikoonate, took the name of Gongensama. Under him the policy of Taiko was continued. The Christians, foreign and native, feeling sure of their ground, openly defied the Government, and in so doing brought upon themselves a terrible persecution. Finally, when it was discovered that an extensive conspiracy existed to transfer the country to the rule of Portugal, a decree ordered that the " whole race of the Portugese, with their mothers, nurses, and whatever belongs to them, shall be banished for ever."

In 1639 the Portugese were totally expelled, and their profitable trade passed into the hands of the Protestant Dutch. The year 1640 saw the last great struggle. In the province of Simabara, near Nagasaki, a large number of Christians arose in insurrection, and seizing a fortified position, bravely defended themselves against the Government until the place was taken with the assistance of the Dutch. The entire besieged population, men, women, and children, were destroyed, preferring death to life bought at the cost of recanting. The law of Gongensama is still unrepealed; it prohibits any foreigner, under pain of death, from setting foot on Japanese soil, and renders it lawful for any subject to kill any one of the hated race.

In return for the shameful assistance given by them in this massacre, the Dutch, thenceforth despised by the Japanese, were indeed allowed to monopolize the foreign trade, though only under great restrictions and indignities.

From that period till 1854 Japan has preserved an entire seclusion from the outer world, no native being allowed to leave the country, and, excepting the Dutch imprisoned at Decima, no foreigner to enter it.

Repeated efforts made by England and Russia, with a view to establish friendly intercourse, have met with failure, and, in the instance of Golownin, with the imprisonment of the envoy. During two centuries Europeans were looked upon only as the descendants of those who brought so much misery into the empire, and who nearly succeeded in destroying its independence. But most of all is our religion hated, not because of its doctrines, but because the Government looks upon it still as being the great political lever it certainly was two centuries ago. Nor are their fears of the missionaries altogether unfounded. The penalty of death imposed on all Japanese who listen in any manner to instruction in Christian doctrines, is a barrier which not only the Romish but many Protestant missionaries would gladly see removed by the sword, were there no other cause for war.

During this long period of seclusion the Japanese obtained, through the Dutch, information concerning the condition of Europe, and during the past fifty years an increasing number of students have devoted themselves to the study of theoretical and applied science, in Dutch works and translations. Thus a party of some strength, including even daimios, would have been glad of intercourse with the outside world, for the sake of the benefits to be derived from it, had it not been for the fear of serious political consequences.

The existence of this party may have facilitated the negotiations of Commodore Perry in 1853–4. The treaty then concluded gained for American ships the right to obtain supplies and to trade under restrictions at Simoda and Hakodade, where consuls were allowed to reside. Soon after this England obtained similar privileges at Hakodade and Nagasaki, as did also the Russians, while the Dutch received greater freedom at Decima. In 1857 Mr. Townsend Harris negotiated for American vessels the right to enter the port of Nagasaki. In 1858 Mr. Harris succeeded in reaching Yeddo, and during the first half of that year, unsupported by armed force, he gained after a long struggle a diplomatic triumph, which places him on a level with the most famous European diplomatists in the East. A few weeks later the Earl of Elgin arrived and concluded a new treaty. By the treaties with America and England the ports of Kanagawa, Hakodade, and Nagasaki were opened to trade with those countries after July 1st, 1859. Negato, or some other port on the west coast of Nipon, after January 1st, 1860, and Hiogo, the port of Osaca, after January 1st, 1863. Subsequent treaties with France, Holland, Prussia, and Switzerland, have opened these ports to subjects of those countries.

These treaties grant the right of residence at Yeddo, and of travelling freely through the empire to the diplomatic agents of the treaty powers, and to the subjects of those powers the right to lease ground at the open ports, to build, trade, practice freely their respective religions, and enter the country to the distance generally of ten *ri*, or twenty-five English miles.

Nearly a month had passed after our arrival in Japan before we heard directly from the Government. Mr. Harris had written to us that they were for some reason opposed to our visiting Yeddo. We found it impossible to account for the delay of the Government in assigning to us our duties, the more so that they were, from the time of our departure from America, paying at the rate of a viceroy's salary.

It seems that an unforeseen trouble had arisen in the minds of the authorities concerning the social position we were to occupy. In a country where rank, from the god-Mikado to the lowest tide-waiter, tapers off in an unbroken perspective of princes and officials on one side, and spies of equal rank on the other, this question had necessarily to be settled before the first interview, by the etiquette of which our relative positions would be assigned. Were mining engineers and geologists mechanics, or were they officials? and if so, what position did they hold in the civil or military scale in the United States? In despair, the question was finally submitted to Mr. Harris, who very diplomatically and considerately told them that were Commodore Perry (whom they knew) and ourselves at his house, he would treat us with the same consideration that he would the Commodore.

This settled the question, and we received a notification that the future Governor of Yesso would come from Yeddo to call upon us. On the appointed day an officer arrived to announce the coming of the Governor, and soon after the loud jingling of the iron staff and rings of the street-warden gave notice of his approach. He came with a large retinue of officers, all of whom, excepting his immediate attendants, remained outside. The Governor Kadzu-ya-Chikungono-kami, and his Ometzki, with three or four officers, seated themselves according to rank, with several scribes behind them on one side of the room, while we took seats opposite them, the Governor's interpreter being in the middle.

The Governor hoped we had recovered from the fatigue of our long journey; he had been told that we had met with head winds, and had made a stormy voyage. It was very kind in us to come so far to give the Japanese instruction in mining.

We replied that we had had a very rough voyage of ninety days, but that the interest we had found in everything we saw in his delightful country had quite restored us. We anticipated much pleasure in doing what we could in the field to which the Japanese Government had called us; we felt highly honored by the appointment.

Several servants now entered and placed in a row two light and gracefully-woven baskets of oranges, and two boxes, each containing about two hundred eggs. After asking us to receive "these trifling presents" and receiving our thanks, the Governor introduced business, by enquiring whether on approaching the coast of Nipon we had been able to judge by the color of the sea or the taste of the water or fish, or by any other means, of the wealth or poverty of Japan in metals. He seemed a little surprised at our negative answer. This was the first of a long series of similar questions I had to answer in interviews with Japanese officials, and the Board of Foreign Affairs at Pekin; they showed that these people, who have for thousands of years sought the philosopher's stone and the elixir of life, suppose that the scientists of the west possess a key to open a royal road through the secrets of nature.

After informing us that the Government had sent for a steamer to take us to Yesso, the Governor asked whether either of us had visited the mining districts of Europe. When told that I had made them the subject of several years' study, he was much interested, and asked many questions concerning the mines, and the manner of working them.

Kadzu-ya-Chikungono-kami, with whom we were to have a great deal of intercourse on Yesso, was the type of a Japanese gentleman. He had a handsome face, with a fair complexion, and an exceedingly kind expression, which always reminded me, as did indeed his manner and appearance generally, of Pius IX. as he was twelve or fourteen years ago. In addition to this he had the modest and easy manner which marks the man of social culture in all countries, and especially in Japan.

The next morning the Governor returned, by appointment, to examine the instruments, etc., forming our outfit; during several hours he wandered among theodolites, levels, chronometers, sextants, barometers, etc., asking an explanation of each object, and expressing the wish that he might be able to give time to the study of science. During this interview, as in that of the previous day, every word said was written down by the attendant scribes, while some of the officers amused themselves by sketching the novel display. The same day we received a call from one of the earlier embassadors to America, accompanied by a former Governor of Yesso. The first spoke much of his visit to the United States, and of the pleasure it had given him.

Having learned that it would probably be several weeks before we would be sent to Yesso, we determined to see something of the surrounding country, and naturally planned our first excursion so as to include the nearest mountains, the Oyama, on the edge of the treaty limits. Accompanied by Mr. Frank Hall and Mr. Robertson, with our Japanese servants and bettos, or running footmen, we made an early start from Yokohama.

Crossing a broad marsh by the costly causeway which the Government had built to render Yokohama accessible to Kanagawa, we passed through the latter town and were soon in the country. Our bettos led the way on foot, acting as guides, and running at the rate of a four and a half or five mile trot. These grooms deserve a passing description. They are a luxury permitted only to officers, whose horses they generally lead by the bit on all formal occasions, for the Japanese official rides fast only when on important business, or when in the absence of spectators a fast trot or canter may be indulged in without loss of dignity. Foreigners have adopted the custom, much to the astonishment of the Japanese, who look with wonder on a European merchant riding in a saddle and keeping running footmen, both of which luxuries are forbidden to any native not graced with two swords.

As we kept up a brisk trot wherever the road permitted it, our bettos gradually relieved themselves of the little clothing they had worn at the outset, and they now appeared in a costume worthy of a New Zealand chief. They were tattooed from head to foot, and there seemed to be as much rivalry among them as to whose back should present the most varied picture, as there was in out-doing each other in swiftness of foot. My betto, who was one of the fastest runners, was covered with an elaborate representation, in bright red and blue, of a lady and a dragon, the head of the latter peering forward over the right shoulder, while the body of the monster, extending down the man's muscular back, wound its tail around the left leg and foot.

The country we were travelling through was part of the low table-land extending from the bay of Yeddo to the Oyama mountains, but was less cut up by ravines than along the route to Kamakura, and there was consequently little rice culture. For several miles a large part of the surface was occupied by a young forest growth, with fields devoted to the cultivation of rape seed, wheat, buckwheat, etc. Soon we came into a more populous district and through small villages, with substantial farm buildings and fire-proof storehouses. Through these places we rode at the head of an amused crowd, whose size was limited only by the extent of the population.

Large numbers of mulberry trees now showed that we were entering the silk district of Hachiogi. The country was divided into small fields, by rows of these trees crossing each other at right angles, leaving the squares thus enclosed open for the cultivation of grain. They are planted a few yards apart, having the trunks cut off at a height of from one to five feet from the ground. This dwarfing process not only hinders them from shading the adjoining grain, but is said to improve the quality of the leaf.

Occasionally a well-built stone wall, enclosing extensive and wooded grounds, and broken by an imposing gateway, showed that we were passing the home of some man of more than ordinary rank. In building walls the Japanese show a great deal of both taste and skill, although the masonry is among them confined almost exclusively to substructures, gateways, and tombs. Indeed, the prevalence of earthquakes prohibits the use of either stone or bricks for houses. Where a suitable rock can be obtained, walls are constructed of large and well-dressed blocks, neatly laid together without mortar; but where the country furnishes only rubble or stone of irregular shape, they are used with mortar in such a manner that while the stones nearly touch each other, the white cement seems to occupy the greater part of the surface and produces a very beautiful effect. In building sea walls of dry masonry, large blocks of lava cut into truncated four-sided pyramids are used.

The fences surrounding farm-houses are always exceedingly neat; sometimes they are well-kept hedges of living bamboo, but more generally they are formed of interwoven bamboo and reeds.

Toward evening we reached Hachiogi, a large town, and stopped at the best looking inn, where we were shown to a large room on the second floor. As foreigners generally insist on wearing their boots on the delicate Japanese mats, it is difficult for them to gain admission to any house where the proprietor has once had his floors disfigured, and when admitted they usually receive the poorest rooms. While we were eating, and till late in the evening, we were surrounded by more people than we could have wished for. As I was about to pass my first night in a Japanese house, I watched anxiously the preparations for sleeping. These were simple enough: a mattrass in the form of a very thick quilt, about seven feet long by four wide, was spread on the floor; and over it was laid an ample robe, very long, and heavily padded, and provided with large sleeves. Having put on this night-dress, the sleeper covers himself with another quilt, and sleeps, *i. e.*, if he has had some years' practice in the use of this bed.

But the most remarkable feature about a Japanese bed is the pillow. This is a wooden box about four inches high, eight inches long, and two inches wide at the top. It has a cushion of folded papers on the upper side to rest the neck on, for the elaborate manner of dressing the hair does not permit the Japanese, especially the women, to press the head on a pillow. Every morning the uppermost paper is taken off from the cushion, exposing a clean surface without the expense of washing a pillow-case.

I passed the greater part of the night in learning how to poise my head in this novel manner; and when I finally closed my eyes, it was to dream that I was being slowly beheaded, and to awake at the crisis to find the pillow bottom-side up, and my neck resting on the sharp lower edge of the box. During my stay in the country I learned many of its customs, mastering the use of chop-sticks, and accustoming my palate to raw fresh fish, but the attempt to balance my head on a two-inch pillow I gave up in despair, after trying in vain to secure the box by tying it to my neck and head.

Early the following morning we strolled through the town, looking in at many of the shops. In these we saw none of the choice lacquer ware and porcelain which are sold at the ports visited by foreigners. There were few articles of luxury, but mostly the objects of necessary consumption, as grain, vegetables, dried fish, sea weed, native cotton and silk stuffs, copper, iron and earthen-ware, and common china, and lacquer work. A sign exposed in front of an apothecary's bore in gilded Roman letters "Van Mitter's Medicines," and looked to us much as the characters on the sign of a New York tea-store must appear to a Chinaman.

On our return to the inn, a man brought a card covered with eggs of the silk-worm: it was about ten inches by fourteen, and contained, according to the owner, 80,000 eggs; the price was one dollar. Our hotel bill for four persons, four horses, and five servants, was five and a half dollars. As we rode out of the town the streets filled rapidly with a crowd, which grew larger and larger as we proceeded.

Every house turned out its quota, every cross-street poured in its thousands, until a surging sea of heads filled the street behind us. "To jin! To jin!" (Chinaman! Chinaman!) greeted us on all sides, till we were almost deafened. If one of us stopped and wheeled round, the effect was laughable: the whole crowd, now as eager to run away as they had been to follow us, turned, and those behind cried "forward," while those before cried "back;" till we left them tumbling one over the other, all laughing, crying, and yelling at the same time. There was no intention to insult us, as often happened in the fishing villages where men and children would run after us, yelling "bacca! bacca!" (fool! fool!) In both Japan and China the farming population is the best behaved toward foreigners.

After a ride of several miles over a plain which was little cultivated, we descended into a picturesque valley, and soon came to a small temple, which looked with the beautiful grounds surrounding it so inviting that we entered. Two buildings, flanking the entrance, contained the usual gate-keepers, colossal images with horrible faces, brandishing weapons and standing on impossible lions. Near the middle of the open space stood a shrine, with a beautifully-executed gilded bronze image, about sixteen feet high, of Budda standing on the lotus. On one side there was a large bronze stork on a tortoise, and on the other a graceful vase of the same metal.

The main building was a Sintu temple. A series of pretty water-color paintings, in which dragons, warriors, and mermaids predominated, hung on the walls; there was one image, that of an ugly man with a demoniacal face, who we were told by the polite priest was the devil.

A few miles further on, the road entered a small village, where, at the inn, the old landlady and several pretty waitresses came out and asked us to dismount. Such an unusual reception made it evident that no foreigners had visited this place before; so getting down, we removed our shoes and entered the neatly matted rooms. We were received in the same manner that is usual among Japanese: the landlady came first, and getting on her marrow-bones and touching the floor with her forehead hoped we were well and had had a pleasant journey; then came a remarkably handsome waitress who, after much bowing and many polite questions, went out for refreshments. First confectionery was brought in (for in Japan this precedes everything else), and after that soup, boiled rice, eggs, sea weed, and stewed clams.

Late in the afternoon we reached the village of Koyasu, built on the hill-side at the foot of the Oyama. As in many mountain villages in Japan, the main street went directly up the declivity by a series of narrow steps and terraces. Up this difficult road we urged our horses, apparently without attracting any attention from the inhabitants. To our surprise not a child followed us in the street, and the few people we passed continued their occupations without looking up. This was something so unusual that we were at a loss to understand the reason, till on applying at the first inn we were refused entrance, when we concluded that the police were at the bottom of the affair. The hostess met us at the door and informed us that her husband being away at Yeddo, and there being absolutely nothing to eat in the house, and no servants, and as the house was being repaired, it would be impossible to receive us, but we would find better accommodation a little further up the street; so we climbed a hundred steps or more to the next inn. Here the hostess appeared and regretted the impossibility of entertaining us: her husband had died that day; but there was a much better place, she said, a little higher up.

Although it was raining furiously, and we were already drenched to the skin, we rode perseveringly up stairs. Nearly half a mile of climbing up the slippery stone steps brought us into the evening, but no nearer to a bed; every inn seemed to have been suddenly visited by an afflicting angel, prostrating the proprietor, till in one place the gates were rudely shut in our faces and we were warned off. To think of riding back ten or fifteen miles in a rainy night was out of the question, so we determined on returning to the house where we had first been turned away, and obtaining quarters by politeness if possible.

Inwardly cursing the *yakoninerie* (as Sir R. Alcock aptly calls it) of the police, we rode our sure-footed horses down the half-mile flight of stairs, to the place where we had made our first trial. Here resolutely dismounting, we waited, while Mr. Hall, who spoke the language well, besieged the hostess. By persuasive politeness he carried the point, where force would probably have failed, and been followed by serious results. Once in, we were treated well, not only by the hostess, but by the landlord also. As we were eating, a sharp shock of an earthquake shook the house, which vibrated for some seconds. No one becomes, I believe, accustomed to these phenomena; the uncertainty which hangs over all the phases of an earthquake-wave darts through the mind of man as well as brutes a ray of terror, which seems frequently to precede the first shock. It has often been remarked in connection with the more fearful of historical earthquakes, that before a shock has been felt the entire population of a city have rushed from their houses at the same instant, as if driven by an instinctive impulse. Certainly animals are warned of the approaching danger before man feels even a tremor, a fact which may be explained by their greater sensitiveness; and it may be that the senses of man, especially in regions where he lives in a chronic state of expectation of these convulsions, are open to impressions so delicate that they affect only the inferior machinery of the brain.

Japan is one of the great centres of earthquake action, and the dates of the destructive shocks occupy a considerable portion of their chronological records during more than two thousand years. An eruption of the volcano Asamayama, in Shinano, in 1783, was accompanied by a fearful loss of life; thousands of people were swallowed up by great chasms which rent the earth, and into which they were plunged in escaping from lava, ashes, and torrents of boiling water. In 1854 the Russian frigate "Diana" witnessed in the harbor of Simoda an earthquake whose centre seems to have been submarine. Three immense waves rushing in from the sea covered the highest trees, and dashed the native shipping to pieces on the inland hill-sides, while in their return they scoured out the harbor to its rocky bottom so that it is said anchors can no longer find holding ground. The frigate was "spun round and round at anchors," and left almost a wreck. The waves produced by this shock translating themselves across the Pacific ocean, recorded their dimensions on the tide guages of California. From the elements thus afforded, of length of wave and time of transmission, Professor Bache was able to calculate the mean depth of the North Pacific. The same wave swept across the China Sea and up the Yangt'z Kiang.*

* Edkins, in "Year-Book of Facts," 1855.

Owing to the frequency of these phenomena the houses are necessarily built of wood, which causes all great shocks to be followed by fearful conflagrations, and proportionate loss of life. Everywhere the traveller meets with the vestiges of these commotions in fallen tombstones and granite columns. In the grounds of a temple in the western suburb of Yeddo, I observed a large monolith which had been turned nearly 45 degrees on its base, presenting an instance similar to that observed on the obelisks of a Calabrian convent. This last has been cited to prove that there are sometimes gyratory shocks. In both instances it is probable that the turning was produced simply by the rocking motion imparted to stones whose centres of gravity were out of the axial line.

In the morning we set out on foot to climb the mountain. The temples near the summit have great celebrity, and are visited by many pilgrims. The stone steps are said to extend to the highest point. After about half a mile of climbing up the street of stairs through the village, an officer joined our party, and seemed disposed to make himself agreeable in answering questions. A little further on we found ten or twelve officials drawn up in a line across the street, near an inn. With a great many bows they pointed to the open door, and pressed us to enter and take some refreshments. Of course we could not refuse; the lion in the path was too strong to be turned by force.

When we had taken our places on the mats, the officers, seating themselves in a semi-circle between us and the door, ordered confectionery and tea, which were produced so quickly that it was evident they had planned the whole thing beforehand. We soon came to business: we asserting our wish to visit the temples, and our right to travel twenty-five miles from the port; they "regretting" that their instructions were to consider Koyasu the extreme limit, as it was twenty-five miles by the road. Of course we had to yield; but we effected a compromise by promising to return if they would allow us to visit a neighboring hill to see the view. Reluctantly agreeing to this they led the way, and we had gone some distance before we found that they were taking us back by another road. Determined not to be outdone in this manner, we insisted upon seeing the view, and starting back over the fields reached a small eminence, where there was a fine look-out over the plains between Wodawara bay and the bay of Yeddo. Expressing ourselves satisfied with this, we turned our steps down-hill and entered the main road, where we found that a large canvas curtain with the arms of the Tykoon had been stretched across the street, and a guard-house erected.

In descending the steps our attention was drawn toward a group of fifteen or more representations of the *phallus*. They were of sandstone, from a few inches to two feet long, and stood erect around a central column containing a cavity either intended to hold a lantern or an incense-burner. The *phallus* enters largely into the symbols of the popular religion, if one may judge by the great number of representations of it exposed for sale. It would be interesting to know whether this is a feature of the older religion of Japan, or whether it was introduced into the country from India. I believe there is no trace of it in either China or Tartary, and the fact that it is incorporated into the Sintu ceremonies would seem to show that it existed here before the introduction of Buddism. The wide geographical range which this symbol occupied in antiquity from the earlier and later mysteries of Greece, Rome, Samothrace, and Egypt to India, and as it would seem to Central America, renders its discovery in actual use in a country where it co-exists with a very ancient religion exceedingly interesting.

The Yakonins sent a spy after us in the person of a man who pretended he was going to Yokohama on business, but we soon left him behind. In the afternoon we reached a river which could be crossed only on a ferry; a flat-boat was there, but the ferryman refused to take us over, and it was not without some difficulty that we succeeded in crossing by ourselves. News of our invasion had gone before, and at the first town we were met by wondering officers and wardens with their jingling staves of iron, to whom however we did not give a chance to repeat the hospitalities we had received from their colleagues in the morning at Koyasu.

Here we entered the *tokaido*, the great highway which follows the eastern coast from one end of Nipon to the other. There is a net-work of these thoroughfares by which the coast and mountain provinces are connected among themselves respectively and with each other. They would be necessary, if only as military roads, to accommodate the transit of the army which each prince is obliged to take with him on his yearly journey to Yeddo. These highways, so important from both a military and commercial point of view, are part of the imperial domain, though they traverse the territories of almost all independent daimios.

As wagons or carts are next to unknown, these roads are intended only for pedestrians and horsemen, and are not always in perfect condition in the rainy season. They are made broad in order that the trains of two princes may conveniently pass each other.

The tokaido is lined on either side with villages, the larger of these extending their suburbs in each direction one or two miles. Thus for a great part of the distance the highway presents the appearance of a city street. But at intervals the traveller comes into the open country, where, as he moves onward on horseback or in a norimon, shaded by ancient elms and oaks, he may enjoy the ever-varying scenery, and turn his eyes from lovely hill and dale, woodland and green terraces, on one side, to bold headlands and island-dotted bays on the other. The scenery along the coast of southern and central Japan is as beautiful as it is peculiar. The coast is very bold, and indented with thousands of bays and fiords. The surf is dashed to foam on countless rocks covered with a gorgeous carpeting of bright-colored sea mosses and shells. There are islets worn by time and wave into fantastic shapes, and islands rising with high, vertical walls, capped with a dense mass of trees and plants, which overhang the precipice in their luxuriant growth. Here and there a wooded island, rising like a pyramid of verdure, is capped with an ancient temple, made accessible by long flights of stone steps, which, beginning under an archway on the beach, climb the steep hill-side, half hidden by the overhanging trees. The general absence of beach, the dark volcanic rock and rich shades of green, combined in every variety of outline, surrounded by the sapphire blue of a deep sea, and covered by a sky like that which vaults the Mediterranean—these are distinctive features of Japanese marine scenery. In the fury of a typhoon it is as awful as it is enchanting in a calm. The Suwonada or inland sea, which separates Nipon from Kiusiu and Sikoku, is described by all who have passed through it as being beautiful beyond description.

But to return to the tokaido, under the shade of whose elms we are trotting. Groups of travellers are strung along the road; here and there a horseman riding, if he bear two swords, astride a saddle with a peculiar heavy stirrup of iron, his horse's mane dressed like a cheval-de-frize with paper cord, and its tail carefully encased in a bag; or if the rider be a merchant, he is perched cross-legged on a high pack-saddle, and carried slowly by a sorry beast. Another group of daimios' retainers and baggage-bearers, separated from the main train, loiter at a roadside booth, drinking tea or saki, and scowling at the passing foreigners. As we canter gently onward we overtake an humble traveller, bent up in the basket cango, which, slung under a pole, is borne by two men at a trot, who have concluded that it is easier to carry clothing on the cango than on their backs.

Soon a rise in the road shows us a larger group slowly ascending the hill before us. From the number of retainers it seems to belong to a man of high rank, perhaps an inferior daimio. A considerable number of soldiers and men bearing lances, spears, tridents, and other insignia, on long poles, are straggling along the road escorting a large norimon, behind which a caparisoned horse is led by grooms. Richardson had not then been murdered for trying to pass the train of a prince, so following the rule of the road we cross to the right side, and pass the cortege. Strolling mendicants and begging priests, with bells or rattles, sturdy story-tellers and pretty-faced bikunins, or travelling nuns, as they are charitably called, make the tokaido their home, and find on it the means of subsistence. I never learned whether the story-tellers have the power of improvising, though I have reason to believe that they have, since I felt more than once that a laugh was raised in the streets at my expense by these popular characters.

Much mention has been made by travellers of the mendicant nuns or bikunins, of whom I saw several; they are generally young and pretty, though not always so charming as they have been represented. Kaempfer has described them: "We also met several young bikunins, a sort of begging nuns, who accost travellers for their charity, singing songs to divert them, though upon a strange, wild sort of tune. They will stay with travellers as long as they may wish for a small matter. Most of them are daughters of the yamabushi, or mountain priests, and are consecrated as sisters of this holy begging order by having their heads shaved. They are neatly and well clad, wearing a black-silk hood upon their shaven heads, and a light hat over it to defend their faces from the heat of the sun. Their behavior is to all appearance free, yet modest, neither too bold and loose, nor too dejected and mean. As to their persons, they are as great beauties as one shall see in this country. In short, the whole scene is more like a pretty stage comedy than the begging of indigent poor people. It is true, indeed, their fathers could not send out upon the begging errand persons more fit for it, since they know not only how to come at travellers' purses, but have charms and beauties enough to oblige them to further good services. * * * They are obliged to bring so much a year of what they get by begging to the temple of the sun goddess at Isse, by way of tribute." *

It was already late in the evening when we rode through Kanagawa and over the long causeway to Yokohama.

The greater part of my time was spent in trying to learn Japanese. I soon saw the hopelessness of attempting to master the written language, as the task of wading through hundreds of varied and obscure letters of the running hirakana, in addition to some thousands of Chinese characters, was one requiring years of patient toil where I could spare only months, and one which had not then been accomplished by any foreigner. My object was simply to learn the vernacular. The pure Japanese language is considered by Klaproth and other leading authorities to stand alone, forming a family by itself, whose nearest relationship, though very remote, seems to be with the Mongolian and Manchu. Siebold and others have tried to trace analogies between it and some South American tongues, as those of the Incas and some Brazilian tribes, and resemblances have been pointed out between it and some Californian and South Sea dialects. But these analogies are based rather on coincidences in words than on grammatical structure, and the former have now far less weight with philologists than the latter. And this calls to my mind a remarkable coincidence, which shows how unreliable results must often be which are obtained by a simple comparison of words. The Japanese word signifying anger is *ikari*, while an anchor is also *ikari*,

* "Japan; an account, Geographical and Historical." Chas. MacFarlane; quoting Kaempfer.

a coincidence in the double application of words which is certainly not based on any generic affinity between Japanese and English.

Spoken by a Japanese lady, this language is as soft and almost as musical as Italian; but when sung under your windows by some half-drunken wight, who finishes each line with an explosive abruptness, suggestive of a punch in the stomach, it .s anything but harmonious. The verbs are easily formed, a large part by the combination of auxiliary and intransitive verbs with nouns, prepositions, etc., as *wakaru*, understand—from the noun *wake*, meaning, and *ari*, to have; *sh'ta-n-iru*, stoop, humble, from *sh'ta*, below, and *iru*, to go. Every verb has a form of etiquette and a familiar form, each of which has an independent inflection. The polite form is obtained by suffixing the particle *mas* to the root, as *aru*, *arimas*, or more politely *go-z-arimas*,—all three of them forms of the present tense of the verb to have. The verbs are not inflected as to either person or number. There is no distinction for gender in the grammar, though sex is indicated in some words by particles. The plural is formed, in nouns and pronouns, by suffixes, as domo,tachi, *watakushi*, I; *watakushidomo*, we. Nouns and pronouns are declined by the addition of suffixes, as *ten*, heaven; nominative, *ten-wa*, or *ten-nga*, heaven; possessive, *ten-no*, of heaven; dative, *ten-i*, or *ten-ni*, to heaven; accusative, *ten-wo*, heaven; ablative, *ten-de*. While in some respects there is great simplicity in the Japanese grammar, as in gender and number, in others it is very complicated, as in its verbs, and in the endless number of representative words used for different classes of objects in connection with the cardinal numerals.

With the introduction of the classical literature of China into Japan began the incorporation of many Chinese words into the native language, and at present even the vocabulary of the lower classes contains a large number of these, in addition to the corresponding native words. But in the official language, the proportion is so large that it becomes nearly, if not quite, unintelligible to the lower classes. All official writing and important literature is written in the Chinese character, often modified for inflection, etc., by Japanese letters. Good penmanship is one of the first requirements of a Japanese gentleman or scholar, and a well-penned character or sentence is often considered as much a work of art as a fine painting.

CHAPTER VIII.

POLITICS.

During our stay at Yokohama we might undoubtedly have seen far more of the country had we chosen to ask for the right to make excursions in our character of foreigners in the Japanese service, a step we did not wish to take before we should have performed some of our duties. As subjects of a foreign power we had no right to pass the narrow treaty limits, nor would it have been always safe to have done so even under the protection of a Government permit. The relations between foreigners and natives were daily becoming more complicated, and a civil war was threatening to break out at any moment. Foreign ministers, in the general obscurity that hides the whole political and social organization of the empire, not knowing whether our enemies were in the Government of the Taikoon or among the daimios, distrusted both alike. Under the pressure of the anti-foreign party of powerful princes, the Yeddo Government was losing ground, and the Taikoon menaced with disgrace, should he not withdraw at least the greater part of the privileges granted to Western powers. To understand the condition of Japan at present, and the standing of foreigners in it, as well as the prospect of increasing benefits to be derived from our intercourse with that country, it will be necessary to give a brief outline of this political organization, so far as our information on this obscure subject will permit.

From the time when Jinmu, establishing himself as a deity, Son of Heaven, founded the present dynasty and its divine prerogatives, down to the twelfth century, the power transmitted to his descendants appears to have been sufficient to enlarge and govern the empire, to carry on foreign wars, and to control the growing strength of the princes, among whom the land seems at an early date to have been divided into fiefs. In the natural course of a developing feudalism the power of the Mikado waned before the combinations of feudatory lords, who were fast becoming independent princes, till in the twelfth century the balance threatened to be lost, and the imperial power to be buried amid internal strife. We have seen how Yoritomo, entrusted by the Mikado with extraordinary power, succeeded in giving a temporary check to these internal troubles, and in laying the foundation on which was to be built the rival taikoonate. The check given by Yoritomo to the daimios was merely temporary; it remained for the strong hand of Taikosama to restore the balance, not as between the princes and the Mikado, but between them and the taikoonate; the latter, while continuing the nominal power of the supreme emperor, using this as a makeweight in the scale.

Sprung from the people, Taiko, even while founding as he vainly hoped a line of sovereigns, could have little sympathy with the great princes, who were alike dangerous to the empire and to the newly-established power. He found the integrity of the empire threatened by the independence of these daimios, while the allegiance of people and princes was being transferred to the Church of Rome. To break these powers was his task. The uprooting of Christianity was merely begun by him; it was left for his immediate successors to crush out a religion that was menacing the independence of the land. The policy introduced by Taiko, and carried to completion by the more powerful among his successors, consisted in subdividing the sixty principalities, until they now number more than six hundred. To facilitate this work he engaged the empire in a war with Corea, in which the most dangerous daimios were drained of their resources to an extent that rendered them temporarily harmless. How many of the six hundred daimios hold their lands in fief from the Taikoon is not known to foreigners, but it seems that daimios of this class form the military barrier which defends the court of Yeddo.

Within this wall is the intricate machinery of the Government; and here we come to the large class of hattamoto—the bureaucracy of Japan. These are the officials proper—not daimios, but salaried servants of the Taikoon—receiving their pay in rice, money, or land. They form the three arms of the service, and a list issued monthly publishes the promotions and changes made in their numbers.

Among the many checks placed on the daimios, the most important is perhaps the obligation to live half the time at Yeddo, while during the other half they are forced to leave their families at the capital as hostages. The large standing army each prince is obliged to maintain, at home and at Yeddo, is a constant drain upon his resources. They appear to be prohibited from visiting each other, and all intercourse between them seems to be rendered difficult, with a view to prevent coalitions. But these feudatory lords still have an immense power, and recent events have shown that however absolute Taikosama and his first successors may have been, the Taikoon of the present time is far from being so supreme as has been supposed.

The Siogun,* or Taikoon, holds the fourth rank from the Mikado, from whom he receives his investiture. Next to the Taikoon comes the Council of the Kokushi, consisting of eighteen or twenty-four daimios, among whom are some of the most powerful members of the ancient aristocracy. These are the representatives of the Mikado at Yeddo, and are said to take no active part in the Government, but rather to form a consultative body, whose duty it is to advise upon questions where their own and the Mikado's sanction is necessary, as in the instances of the treaties with foreign powers, when intercourse with these had been prohibited by the laws of Gongensama for more than two centuries. Next comes the Gorogio, called the Cabinet of the Taikoon, composed of five daimios of the third class, seemingly chosen from the newer aristocracy. Subordinate to the Gorogio there is a council of eight ministers, also daimios, but of inferior position, whose functions are supposed to be purely administrative.

After the second council come the Buñios, of whom there seems to be a large number holding a great variety of offices. A number of these, under the name of Gaikoko Buñio, Governors of Foreign Affairs, are said to correspond, to a certain extent, to the British Under-Secretaries of State, and the American Assistant-Secretaries. From the class of Buñios are appointed the governors of towns and judges. The larger part, if not all, of the offices inferior to the above are filled from the hattamotos.

* In this sketch of the organization of the Yeddo Government, I have followed Sir R. Alcock's work, "The Capital of the Tycoon," and the author of the App. D, in the same book.

Almost every office is duplicated, perhaps every one below the Taikoon. Every officer who holds a position of any responsibility, down to the subalterns of the custom house, is attended by a metzki, or an ometzki, according to the rank of the officer. These have generally been called spies by foreigners, but they are more properly auditors, and they constitute not only a powerful check against misconduct in office, but are at the same time official advisers on all questions. They are, at least sometimes, promoted to fill the positions of those whose auditors they have been. At the consular ports there are several metzkis, whose duty it is to be present at all interviews between foreigners and any official. These report to the ometzki, whose duty it is to attend the Governor. The ometzki reports to a board of o-o-metzkis at Yeddo. Once a year members of this board make tours of inspection through the empire.

But apart from this open system of control there is a net-work of espionage spreading its secret meshes over every part of the empire, and surrounding the actions of mikado, daimio, and official, and, to a certain extent also, of the people. Working in profound secresy, the spy adopts the apparent position most likely to further his object. One of the embassadors to the United States was at one time a spy of this class in Hakodade, circulating among the inhabitants in the disguise of a pedlar.

So much for the machinery of Government; concerning the population, whose political and social life it controls, our information is not much more definite. They are divided into classes, not indeed as strongly marked as are the castes in India, but still fenced in with all the restrictions of feudalism. These classes are said to be eight in number, viz:

1. The daimios, many of whom hold large territories in the administration of the affairs in which they are virtually independent, possessing despotic power over the lives of their subjects. These princes rank according to their revenues, which, estimated in kokos* of rice, vary from 1,200;000 to 10,000 kokoas (£769,728 to £6,400.) †

2. Hereditary nobility, not daimos, holding their estates in fief from daimios or the Taikoon, and obliged to furnish fighting men in proportion to the value of the estates. This class is,

* One Koko equals about 100 lbs.

† Alcock's "Capital of the Tycoon," App. D.

I believe, the hattamoto, at least those in it who are vassals of the Taikoon.

3. Priests of all sects.

4. Soldiers, vassals of the nobility.

The members of these four upper classes have, among other privileges, those of wearing two swords and Turkish trousers, and may ride on saddles.

5. Professional men, as physicians, government clerks, etc.

6. Merchants of the higher class, who, although possessing perhaps the greatest wealth of any class in the empire, are looked down upon by those above them, from whose ranks they are excluded. Still some of the great merchant families in which wealth has accumulated for many generations, affect considerable state in travelling, and it is not impossible that some among them may hold a social position somewhat analogous to that of a Rothschild in aristocratic Austria.

7. This class includes smaller dealers, mechanics, artisans, and artists.

8. Peasantry and day laborers of all descriptions.

Below these there is a class composed of workers in leather, who are pariahs, living in suburbs, separated from the rest of the inhabitants, and not allowed to enter even a roadside inn; they furnish the executioners.

There is another subdivision into classes which has rather reference to classification of occupations in the abstract, viz: war, agriculture, scholarship, trade.

The great mass of producers and manufacturers, forming a class far below the consumers, are merely tolerated, and their position is not much better than serfdom. The common soldier enjoys privileges which the merchant, often far better educated and richer, may not hope to see accrue to either himself or his descendants. One would suppose that in absence of the ability to pass from the lower to the higher ranks all incentive would be wanting for the accumulation of surplus wealth, in a country where dress and most expenses are regulated by sumptuary law; but this does not seem to be the case.

The government of the empire is best described by calling it a feudalism of the most despotic kind, while at the same time it is doubtful whether any other people ever before prospered and lived as happily under a feudal and despotic government as do the Japanese.

The relation between the tenant and his landlord is not well understood; it is known that rent is paid in kind amounting to more than half the crop, the land being frequently surveyed to determine the share; this applies to rice, other crops being paid in money.

We have then two great opposing elements, the Taikoon and the daimios, and between them the nominally acknowledged suzerain of both, the Mikado. The power of the Mikado is moral, but even as such it is immense, and in it would seem to lie the balance. This power existing in the prestige attaching to the Mikado, as such, appears to be independent of any individuality, and is consequently valuable only as an instrument in the hands of one or the other of the opposing parties. During times of peace, when the national machinery runs smoothly, the Mikados go through the tedious routine of living and dying, toy sovereigns with a toy court; but when some grave question arises, as of late years, he becomes the object of intrigue, and the most important problem appears to be who shall then control his mandates.

Although much depends upon the individual character of the Taikoon, still the greater part of the power of the Yeddo Government lies in the hands of the Council of Kokushi and the Gorogio, and above these, as it would appear from their action concerning the treaty with Commodore Perry, is the voice of the assembled 600 daimios, to be consulted on questions of the deepest importance. From this it will be seen how difficult it is to find the true seat of power. The reins seem to lie in the hands of the Taikoon, and the power of this to be limited by combinations among the daimios, and by the action of these through the voice of the Mikado. A system of intrigue and espionage at the court of Miako and among the daimios has until lately been sufficient to maintain the nice balance established by Taikosama. This certainly seems remarkable, when we consider that each prince keeps a large standing army, and controls his own territory.

Many explanations have been attempted of the causes lying at the bottom of the troubles that have attended recent intercourse between foreigners and Japanese. Sir Rutherford Alcock, for three years British Minister to Japan, supposes that the Government yielded the treaties solely under the belief that a refusal would be followed by a war with all the powers demanding intercourse, and that they yielded with the intention of expelling foreigners so soon as they should feel strong enough. With all due respect for the opinion of one who has had three years of diplomatic intercourse with the Yeddo Government, I cannot but think that this judgment is unjust. Another explanation seems to me to accord much better with the course of events which followed the making of the last treaties.

For many years an increasing number among the upper classes had been students of foreign sciences and arts, to such an extent as they could profit by Dutch works on these subjects and translations from them. If there were no daimios among this number, several of them encouraged these studies and endeavored to turn them to practical account in building ships and steamboats, in casting cannon, and in establishing manufactories of different kinds. Thus some of the great princes, whatever they might think of the foreigner, had evidently begun to appreciate the material features of his civilization, and they undoubtedly saw in foreign trade a means of strengthening themselves and increasing their revenues. This is proved by the fact that they have shown themselves exceedingly eager to buy foreign steamers and sailing vessels, and that their tenants have been allowed to turn their attention to the production of such articles as have at different times been most in demand for the Western markets. I know of no reason why this remark should not be true of all the daimios.

The Yeddo Government also saw in foreign trade the source of a large revenue, at the same time that their knowledge of Western affairs and the march of events on the shores of the Pacific taught them that the time was fast approaching when seclusion would be impossible. It is not likely that the making of the treaties was at the time very seriously opposed. But a violent opposition broke out afterward. The cause of this appears to have been much more in the restrictions placed by the Government upon trade between the daimios and foreigners, than in any hatred felt by the former toward the latter. The Government, ever jealous of the princes, while it could not prevent these from buying steamers, would not allow them to employ a foreigner in any capacity, thus rendering the loss of costly vessels almost certain, a loss which the Government may have regarded as a desirable drain on the owners' resources. They were restricted also in the purchase of arms, and finally, not only were the daimios prohibited from sending any of their subjects abroad, but all their products destined for the Western market could reach the foreign merchant only through the hands, or under the surveillance of Government employés, and they charged the Government with retaining the lion's share of the profits.

These restrictions could not but excite the jealousy and opposition of the daimios. Among the first results of foreign intercourse was a complete revolution in the relative values of labor and its products, a condition of things which weighed heavily on a large part of the population, especially in the interior. Silk, one of the great articles of export, nearly doubled in value at the ports from 1861 to 1864. The demand for cotton produced by the American war, raised the price of this necessity from a few cents to over thirty cents per pound. It was the same with almost everything for which there was a demand for exports. Thus in Japan, which had been one of the cheapest countries in the world, the prices of the necessities of life were suddenly raised to nearly an equality with those in the dearest markets. The effect of this was to bring great profits to the Government and to those standing between the producer and foreign shipper, while the producer was obliged to pay for necessities and luxuries prices out of all proportion greater than the increased value of his products. Naturally, in the absence of extraordinary hindrances, time would equalize the relations between labor and its products, but, at best, it would take years for an equilibrium to establish itself through the whole country. The value of labor on Nipon is unknown to me, but at the mines on Yesso, where it was said to be much dearer, miners received 5 cents, common laborers 4 cents, overseers 7 cents, and women 2 to 6 cents daily—each receiving daily rations of the value of 4.5 cents. On Nipon, rice, the mainstay of life, was worth until recently about one cent per pound. If the rise in prices bore heavily on the laboring classes, accustomed to live in the strictest simplicity, it weighed still more upon the immense population of less patient retainers and Government employés, whose pay had hitherto enabled them to dress in silk and indulge in luxuries. Having no interest, present or prospective, in foreign intercourse, they soon became exasperated at a state of things which plunged them into a condition of relative poverty, since their pay remained stationary.

In addition to these causes for internal troubles, there were intrigues among princes, who sought to aggrandize themselves at the expense of the Taikoon. These, finding a powerful lever in the rising unpopularity of the course pursued by the Yeddo Government, brought it to bear at the court of the Mikado, and all the more effectually that the making of the treaties had been without the consent, and probably in defiance, of that sovereign.

These intrigues culminated in the organization of an opposition sufficiently strong to control the Mikado, before whom the Taikoon was summoned to appear. In the conferences of the great lords of the empire, assembled at Miako in 1863 and 1864, several of the daimios appear to have openly advocated the removal of all restrictions on foreign trade, and the opening of the whole country. But the decision of the majority resulted in a decree of the Mikado, commanding the Taikoon to release the princes from obligation to live with their families at Yeddo, and ordering these to turn all their resources toward preparations for war, with a view to the expulsion of the "barbarians."

Foremost among the opposition was the Prince of Chosiu, whose batteries at Simonoseki command the inland sea. This daimio precipitately began hostilities, which soon brought him into war not only with foreign powers by firing on their vessels, but with the Taikoon, and, by his attempt to seize the person of the Mikado, with the court of Miako. The empire was threatened at the same moment with both a civil and a foreign war. It became evident how little real power the Yeddo Government possessed when opposed by the daimios and the Mikado. The open ports were threatened with constant danger, trade was at a standstill, and the Government was pressing the abandonment of Yokohama by foreigners.

A combined attack made by the foreign squadrons upon Simonoseki resulted in the immediate humbling of Chosiu, and changed the whole complex of affairs. The Taikoon was strengthened by the humiliation of his chief opponent, and from that time the course of events was progressive.* One of the most significant results of this change in the political current was the decree which soon followed, permitting Japanese to go abroad—leaving the country, even when carried away by storms at sea, having been always a capital offence. That it has been, throughout, the intention of the Yeddo Government to extend their relations with the outside world, is shown, I think, by the fact of their purchasing foreign merchant-vessels, with the intention of opening a direct trade between their own merchants and other countries. Two voyages of this description were made—one to the Amoor river, the other to Shanghai. The intention of the Government was to open the way for a direct trade in which Japanese merchants should compete with the foreign shippers. The history of the past nine years has been marked by many acts of violence which have tended to widen the breach between the Japanese and foreigners. A few of these have perhaps had a direct political origin, but the greater number, if not all, have been acts of revenge, in which the victims were the provokers, or have suffered for the deeds of other foreigners. Even the attempted assassination of Sir R. Alcock is ascribed by that gentleman to the wish of a daimio to be avenged on a foreigner of rank for having been forced to demean himself by having an interview with the commander of a Russian man-of-war. The murder of Richardson, which was so fearfully avenged by the British fleet at Kagosima, was another instance of the same class. Shimadzo Saburo, representative of the powerful Prince of Satsuma, had been to Yeddo as bearer of a message from the Mikado. Returning after unsuccessful negotiations, his large retinue was met by a party of foreigners. In order to avoid any collision, the Government had requested foreign ministers to warn their countrymen of the danger of riding on the tokaido on that particular day. A party of three Englishmen and one lady, disregarding the warning, met the train beyond Kanagawa, when, as would appear from the language of the lady, the soldiers tried to crowd the party off from the road—a proceeding which was resented by an attempt to break across the double file of retainers. The latter,

* Since the above was written great changes have taken place. A revolution has been begun, of which we cannot foresee the end. The Taikoon Government has, at least for the present, disappeared. It remains to be seen whether the foreign Ministers have acted wisely in using their influence in the furtherance of this revolution, in which the country seems likely to be resolved into its feudal elements.

drawing their swords, cut down Mr. Richardson, and the remainder of the party escaped only with several wounds. Richardson, at first wounded, was afterward killed, by the order, it seems, of Shimadzo Saburo. Had a Japanese of any rank tried to cross a similar train he would have been cut down in like manner; but it appears from the language of the lady, *immediately after her escape*—language quite different from that of the subsequent affidavits of the party—that there was an attempt to force a passage across the train by riding down the soldiers. Certainly it would seem that some such provocation was given, since another foreigner, a few minutes in advance of this party, met the train, and passed it without the slightest trouble. The affidavits of the party, however, represented the attack as having been wholly unprovoked; and, acting on this, the British Government prepared to avenge the assassination. Satsuma was responsible for the act, and to his capital, Kagosima, the fleet was sent, to demand the payment of £25,000 as indemnity, and the execution of the murderers. After two interviews with the officers of Satsuma, in which the latter blamed the Taikoon's Government, and proposed that a commission should examine into the indemnity question, the Chargé d'Affaires placed the matter in the hands of the admiral, who seized as pledges three steamers belonging to Satsuma. The Japanese, regarding this as an act of hostility, opened fire, when the admiral signalled to have the steamers burned. In the midst of a fierce gale, the squadron brought its guns to bear on the town.

"At this time the storm was raging with great fury; the town had been fired by the shells and rockets of the fleet, and the wind was carrying the flames swiftly through the streets. A dreadful spectacle was thus presented. The three [captured] steamers were on fire, as were also five large Lewchew junks, to which the gunboat "Havoc" had separately applied the torch, and the city stretching away over three miles was in flames, which were seen also to envelop the green trees on the hillsides. The foundry and machine shops, a mile in extent, were also on fire, and the fury of the flames kept pace with that of the storm. The next morning the fleet opened fire again on the town and batteries, some of which feebly responded. Several shells were thrown into the palace, which is believed to have been destroyed, as flames were seen to issue from it as the fleet left." The account from which I quote adds: "It was thought that sufficient had been accomplished by way of punishment, and that further proceedings would be regarded as vindictive!"

The attacking squadron suffered severely, and lost fifty-six officers and men. The loss of life among the population of the city is said to have been very great, as no notice whatever was given of the intended bombardment. Indeed, scarcely thirty-six hours passed between the arrival of the fleet and the attack. Thus many lives were lost, and a city laid in ruins, and with it the extensive machine shops—the nucleus of foreign civilization in Japan—all because a foreigner had been killed in attempting to do that which law and custom punish with death in Japanese subjects. When a young Englishman was shot down in Rome by a French sentinel whom he approached, not having understood the challenge, did any one think that offence called for the bombardment of a French city? It was in fact in perfect accord with the policy followed by the West in treating with the East. When an Englishman, or an American, or a Frenchman—starting from the firm belief that all orientals are infinitely beneath his own race—assumes that they have no rights he is bound to respect; ignores the fact that, as a stranger, he is tolerated in their land by courtesy or necessity, and forcibly attempts to assert that superiority; he should be taught that he does so at his own risk. As with the individual, so with the nation. The representatives of the Western governments are clothed with almost sovereign power, and are only too often also imbued with the prejudice of race. That which they would not dream of doing in the face of an European power, they often do not hesitate to practice toward a weaker oriental nation—constantly violating international law at the same time that they demand of them an observance of it. Thus at Kagosima we find the fleet arriving on the evening of the 11th. Negotiations during the 12th resulted in a letter which did not refuse compliance with the weighty demands of the English, but proposed the appointment of commissioners by Satsuma and the Taikoon to determine whether the former was responsible for the murder, or the latter from not having stipulated in the treaties that foreigners should not be bound to observe the same rules of the road that are obligatory among the natives. This letter was evasive, and early on the 13th the steamers of Satsuma were seized without any notification that they were taken as pledges, and not as a declaration of war. This is resented by a brisk fire upon the squadron. The admiral forthwith burns the three prizes and other shipping, and within half an hour has begun a fierce bombardment, not of the batteries only, but of a large city, amid whose converging flames thousands of innocent people find their death. Surely these things are done quicker in eastern than in western waters; and what can prevent hasty action where all depends on one word from one man, and where that word, on which hang the lives of thousands, may depend on the state of that man's digestion?

Leaving justice out of the question, the material interests of the West require a thorough change in its policy toward orientals. Throughout eastern Asia we have to deal with people on whom, at present, we are far more dependent than they are upon us; at the same time we are hoping to create among them the principal markets for the products of our industry. The creation of such markets presupposes the creation of wants, which are wholly inconsistent with a condition of decay, and which can be gratified only by the products of an industry of which a vigorous national vitality must necessarily be the basis. Everything that tends to impair that vitality, whether it be the indirect encouragement of anarchy, through the weakening of the government, or by the forced introduction of opium, operates directly against the interests of the West. Both justice and our own interests demand that our diplomacy with these people shall start not from the assumption that they are an inferior race; but that, owing to continued isolation, they are now a century or more behind us—and this not in all things, but in a few of those essential points of our civilization at which Western nations have successively arrived at recent dates. Starting from this point, and looking upon them as capable, under favorable circumstances, of rising to the average level of Western countries, it will be the duty of the West to render the conditions necessary to such an elevation as favorable as possible. The cunning of the Japanese or Chinese statesman, by which he seeks to compensate for his nation's weakness, not only in exciting jealousies among foreign ministers, but in a thousand other ways, must be met by a just and united action on the part of the representatives of the West. While we exact from them the observance of treaty stipulations, we must first see to it that those stipulations are just; and, next, our policy must be such as will tend to make these governments independent of foreign military aid, in either external or internal troubles. Thus, by strengthening the power of a government, we shall both remove from it the cause for a deceitfulness which arises from conscious weakness, and shall render it able to meet its treaty obligations. Such a policy requires a co-operation not only among the foreign representatives, but also among their respective governments; and surely the problem which it alone can satisfactorily solve is sufficiently important to demand for it a careful consideration. The problem is nothing less than this: there are two healthy nations, representing more than one-third of the human race: shall we do that which lies in our power toward maintaining them in a healthful condition and raising them to the rank of equals, or shall we stand by and see them sink into a state of decay, in which for centuries they will be not only useless to the world, but a curse upon it? We shall see, in speaking of China, that this desirable change of policy was inaugurated by the foreign representatives at Peking. Could the home governments be brought to see the importance of the change, as did the broad-minded statesmen who originated it, it would be alike well for the future of the East and for the world at large. What Turkey is to-day to Europe, eastern Asia, if not rendered self-dependent, will surely soon be to the world.

I would here remark that as England, of all western countries, has long played the most important part in the East, comments on Western diplomacy in that part of the world are almost synonymous with comments on English diplomacy. But I am instigated by no feeling of animosity toward England in my remarks, for I consider her simply as the exponent of the whole West. England has built up the commerce of the world; and if in doing, as she has done, almost the entire police duty of the Eastern seas, and in opening new countries to trade with all the world, she has committed many acts which may in future be considered as stains on her flag, it must be remembered how great are her interests there at stake, and that what she has done we might also have done under less excusing circumstances.

CHAPTER IX.

EXCURSIONS.

TOWARD the end of April I joined Mr. C. Maximowitch, a distinguished Russian botanist and explorer, in making an excursion to Inosima, on Wodowara bay. A pleasant ride along the western shore of Yeddo bay brought us to Outzu, or the peninsula of Sagami, where, leaving the sea, we turned to cross over to Wodowara bay. There are extensive fortifications at this place, and we had barely passed behind these when several soldiers rushed out after us with drawn swords. They were fortunately on foot; and, finding that we did not stop, they sent a runner to give notice of our coming. This fellow shot past us, and although we kept up a travelling trot, he reached a village four or five miles off a few minutes before we arrived. But we were half-way through the place before those who might have turned us back could be astir. The warden, with his jingling staff, on his way to stop us, started back at the sight of two foreigners, and before he could recover we were beyond the village.

It is impossible to ride anywhere in Japan, off from the tokaido, without being aware of the difficulties an invading army would meet with. Excepting the few great arteries, like the tokaido, the roads are mere bridle paths, winding among rice fields, which, at most seasons, are deep sloughs of mud.

When we came in sight of the sea, a view presented itself in which I immediately recognized a scene familiar to all who have seen much of the Japanese lacquered ware. Before us lay the smooth water of Wodowara bay. A mile or more from us a long, low neck of sand joined the beach to the rocky island of Inosima. Far away over this neck, and the bay beyond, rose the lofty and graceful cone of Fuziyama. This view of the mountain is a favorite subject of Japanese artists. The annexed sketch is taken from this point. The most perfect of volcanic cones, rising, no matter whence you see it, above a beautiful intervening landscape, it is with reason an object of national pride, and the subject of innumerable sketches and verses.

Sir R. Alcock and the Europeans of his party are the only foreigners who have ascended Fuziyama. They determined the height of the highest peak, by the boiling point and aneroid, to be 14,177 feet above the sea, and estimated the depth of the crater at 350 feet. The last eruption was in 1707, and six months afterward the mountain Ha-e-san was thrown up on its flank. Other great eruptions took place in A.D. 1032, A.D. 800, and A.D. 781.

INOSIMA, AND MOUNT FUSIYAMA, FROM A JAPANESE SKETCH.

This mountain is the resort of thousands of pilgrims from the common classes; but according to the British minister it is considered beneath the dignity of a person of rank to make the ascent. Indeed, I believe that the upper classes are generally Confucianists, while Fuziyama is sacred in the Sintu religion.

A pleasant canter along the firm beach brought us to the sandy neck, and over this, between two lines of surf, to the island. Here we passed under the inevitable temple gate-way or arch; this one was of bronze, and its unusual size and workmanship showed that we were entering upon very sacred ground.

9

The island is about two hundred feet high, and a quarter of a mile or more long, three of its sides being precipices. From the sacred portal we ascended the steep street between a double row of inns, at one of which we left the horses, and continued the excursion on foot. Temples with large paved squares in front of them, filled with pilgrims, booths of shell dealers, small tea-houses, and fragments of overturned gateways—records of earthquakes—lined the street on either side.

The island is cleft by a great chasm, which is now partially re-filled with detritus. But the celebrity of the place arises from a long, tunnel-like cave, passing at the level of the sea nearly through the island, and excavated by the waves along a system of cracks in the sandstone. The cavern is about 500 feet long, but the waves rush into it through a long, deep chasm, a continuation of the cave without the roof. Here is the home of the sea-god, of whom there are many images in the dark recess. Truly, a more appropriate place could scarcely be found than here, where the waves of a stormy sea must enter with awful force and reverberating thunder.

Walking back to the inn, we were struck with the beauty of many of the shells exposed for sale; among these were the delicate, smooth scallop, with one valve white and the other purple, and the paper nautilus. In these waters are found also the fragile and hair-like vitreous coral, and the beautiful fluted dentalium.

On our return we visited the Daibutz at Kamakura, and, crossing thence to the tokaido, reached Yokohama. During my absence a vessel had arrived, bringing Mr. Pruyn, the successor to Mr. Harris, and the consuls for Yokohama and Hakodade. As this ship was going to Yesso, we proposed to the Government to send us by it, and they immediately dispatched a Governor of Foreign Affairs to Yokohama, to give us our instructions.

After our business was transacted I asked the Governor what objection there could be to Mr. Blake and myself seeing Yeddo. I was not a little astonished when he replied that there was not the slightest objection, and expressed surprise that we had not already visited the capital. He informed us that, should we wish to go thither the following morning, he would give orders to the Governor of Kanagawa to provide us with an escort. We accepted the offer, although it would allow us only one day at Yeddo, including the journey.

Early the next morning, accompanied by six officers and eight bettos or running footmen, we set out for the capital. With the exception of a few short interruptions, the road between Kanagawa and Yeddo is lined on both sides with houses, forming under different names one long, narrow village. A short distance beyond Kanagawa we passed the place where, a few months later, Mr. Richardson was killed.

Away from the tokaido, the country lying only a few feet above the bay is a broad expanse of rice plantations. The horizon is bounded on the west by the low green bluff of a table-land, which, approaching the sea near the southern limit of Yeddo, furnishes elevated ground for the city, while to the numerous valleys in this plateau Yeddo owes much of the agreeable variety and picturesqueness of its scenery.

Our escort conducted us to the American legation, where we were hospitably received by Mr. Harris, from whom we learned, much to our disappointment, that we had visited Yeddo upon the one day in all the year when it would be impossible for us to either cross the city or approach the castle, since on that day the Taikoon would visit a favorite palace, and the Government had requested that no foreigners should enter the heart of the capital. I felt this disappointment less than I should have had I foreseen that I was to leave Japan without revisiting its metropolis.

The legation occupied the large reception rooms of a temple built for the use of those daimios whose ancestral tablets were here preserved. For the protection of the minister, the grounds were surrounded by a double stockade of bamboos. Between these walls a strong patrol was constantly on duty, and from 150 to 200 soldiers, furnished by the Taikoon and a daimio, were always on guard. Piles of combustible materials were scattered through the grounds, by which, in case of an attack, a brilliant light could be produced. In the midst of dangers requiring precautions of this kind did Mr. Harris live in Yeddo, after the withdrawal of the other ministers, himself and his interpreter, Mr. Portman, being the only Europeans in the great city.

The grounds of the temple were large, and contained some beautiful specimens of Japanese gardening, consisting of dwarfed trees and rock work, with ponds containing gold fish and silver fish. Several of these were more than two feet long, while some of the smaller ones proudly steered their way by means of lobed tails longer than their bodies, and apparently as delicate as lace.

The excursion we made at the suggestion of Mr. Harris, while it showed us only a small part of Yeddo, led us through the daimio quarter. One feature that struck me was the abundance of large trees, many of them primeval forest pines, which met the eye at every turn, crowning the low hills or rising from the grounds of a daimio's yaski. The enclosures are very large, and one may ride miles between the low black barracks that surround them. Of the space enclosed only a casual glimpse is vouchsafed by an open gateway. In these enclosures many small standing armies are scattered through Yeddo, and it is said that military drill and artillery practice are here kept up as regularly as among western armies. Should the system be destroyed which so perfectly balances these forces, it seems almost certain that Japan, with its feudal lords and their mountain-bound territories, will undergo a most destructive period of anarchy.

Although I was nearly all the day in the saddle, I saw but little of Yeddo excepting the streets leading through the daimio quarter and the western suburbs. Here we rode for miles through what was half town, half country. The houses were all neat villas, standing some distance from the road. They were protected, but not hidden, by hedges of living bamboos and other plants, while the grounds enclosed were shaded by carefully cultivated trees, and ornamented with the choice flowering shrubs of the country.

As we turned our steps homeward, and re-entered the long suburb on the road to Kanagawa, the escort pressed upon us the necessity of keeping together, as the drinking-houses of this quarter were always full of the drunken retainers, who are a constant source of terror to the peaceable inhabitants. A somewhat startling illustration of the habits of this class offered itself more suddenly than was agreeable. A party of eight or ten dashed into the street just ahead of us, flourishing their drawn swords and acting like devils. Fortunately they were either too drunk or too much bent on cutting each other to notice us.

It was late at night when we reached Yokohama. We had

gone fifty-four miles since the morning, and we had been to Yeddo, and had ridden sixteen miles in the city; we had probably seen less of its interesting points than any other traveller before or since. One only out of all our running footmen returned with us, having kept ahead of his horse during the entire journey. The varied picture of life offered by a great city, even though seen from a distance, leaves a more vivid impression on the mind of a traveller, and supplies, perhaps, more suggestions for his appreciation of a people, than any other phase of a journey. But knowing as little as do foreigners of the social life and manner of thinking of the Japanese, it is impossible to give a just description of their character. The opinion of each traveller is generally based on the strongly-impressed incidents of his experience. On his first excursion he hears the universal salutation, "Ohaio!" good morning! which he receives from children, and enters in his journal that the Japanese are an exceedingly hospitable people. Soon he finds that the exclamation is quite as often, "bacca! bacca!" fool; or "tojin! tojin!" Chinaman; and when the novelty of their appearance has worn off, he becomes vexed at the immense crowds of men, women, and children, which, attracted by the novelty of *his* appearance, follow him through the streets, and nearly crowd him out of his quarters at the inn, in their anxiety to see him eat, drink, sit, and stand, even waiting for him to undress to see whether the barbarian is made like themselves. If he lacks patience, the virtue above all others necessary to the traveller, he is likely to resent this treatment by violence, and to get a pelting with mud or stones for his reward. Such treatment causes a change in his estimate of the people, and the world is informed that the Japanese hate foreigners.

He sees the "social evil" at the tea-houses, and visiting the public baths finds both sexes bathing in common, without the refinements adopted at Newport or Brighton, and the world learns that modesty, and consequently all other virtues, are unknown to the Japanese—that they are sunk to the lowest depths of vice to which even a heathen people can sink.

But the thoughtful traveller learns in the first stages of his wanderings, that the more distant the relationship between two races, the more difficult is it to measure them by the same standard. To describe a people we must first know their inner life—

how they act and how they think, what are their home relations, and what their virtues and vices—for to these a nation's character may be reduced. Before we can pass judgment upon their character, or compare it with our own, it is necessary to analyze their virtues and vices, to find out how much of these is absolute and how much conventional, when compared with the West; and when, after submitting our own to the same analysis, we have reduced both to their simplest expressions, then and not till then may we institute a comparison.

But ignorance of these data does not prevent my giving to the reader the impressions gleaned during a closer intercourse than foreigners have generally had with the natives.

In the nervousness of their temperament they differ widely from all the other peoples of eastern Asia; and, although we are ignorant of their literature, enough is visible in their art to show that in imaginativeness, as well as temperament, they approach more nearly to the Hindoo race than does any of the Mongolian branches. In this fact lies the secret of the rapidity with which not only the Buddist, but, later, the Christian religion took root among all classes. And in nothing is the difference between the Chinese and Japanese more marked than in this matter of religion; for while in China the early popular faith, after the lapse of thousands of years, sank to its already ancient condition of a State ceremonial, and was supplanted by the materialism of Confucius, leaving only a few vague superstitions floating in the popular mind, the race between Buddism and Confucianism, continuing nearly as long in one country as in the other, has in Japan always been to the advantage of the former.

This same characteristic feature of the national mind may again render easy the introduction of Christianity clothed in the splendor of the Roman ritual, an event which none but the most sanguine can anticipate for China.

The writers on Japan, of the sixteenth century, could not say too much for the truthfulness, frankness, and gentleness of the natives. Nor do I think their pictures of the people so extravagantly colored as some later writers would have us believe. There is a modesty and refinement, extending far into the lower classes, and, accompanying these qualities, a far greater regard for truth than is generally found among orientals. Unfortunately, this remark cannot hold good in regard to official intercourse in a country where intrigue is an arm of the Government.

But Japan is a country full of contradictions, according to our standard. It is pretty certain that female virtue stands quite as high among that people as among any other, and higher than in some western countries; and yet accompanying this we find parents selling their daughters to licensed houses of prostitution, which abound to a great extent, showing that any excess of virtue in one sex is perhaps counterbalanced in the other. As repulsive as is this Japanese feature of the social evil, it carries with it mitigating circumstances which are wanting in other countries. The victims, who are always from the lower classes, are sold from poverty, and being themselves entirely irresponsible for their position, none of the disgrace attaches to them which drags the unfortunates of the West into the lowest depths; on the contrary, they are sold in childhood for a limited number of years, and as the proprietors of the establishments are obliged to have them instructed in every branch of female education, they often marry into the class in which they were born. Parallels to both these modes of entering and leaving this kind of life are not wanting even among the families of poor officials in some parts of eastern Europe. The anomaly is in the laws which permit in the husband that which they punish with death in the wife.

Japanese houses are built on one model, differing chiefly in size and costliness of material, while, from the palace down, there reigns a rigid simplicity in form and furniture. The frequency of earthquakes necessitates the use of the lightest materials, and these are wood and paper, and with these substances the danger from fire is so great that costly ornamentation would be thrown away. According to Sir R. Alcock, fires in Yeddo are so frequent that the whole city is burned down and rebuilt every seven years, and the same rule probably holds in other towns. Fire insurance is unknown, and though there are brave and well-organized fire-brigades, they can, with their small hand-pumps, do little to stay a conflagration raging in such light materials.

The dwellings are one or two stories high, with a verandah running all around. The size of the rooms is regulated by the number of mats; and as these are always six feet long by three wide, the area of the room must be planned to admit a given number of whole mats. The rooms are divided by sliding doors of paper, stretched on a slight frame, which rolls easily in grooved beams in the floor and beneath the ceiling. These doors often form the only partition walls, and by removing them the whole building may be thrown into one room. The mats are made up of several layers of course matting, covered by one of a fine white grass, the whole being about two inches thick, and bound at the sides with a border of dark cloth. This forms a firm and elastic covering for the floor. The wood-work of the outside is painted black, when painted at all; but, in the interior, wax, oil and lacquer are used to produce ornamental effect, in connection with the grain of the wood. Beams of the ceiling and upright posts are often carved, but more generally lacquered or waxed; sometimes the timber is only partially squared, a portion of the bark being left on, and a curious effect produced by lacquering this with the rest. The paper of the sliding doors is often a picture-gallery in itself, representing landscapes, or birds and flowers, often admirably done in ink or colors.

Nearly every room has one end devoted to a recess, one-half of which is a closet for mattrasses, etc., in bed-rooms, and the other half a niche with a hanging scroll, bearing a picture or verses; underneath this stands a low rack for swords. The rooms are heated with charcoal, either in an elegant bronze brazier, or in an iron pot in a box of sand, sunk into the floor.

Thus easily is the furniture of a Japanese room summed up. As simple as it is, these houses have the charm of neatness. No dust is visible, least of all on the floor; and if the rooms look empty, they also look airy. The reader will have remarked the absence of chairs and tables—of these the Japanese has no need. Never stepping on a mat other than in his stockings, he always has a clean floor to sit on; and here, with shins doubled under him, and using the hollow of the feet for a chair, the native will sit by the hour, smoking and gossiping over tea or saki, or playing chess.

In neatness I do not believe that the Japanese are surpassed by any people; and if "cleanliness is next to godliness," certainly the daily parboiling to which every one of the population submits himself may go far toward absolving them from other sins. Every house has its bath—a simple tub, large enough to allow one to sit down with the knees doubled. A copper tube passing through the water at one end, and having the bottom perforated for a draught, contains a little burning charcoal, which soon heats the bath. Toward evening this is warmed, and the household, beginning with the master and ending with the servants, take their turns.

Although every house has its tub, the towns abound in public baths, where, for a trifle, a more luxurious scrubbing can be had. And these public places are an institution of the country quite as remarkable as any other. There is a door marked "for men," and one "for women;" but this distinction ends after crossing the threshold, for, on entering, men, women, and children are seen scrubbing each other, enjoying cold and hot douches, and making a perfect babel of the room with their loud chattering and laughter.

This custom, shocking as it seems to an European, appears to be perfectly compatible with Japanese ideas of modesty and propriety, and a Japanese lady of undoubted virtue finds nothing wrong in the practice. I shall long remember an incident which convinced me of the truth of this statement. During my stay at one of the mines on Yesso, where there is a hot spring, I went one evening with one of the officers of our staff to take a bath. The small spring-house had an outer room for servants and miners, and an inner compartment for the officers and their families; but this division was only above the water, which ran from the spring into a box about three feet deep and eight feet long. As we entered the inner compartment we found the wife of the chief officer bathing with her children. Before I had time to withdraw, the lady came out; and, politely offering us the bath, remarked, that as there would not be room for all of us, she would go with the children to the other compartment. The whole thing was done so gracefully, and without the slightest embarrassment on her part, that I began to wonder from what direction would come the next shock to preconceived ideas of propriety. *Honi soit qui mal y pense* is perhaps as applicable in a Japanese public bath as in the galleries of sculpture of the Vatican.

Much of the healthful effect of the daily bath is neutralized by the absence of under-clothing that can be often changed, as white under-garments may not be worn by any one beneath the rank of a Buñio.

It is possible that the prevalence of skin diseases, to which the Japanese are subject, is in some manner connected with the bath-system. Besides the common itch, there is a kind of similar disease, peculiar to the country, I believe, which is very obstinate and difficult of cure. The whole empire seems to enjoy a healthy climate, which has generally secured them from epidemics. These have however sometimes swept over the country; and among them measles, apparently epidemic, appears to have been the most common. Notwithstanding the proximity of Japan to China, which is one of the centres of cholera, there appears to have been but one cholera season previous to the opening of the ports. This freedom from the great Asiatic scourge is certainly remarkable, when we consider that, although houses and streets are exceedingly clean, the practice of preparing liquid manure in large open cisterns, of which there is one in every field, would with us be thought sufficient of itself to generate the disease. At certain seasons, indeed generally, this custom makes it almost impossible to enjoy a country walk unless one be gifted with enduring nostrils. If it be true that the germ of cholera is a fungoid body, transmitted through the air, one might expect to find it brought by the S. W. monsoons from the delta of China. What the wind can do as a medium of transportation is well illustrated by its power of carrying dust and volcanic ashes to a distance of hundreds of miles. On the 31st of March, and 1st of April, 1863, there was a great dust-storm on the plain around Peking, in which people lost their lives. The air was darkened, and the dust fell several inches deep, the wind being from the northwest. During the same days the air was filled with a dust fog at Shanghai, and at Nagasaki, where I then was. At Nagasaki the wind blew from the west, and during both days what appeared at first to be a fog obscured the sun just enough to permit one to distinguish the spots on its red disc with the naked eye. On the third day it was found that a deposit of dust had settled, so fine as to be imperceptible excepting on the fresh white paint of a yacht.

This phenomenon occurring at Nagasaki, more than 700 miles from its source, was observed at points much more distant at sea.

These dust storms had been supposed to have their origin on the Gobi desert; but I found in 1864, while travelling beyond the great wall of China, between the Gobi and the plain of Peking, that the strong northwest winds blowing from the desert reached the plain quite free from dust, and that it was not until it struck the cultivated plains of northern China, at a season when the dry loamy soil was unprotected by crops, that it raised great volumes of dust, similar to that described. The dry climate of northern China is comparatively free from cholera.

During all my travels in Japan I noticed only one case of goitre. It is true that I did not visit any limestone regions, but a great part of the population live in shaded and damp valleys; so damp that a freshly-polished boot is covered with mould in forty-eight hours. If there be any connection between absence of iodine and presence of goitre, it may be that the universal consumption of sea-weed as food, or presence of iodine in water coming from the recently raised marine volcanic tufa which prevails on the coast, may have something to do with the immunity the Japanese enjoy from this disease. Goitre abounds in the limestone hills west of Peking, in a very dry climate.

That tape-worms do not come from pork only, would seem to follow from the statement of a Japanese officer at Hakodade, that officials sent from Yeddo to Yesso generally become troubled with these parasites. The Japanese eat little meat, never pork in any form, but they are not so scrupulous with regard to bear's flesh. Troubles of the eyes are common, and many blind people are seen in the streets, recognizable by their shaven heads and long sticks.

That the Japanese do not die off *en masse*, is no fault of their physicians, for these are little more advanced than their brethren in China, and in the latter country the most profound ignorance of anatomy and physiology rules, at least among the old-school doctors. A considerable number of physicians now practice medicine as learned from good Dutch teachers and foreign works on the subject; but in view of the great difficulty that attends the study of the body, by the aid of dissection, in Japan, their knowledge is not deep.

Although pills to insure longevity form part of the Japanese materia medica, immense cemeteries prove that even long lives must end. These cities of the dead were always interesting to me. Often built on the side of a hill, covering a large area, and commanding a fine view, their neatly-kept avenues offer the place for quiet walks, where one is sure to find none of the revolting sights so common in similar places in China. In all that relates to their dead, the Japanese exhibit a refinement one does not expect to find out of Christian countries. Thus we find great care bestowed on the tombs, and much taste and art displayed in their construction. Thousands of small paved terraces, surrounded by stone balustrades, form family lots containing commemorative stones of every shape and size, and every variety of proper ornamentation. The sculptured inscriptions in the Chinese character always excited my admiration, the execution being much more finished than is common with us.

On the night of the festival corresponding to All Souls' Day, the cemeteries are illuminated with myriads of lanterns, which, seen from a distance, produce the effect of as many openings into a mountain burning within. Cremation and interment seem to be about equally practiced, though it does not appear which is the more ancient custom.

But the reverence they show for death does not prevent the Japanese from getting all the enjoyment they can command out of life. Festivals abound: there would seem to be one for every temple; and in the absence of these, holidays, marriages, theatres, performances of jugglers, acrobats, and wrestlers, furnish the needed excitement for the people. In pleasant weather, picnics, on water and land, enlivened with music, are an unfailing resource.

The wrestlers appear to be retainers of daimios, and are trained from youth to their occupation. They are certainly men of great strength, but it was always a question with me how strength could exist under such masses of fat as they seem to be made of. In their exhibitions they are naked, excepting a belt drawn tightly around the loins, forming the only means of obtaining a firm hold of each other. It is doubtful whether they are as strong as the more muscular native stevedores, who trot along all day, bearing two or three hundred pounds of tea or copper, in loading ships. Among the Japanese acrobats and contortionists, one may see nearly all the feats familiar to similar performers with us, and many others, requiring great skill and courage, and the jugglers are probably not excelled by their brethren of India and Europe, in tricks that require extreme delicacy of manipulation.

The theatre is considered one of the best reflectors of the popular mind. In Japan, as in China, the performances begin early in the day, and end late at night, the large audiences showing how popular is this amusement. The plots are nearly always intrigues at court, resulting in promotion or death of the heroes, or the exploits of great warriors and robbers. The public taste demands, and is gratified by, the profuse display of gory heads and dripping swords. The favorite pieces contain a great deal of "blood and murder," and not unfrequently scenes that border on extreme grossness, which are viewed with as little embarrassment by neatly-dressed matrons and daughters as the sallies of "Genevieve de Brabant," or the "Grande Duchesse" excite in a western audience. The same vein seems to run through the immense range of light literature, illustrated with woodcuts, that often approach the obscene. Although I have been told by Japanese that the families of the upper classes do not witness this kind of theatrical representations, and are guarded against access to corresponding works of fiction, still there is no doubt that there reigns throughout the female population an absence of that moral refinement which, with us, is considered so necessary as a safeguard for female purity.

The ruling vice in Japan is, undoubtedly, drunkenness. It pervades all classes, though it is confined by the force of public opinion to the male sex. On a festival of the third day of the third month women are indeed allowed great license, and in their harems, from which on that day even their lords are excluded, they may indulge to any extent in the forbidden cup; but a woman of the lower class who should be found drunk at any other time, would expose herself to a severe beating from her husband, while were she of the higher class she might die by the sword of her spouse. The only fermented liquor used is, I believe, the saki, distilled from rice, and differing from the Chinese tiu or samshu in that while it is weaker it often contains much of the poisonous oil of distillation. It is always taken warm, and the better kind is not disagreeable to the taste. Few Japanese are fit for business in the evening, and during the afternoon many streets in Yeddo are rendered wholly unsafe by the troops of drunken retainers, whose drawn swords are the terror of the inhabitants.

With all their faults the Japanese are a generous people, brave, and capable of enduring great hardships, imaginative and impulsive rather than reasoning; while in their enthusiastic attempts to learn foreign sciences and arts they contrast strongly with the Chinese, and vouch perhaps for a rapid and progressive revolution in their civilization.

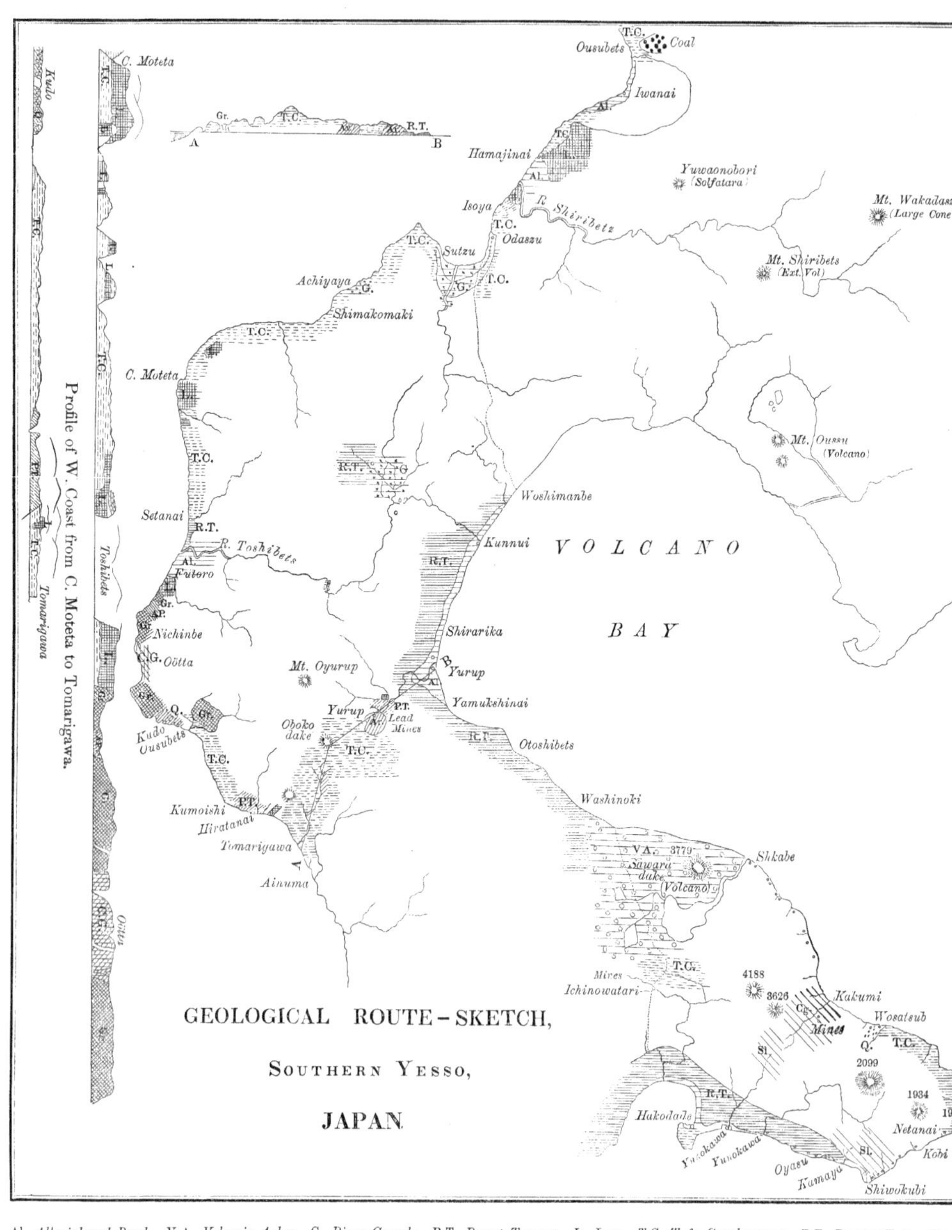

Al. *Alluvial and Beach.* V.A. *Volcanic Ashes.* G. *River Gravels.* R.T. *Recent Terraces.* L. *Lava.* T.C. *Tufa Conglomerate.* P.T. *Pumice Tufa.* ⁘ C
Ar. *Metamorphic Argillite.* Q. *Quartzite.* Sl. Cg. *Clay Slates and Conglomerate.* C.G. *Conglomerate and Granulite*
A.P. *Aphanitic Rock.* Gr. *Granitic and Syenite Series.*

CHAPTER X.

FIRST JOURNEY IN YESSO.

BIDDING good-by to our hospitable friends, Messrs. Brower and Benson, and to Dr. Simmons, to whose kindness I owed much of the pleasure of my visit, we sailed on the "Ringleader" for Yesso, and entered the harbor of Hakodade after a short and pleasant voyage. This town, the northernmost of the open ports, is built on the foot-slope of a rugged peak of trachyte, which, rising 1,150 feet, overlooks the straits of Tsungara, and commands a view of the hills of Nipon. This island-like peak is connected with Yesso by a low sandy neck, thus forming a harbor several miles broad, and accessible for the largest vessels.

Quarters were assigned us at the custom-house pending the building of a house suitable for our dwelling, offices, laboratory, etc.

As the object of our engagement with the Government was the exploration of its lands on the island of Yesso, and the introduction, if found advisable, of foreign methods of mining and working metals, it became necessary to make a general tour of observation through those lands. Accordingly, on the 23d of May, we set out on our first official journey. The Government had attached to us a staff of five officers, who were at the same time assistants, escorts, and pupils. Two of these, Takeda and Oosima, were chosen as having distinguished themselves in the study and application of European science; two others, Tachi and Yuwao, were officers of the mining department of the revenue office; the fifth, Miagawa, accompanied us in the capacity of both interpreter and student. Besides these, an ometzki was sent, nominally, and I believe really, to either control or advise the officers.

With our servants we made a train of eleven horsemen as we rode through the long paved street of Hakodade.

Crossing by the sand neck to the main island, we cantered over the firm beach to Arikawa, passing through straggling hamlets of fishermen. Here oil was being made from tons of reeking herrings, and we threaded our way among a labyrinth of drying nets, and under myriads of noisy ravens and crows. These birds enjoy absolute security in all Japan.

Welcome as scavengers, they are little feared by the farmer who by a simple contrivance frightens them from the crops of his small fields. I never see a crow without being reminded of a manner of killing them I saw practiced in Corsica. Small cones of stiff paper, with pieces of meat glued in the bottom, and smeared with glue above these, are placed open-end up in holes in the field. The unsuspecting raven, plunging its beak deep into the meat, draws forth not only the morsel but the enclosing cone, glued to the feathers of its neck; thus blinded the bird rises in the air till it falls exhausted near the place where it was entrapped.

A broad crescent-shaped plain half encircles the bay of Hakodade, and rises gently from the water to the wooded hills of the interior; its green surface, covered with a heavy growth of tall, rank grasses, forms, as seen from Hakodade, a beautiful middle ground between sea and mountain.

Leaving the beach we ascended the Ari, a small river, to the village of Ono, on a broad, swampy plain, one of the few places on Yesso where agriculture is followed.

Until within a few years the island formed the domain of the Prince of Matsmai; but by an imperial decree it was subdivided among the five lords of Matsmai, Sendai, Tsungara, Nambu, and Awa, the Government retaining a considerable part for itself. It was inhabited only on the coast by fishermen; and as the proceeds of their labor were very profitable, all other pursuits seem to have been forbidden. Since the partition, the Government has turned its attention to colonization from Nipon, and to the encouragement of all the occupations necessary to develop its resources. With this end in view, it has offered many inducements to farmers and others, supplying them with land at a reasonable rate, and distributing among them horses, for which they are bound to furnish relays to officials travelling on Government business. Thus at Ono there are already several farms cultivating an inferior kind of hardy rice, and enough silk is produced to supply the raw material for a factory.

From Ono we sent back our own horses, and the next morning began our experience with the vicious brutes of the country, which, being unaccustomed to foreigners, did all they could to throw us. The Japanese horses are small and strong, but badly built, and are evidently the degenerate offspring of the Tartar stock. As they are always entire, their worst qualities are generally the most apparent. There is an improved breed on Nipon, which supplies really superior animals for the stables of the daimios and high officers. The frame of the Japanese saddle is very similar to that used by the Chinese, and, like that, is derived from the Tartars, who seem to have furnished the model for saddle-trees to all the world, if we except the English variety. After a short ride through a wooded valley we reached the lead mines of Ichin-owatari, lying at the entrance to a rocky ravine containing a wild mountain torrent.

The ore is galena, associated with zinc blende, iron pyrites and copper pyrites, the body of the veinstone being mainly magnesite, while the rocks enclosing the veins are calcareous argillites and a greenstone. In all Japanese mines the absence of pumping machinery prevents mining to any considerable depth below the level of the adit. The galleries were tolerably well timbered, though low and narrow. Owing to ignorance of the use of powder in blasting, their means of attacking the rock were—till the application of powder in mining was introduced by us—confined to the use of pointed instruments: a miner's pick with one point, a hammer, and a gad with handle, completing the outfit. The ore is roughly assorted by hand, and then passed under dry stamps.

I was not a little surprised to find, in the mountains of Japan, stamps constructed on the same principle as those of Cornwall and Germany, though far inferior in point of efficiency. They were worked by an overshot water-wheel, turning a cam shaft. The stamped ore is sifted and sent to the washing house, where it is concentrated in wooden pans, generally by women, to a very pure schlich. The furnace in which the ore is smelted is a cavity in the ground lined with a mixture of charcoal and clay, and forming a crucible, about fourteen inches broad by ten inches deep, with under-drains. In front there is an earthen shield to reflect the force of the blast, which enters through a clay nozzle from a box-bellows. The smoke and fumes of lead and sulphur pass off through a chimney.

In smelting, the crucible is filled with burning charcoal, and on this is thrown the ore to the amount of eighty pounds. When this is about half melted, twenty-five or thirty pounds of pig-iron is added in small pieces, to combine with the sulphur of the galena, and when this is partially effected the whole is stirred. After about two hours the blast is stopped, the coals are withdrawn, and water is thrown on the bath to cool the first layer of matte. This is repeated six or seven times, till the surface of the lead is free, when the metal is cast into bars, the matte being thrown away. In this operation we have the simplest form of the "precipitation" process, the Niederschlag Arbeit of the Germans.

These mines are very poor, their greatest production having been in 1860, when during a few months it averaged 600 pounds of lead daily. At the time of my visit it was about 80 pounds. As a curiosity I give below a schedule of the daily expenses at these mines:

Thirty miners, averaging 6 cents each	$1 80
Thirty coolies, at 8 cents each	2 40
Seven overseers, at 5 cents each	35
One carpenter, 8 cents	8
Twenty-six ore-dressers, averaging 3 cents each	78
Two men at the stamps, at 4 cents each	8
One smelter, 8 cents	8
Two smelter assistants, at 4 cents each	8
Two hundred pounds of charcoal, 17 cents	17
Thirty pounds of inferior pig-iron,	16
	$5 98

Rations of rice and miso, a substance used for soup, are supplied to the workmen. Low as are these wages, they are higher than in the mining districts of Nipon.

Leaving the mines, we returned to the main road and ascended the water-shed of the peninsula which divides Volcano bay from the straits of Tsungara. The top of the ridge commands a fine view, reaching on the south across the straits to the hills of Nipon, while in the north rises the volcano of Komangadake, with a beautiful lake nestling in the wood and meadow at the foot of the long slope of the cone. A vegetation almost tropical in its luxuriance, overhangs the banks of this picturesque water.

Riding a short distance beyond the lake we stopped at Skunope for the night. Here we were kept waiting one day, owing to the failure of the warden of the village next beyond, to provide horses. I must remark that this was the only instance in which we were delayed on any of our journeys in Japan from this cause, and it appears that the delinquent in this case was severely punished for the neglect. A courier always preceded us by two or three days, bearing a requisition for horses, and notifying the inns at which we were to stay, to receive no other guests. On the journey a messenger was sent out every evening to give additional notice. As this was our first official journey, the Government had ordered that we should receive the same honors in passing through towns, that are shown to the Governor on his annual trip. Thus we were met by the wardens of villages at the town limits, sometimes two or three miles distant from the houses. These men coming on foot, went down on their knees as the train approached, and then, after touching the ground with their foreheads, jumped up and led the way to the inn. Independent of the fact that a European must feel more disgusted than honored, by having a man kneel before him in the dust and mud, these men were a great nuisance, as Japanese ideas of dignity required us to follow them at a walking pace.

Japanese despotism has trained the people very thoroughly in the art of falling instantaneously on their marrow-bones. It is astonishing to see the effect of the magic word "*sh'taniro!*" "kneel" upon a dense crowd, when a person of high rank is passing; as if by enchantment every gaping, laughing, and chattering native is prostrated, and a deep silence reigns, broken only by the jingling rings on the warden's iron staff, and the solemnly-repeated warning, *sh'taniro! sh'taniro!*

In most of the villages we found small heaps of white sand scattered along the streets, which we were told was intended as an honor for us.

On the second morning our horses came, and we set out on the way to the volcano. As we were obliged to pass through the intervening forest, a party of coolies went before us with axes, to clear a route through the underbrush. For several miles we were in a dense wood in which the predominating trees were noble specimens of magnolia, beech, birch, maple, and oak, with large vines of grape, ivy, etc., twisted around their trunks and hanging from the boughs.

We came out of the forest at the beginning of the gentle foot-slope of the mountain, and found ourselves on a bed of pumice that extended from where we stood to the summit of the volcano, in the shape of a stream several hundred yards wide. Leaving the horses here we began the ascent over the surface of the pumice-stream; it was easy enough at first, but the slope soon became steeper, and we made slow progress during the last half of the ascent over the loose material. Large trunks of dead trees, some fallen and others standing, surrounded with pumice several feet above the root, showed that a growth of heavy timber once covered the sides of this mountain and was killed by an eruption.

We reached the edge of the crater at a point below the highest peak, the latter being 3,779 feet above the sea, according to the marine charts. I was told that this volcano was formerly a more perfect cone of greater height than at present, but that seven or eight years before our visit, it fell in; the occurrence was accompanied, or preceded, by a severe earthquake and an eruption of hot water and pumice, causing the loss of several lives at a distance of several miles. The ashes of this eruption were carried, by the higher air-currents, to the Kurile islands, the nearest of which is about 250 miles distant in a northeasterly direction. The crater is now several hundred feet deep, with steep walls, and entirely open toward the sea on the east side. Its bottom is formed by a broad plain elevated in the centre—a rudimentary inner cone—which extends with an unbroken slope through the opening down to the sea-shore.

This plain is traversed in all directions by great cracks, distinguishable, from the summit, by rows of steam jets issuing from between their raised red-and-yellow edges.

The view from Komangadake is grand. On our left the shore of the beautiful Volcano bay forms a long and sweeping curve, while parallel to this the mountains in the background, covered with dense forests, appear in all the shades of green, blue, and purple as they stretch away toward the distant horizon. Far away over the bay, rising as it were from the sea, are several symmetrical cones, long extinct, while nearer, though seemingly among them, rises the semi-active Oussu volcano in ruins, its sulphur-coated cliffs glistening, even at this distance, in the sunlight.

Although it was the 29th of May a few patches of snow still remained in the inner ravines of Komangadake.

Following a talus of pumice we descended into the crater and crossed the plain to a point where the largest volume of vapor was emitted. This, as we found, arose from an inner crater or pit about 600 feet in diameter, with precipitous sides exhibiting the stratification of the pumice plain. We examined next the long cracks that marked the surface of the plain like a network of gigantic mole-hills. In approaching these, the ground trembled and answered with a hollow sound to each foot-step. The crevices, often open, are in places closed over at the top by a deceitful arch of sulphur and drifted sand. Breaking through these arches we exposed gorgeous cavities lined with dense, yellow masses of sulphur crystals too delicate to bear the shock of a breath. The action of the steam, charged with sulphuretted hydrogen and sulphurous acid, has altered the pumice near the cracks to a bright-red clay, and formed efflorescences of iron-salts, and alum.

The appearances are that this mountain has been a ruined cone, which was rebuilt by an eruption of pumice, to be again broken down, and its skeleton of trachyte given over to the mighty leveling force of solfatara gases.

As we were cantering homeward through the woods, in single file, an incident occurred which might have caused the death of one of the party.

As I was riding at a brisk gallop, a short distance in advance of the others, I saw, too late to avoid it, a grape-vine hanging like a swing forty or more feet long, and its lower end just high enough from the ground to strike my stomach. To cry out a warning to those behind, and give the swing a push into the air, was the work of an instant, but it was too late; the returning vine embraced Takeda, and, as I looked back, his horse had gone from under him, while the force of the shock expended itself in causing him to make several somersaults around the loop preparatory to a tremendous flap on the ground. His swords had fallen from the scabbards, and he narrowly escaped being transfixed by one of them, which stood point up, its hilt buried in the moss.

The road from Skunope to Volcano bay led us through a dense

forest of magnificent trees, over two or three swamps which we crossed on corduroy roads, and along the banks of a small lake whose surface was covered with water-plants, and its edges hidden under drooping foliage. The last few miles of the way lay through a more scanty growth of small trees springing from a soil of less decomposed pumice. Finally we came to the shore of Volcano bay. This truly beautiful arm of the ocean received its name from the three volcanos that rise on its circumference, and the fact that as many more perfect cones of extinct volcanos are visible from its centre, renders the name appropriate. The Japanese call it Edomo bay.

Turning eastward we skirted the southern shore, and passed the base of Komangadake (called also Sawaradake), which slopes gently into the sea, deflecting the shore line in a semicircle toward the north. The northern slope of the mountain was formerly covered to near the summit with a heavy growth of timber, represented now by a forest of dead trunks extending over many thousands of acres. The trees were probably killed by a shower of hot pumice, which still covers the surface to the depth of from six to twenty-four inches. On most of the trunks the bark is intact, showing no signs of the action of a high degree of heat. Seven or eight years had passed since the destroying shower, and a fresh undergrowth was starting, among which creeping plants, apparently the first to spring into life, were already winding their spiral course around myriads of dead giants.

Sections of the soil exposed in gullies showed that this last shower was only one of a long series, some of which were on a much greater scale, and must have carried destruction over a far wider area.

At a short distance from the foot of the mountain slope we reached the hot sulphur springs of Shkabe. There are several springs rising on the beach, and in a small rivulet. They are housed over and visited by many invalids, who parboil themselves in water where the thermometer rises to 70 and 75 degrees of the centigrade scale, or 167 degrees F. No people are fonder of the use of hot springs, both for pleasure and as remedial agents, than are the Japanese, and in no country are they more abundant than in this group of volcanic islands.

Beyond Shkabe we left the semi-circular plain which surrounds the volcano, and our way now lay along the shore, the gentle surf from the sea playing around the feet of our horses, while on our right hand arose the green hills of the peninsula.

The sandy beach was in places covered with a thick layer of the black grains of magnetic iron concentrated by the surf, from the detritus of volcanic rocks, containing a small per-centage only of that mineral.

Leaving the sea-shore at the mouth of the Kakumi creek, we ascended this stream, whose clear waters, flowing over a bed of snow-white porphyry, looked like milk. A short ride brought us to the buildings of the Kakumi mines. The day of our arrival here was the festival of children. Before the dwelling of the officer in charge of the mines, a dragon and fish were flying at the top of a long pole, and the presents to the baby-son of the house were displayed in the entry; they consisted of toys in imitation of the various insignia of high military rank. Kakumi also has its warm spring.

The next day we visited the mines, neither of which were being worked. The first, a gold mine, gave little promise, even with the cheap labor of the country, and we began a long walk up the creek to the other, which had been opened on a copper vein. There was no road and rarely a path, much of our way lying in the bed of the stream or through a dense underbrush dripping with the night's rain. This vein, which had been explored by an adit, contained copper pyrites to an extent which would not justify work in a country where labor and materials are dear, but which rendered a profit possible in Yesso. Being surprised by a heavy shower on our way back, I was not a little amused at the readiness with which the Japanese improvised umbrellas by covering themselves with the immense leaves of a large plant, resembling the dock, growing to the height of nine or ten feet, with leaves several feet in diameter. On this occasion, and subsequently, I found in them an excellent substitute for both umbrella and rain-coat. The Japanese always carry rain-coats of strong oiled paper or silk, which are light and tolerably durable as well as cheap, qualities which are also combined in their paper umbrellas.

From Kakumi we returned to the bay, and riding eastward to Wosatsube, embarked in a boat, the precipitous character of the shore rendering it impossible to continue by land, even on foot.

Here a low point of fantastically curved beds of hornstone breaks the surf. Our boat was worked by sixteen oars and sculls, and the strong arms of the boatmen made it fly over the water, keeping time in its vibrations to the swaying and the song of the naked sailors.

Added to the charm of novelty, this water journey had that of the wildly picturesque coast scenery. The boat kept as close as possible to the shore, in its shade indeed. Far down in the clear waters we could see great rocks surrounded by darkness, and covered with sea-weed in leaves fifty feet long, almost motionless in the deep. Every now and then a trough of the rolling swell would lay bare, in the whirling waters, some rock taller than the rest, carpeted with a dense mass of sea-moss, shells, and sea-anemones, brilliant with splendid colors, which show their beauty for a minute to the daylight, to be reburied in a whirlpool of returning waves. Cliffs hundreds of feet high, of brown, columnar lava, rise from the deep, caverns resound the thunder of the waves, while great stains of red and black are half hidden by the green masses of moss, vines, and flowers that find root-hold even on the face of the precipice. Add to these the many waterfalls leaping from the woods above to the sea below, a clear blue sky and the graceful column of vapor rising from the distant volcano, and you have a faint outline of the scenes though which our wild and naked sailors made us skim over the waves.

The rocks forming the shore cliffs are volcanic tufa conglomerate deposited under the sea, and containing lava-streams all of trachytic origin. The skeleton of the peninsula, however, is made up of very old clay slates and sandstone, with massive bodies of greenstone.

We landed in a little bight at the fishing hamlet of Totohoke, and the next morning began, on horseback, the ascent of the volcano of Esan, a very active solfatara lying at the eastern point of the peninsula. As the mountain is barely 2,000 feet high, and the entrance to the crater much lower, we soon reached the Government sulphur-works.

Although Esan must once have been a volcano of large size, and the source of the great deposits which form the sea-margin for several miles, I saw in its crater and walls no pumice and no rocks readily recognizable as products of recent eruptions. On the contrary, it is a volcano in ruins, and in which the destructive agencies are still working on a grand scale. The large crater is divided by a high ridge of detritus, and in both the compartments thus formed, countless jets and columns of steam and gases issue from the wall, from the detritus, and from the vaulted mud-vents. The air is loaded with sulphurous acid, and a small stream of limpid water, which issues from the crater, is strongly impregnated with the same acid and with astringent salts.

The walls of the crater are rapidly disintegrating and falling, to be converted into clay, impregnated with sulphur, alum, and other salts, products of the action of acid and steam on each other and on the rocks they are decomposing. Everywhere the scene is one of ruin. Here is visible on a grand scale the decomposing action of sulphurous acid and steam, the effects of which are seen in the altered trachytic rocks of Hungary, and still progressing on a smaller scale in the Neapolitan solfatara. Nowhere have I seen so well exhibited the levelling power of nature when she brings into steady action her more active agents. Steam surrounded us on all sides, issuing in jets from the sides of the crater and rising slowly out of the taluses of debris, as the smoke rises slowly and silently from the ruins of a mighty conflagration.

The main vents are small mud-craters or geysers in the centre of one of the compartments of the great crater. They are springs or pits, each covered by a great vault of hardened mud, like an immense bubble or inverted bowl, from ten to twenty-five feet high, the sides and roof from six inches to two feet thick. They quake with the constant reverberation of the struggling gases and mud, the last rising to near the surface, and sometimes bursting out in a shower of thick drops. Through the small openings in these vaults issue volumes of steam, highly charged with sulphuretted hydrogen, and at intervals glimpses of the interior exhibit the surface lined with sulphur in massive layers, splendid with crystals or drooping with long stalactites of the yellow mineral.

From one of these vaults I traced a mud stream, evidently the last feeble attempt at an eruption, and the date of this was not known to the sulphur-diggers. Whenever new vents are formed, mud and large masses of rock are ejected with much violence.

The sulphur works are supplied from the talus formed by the

ever-falling walls of the crater, and this material contains from twenty-five to sixty per cent. of sulphur in layers and impregnations. Without further preparation than being broken into pieces, it is melted in iron pots, where the impurities sink to the bottom, and the top is ladled out into shallow depressions in the ground and left to cool. As this product is still impure, it is re-melted in similar pots and then strained through sacks into tubs, where it cools. The blocks thus obtained are broken, and the centre, which is yellow and highly crystaline, goes to market; while the surface, to the depth of one or two inches, being dark and perhaps less pure, is re-melted. The production amounted at the time of my visit to about 5,600 pounds daily. According to the books at the works, the cost of production amounted to about $6,43 per ton of 2,000 lbs., the same quantity selling for $24 in the Hakodade market.

Leaving this scene of destruction, we descended to Nietanai, on the shore of the straits of Tsungara. The next morning, riding along the sea-shore, between Nietanai and Kobi, I discovered in the bluff a deposit of white infusorial earth, specimens of which I submitted to Mr. Arthur M. Edwards. The results of that gentleman's investigation * are exceedingly interesting, bringing to light a close resemblance between the organisms contained in this deposit and those in the stratum under Richmond, Va., and a still greater similarity, extending to identity of species with those of the extensive deposit in California.

At Kobi, as at many points on the coast, large quantities of magnetic-iron sand are concentrated on the beach by the surf, and a bed of the same material, much oxidized, crops out in the bluff deposits, which are themselves raised beaches. The Imperial Government, wishing to manufacture cannon for the defence of Yesso against the Russians, commanded Takeda, an officer afterward attached to us, and one who had done much to advance in his country the knowledge of military engineering and navigation, to build a furnace on the foreign plan, for the purpose of smelting this ore. Such a thing had never been seen by a Japanese, but without further plans or specifications than were given in a Dutch work on chemistry, Takeda built a fur-

* See Mr. Edwards' letter, in appendix No. 3 to "Geological Researches in China, Mongolia, and Japan," by the author. Smithsonian Institution, 1866.

nace about thirty feet high, after a really fine model, with a cylinder blast, moved by an excellent water-wheel. Unfortunately, owing to the absence of all details on the subject in the only book he had, the blast was far too weak, and the bricks not sufficiently refractory. The furnace thus proved a failure, after smelting a few hundred-weight of iron. The incident, however, will serve as an illustration of Japanese enterprise. Another of our officers, Oosima, by dint of repeated experiments, carried a similar undertaking to a more successful issue in the province of Nambu.

The southern side of the peninsula is entirely different from the northern. Facing Volcano bay the rocks are volcanic, overhanging the coast in high cliffs, which form the abrupt termination of a densely-wooded table-land or terrace. On the southern side the grassy pyramidal or rounded hills of the older metamorphic rocks slope off to the straits in the eastern half, while as they trend westward they are separated from the sea by a low and gently-sloping terrace of recent clay deposits. Both the terrace plain and the southern exposure of the hills are barren of trees.

Along the shore of the straits we discovered several promising veins of copper pyrites in the clay slates already mentioned, and in the further exploration of which we subsequently made the first application of powder to blasting in Japan. Returning to Hakodade we completed the circuit of the peninsula and our first excursion.

We were now detained more than two months at Hakodade by the prevalence of measles over all the island, and in the families of the officers attached to us. During this time we gave regular instruction to our assistants in the branches bearing on mining and metallurgy, an occupation which, at the same time, gave me some insight into the intellectual capacity of the class represented by these men. The difficulties to be overcome were very great, as we were teaching subjects of which but few of the technical terms have Japanese equivalents, to students who were ignorant of the elementary branches, which necessarily precede the study of applied sciences. But they showed generally anxiety to learn, as well as rapid comprehension of what was taught. Takeda had studied mathematics in Bowditch's "Navigator," using an English-Dutch and a Dutch-Japanese dictionary, and had mastered that book so thoroughly that it was literally indexed in his mind, and he was able to calculate longitude from an eclipse or an occultation as easily as from an altitude or lunar distances; but this knowledge was purely mechanical, and mathematics from a philosophical point of view was a new field to him, though when he took them up in this spirit he exhibited for the study a mental power which I almost envied him.

Our interviews with the Governor and his council took place alternately at his palace and in our own quarters. At the palace they were always accompanied with tea and refreshments, and often with a Japanese dinner, while the short pipe of the country was in constant use. This is quite an important weapon in diplomacy, and a Japanese minister or governor never fails when pressed with a question, to gain time for reflection in filling and lighting a pipe of their fragrant tobacco. As official interviews occur very frequently between the authorities and foreign representatives, the former have gradually formed a strong liking for European cooking, and in order not to appear ill at ease in the use of western table-furniture, the Governor and his council had, at times, dinners prepared in European style to practice the use of knives, forks, spoons, and glasses, and in giving toasts. They are very fond of champagne.

The Governor and all the high officers about him were gentlemen whose dignified bearing and refinement and suavity of manner would grace any western society. And I remarked that, as a rule, they showed consideration toward inferiors and servants, never exhibiting the passionate outbursts so common among Chinese officials, a difference, perhaps, partially arising from the consciousness of power with the Japanese. The governors never lose self-possession in presence of the sometimes excited and rude language of some western representatives. On one occasion, in answer to my question whether this self-possession were inborn or the result of education, the Governor replied that it is made one of the most important features of training, from the earliest childhood through life. Indeed, so delicate is the sense of personal honor in the official class, that the wounded feelings of an equal may easily cause him to retaliate by *hara-kiru*, thereby forcing the offender to perform the same operation. The necessity for self-control thus rests on a basis not less strong than the love of life.

Formerly, in committing *hara-kiru*, the suicide actually ripped open his bowels; at present, he simply scratches the abdomen, drawing blood, while an attendant, dressed in white, gives the death-blow with a sword

CHAPTER XI.

RELIGIONS OF JAPAN.

Of the Japanese religions, very little is known by Europeans. At present, besides many sects of Buddists, we find Sintuism and Confucianism. Toleration has always marked the relations between the Government and the followers of different faiths. Christianity was, indeed, rooted out, but its priests could blame only their own abuse of the encouragement they long received.

Whatever may have been the earliest religion of the Japanese, Sintuism, (Shintau,* Chinese; kaminomitchi, Jap., way of the kami, gods or spirits,) was that which formed the basis of the spiritual-political government founded by Jinmutenno, in the seventh century B.C.

From the vague knowledge we have of their cosmogony, it should appear that out of nothing there arose a self-created supreme god. But this deity, like Brahma in the Indian trinity, withdrew, leaving two other gods to accomplish the material creation. The universe was then ruled during myriads of years by seven cosmical gods in succession—Ten-sin-szchi-dai. The last of these, having a wife, became the progenitor of the human race. To create a habitable earth, he plunged his spear into the waters, and from the drops which fell congealed from it was formed Japan. The government of the world now passed into the hands of five successive gods, Dai-sin-go-dai, who during more than two million years ruled the earth, and to the last of whom in union with a mortal, was born Jinmutenno, the first of the Mikados. The first of these five rulers was Tensio-dai-jin, the goddess of the sun, daughter of the last of the preceding seven.

It is quite possible that this cosmogony is a foreign element, devised as a foundation for the heavenly claims of the Mikados; and, as it has been supposed that Jin mu was a foreigner, it is not impossible that under the early emperors a mixture of imported

* According to Siebold.

and native beliefs may have taken place to found Sintuism, the state religion.

The earliest expression of the religious idea in Japan was, probably, a worship of spirits and animals, a mixture of Shamanism and Fetichism.

It is not clear what position the primeval gods hold in the Sintu worship; but the Mikado is superior to most, if not all, since the gods are all obliged to attend him every year in the tenth month, which, for this reason, is called kamimatsuki godless. During this month there are no festivals, as the gods are supposed to be absent from their temples. The Ten-sin-szchi-dai and Dai-sin-go-dai are excepted in this service.

The sun goddess is the great divinity who, it seems, may be worshipped only through the mediation of her lineal descendants, or of the kami, born gods or canonized. All these kami have temples dedicated to them, generally small shrines closed with grating and containing a mirror and tassels of white paper, as emblems of purity. At Isye is the principal temple of the sun goddess, surrounded by a great number of smaller ones. Every village appears to possess a shrine, and one is often found within the precincts of Buddist temples. No images are set up for worship. The whole cultus is obscure; the functions of the priests, who bear the titles "god keepers" and "messengers of the gods," are not known to foreigners. The sun goddess is the highest; and as she may be worshipped only through the mediation of the Mikado, or of the kami, consisting of 492 born gods and some thousands of deified mortals, there is no need of an interceding priesthood or of images.

At a small village on Yesso I happened to see something of a Sintu festival. A vista of temple gate-ways leading to a small shrine was lined with box lanterns eight or ten feet high, supporting similar horizontal ones overhead. Among the countless decorations painted on these paper transparencies, were many representations of the phallus. During the afternoon a procession left the temple bearing the inner shrine. A staff-bearer preceded, followed by a man carrying a stand to receive gifts. Next came two men with sticks, from which hung ornaments of white paper, and after these a drummer, fifer, and cymbal-bearer. Behind these strutted the "god keeper," fantastically masked with flowing white locks, and a nose six or eight inches long projecting from under a helmet. He wore high stilt-shoes, and bore a large spear in the right hand. Following the god-keeper came a number of retainers leading a caparisoned horse, and bearing spears, bows, and guns, the insignia probably of the priest's office. Strangely enough, the man who represented the god-keeper was merely a cooly, hired as a substitute; the true priest, if such he may be called, walked behind the procession in civilian's dress.

During the day and evening, worshippers, dressed in their best clothes, approached the shrine after washing their hands at a small tank. Throwing a few coins into the gift-box, they prostrated themselves, uttered a short prayer, rang the shrine bell three times and withdrew. The approach to the temple must be made with a pleasant face, and indeed there seems to be an entire absence of asceticism in the Sintu cultus. Offerings of rice, wine, etc., are brought; but if the custom of offering sacrifices was ever developed to a further extent, it has been modified by Buddism.

The duties enjoined by this religion are said to be: "1. Preservation of pure fire, as the emblem of purity and means of purification. 2. Purity of soul, heart, and body. The purity of the soul is to be preserved by a strict obedience to reason and the law; the purity of the body, by abstaining from everything that defiles. 3. Exact observance of festival days. 4. Pilgrimage. 5. The worship of the kami, both in the temples and at home." "Impurity is contracted by associating with the impure, listening to impure language, by eating certain meats, by coming in contact with death or with blood. Whoever is stained with his own or another's blood is impure for seven days, *i. e.*, unfit to approach holy places. Whoever eats the flesh of any four-footed beast, deer only excepted, is impure for thirty days. On the contrary, whoever eats a fowl, wild or tame, (water fowls, pheasants, and cranes excepted), is impure for only one Japanese hour." * Attending a dying person, killing a beast, or approaching a corpse, renders impure for one day. The nearer the relationship to the dead person the greater the impurity.

The worship of ancestral spirits is general among the Japanese, and is apparently identical with the Chinese custom, but in what relation it originally stood to Sintuism is unknown to us. It

* "Japan." Charles MacFarlane.

forms there, as in China, the household worship. A festival of this cultus, the feast of the dead, reminding one of All Saints' Day, occurs yearly. During three days the departed spirits return to their former homes, and on the last night every house sets afloat on the waters a little boat containing rice, wine, etc., for the departing spirit, while lanterns on every tombstone illuminate the cemeteries.

Side by side with these ancient forms exist remnants of Fetichism, perhaps as traditions of the earliest belief of the people. Certain animals are kami, and even stones may be chosen as such. No Japanese will kill a water-snake, at least those living in and near warm springs, of which they are looked upon as the gods. Whenever we caused excavations to be made for mining purposes, the common miners chose from the rubble the most water-worn rock and set it up as the kami or rather fetich of the place.

Besides these, there are the remains of an extensive system of demon-worship, also of great antiquity, in which good and evil spirits play an important part, and which seems, in connection with the worship of ancestors, to be of the same origin with the Shamanism of the Mongolian family. These demons, represented under conventional forms, occupy an important place in Japanese art.

Even in the little we know of these ancient forms of religion, it is impossible not to see in them an incongruous mixture. While the greater part of them probably belong to Mongolian Shamanism, we are reminded of the Arians in the cosmogony, in the worship of the sun, and in the veneration of the phallic symbol, as well as in the order of nuns,* the proceeds of whose mode of life go in part to the temple of the sun. It should appear that the religion of the Mikados is an offshoot of the early worship of sun and light, which in antiquity was practiced in central Asia, and which, at different times, seems to have been common to all the agricultural tribes from the Nile to Peru. Unlike the course of development among other peoples, it does not seem to have grown into a dualistic belief; the sun goddess is worshipped as the mother of the human race, as the positive deity, without the awful rites of Siva and Kali. It is probable that there was no distinct idea of a hell until this was introduced by Buddism.

That a future life was believed in, is shown by the ancient cus-

* See page 111.

tom which required the wives, concubines, and attendants of the Mikados to commit suicide at his death, a fact that reminds us of the similar custom among the Incas of Peru, and the burning of widows in India and among the Phenicians.

A careful study of the early religion of Japan cannot fail to produce most interesting results to the ethnologist.

In the year A.D. 285 the works of Confucius were introduced by the philosopher Wani. While the philosophy of Confucius has done much toward moulding the ethics of Japan, its skeptical tendency has been confined to the higher classes, among which it has come to number a large sect of atheists.

But the religion of the Japanese people is Buddism, derived through Corea from China, and subsequently developed by priests who travelled to its source in India. The early missionaries of this faith, disregarding hardships and dangers, penetrated, as zealous apostles, through all eastern Asia, spreading their doctrines broadcast over fields in which they took root the more readily that the teachers were ever ready to engraft on them the pre-existing superstitions. As Buddism, in its different forms, has had an important effect on all the people of eastern Asia, it may not be amiss to give here a brief outline of it.

At the time of the birth of Budda, in the sixth century B.C., Brahminism, developed out of the sun and light worship of the Arians, was flourishing in all India, and supported like an arch of adamant the oppressive system of castes—a system which, based probably on the original relations between the conquering Arians and the subjugated aboriginal tribes, has been the bane of India, from the time of that conquest to the present day. Brahminism taught that Brahma, the one supreme deity, feeling a desire to create, developed into a god-head of three persons—Brahma, creator; Vishnu, preserver; and Siva, destroyer—and that the whole world was created not only by this deity, but out of him, and is, in fact, part of his essence. According to the Brahminical view, all creation was the result of a sinful desire on the part of Brahma to produce; and existence is an evil which ought not to be; indeed, their abstract philosophy teaches that it is a dream. But, creation being effected, or at least seeming to be, the whole course of existence, material and immaterial, is a preparation for the remedying of this evil by the final re-absorption of all things into the divine essence; and this could be effected only by transmigration—by a long-continued purification through birth and regeneration of each individual soul in the various forms of life in plants, animals, and men. Out of the demand of the popular mind for a more explicit system of punishments and rewards, arose a belief in a heaven for the righteous, and a graduated hell for the wicked. But these were not eternal conditions—heaven, earth, and hell were finally to be re-absorbed into Brahma, and all individual existence to be lost in the original essence from which it sprang. A leading doctrine of this religion is the salvation of man—that is, his final absorption into the divine essence, through his own exertions, and from this doctrine grew the asceticism, which, developing to its highest degree in self-sacrifice, has long formed the second destructive worm at the root of Indian civilization.

Budda undertook the reformation of the world, the abolition of caste, and of the shedding of blood in sacrifices. His name was Sakyamuni. He was born a prince,* and is said to have been prompted to meditation by meeting in one walk an old man, a sick man, a corpse, and a priest. Determined to find by meditation the cause of the four great evils—birth, sickness, old age, and death—he secretly left his family and possessions to study among the Brahmins. After six years of deep thought, aided by fasting and mortification, he found that Brahminism offered no solution of the problem. Finally, after throwing off the shackles of the Brahminical philosophy, he attained the essence of knowledge and became Budda, sage.

The original dogmatics of Budda and his disciples, the result of this long meditation, is substantially this: † there is no existence, no substance, no world; consequently all that existence pre-supposes is wanting: there is no first cause, no deity. All was nothing, is nothing, will be nothing; all things are unreal, and non-existence is the only reality. The presence of the ever-changing world is only a conceit, a result of the belief in its reality. ‡ All that exists, *i. e.*, seems to exist, is subject to the four great evils: birth, sickness, old age, death, and to the pains arising

* The earliest Buddist writings speak of him only as a man; but the mythology with which the religion was early corrupted, represents him as an incarnation of Vishnu, who entered his mother's womb in the form of a five-colored ray of light.

† "Scherr Gesch. der Religion," I. 229.

‡ Lassen after Hodgson. Ind. Alterthumskunde, II. 461.

from these. The world and life are only a sorrow. To relieve this sorrow, man feels a longing, which gives birth to pleasure and passions. In the complete destruction of this longing consists the redemption from sorrows, which are ever being born anew. This destruction and redemption is approachable only through the six perfections: wisdom, virtue, activity, charity, patience, and brotherly love.* Salvation results from the union of the highest wisdom with the most virtuous action. But salvation is nothing else but nirvana, *i. e.*, the entire extinction of man—the return of the individual nothing into the primeval state of non-existence.

During nineteen years Budda travelled through India, followed by disciples, preaching his doctrines, recognizing no caste, teaching human equality, virtue, and brotherly love, and planting the seeds of a religion which was destined to number hundreds of millions of followers. He died in his eightieth year, after having won many disciples among all classes. Budda left no writings; but, as in the early Christian church, his doctrines were written by his immediate followers, and in three great ecclesiastical conferences, the last B.C. 146, the dogmas, discipline, and course of missionary labor were established. †

In its original form, Buddism taught that existence was an evil, the world a vale of sorrow, and the release from this evil was attainable only in the nirvana, *i. e.*, the condition of extinction of the soul, or of its consciousness. This blessedness was open to those who became Buddas by observing the ten commandments, viz: 1, thou shalt not kill; 2, thou shalt not steal; 3, thou shalt not be unchaste; 4, thou shalt not lie; 5, thou shalt not bear false witness; 6, thou shalt not swear; 7, thou shalt not speak evil; 8, thou shalt not covet; 9, thou shalt not take vengeance; 10, thou shalt not be superstitious, *i. e.*, believing in gods.

But this was too unsatisfactory; and to satisfy the moral necessity in the Indian mind for a belief in future punishments and rewards, the doctrine of the transmigration of the soul, and ultimately of a paradise and hell, were taken from Brahminism, with many other corruptions; and as the new faith spread beyond the confines of India, a whole hierarchy of saints, with a queen of

---

* Burnouf. "Introduction a l'Histoire de Buddism," I. 153.
† "Scherr. Gesch. der Religion;" a work I have used freely in this sketch of Buddism.

heaven at their head as in Catholicism, was built upon the spirit-worship of the converted peoples. And it was to this plasticity that the religion owed the facility with which it spread over eastern Asia.

Thus Buddism modified its absolute negation of immortality to the extent of lengthening out existence by means of transmigration as a purifying process, preparatory to extinction in the blessed nirvana. The soul wanders through six classes of animated beings, viz: genii, demons, men, quadrupeds, birds, and creeping animals, ascending or descending, according to merit or demerit. It is open to all to become Buddas, through their own exertions after wisdom and virtue, aided by the purification of transmigration. But there are several degrees among the Buddas to be gone through before entering the nirvana. At present Sakyamuni is the highest, and under him are three bodhisvatta, *i. e.*, possessors of the essence of wisdom. They have reached the entrance to the nirvana, but are not yet freed, being obliged to be born again and again on earth to advance the work of salvation. On this basis, especially, rests the whole organization of Lamaism in Thibet and Mongolia, where these Buddas re-appear in the persons of the Grand Lamas.

Strictly, all Buddists should be beggars, celibates, and ascetics. Practically, these conditions are followed only by the priests and a large number of hermits.

At an early date, probably in the conferences already mentioned, the organization of the Buddist church and its discipline received the main features which have lasted to this day. The divisions into active clergy and monks, all celibates as well as nuns, the ranks of the clergy, the ritual, veneration of relics, intercession through saints, confession though not auricular, organization of monastic and conventual life, use of the rosary in prayer, shaving the heads of clergy and nuns, the synods and church councils, the clerical costumes especially in Thibet, the sermons in Japan, ringing of bells for matins and vespers—all bear the strongest analogies to their counterparts in Catholicism. The temple service, with sprinkling of holy water, burning of incense in censers, and with chants, resembles high mass.

The resemblance is so strong indeed that Abbé Huc, a zealous and learned Catholic missionary in Thibet, was forced to admit a community of origin, though while in one part of his narrative he supposes that a Nestorian missionary introduced the Catholic ritual into Thibet, in another place he attributes it to the agency of Satan. But so many of the features in which Buddism resembles Catholicism are common to all the branches of the former, branches which diverged even in the middle of the first century, that one is forced to the conclusion that western ritualism and much of the superstition on which it is based is of Pagan birth.

Buddism, as we have seen, entered China in the middle of the first century, and thence, through Corea, it reached Japan in the sixth century. In these countries it has retained more nearly its external Indian form. It entered Thibet also at an early date; but obtaining there control of the state, the doctrine of transmigration was carried to a logical consequence in the incarnation of the bodhisvatta in the ruler under the title of Dalai Lama. It is in Thibet that the strongest analogy obtains between the Catholic and Buddist hierarchies, culminating at H'lassa, as at Rome, in a temporal and spiritual sovereign. In the fourteenth century Thibetan Buddism was much purified of its corruptions by Tsongkaba,* a reformation which extended only through Thibet and Mongolia.

In its earliest form a rigid, comfortless Atheism, with the mildest and most humane of moral codes, it has everywhere engrafted upon its stock foreign superstitions until its temples are pantheons. Still, as in most religions, the unalloyed doctrines of the founder are studied as a mysticism by a few of the more learned in the priesthood. In every country where it has found foothold it has left more or less of its impress on the people. In Thibet, where one-third of the population are said to be in the clerical ranks, the effect of the reformation is still visible in thousands of ascetics seeking salvation through hermit life and severe mortification of the flesh, and in the law requiring women to render themselves hideous when out of their homes. In Mongolia the humane doctrines of Budda have made a peaceful, hospitable, and kind-hearted race out of the descendants of those hordes which during the middle ages were the scourge of the eastern world, from the Pacific to the Atlantic, from the Arctic to the Indian ocean.

In China it has had less effect on the people. The Chinese

* "Huc's Travels in Thibet, China, and Tartary."

mind, the exact reverse of the Indian, had early formed for itself the moral code of which Confucius was the exponent; while Tauism, with its mixture of early native and Brahminical superstitions, supplied as much of the supernatural as an utilitarian people could require; but among the teeming population there were certain fields open for it, and to these it adapted itself. Even in China enough are found to fill its monasteries, and the priests of the countless temples are supported by the sale of charms, by giving theatrical representations, performing funeral services, and feeding the spirits of the dead on All Saints' Day.

It is said that the early Buddist missionaries in Japan obtained the imperial favor by announcing that the Mikado was an incarnate Budda, thus making him the head of their church as in Thibet. But, though not disturbed by Government, it suffered a long persecution from the people. Its usual elasticity causing it to adapt itself gradually to the popular mind, and the fact that it offered more distinct promises of a future condition, enabled it ultimately to overgrow Sintuism, and to spread wider and deeper than the utilitarianism of Confucius. Buddism may now be said to be the religion of Japan, though it must be used as a generic title, numerous sects having sprung up under the lax supervision of its nominal head.

In Japan, Buddism has not merely taken into its hands the performance of the native ritual—it has spread widely its influence, especially as a means of moral instruction in families. Its temples are crowded not only on festival days, but regular and frequent sermons by day and in the evening are attended by attentive congregations, chiefly of women with their children; and in this way religious instruction, which, though Pagan, inculcates many of the moral truths that form the basis of Christianity, is extended to the family circle. Religious training, left to the mother and the temple sermon, begins when the former carries her baby to the temple, thirty days after birth, to make its first offering of a few coins. Alcock has described the funeral of a Japanese interpreter of the British legation, in which he dwells upon the points of resemblance it bore to a Catholic ceremony.

It is said that in Japan, Buddism has developed a more defined idea of heaven and hell than elsewhere; certainly the illustrations of hell-torment in Buddist books might have served as models for Dante, so much do they resemble the monkish fancies of mediæval Europe. But for the same reason that Buddist asceticism, which flourishes in Thibet, found a slight foothold in Japan among the pleasure-loving Japanese, this dualistic conception has never produced the gloom which with different degrees of darkness has accompanied a similar conception in the west, from ancient Egypt to modern Scotland; much less has it developed the fearful rites of Moloch and Astarte, of Siva and Kali; indeed, the Japanese mind was wanting in the qualities necessary to originate or grasp a distant personification of the evil principle.

The fact that Sintuism forbade the use of meat as food, rendered it the more easy for the Buddist religion to inculcate its doctrines against taking life. Certainly the gentle doctrines of Budda must have done much toward making of the Japanese, outside of the soldier class, the quiet and kindly people they are.

The strong resemblance between Japanese Buddism and Catholicism, existing in the idea of a supreme God and the miraculous incarnation and birth of a Saviour, in the doctrine of future rewards and punishments, in the ritual and church organization, in the worship of saints and a queen of heaven—all these may be the ingredients of a soil in which Christianity would flourish.

We have seen how successful were the efforts of the followers of Xavier; could they have copied the example of their Buddist predecessors by proclaiming the Mikado as Vicar of Christ, and have renounced all political designs against the independence of Japan, Miako might to-day be a rival of Rome, the centre of an eastern church, and the Mikado the head of a powerful hierarchy.

CHAPTER XII.

SECOND JOURNEY IN YESSO—THE WEST COAST.

TOWARD the end of July the measles were so far on the decline throughout the island that we prepared a more extended journey of reconnoissance. On the fifth of August we left Hakodade for the west coast.

Our first day's ride was over a part of the road followed on the previous occasion, and brought us to our first resting-point for the night, Washinoki, on Volcano bay. Leaving this point the next morning, we struck off to the northward, over the beautiful beach which skirts the western shore of this water. The

KOMANGADAKE FROM WASHINOKI.

scenery surrounding this inland sea is beautiful even for the Japanese coast. Jutting far inland from the Pacific ocean, its southern shore from Cape Esan is formed by lofty cliffs, crowned with dense forests as far as the volcano of Komangadake. Thence the coast-line sweeps in a circle of some forty miles in diameter to Cape Edomo on the north. Terraces, covered here with grass and there with forests of deciduous trees, separate the bay from the rugged range of mountains which divides the waters of the Pacific from those of the Japan sea. The northern horizon is broken by several lofty and symmetrical volcanic cones, while on both shores curling columns of vapor rise with ever-varying shapes from yellow sulphur-coated piles of rock, the only remnants of once active volcanos.

A brisk trot soon brought us to Otoshibetz. Beyond this place the beach is overhung by a terrace bluff, from sixty to eighty feet high, exposing strata of sandy clay abounding in recent marine shells. A large part of these still contained much of their organic matter, and in several instances I found the dorsal ligament of bivalves still elastic when wet.

A further ride of a few miles brought us to the large fishing village of Yamukshinai. Near this place, between the shore and the cliff, there is a marsh several acres in extent, in which numerous tepid springs bring to the surface a mineral oil of the consistency of tar. Here we found several priests, who not only used this product for light, but also in the manufacture of India ink. These old men received us hospitably, and listened with incredulous wonder to our stories of artesian borings, and flowing wells of petroleum.

Before reaching Yurup we passed through a settlement of Ainos, a remarkable race, which is shrinking steadily in numbers before the superior civilization of their rulers. Those of this people whom we saw had been long in close contact with the Japanese, but we were told that they did not differ much from those in the interior. They are of medium stature, and tolerably strong and compact build. The face is broad, the forehead rather low, the nose short, and oftener slightly concave, in profile, than straight. Their eyes differ decidedly from the Mongolian type in shape, and are black. Their color is perhaps a little darker than that of the Japanese; the smallest children are white.

But the most remarkable characteristic of this people, in which they differ from all other races of eastern Asia, is the luxuriant growth of their hair, which is straight, long, and glossy. The men have heavy beards of great length, and moustaches of such dimensions that they form a curtain which has to be raised to gain access to the mouth in eating. The whole body is more hairy than in other races.

The women are short, tattoo their chins, and wear large ear-rings. The Japanese look upon the Ainos with contempt, and give to them a curious origin. According to a traditional myth, the wife of a pre-historic Mikado was banished from Nipon for infidelity. After a long wandering, she found herself alone on the island of Yesso. Here there appeared to her a dog, which became her sole companion, and from the union of this pair there sprang the Aino race. But notwithstanding the degraded position which they are now able to assign to this people, the Ainos were able during more than a thousand years to maintain a vigorous defensive warfare. It is probable that they were the aborigines of the empire: indeed as late as the seventh century they occupied a considerable portion of Nipon. And it was not until about the twelfth century that they were brought into complete subjection by the arms of Yoshitzunè. Their spirit was then broken, and they were practically enslaved by the Japanese. For the last two hundred years at least they have been the serfs of the Prince of Matzumai, who by allowing them no other source of subsistence than that of fishing, has made their labor the main source of his revenue. At present they are a mild, good-natured race, and the early European navigators in the Pacific found no terms too strong in praising the simple habits and virtues of this people.

As we passed through the village we met several men who saluted us in the Aino manner, by stroking their long beards and lowering their hands gracefully from their mouths. The houses or huts are built of poles, covered with brush or rushes; they are rectangular on the ground, and curve at the sides and ends upward to the ridge-pole; each hut is fenced about with reeds. Near each of them is a small building, raised about eight feet from the ground on posts, and serving as a store-house for fish, sea-weed, and so forth. Before many of the dwellings I observed the skulls of bears raised on long poles. This custom is connected with their superstitions, and reminded me of a similar practice described somewhere as occurring among a tribe of Indians in British America. Reverence for this animal has not prevented the Ainos from becoming very skilful in the art of killing them by the use of spring bows, and other means. Sticks cut so that long tassels of shavings hang from the sides, are also connected in some way with their superstitions. They are called *inas*, and are found raised on poles alongside of the skulls of bears, and stuck into the earth near graves.

The characteristics of this people are so little known that it is more difficult to determine their position among the races of man than that of almost any other. It is not improbable that they represent a portion of the ante-Mongolian population of eastern continental Asia, of whom the easternmost islands have become the last foothold, just as the inaccessible portions of the Indian archipelago, the mountains of China and Thibet, and the frozen regions of the northeast, contain the varied remnants of peoples who have no longer place in either history or tradition.

Leaving Yurup in the morning we continued our journey along the beach to Kunnui on the sea. Here leaving the shore we ascended the valley of Kunnui creek. The day was extremely warm, and both horse and rider were tormented beyond endurance by swarms of many kinds of insects. There were large brown flies, nearly an inch long, which inflicted pain, and drew blood through a single thickness of woollen clothing; there were yellow flies barred with black, which buried themselves in swarms in the shaggy hair of our horses, driving the poor animals almost to distraction; there were the common horse-fly, the deer-fly, and clouds of mosquitoes.

Our bridle-path lay for several miles through a swamp, covered with a dense growth of weeds, eight or ten feet high. Among these there is the plant I have already mentioned, with a strong leaf, often nearly four feet in diameter, which frequently serves the Japanese as umbrella or parasol. At length we crossed into the valley of the Toshibetz, and descending by a most villainous road, where the horses floundered in mud to the saddle-girths, we reached the dwelling of the officer who had charge of the gold mines of Kunnui. The hospitality of this gentleman was very acceptably shown in the form of a salmon over two feet long, which had just been speared in the Toshibetz. The next day we started for the gold washings, in a log canoe, with sides of neatly-fitted boards. Two Ainos, a man and a bright-eyed boy, pulled us skilfully and rapidly against the strong current of the mountain torrent. This region is clothed with a forest of maple, beach, birch, oak, magnolia, elms, and wild mulberry trees of large size and thrifty growth. But these beautiful woods are rendered almost impenetrable by the dense growth of a kind of bamboo, which grows from eight to twelve feet high, and so compactly that it is impossible to see more than two or three feet into it. The gold is found in a deposit of sand and gravel, which at one time has formed a broad plain occupying the whole valley of the Toshibetz, but in which the river and its tributary creeks have cut their channels to the underlying rock. Geologically the deposit is very recent, overlying in places beds of sandy clay, which are the equivalents of the terrace deposit near Otoshibetz. and like this latter abound in shells of living species in which the organic matter and ligaments are also still preserved. The auriferous gravel contains varieties of granite in chloritic and micaceous slates, quartzite and amygdaloid with geodes of chalcedony, and rolled fragments of binoxide of manganese. The concentrated sand of the washing is chiefly magnetic iron and zircon. The manner of working is ingenious, and will be understood by referring to the annexed diagram. The bed of a rivulet is chosen for the work. A reservoir (*a*) is dug and dammed, and the bed of the stream (*b*) cleaned out and made regular. This done, the auriferous banks (*d*) are broken down into the stream, where the force of the current concentrates the gravel, carrying off the sand and clay. The workmen then place themselves in pairs (*g*) up and down the stream, near and below the broken-down bank. Each man is provided with a coarse mat, about two feet long by one broad, which he places lengthwise in the stream, keeping it down with one foot, at the same time partially stemming the current. He then hoes the gravel on to the mat, much of the old gravel going off below as fresh material arrives from up stream. At intervals the mat is carefully removed and washed out into a very shallow tray on *batea*, made from a board about eighteen inches long, and one foot wide, hollowed out, and having a circular depression near one end in which the workman concentrates the gold. In this manner the gravel is pretty well exhausted of its gold, very little being caught upon the lower mats. The working progresses sideways into the deposit and up stream, and the current is kept near the banks, as these recede from the centre of the rivulet. As the space between the banks widens, all the coarser material that is not carried beyond the workings by the current is built up into a pile of loose masonry (c), which, increasing in length and breadth as the work advances, forms an island.

The returns from these washings are very small, and even with the cheap cost of labor barely pay more than expenses. This, however, is probably owing to the fact that this whole region had been very thoroughly washed over in ancient times, though when and by whom does not appear to be known. Broad and deep canals of considerable length are still visible in the dense forest, and we found every indication that an extensive and well-arranged system of "ditch-digging" had once existed through this region. All these workings are covered with a heavy growth of trees, apparently not differing from the surrounding forest, either as to kind or size. Trees eighteen inches in diameter were found growing in the bottom of the now dry canals. The same method of washing the sand and disposing of the rubble as that described above appears to have been used by these old miners.

On our return to the house we found each member of our large train rejoicing in the possession of a long string of fine speckled trout; among these were some fish which resembled closely the cat-fish of our own rivers.

The next day was a fast, corresponding somewhat in the Japanese calendar to All Souls' Day of the western church. At this time the spirits of ancestors are supposed to visit the homes of their earthly relatives. In the evening a fire is built at the entrance, to guide the spirits in; and the next day another is built to conduct them out. This is the simple form of the ceremony in the wilderness. In the cities and towns the houses and cemeteries are illuminated, and on the sea-shore every family launches a mimic vessel, loaded with rice and wine, to feed the departing spirits on their voyage to the other world. During this fast the Japanese live entirely on vegetables, eating neither fish nor eggs.

Being ready to continue our journey we retraced our steps toward Volcano bay, running again the gauntlet of mud-holes and flies. Of these last the yellow variety, which gave us the

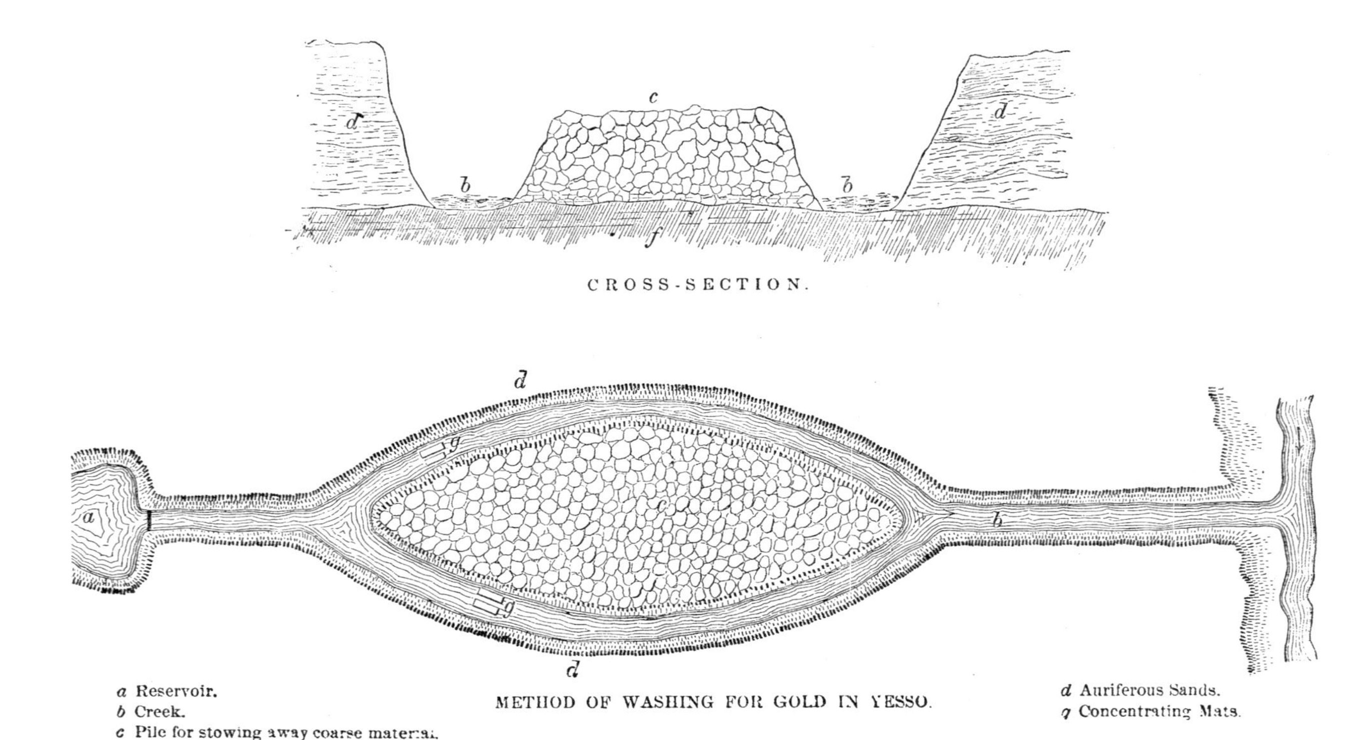

METHOD OF WASHING FOR GOLD IN YESSO.

a Reservoir.
b Creek.
c Pile for stowing away coarse material.
d Auriferous Sands.
g Concentrating Mats.

most trouble, left us as soon as we came within the influence of the sea-breeze. At Kunnui on the sea, the fishermen were busy in packing in straw bags, and loading into junks, immense quantities of herrings, from which the oil had been expressed. This refuse is shipped as a manure to Nipon. Clouds of ravens, the constant attendants of the fishermen, hovered over the beach. We reached Woshimanbe, our sleeping place, early in the afternoon. Here taking a boat and rowing a short distance out on the bay, we had a fine sun-set view of the north and west shores. We could see distinctly the sulphur-coated cliffs of the great solfatara of Mount Oussu. This ragged pile is evidently but the remnant of a volcanic cone, which must once have been of great size. Far inland and north from Mount Oussu we could clearly see the towering peak of Shiribetz. This is a perfect cone, regularly truncated, and rising apparently from the plain. Unlike the greater number of Japanese volcanoes, its activity seems to have ceased soon after the formation of the cone. It is clothed to the summit with a dense vegetation, which at the distance from which we saw it, seemed like purple velvet and the rays of the setting sun. Its height is great, probably between six and eight thousand feet, and its symmetrical form entitles it to a place among the picturesque volcanoes of the world.

Leaving Woshimanbe and Volcano bay, we turned northwest to cross over to Odaszu on the Japan sea. The road was hardly passable even on horseback. The long trains of pack-horses, fastened together in single file, soon convert a road into a succession of deep holes, separated only by narrow partitions, and filled with soft mud, which the sinking feet of the horses churn up at every step into the rider's face.

After a tedious ride we reached a solitary farm situated in the plain on the water-shed. The establishment of these farms, together with the granting of many privileges to their occupants, is one of the wise means by which the Government is endeavoring to colonize the island, which has hitherto been productive only in its fisheries.

Here we embarked in two small boats and descended a shallow and rapid river. For several hours we passed between banks, now low and overhung with water-willows, now high and clothed from the river's edge with beautiful forests. As we glided down the shallow rapids, I noticed that the bottom was covered with closely-packed colonies of unios. Gradually the steep banks receded from the river, and the valley opening out before us was occupied by broad terraces sloping gently toward the sea.

At a point a mile or two above the mouth of the stream we came upon a relay of horses which had been sent out to meet us, and which carried us to the village of Odaszu.

We had hardly arrived when an officer appeared, announcing that the magistrate of the district would soon wait upon us. He came immediately with all his retinue, and entered our apartments with two or three officers. In our interviews with those officials who had been in the habit of meeting foreigners, we had always adopted the usual compromise between foreign and Japanese etiquette; but we now were to receive an officer who knew nothing of this compromise, and to whom a shake of the hand would have seemed as ridiculous a proceeding as the salutation by rubbing noses seems to a European newly arrived among the natives of the South Sea islands. There was no escaping it; it was clear we would have to conform to the complicated Japanese ceremonial. Accordingly we ranged ourselves and the officers of our escort in a row, squatting upon our marrow bones, while our visitor and his attendants faced us in another row, exactly five feet distant. This done, using our knees as pivots, every man threw his body forward, with the palms of his hands resting on the mat, and regarding his vis-a-vis for an instant, lowered the head till the forehead rested on the floor. In this position each side murmured in a low tone the customary formula, and then raised the head just far enough to see that the other side was being equally polite. Another lowering of the head, and another formula, and the ceremony was ended. Returning again to the usual sitting position, not without a strong tendency to vertigo, on my part at least, we began an informal conversation, assisted by the fragrant tea and tobacco of Japan. Our visitor soon left us to rest from the fatiguing journey of the day.

Our route now lay northward along the western coast of the island. The road to Isoya was very rocky and difficult of passage. We found it, however, very picturesque, winding along the sea-shore, now over a narrow, pebbly beach, overhung by high and ragged cliffs, and now cut through projecting points of rock. Beyond Isoya, leaving the shore, we ascended by a narrow trail to the top of a high promontory, which here juts out into the sea. From this ridge, which is barren of forest, we could see far inland up the broad valley of the Shiribetz river. The plain, and the gently-sloping sides of this beautiful valley, are covered with a compact growth of the cane already mentioned, giving to it the appearance of a green savannah, through which meanders like a silver thread the clear mountain stream. Descending to the plain we were ferried across the river, which it seems is navigable for some distance for flat-boats.

The northern wall of the valley is formed by a lofty promontory called the Raiden. Here, leaving the sea-shore and rising by a rugged path, we reached the surface of a terrace, a barren plain bestrown with fragments of volcanic scoria.

The road up the side of the mountain proper was one of the worst on the island, and was in many places little better than a flight of rocky steps. This mountain is composed of beds of trachytic lava and tufas, and the soil formed from a disintegration of these rocks supports a noble growth of the beautiful forest trees of this country.

After a precipitous descent into a deep gorge, we reached, before sunset, the hot springs of the Yunonai. Through this ravine there runs a small torrent which has its source in the crater of the solfatara of Mount Iwanai. Where our route crossed this creek there are several hot sulphur springs, and a small inn, a branch of the principal hotel of Iwanai. The springs have temperatures varying from 40 to 50 degrees C. In the warm detritus which surrounds these, there harbor countless snakes, of which the cast-off skins are visible in every direction, on the ground, and fluttering from every bush. These reptiles are respected by the natives, being looked upon as the divinities of the springs—a remnant, probably, of the old nature-worship of the country.

Here, as at Kakumi, the hot springs stand in close connection with the snow-white quartziferous porphyry. This rock is impregnated with iron pyrites, which in places is represented only by cubical cavities containing sulphur.

Another long and difficult ride over the northern part of the Raiden brought us to Iwanai and the broad terrace plain which rises from the sea to the inland mountains.

Iwanai is one of the principal towns on the island, and is the residence of a magistrate. This officer waited upon us as soon as we arrived, and we went through a repètition of the customary ceremony, but this time with a more practical result; for we had to make requisitions on him for the necessary animals and guides to take us to the volcano of Iwaounobori. Early the next morning the guides were in the court of our inn with twenty-six saddle and pack-horses. With this long train we soon filed through the streets, objects of silent wonderment to the population. A ride of a few miles over the grassy plain brought us to the mountain, and here began a road the like of which it would not be easy to find outside of the island of Yesso. It had been cut the year before through the dense undergrowth, and consisted of mud fully two feet deep, in which countless stumps of cane stood like so many bayonets.

In the midst of the mountains an unexpected view burst upon us. We suddenly left the forest, and there lay beneath us a beautiful lake, hemmed in on all sides by gentle mountain slopes, clothed only with bamboo cane, but this so dense and green that it had all the appearance of long, waving grass. Through an opening in the hills this green landscape was brought into sharp contrast with the towering pile of black and gray crags and cliffs, coated with glistening sulphur, or striped with bright bands of red and yellow. From this massive ruin countless columns of vapor were rising, at one moment separately, at another intermingled by the breeze, and we knew that we were approaching one of nature's grandest laboratories. Skirting the lake and crossing the low pass we reached the sulphur works at the foot of the mountain before dark.

It is worthy of remark that on the plain at the foot of the mountain we found a large area covered with wintergreen, bearing white berries. The occurrence of this genus, gaultheria, which is unknown on continental Asia or Europe, is another striking point of resemblance between the floras of northern Japan and the United States.

We attempted an ascent of the mountain to get a view, but were rewarded only with a thorough drenching from the fog, which suddenly settled round the summit.

The next morning we all made the ascent. Iwaounobori is a

true solfatara of grand dimensions. It is the remnant of an ancient cone, which must have been of great height, and it is the centre of a large volcanic region which surrounds it, with the varied and peculiar scenery belonging to such districts. From the summit, fifteen extinct cones, and probably many more volcanic mountains, are visible; among these the distant peaks of Esan and Komangadake rise distinctly on the horizon. Nearer to us was the magnificent cone of the Shiribetz, second only to the Fuziyama in beauty; while between this and the mountain on which we stood lay the broad green valley of the Shiribetz, remarkable for its long sweeping horizontal and vertical curves. Afar off to the east the horizon was broken by a range apparently running north and south through the middle of the island.

While I was lost in the great beauty of the scene spread out before us, I became more strongly impressed by the difficulties which we would have to contend with in our exploration of the island. The presence everywhere of the dense undergrowth of cane seemed to render the interior inaccessible.

As I have already said, this mountain is only a part of the skeleton of a former cone of large size. Of the symmetrical mantle of ashes which once covered it, only portions of the foot-slope are now visible around the base. The present mountain is a great mass of trachytic rock with several culminating points, connected by small ridges, and has a number of crateriform depressions. The sides are broken with perpendicular cliffs several hundred feet high, and cut into by deep and narrow gorges. The depressions on the summit, which indicate, perhaps, the position of former outlets, are now filled to the level of the lip with sand and clay, forming plains surrounded by rocky walls.

The Iwaounobori is the central one of three volcanos, which lie in a line running about N. N. W. This is also the course of a broad belt within the limits of which the solfatara action is most developed, both across the summit and upon the sides. The rock within this belt, wherever not covered by the products of decomposition, is traversed by countless fissures, more or less filled with sulphur, and wherever the filling is incomplete there issue forth jets of steam and gases. These jets showed on every trial a temperature of 98 degrees C. The steam has a strong odor of both sulphurous acid and sulphuretted hydrogen. It has an acid reaction on litmus paper, which is especially strong when drops that condense on the sulphur-crystals around the orifices of the jets are tested. Beautiful crystals of sulphur formed rapidly on the bulb of the thermometer. Excepting at the steam vents, the fissures are closed with sulphur at the surface; but by breaking in to the depth of a few inches cavities are exposed, lined with a bristling mass of the straw-colored crystals of this mineral. On a precipitous part of the exterior of the mountain, where a large mass of the rock seemed recently to have fallen off, I saw an interesting exhibition of the action of the gases. The rock is seen to be traversed by a perfect network of sulphur veins (*a*), which seem to occupy the positions of the cracks common to all rock. The trachytic character (*b*) is tolerably well preserved in the centre of the block, but towards the circumference the rock is more and more disintegrated, and has assumed the form of concentric layers, the outer shell being changed to a white earth. It seems not improbable that this condition may exist through a large part of the mountain, thus forming a great *stock-werk* of sulphur.

The only way in which I can account for this structure is by supposing that the disintegration of the rock, which formerly occupied the spaces now filled with sulphur, took place when the water, which now appears only as steam, stood at a higher level in the mountain, making it a mud volcano, like Esan, and exuding the products of decomposition as fast as formed. On the withdrawal of the water to a lower level, the abandoned net-work of fissures was filled with sulphur by the decomposition of sulphuretted hydrogen.

At another place, in the walls of one of the small craters near the summit, there is an instance that would seem to illustrate the action of the gases and steam without the presence of water as such. Here a black rock, which occurs in dykes at several points on the mountain, is visible in different stages of alteration. In places it was observed to have the concentric structure assumed by many rocks during the first period of disintegration, and by which the polygonal form of the blocks into which all bodies of rock are subdivided, is lost as each succeeding shell is removed. In this case the outer shell is white and earthy. Again the same rock was found altered, to the centre of each block, the shape re-

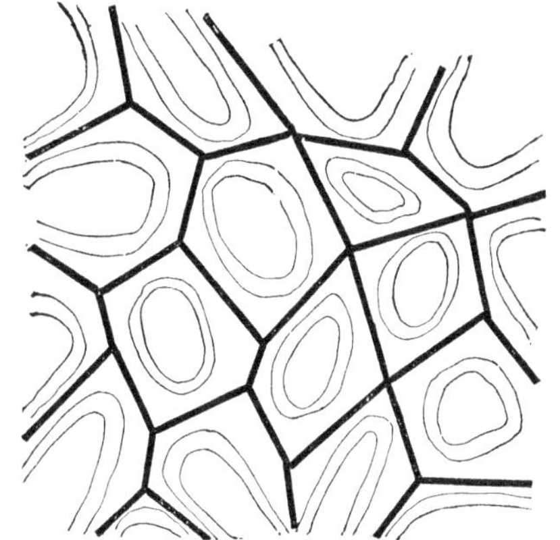

CHANGE FROM POLYGONAL TO SPHERICAL FORMS, IN ROCK-MASSES.

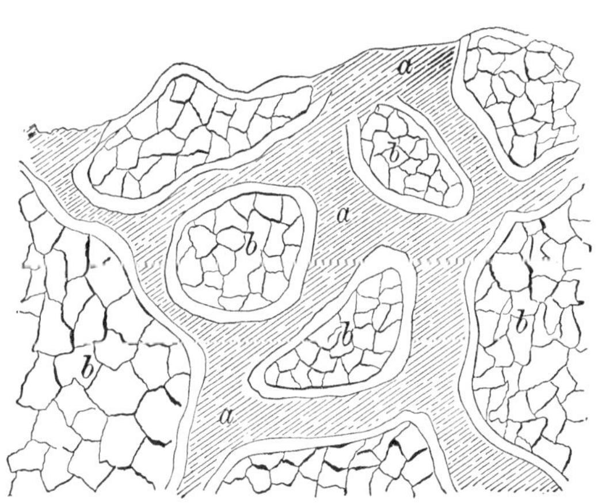

MANNER OF OCCURRENCE OF SULPHUR.

a Sulphur. *b* Rock.

maining, to a soft, pasty, white clay, quite tasteless. Often in the centre of a snowy-white mass of this clay, would lie a core, equally soft but black, the line of separation between the colors being well marked. In places where the alteration was in the first stage, an alum-salt was found, producing an efflorescence on the surface of this black rock, possibly as one of the first products from the decomposing felspar.

On the west side of the peak, in the valley which drains the craters, there was formerly a spring of chalybeate water, which has left a large deposit of hydrated oxide of iron, filled with leaves and stems of cane, apparently of the same species that now covers the surrounding country.

After taking lunch near the small shrine of the San Gin (mountain god), we descended to the sulphur works. Here also some one has worked in ancient times, and an old iron cauldron of great size, which was found half-buried at this spot, is now used for the evening bath-tub. It is mounted over a furnace in the open air. When the water is heated to the right point, the bather gets in, and presents, as seen through the smoke, a scene which reminds one of pictures of boiling martyrs of old.

The Government has sulphur works on this mountain, in which fourteen cauldrons are kept at work. The monthly production is about 64,000 pounds, at a total cost of $183 25.

Returning to Iwanai, we left the next morning to continue our journey northward along the coast. A broad, pebbly beach, between the terrace plain and the sea, extends as far as the mouth of the Shiribuka river—a stream which is navigable for canoes. After crossing this we came again to the precipitous cliffs and craggy head-lands which characterize the west coast. Our journey was made partly on horseback, and partly by boat, the headlands being often impracticable for roads. In this manner we reached the small fishing village of Ousubetz. Leaving the sea the next morning, we ascended the bed of Kaiyanobetz creek. About a mile from the shore we came upon a series of sandstones and shales, enclosing three seams of superior bituminous coal, the largest bed being about four feet thick. We spent the hour before sunset in rowing among the rocks off Ousubetz, admiring the richness in form and color of the marine life exhibited in the fissures and on the sides of the rough rocks. Brilliant starfishes and shells were clustered in the bright and many-colored sea-mosses, out of which grew, like beautiful flowers, large sea-anemones. Many fishing-boats were engaged in taking the haliotis from the rocks. This is done by means of a long, three-pointed spear. We found this mollusk to be an excellent substitute for oysters when made into soup. The Japanese are very fond of this, as they are indeed of almost everything that lives in the sea. Sea-slugs (beche-de-mer), cuttle-fish, sea-urchins, and sea-weed of many varieties, would serve to head a long list of marine animals which are, in reality, excellent food. They occur on many coasts, including our own; but the Japanese alone seem to turn them to practical account. The same remark might be applied to the vegetable productions of the forests. In one class especially, the cryptogams, there seems hardly to be a variety —whether growing in the forests, or even on the wood-work in mines, or cultivated in gardens—which does not find its way into Japanese soups.

CHAPTER XIII.

SECOND JOURNEY IN YESSO.

THE summer was now so far advanced that, much as we wished to visit the northern part of the island, we felt that to continue our journey, which was purely one of general reconnoissance, would give us too little time for work at the mines before the setting-in of winter; we therefore concluded to return. A boat, propelled by eight oars and four skulls, aided by a large sail, brought us rapidly across the bay to Iwanai.

As we were to continue our journey by sea, we were now at the mercy of the weather, which for two days prevented our starting. This delay, however, gave me the opportunity of seeing the ceremonies of a great Sintu festival, which I have described in a previous chapter.

On the 25th of August a smooth sea tempted us to start on our journey by boat. We were soon passing under the rocky cliffs of the Raiden. The northern part of this mountain is formed of the volcanic tufa-conglomerate, covered by a great bed or perhaps several flows of lava, often exhibiting columnar structure. In places, beds of lava seemed to be inter-stratified with conglomerate.

At about half the distance between the northern and southern sides of this highland a large amphitheatre or crateriform valley opens toward the sea. South of this the cliffs, less high, consist of the conglomerate, and in the perpendicular walls are visible many small but regular dykes with transverse columnar structure, and in places dislocated by faults. The conglomerate strata have a considerably south-westerly dip, and as we approached the southern flank of the Raiden, near the village of Hamajime, they disappear under the sea. Over-lying this formation, and composing the mountain above, is a gray volcanic rock, possessing a tabular structure, which gives it often a stratiform appearance near the bottom; but in the upper half of its thickness, the plates curve irregularly upward, presenting their edges toward the upper surface of the bed.

This mountain is a high flat ridge, running nearly east and west, between the valleys of the Shiribetz and the Shiribuka rivers, and on it is the Iwaounobori, and at least one more volcano.

These volcanic rocks, especially the tufa-conglomerates, are characteristic of a greater part of the Japanese coast. They were deposited at a time when this long range of islands was submerged to such an extent that only the higher points, most of which are volcanos, showed themselves above the sea. What is now a range of large islands, was then a long archipelago, consisting in the main of super and submarine volcanos. In the straits separating these countless islands, and upon the submerged slopes flanking the main range toward the Pacific on the one side, and the Japan sea on the other, there were deposited the ashes ejected from these vents, commingled with the debris which was being constantly formed along the shore-line of the islands. The eruptions of lava from the sub-aerial and sub-marine volcanos flowed in streams over the surface of these deposits, to be again covered by other beds of detritus and ashes. In the neighborhood of active centres the fissures radiating from these through this deposit were filled by dykes of injected lava. Long submerged and exposed to the action of both the sea-water and springs containing acids and alkaline salts, the mineralogical character and texture of these beds suffered great changes. This was especially the case where the more finely comminuted and more soluble ashes predominated over the rolled fragments of harder rock. The results of this metamorphic action differ according to the circumstances under which it took place. Thus, near Kumaishi there are heavy beds consisting entirely of pumice, which seem to have undergone but little change; this is perhaps explainable by the abundance of small and perfect crystals of quartz, which would seem to indicate that the pumice itself is highly silicious and insoluble. In other places immense beds have been transformed into palagonite tufa. Again, as in the peak of Hakodade and the neighborhood of the Esan, immense beds, which were unquestionably deposits of tufa, have been so changed by re-crystallization into felspar with horn-blende and quartz, as to become trachytic porphyries.

The subsequent elevation of the Japanese archipelago so far united its countless islands as to form the present group. Many former straits are now passes between inland mountains, from the crests of which the beds of tufa slope off to disappear under the ocean. The action of the sea along the coast has everywhere cut deep into this deposit, breaking the once continuous declivity, and substituting for it the cliffs and fiords, which everywhere encircle the islands that constitute Japan.

This is one of the more recent phases of geological change to which the Japanese group has been subjected. The skeleton of the islands consists of granitic and schistose rocks, apparently of the same age as the similar formations of China and Tartary, and like these either silurian or protozoic. At various points upon the group, tertiary, secondary, and perhaps paleozoic rocks are represented.

Leaving the boat at Isoya we continued our journey the next morning with horses. Riding around the head of the bay of Odaszu, we were ferried over the Shibuta river, our horses swimming behind. Here we entered the domain of the Prince of Tsungara. The broad terrace plain which forms the surface of the deposit of tufa conglomerate is here covered with a heavy growth of a jointed grass from six to ten feet high, while the inland hills are clothed with stunted forests. In crossing the wooded slopes we found abundance of vines of the wild grape and of the *biwa*, which bears a delicious fruit.

In crossing one of the small rivers, near where it empties into the sea, an accident occurred which might have been attended with serious results. The stream was spanned from bank to bank, about fifteen feet above the water, by a bridge constructed only of four large timbers laid loosely side by side. The two inner beams were squared, but the outer ones were left unhewn. On to this narrow bridge five Japanese officers had already preceded me, when I observed that every one of their horses was treading against the side of the outer round timber, and rolling this from its place. Foreseeing an immediate catastrophe, I backed off and gave the alarm. But the warning came too late. The words *abnai! abnai!* had hardly left my mouth when the beam rolled from its place, and the horses plunged with a heavy splash into the torrent below. The riders, with the skill peculiar to Japanese horsemen, landed upon the bridge and escaped unharmed. The animals also suffered nothing worse than a wetting.

I was struck by the more flourishing condition of the inhabitants of the imperial domain, as compared with those of the territory of the Prince of Tsungara. There was a general air of dilapidation in the villages, and of thriftlessness among the people, in the region we were now passing through, which spoke of the imposition of burdens disproportionate to the sources of revenue. The line of demarcation between the two conditions was as sharply drawn as the geographical boundary. The cause could not lie in nature, for the sea, which is in both the only source of revenue, offered its treasures alike to both. The reason most probably lies in the policy of the Taikoonate, which during more than two centuries has been exerted to impoverish the feudatory lords of the empire, by exacting from them the constant maintenance of large armies, and of great establishments at Yeddo. To meet this constant drain, taxation must have been pressed to the utmost, while the means thus raised were in great part expended in the imperial city, and on the road thither; thus enriching countries which are practically foreign, instead of circulating for the benefit of all classes at home. One can hardly conceive of a policy better calculated than this to impoverish and weaken the dangerous elements of a feudal empire, and at the same time to enrich the territory of the central power.

After riding through several of these miserable villages, we came to a point beyond which roads were impossible, and from which we continued our journey by boat. The coast here was a succession of deep fiords and bold head-lands, facing the sea, with high and wood-crowned cliffs. With a breeze which just filled the sail, we threaded our way among countless islets. Nothing but the most intimate knowledge of this coast could have guided us safely through the narrow channels separating rocks which lay bare after every wave, and which almost touched us on either side. But the sense of danger is often lulled by the increasing confidence in one's guides; so here, after having passed several times through places which seemed to threaten certain destruction, we withdrew our attention from the terrors beneath, to the fantastic forms carved by the waves out of the soft rock at the base of the overhanging cliffs, and to the grander view of the long perspective of headlands and islands, forest and sea, drawn out before us.

During the afternoon we had been approaching a chain of high pinnacle rocks, which jutted out from a cape, and which as we approached them were found to consist of symmetrical columns of lava. In the little bay thus protected lay a fishing village, our resting-place for the night. The chief productions of this part of the west coast are *awabi* (haleotis), *erico* (beche-de-mer), *ika* (cuttle-fish), some herrings and pectens, together with sea-weed. The sea-urchin (*nona*) is also very abundant. All these form articles of trade with the other islands, and of export to China. From this point we made a short excursion into the interior.

Continuing our journey now by horse, now by boat, we reached Ousubetz, whence we were to ascend a small stream into the mountains.

At this village there was being built a large penitentiary, to which prisoners from all parts of the empire were to be sent, and where they were to pass their time in working at different trades. This experiment was being tried in imitation of American state prisons.

Our excursion up the valley of the Ousubetz, or more properly up the bed of that creek, was one which showed the difficulty of access to the interior as soon as the very few routes of travel are left. We made the first seven miles with the greatest difficulty on horseback, over the stony bed of the river. Here we found several huts and warm springs; these latter, having temperatures from 54 to 58 degrees C, issuing from porphyritic rock, and containing much lime and iron, are the favorite resort not only of countless snakes, but also of many invalids; and it would certainly seem that any person whose constitution is strong enough to carry him over the road thither from the coast, could not fail to leave this locality with every assurance of having a well-tested constitution.

A very large and cavernous deposit of ferruginous tufu surrounds the springs. In the never-failing heat imparted by the neighboring water to this rock, large families and colonies of harmless serpents live and multiply, enjoying, as the presiding genii of the place, a perfect immunity from harm. Their cast-off skins cover the ground, rot in the water, are entwined among the plants, or dangle as streamers from every hole.

These springs are frequented by bathers during the spring and autumn, when insects are least troublesome, the visitors paying the owner for the privilege of using the water.

Leaving our horses at this point, we continued our journey on foot. For several miles we waded almost uninterruptedly in the stream, the water often rising nearly breast-high. The object of this excursion was to examine certain mineral deposits which had been reported to the Government as existing in the valley. But after we had nearly exhausted both the afternoon and our strength, the guide confessed himself unable to find the place, and we retraced our steps. The valley of this river lay between nearly vertical walls of amygdaloid and porphyries, a structure which, by forcing us to follow the bed of the torrent, rendered our journey exceedingly difficult.

The next morning we returned to the sea-shore, and continued southward to Kumaishi. Here for a distance of some miles the terrace formation changes character; its usual gloomy conglomerate tufa is replaced by pumice, the snow-white cliffs of which presented a new feature in the coast scenery.

While rowing off the shore I was struck by a peculiarity connected with this tufa. There are in the deep water many rocks, whose surfaces are just exposed at low tide. They are flat, and from a few feet to several yards in diameter, the tops and the sides for some feet below the surface being thickly encrusted with mussels, and a variety of those organisms which flourish between tides. Below the area thus protected, the action of the sea upon the soft pumice has progressed until the supporting material of each encrusted rock is little more than a slender column.

At Tomarigawa we left the Japan sea and turned eastward to re-cross the mountains. The western slope is deeply sulcated by ravines, which at a short distance from the sea expose the granitic and other rocks, the irregularities of the surface of which have been filled up by the volcanic tufa conglomerate. Our route lay mainly along a very narrow ridge of this conglomerate, which in places became so sharp that the road had to be built up with rubble and brush.

The forest had the usual dense undergrowth of cane. While we were threading our way along the narrow path, a large bear met us, coming from the opposite direction, and caused a great commotion among our horses. He was evidently as much startled as we were, for with a rapid shuffle he disappeared in the thick undergrowth, and the noise he made showed the speed with which he descended the hill. These animals are very numerous, and only a few days before some of them had eaten a horse at the neighboring mines.

Before evening we reached the mines of Yurup, in a valley on the eastern slope of the mountains. Here the volcanic conglomerate has been removed by erosion over a large area, exposing an extensive development of black metamorphosed argillite in vertical strata, associated with broad bands of greenstone. True fissure veins traversed both these rocks, bearing galena, zinc-blende, and pyrites of iron and copper, associated with quartz, calcite, carbonate of manganese, and more rarely barytes. These veins, which, with a width of from two to eighteen inches, are tolerably regular in the greenstone, split into parallel threads in the argillite. A considerable area has been worked for lead, but here as at Ichinowatari the deposits are very poor. The highest production ever attained was about four tons per month, but at the time of my visit it was less than two. The processes of separation and smelting are the same as at Ichinowatari. The following schedule of the daily expenses is inserted as a curiosity. The laborers are supplied by the Government with rice:

DAILY EXPENSES OF THE YURUP LEAD MINES.

Accountant clerk	$ 0 05
Head miner	07
Twenty five miners, at 5 cts	1 25
Eighteen Coolies, at 4 cts	72
Thirteen women, ore dressers and washers, 2 to 6 cts	45
Daily consumption of iron	12
" " " steel	04
" " " mats and ropes	06
Total	$ 2 76

Here we made the first application of powder to mining that had ever been attempted in Japan. The men learned readily the art of drilling, but could not be persuaded to take any part in the charging, tamping, and lighting of the first hole. They would not even stay to watch the process, but left the mine in a body. They came back immediately after the explosion, fully expecting to find the works fallen in, and the rash foreigners buried in the ruins. Their delight was indescribable when they saw the result of the blast, which, at the cost of an hour's labor, had accomplished more than they were able to do by their own process in a day. After this they stayed to learn all about the tamping and lighting, and very soon went through the whole operation without assistance.

It is remarkable that the use of powder for blasting should have remained so long unknown in China and Japan, in which countries this explosive material has been used for other purposes since very early times. It was amusing, too, to find the Japanese Government in 1862 urging the same objections to its use in mines that were put forward under similar circumstances by the governments of Europe two or three hundred years ago. It was not without some difficulty that we obtained permission to make the trial. The result was so successful that before I left Japan I was told that many princes had sent men to Yurup to learn the new process.

The empire is very rich in deposits of useful metals, and upon the island south of Yesso, these, including iron, have been worked since very early times. The Japanese being very skilful in mining above the lowest attainable water level, have found and worked countless deposits, exhausting them down to the point at which the water compelled them to leave.

The natural result of this is, that large numbers of veins bearing gold, silver, lead, and copper, have been abandoned when most productive. Indeed, it would seem that only the introduction of pumping machinery is necessary to raise to a high point the production of these and other metals. In this direction, therefore, I turned my first attention. As the Government considered it dangerous for us to visit the mining districts of Nipon, I decided to introduce such improvements as could be constructed in a simple form at the mines of Yurup.

Unfortunately, the lateness of the season prevented my doing more than making the preliminary surveys, and the termination of our engagement soon after this rendered it impossible to give other than theoretical instruction in this important branch of mining.

At Yurup there are also two warm springs with a temperature of 46 degrees C. The water is used in winter for washing the ores, and for this purpose is conducted into a large tank built in one corner of the ore-house, where it serves also as a bath.

The road from Yurup to Volcano bay lies for some distance through deep and narrow gorges, in which it is in places cut out of the solid rock; but as we approach the sea the valley widens and becomes a fertile river bottom, upon which there were already two or three farms. Among the products of these is the hardy variety of rice, which in Japan and China is cultivated in a climate resembling that of the northern United States. Coming at Yurup into our previous road we returned to Hakodade, which we reached on the 14th of September.

The remainder of the autumn was passed at the mines, Mr. Blake returning to the gold washings of Kunnui, and I to the lead mines of Yurup.

During this time there was growing the revolution which has since broken out with such force that the long prosperous empire is now the scene of dissensions which threaten its very existence.

Among the charges brought against the Taikoon by the anti-foreign party, was one which accused him of throwing the resources of the country open to foreign spies in engaging us. Finding itself losing ground, the Yeddo Government was forced to suspend many of its liberal schemes, and first of all to bring to an end our engagement. This was done in February, 1863. My connection with this Government had been uniformly pleasant, and it was with deep regret that I saw the threatening ascendancy which the anti-liberal party was daily gaining.

As the hour of departure approached, the young officers who had so long been my companions and pupils showed how strongly they felt a separation which threatened to put an end to the study of foreign sciences in which they had become engrossed. To several of them I was deeply attached, and that the feeling was mutual was shown by the tears they shed when the moment of parting came, and which were the only ones I ever saw in the eyes of a man in Japan or China. Takeda, Myagawa, Oosima, and Yuwao, vied with each other in bringing presents, among which were ancient family swords, the choicest of heirlooms, which money could not have bought. It was useless to refuse the acceptance of objects which I knew they prized so much. They were men of high intelligence and cultivated minds, and possessing all the characteristics which with us constitute the thorough gentleman. Myagawa, who had mastered the English and French languages, has since twice been to Europe as interpreter and secretary to Japanese embassies.

During our sojourn in Hakodade I incurred a heavy debt to the greater part of the foreign inhabitants for many acts of friendship and hospitality; especially to Messrs. Walsh & Co., and their agents, Messrs. Stevenson and Wheaton.

Profiting by the kind invitation of Capt. Bassargine, we embarked for Nagasaki in H. I. R. M. corvette "Bogartyr." The weather was very rough, and we had more than usual difficulty in making headway through the straits of Tsungara. Here a strong current rushes perpetually from the Japan sea to the Pacific. During the winter months this and a constant west wind render Hakodade almost inaccessible to vessels coming from the east. After entering the Japan sea and turning south-westward, every day's progress brought us into more southern climates. As we approached the straits of Corea, countless picturesque islands, covered with a semi-tropical vegetation, offered a pleasant contrast to the snowy hills and leafless forests of the northern part of the empire.

It was a beautiful morning at the end of February when we steamed up the long bay of Nagasaki. It had been my intention to go on with the "Bogartyr" to Shanghai, but receiving a kind invitation from Mr. J. G. Walsh, the U. S. Consul, of the house of Messrs. Walsh & Co., I concluded to remain.

Nagasaki is built on the side of a high hill at the head of the long bay of the same name. Its streets in one direction are long and crooked, conforming to the contours of the ground, while in the other they rise in flights of stone steps, ascending the mountain. The upper part of the slope is occupied very generally with temples and temple grounds, and with extensive cemeteries. As seen from the water, the city and its surroundings present a unique and pleasant appearance. Large trees rise from every part of the town, while here and there thick masses of the rich foliage of the camphor tree, or smaller groves mixed with the lighter green of the bamboo, relieve the monotonous outlines of the level roofs of a Japanese town. Above all these the city is overlooked by massive temples, standing on terraced grounds faced with heavy stone walls, and approached by long avenues of steps and sacred gate-ways. Not less remarkable are the cemeteries, always a particular feature of a Japanese town. These, too, lie above the city, and cover the surface of the hill, following all its irregularities, filling ravines, and mantling the summits and sides of promontories, here creeping into the temple grounds, and there setting a limit to the growth of the town. The hills thus occupied are very steep, and have been made available for this purpose only by raising upon their slopes thousands of small terraces, faced with stone. Indeed, the entire side of the mountain is one mass of hewn masonry. It is a city of the dead, and is traversed in every direction by main avenues and lesser streets, always paved with well-trimmed blocks of stone. Each terrace is divided into small lots a few yards square, which are floored with stone and surrounded with tastefully carved railings of the same material. These are family lots; and in each are several monuments in dark-colored stone, of various forms and sizes. Round and square columns, obelisks, human figures, and tablets, are the most common forms, and upon these the inscriptions are tastefully cut in such high relief, or sunk so deeply into the rock, that, like an Egyptian necropolis, this one and the names of its inhabitants seems intended to last through all time.

Till the end of the fourteenth century the site of Nagasaki was occupied merely by a fishing hamlet belonging to a prince of the same name, the ruins of whose palace were in Kaempfer's time still visible upon the hill behind the city. With the extinction of this family its territory became part of the domain of the Prince of Omura. Soon after the arrival of the Portugese, the then ruling head of this house found it conformable to his spiritual or material interests to confer this city upon the strangers, to be theirs for ever. It became immediately a centre of foreign trade, and of the proselyting missions of the Christian church, and a stronghold in which were developed the ambition and insolence of the Europeans, which before long led not only to their own expulsion, but also to the awful persecutions inflicted upon those over whom their influence had been extended. After the adoption by the Japanese of an exclusive policy, they transferred the Dutch factory to this place, or rather to the artificial island of Decima, where they were guarded by gates and police, and treated with great indignity, as the price of being permitted to trade.

Being no longer in the service of the Government, I was debarred from making any excursions in the neighborhood of Nagasaki. My walks were confined to an area of a few square miles, and to runs in a sail-boat along the adjoining coast. The neighborhood of the city is highly cultivated, the valleys and hillsides being terraced. Among the crops I noticed large fields of rapeseed, raised for the oil. The walks through these fields and terraces command beautiful and ever-changing views, and would be delightful were it not for the manure-tanks sunken in the ground, which meet one at every step with the most offensive odors. There are several coal mines in the immediate neighborhood, but as they are on princely domain they were inaccessible to me. After trying in vain to get permission to visit them, I concluded to leave for China, where foreigners had lately acquired the right of penetrating to the interior.

CHAPTER XIV.

AN ESSAY ON JAPANESE ART,

Written to accompany this Volume, by

JOHN LA FARGE.

INTEREST in Japanese art must have much increased, to have made Mr. Ruskin fear some malign influence upon his artists coming from this heathen source; and it is true that many artists are in the habit of looking to it for advice and confirmation of their previous tendencies and efforts in art.

Our first knowledge of Japanese art is not recent. Japanese products have come into Europe for the last two hundred years. In 1664, the importations into Holland of Japanese porcelain, fine specimens, amounted to 44,943 pieces. Japanese museums were formed at Dresden and in Holland; and very good sale-catalogues (*raisonnés*) of the last century, distinguish carefully between Japanese and Chinese work.

They have always been admired, and collected, but like other rare things have had their best merits passed over, because they could be made the objects of a vulgar curiosity. Though they furnish a test, if ever there was one, for discernment in art, those who make it their business to instruct in such matters were silent. Original appreciation of excellence is never abundant; even so late as 1851, Mr. Owen Jones did not include Japanese decoration in his "Grammar of Ornament."

Since then, the opening of the treaty ports has made it familiar to all of us. We have all admired the many objects made lovely by their workmanship: their inimitable lacquers, embodying on their surface a complete school of ornament; their unrivalled ivory and metal work; their porcelains and enamels; their bronzes, of colors unknown to ours, cast and polished beyond our means; their colored printing, contrasting with our own brutal chromolithographs by its frankness, or by a delicacy equal to exquisite hand-work.*

These things all please the eye, as if with the sense of touch. On analysis, besides the wondrous finish, we notice the novelty of the design, its energy, its accuracy, its sentiment, very often the grandeur of its style, very often a stamp of individuality or personal talent, its recalling of natural objects, the enchanting harmony of its colors, and its exquisite adaptation to the surface ornamented.

We feel that we are looking at perfect work, that we are in presence of a distinct civilization, where art is happily married to industry. These accompaniments of every-day life, studied out, reveal a complete school of art. While it is still pure, uninfluenced, and uninjured by new contacts, it will be well to inquire into its value, and to learn what lessons we can derive from it. Its limits seem at this day distinctly traced. What we shall know hereafter cannot contradict the points already made, even if it should very much displace them. Notwithstanding that every nation bears intellectual fruit neither natural nor tasteful to others, this is truer of literature than of plastic art, for this last speaks the more universal language; and without our aiming at a full analysis, the principal characteristics of this decorative art may be here described in some connected order.

Most evident in Japanese art, is the use of a marvellous decoration, the very crown of that power over color always an heirloom of the East, and a separate gift from ours. To Eastern directness, fulness, and splendor, the Japanese add a sobriety, a simplicity, a love of subdued harmonies and imperceptible gradations, and what may be called an intellectual refinement akin to something in the Western mind. If we wish, their works can be for us a store-house as ample and as valuable in its way as the treasures of form left to us by the Greeks. For the Japanese, no combinations of colors have been improbable, and their solutions of such as are put aside by Western knowledge recall the very arrangements of Nature.

* I remember a print in which a silvered sickle of a moon shone through the most delicate gray fog clouds, as correctly edged as if by the photograph, and melting into the very texture of the paper. Over this were faint lines of falling rain, and an inscription perfectly distinct, but as pale as the faintest wash of India ink. If we admire this refinement, what are we to think of that which it addresses in Japan?

Great beauty of color is apt to obscure the structure upon which it rests, and excellence of design is not seldom unrecognized in the works of great colorists. Little as this is felt in the harmonious synthesis of Japanese decoration, Japanese drawings and wood-cuts in black and white allow us to gauge their abstract power of design, and their knowledge of drawing. Stripped of those other beauties of color and texture so peculiar to their precious work, these drawings give us in the simplest way their control of composition, that power in art which affects the imagination by the mere adjustment of lines and masses. Herein their work can be compared to the best, in this the most simple means of expression in art, for by this all its forms and periods are united, and the tattooing of the savage is connected with the designs of Michael Angelo. In fact it is the nearest expression of the will of the artist, which is the very foundation of art. Japanese composition in ornamental design has developed a principle which separates it technically from all other schools of decoration. This will have been noticed by all who have seen Japanese ornamental work, and might be called a principle of irregularity, or apparent chance arrangement: a balancing of equal gravities, not of equal surfaces. A Western designer, in ornamenting a given surface, would look for some fixed points from which to start, and would mark the places where his mind had rested by exact and symmetrical divisions. These would be supposed by a Japanese, and his design would float over them, while they, though invisible, would be felt beneath. Thus a few ornaments—a bird, a flower—on one side of this page would be made by an almost intellectual influence to balance the large unadorned space remaining.

And so, by a principle familiar to painters, an appeal is made to the higher ideas of design, to the desire of concealing Art beneath a look of Nature. It has the advantage of allowing any division and extension, and super-imposition of other and contradictory designs. With another analogy to the higher forms of Art, the Japanese look to more symmetrical arrangement for their graver effects and religious symbolisms. To carry out this subtle conciliation of symmetry and chance, this constant reference to the order of nature requires of course an incessant watching of all its moods and all its details.

The daily record of such attention fills the sketch-books of all artists, and many of the little Japanese books of prints are nothing but fac-similes of such sketches. Whether they are careless or studied, an impression of Nature disengages itself from them all; every one who sees them will be more or less sensitive to a spirit of observation unfamiliar to our more hurried civilization. With the exception of a certain idealized stereotyping of the female face, they have a respect for reality only limited by understanding the necessities of art. Any excess is in the direction of essential laws, and accentuation is a note of Japanese art. If they have not the feeling for plastic beauty that we inherit from the Greek ancestors of our mind, they show a deep sense, a profound knowledge, of the character of the human form; and since drawing may be divided into the drawing of form, and the drawing of motion, they may lay claim to a full and consummate ownership of the latter. If their modes shock our own conventionalities, we cannot gainsay that never before have artists so lived at home with animals and plants; never has artistic skill held under a more subtle sway the thoughtless tribes of sea and air.

The printed sketches of Hoksai, one of their later artists, from some of which the accompanying fac-similes are taken,* are types of the many-sidedness of the Japanese sketch-books. Birds, beasts, insects, and plants—their growth and movements; curves of motion in water—falling, running, or even thrown; the curl of smoke; the ceremony of the Daimios, the shuffling of the Bonzes, the strut of the soldiers, the quarrels of the populace, scenes of home and out-door life, games of children, military exercises; all trades with the workers in them, and deformities born of their work; men too fat, men too thin; landscape effects; studies of architecture and perspective; and especially, and always, all possible positions of the human body are noted down in these little albums. All this is done in a manner which would grace the sketch-book of the best draughtsman that ever lived, with sensitive feeling, a detached mind, and gentle humor.

Art is a necessary exaggeration of Nature, and implies a bear-

* These fac-similes, not chosen particularly for their artistic merits, give besides some imaginary scenes, a page of common Japanese types, and one of occupations and trades. At the foot of one is depicted a dispute about hack-hire, or rather cango-hire, not differing materially from similar comedies with us; above, the figure throwing back his arms is frightened by a ghost.

ing heavily upon certain distinctive points (*caricatura*). A certain grotesqueness marks these Japanese drawings. I do not refer to that side which, in all works of art, marks national differences, and which has for other nations something ludicrous; but there exists here a vein of humor which everything tells us must be a national expression. Their constant and delicate observation recalls with a smile the secret mechanism of actions, from the slight indications of any habit to extravagances of gesture and demeanor which flourish in an open life like theirs. Their hand is light, and never suffers from that Western spirit of caricature which underlines and insists and dwells upon its joke. A few lines give it. If we understand it, so much the better; if not, we shall not have failed in a puzzle or a rebus. We can still admire the accuracy of whatever is detailed, the comprehensiveness of what is suggested, often the grace and beauty; always the swing and energy of the design: for the Japanese draughtsman unites within him what is often separated in the Western artist—the power of representing grace and awkwardness, and a feeling of dignity, with a sympathy for the laugh on things. A Japanese hero strains under a ponderous weight, or a lady flirts her fan, and it is hard to say whether we receive most distinctly the impression of manly effort or of female grace. The summons of the idea is always answered by their imagination; the real bends before their will, though never trampled upon, and retaining all its essential laws. However much the motive, the main forms or the accessories help the story and belong to it, they retain their elementary construction, and their strength or their grace is merely framed by a more feeling line. Hoksai, in the inscriptions alongside of some designs equal in all but beauty to the Greek inventions of the centaur, or the fawn, modestly remarks that it is more easy to draw things that no one has seen, than to represent things that every one sees.* With us, however, this

* A sample of his playful fancy is given in the fac-similes of this book, the two figures carrying a bundle between them balanced upon the nose of one of them. They are called by Sir Rutherford Alcock *gnomes*, rather perhaps suggested by some such description in the work known as the Sinico—Japanese Encyclopedia, of "the Yu-min," the feathered people: "The kingdom of the feathered people lies southeast of the sea, amid rocky precipices. The men have cheeks lengthened out like those of birds; their beaks are red, their eyes white. Wings grow upon them,and they can fly, but they are incapable of going far away or of keeping up their flight for a long time. They resemble birds, but are not born of eggs." These stories account for other creatures of Hoksai, bicephalous semi-cen-

case of imagination is not an every-day matter, though with us, also, the greatest successes in realism have been attained by men among the greatest in imaginative power. The exception with us seems to be an essential character with them, transforming nature, deeply studied and wisely understood. The sum of all this makes up our first impression that the two opposites of realism and decoration form the art of Japan, and that in this successful blending, it takes a distinct place, never before filled in the logical history of art.

Some of the compromises made necessary by this combination are interesting. Chinese art is often ridiculed for its complete absence of perspective; but our own practice of copying paintings, imitated in all their modelling and light and shade, upon the curved surface of our vases, is itself an utterly barbaric notion.

The perspective of the vase destroys the perspective of the ornament, which it is impossible even to see from a proper point of view. The treatment of perspective in Chinese decoration is, therefore, the result of a very sensible idea. But the Japanese have improved upon the usual Chinese manner, and have invented an interesting compromise, in which certain rules of linear or isometric perspective are used with a deep feeling for the actual appearance of nature: and by the use of high horizons, so that the different planes shall come one above the other, they manage to frame large compositions within quite an illusive effect. It is owing to this bird's-eye view that they are able to represent crowds and masses of people with enviable felicity, and give the feeling of open air and expanse to their smallest landscapes.

In the gradual separation of decoration and pictorial art with

---

tauric, many-legged, extensible, accustomed to send their heads on hawking expeditions or using their noses with more than elephantine sagacity, as does the female at the top of this same page. Notice the probability of these impossible creations. In the foremost creature the blending of man's cheek with bird's beak; the bird-like skull under the wild hair. See how the clothes and the wings in both are customary with them, and how the wings indicate a short flight and are merely a help. The man with the nose is not doing anything eccentric for him. He is accustomed to it, but he must of course lessen the weight of his burden and stop its swaying by putting his hand under it. His eyes blink too, and his face is wrinkled by the tension. All this the artist has seen in his fancy; within the memory of his observation he has found the projected head, the bent body, the cautious and balanced tread. Hoksai has, if I may say so, studied the manners of these strange creatures, and in other pictures of the bird-men, they always preserve their character, short-winged and strong-beaked, abrupt in motion, whirring in flight, quarrelsome as the quails they are like.

us there was at least this advantage, that the artist was impelled to the individual study of nature that he might mirror the great world in the little world of his picture.

To different origins we shall reasonably look for the causes which have kept the Japanese artist to flat tints and boundary lines in drawing, and have prevented his pursuing others of nature's appearances, and attempting to give the forms of things by the opposition of light and shade, or the influence of colored light. With the harmony which belongs to all good art, Japanese works, if they do not solve the latter problem, offer at least very successful sketches of such solutions. Their colored prints are most charmingly sensitive to the coloring that makes up the appearance of different times of day, to the relations of color which mark the different seasons, so that their landscape efforts give us, in reality, the *place where*—the illuminated air of the scene of action; and what is that but what we call tone? Like all true colorists, they are curious of local color, and of the values of light and shade; refining upon this they use the local colors to enhance the sensation of the time, and the very colors of the costumes belong to the hour or the season of the landscape. Eyes studious of the combinations and oppositions of color, which must form the basis of all such representations, will enjoy these exquisite studies, of whose directness and delicacy nothing too much can be said in praise.

The possibilities of art resemble very much those of life, and outside of this peculiar art we can imagine many openings. We certainly have in the colossal statue of Daibutz (given in the frontispiece), in its serene ideal of contemplation, a surmise of some one of the things that might have been in Japan.

I have no space to consider whether, if the Japanese have an ideal, it can be contained, as with the Greeks, in the dream of a perfected beauty. The sufficient ideal of realism is character. Nor, any more than in Pagan antiquity, need we expect to find in Japanese art that deeper individual personality—the glory of our greatest art—and which may perhaps be connected (however illogically it has been proved) with the education of the Western world by Christianity. That attempt at bringing to the surface some of the subtlest, deepest, and most complicated feelings of the mind, which is the soul of the works of Leonardo, of Michael

Angelo, of Rembrandt, has had apparently no exemplar outside of modern and Christian Europe.

We shall miss that unconscious inferiority of the artist to his intention which so often gives a naïve charm to early works. Art is a slow growth, as slow as civilization; and the consummation of refinement in certain of their designs, meant to be repeated for common uses, is a sufficient proof that it is old in Japan Besides that, we have its Chinese antecedents, its long intercourse with China which has an ancient art history, and the antiquity of some of the few documents we know. All our judgments have thus far been based upon the pictorial art of Japan, the only accessible to us, and open to any inquirer. The questions regarding other forms of art with them—the social questions connected with the position of art among them—cannot be undertaken for want of room.

Inquiry into Japanese art would give material for appreciation of the social state of the artist-workman in mediæval times and in a military race, or again in Pagan antiquity, and for a study of the advantages and disadvantages connected with a fixed social condition: to which comparison the analogies and differences with their Chinese brethren will add help. But it must now be sufficient to have helped, in any way, to call attention to this art, which helps to bridge the gulf between us and the Eastern gardens. It can be the source of useful influences from a living school, equal to any in the study of nature and the use of decoration; and it offers, to all those willing to put themselves in the proper mood, a new and fresh fountain of imaginative enjoyment.

J. L. F.

CHAPTER XV.

INTRODUCTION TO CHINA.

TOWARD the end of March I embarked on a sailing vessel. I had bidden farewell to the "land of the rising sun." With feelings akin to homesickness I watched the green mountains of Kiusiu and the Gotto islands till the last peak disappeared.

After a few days westwardly sailing, and already at a distance of two hundred miles or more from the China coast, the sea water lost its clearness, and assumed a brownish-yellow color, caused by the suspended silt which is brought by the Yangtz' Kiang and Hwang Ho from the interior of China.

This material is rapidly filling the Yellow sea and the gulf of Pechele. Passing a day or two among the shoals at the mouth of the Yangtz' we finally entered into the Wusung river. We were nearly half a day in ascending to Shanghai. On either side of the stream, high levees, covered with grass, shut out the view of the country beyond, allowing only glimpses of tree-tops and tiled roofs. Many Chinamen and dogs were always in sight on the embankments, and the passage of the river was frequently barred by fleets of junks, their decks literally crowded with diminutive natives, whose stolid faces, shaven heads, long queus, and incessant jabbering, produced upon me an impression which was the foreshadowing of the endless monotony of life and character among this great race.

The city of Shanghai consists of two parts, the old walled town, and the foreign settlement, around which there has gradually collected an immense native population, mostly drawn thither from the surrounding country for protection against the rebels. During this visit I found Shanghai anything but a pleasant place. Through the whole month of April there were incessant rains and fogs, rendering the streets of both cities almost impassable. Still I managed to take several walks through the old town, than which a more filthy place can hardly be imagined. The streets are very narrow, often with mud a foot deep. In China nothing is lost; even the parings of finger-nails and the clippings of hair from the barber's shop are bought and sold for manure. I was therefore not so much astonished as disgusted at the frequent occurrence on the side of the street of large open pits, spanned by planks, and intended for the accommodation of the public and the farmer. Even the better streets, which are paved, are so narrow and so covered with awnings that the sun rarely enters, and in this warm, damp climate they are always pervaded by disagreeable odors.

China is probably in the minds of most people associated with the old picture in the school books, of a man bearing a pole with a basket of rats at one end and one of puppies at the other. It is generally thought of as the home of all that is curious and ridiculous, and as the seat of every kind of vice—views obtained not from the early travellers and Jesuit missionaries, who were close observers and intimately acquainted with the country, but from later visitors who were less observing than prejudiced. Confessing that my first impressions of this strange people and their land were extremely unfavorable, I shall pass them by in silence, giving only those, and in their proper place, which were the result of maturer observation.

The opinions which rapid travellers express concerning the character of a people are only too apt to be but the reflex of those of their fellow-countrymen who are supposed, during a longer residence upon the spot, to have had better opportunity to become acquainted with the inhabitants. But it happens that the prejudice and hate of race are proportionate to the degree of dissimilarity in language, religion, and customs, to say nothing of physical qualities. When, therefore, we find in close contact two races, so different in every respect as are the European and the Chinese, neither understanding, nor having anything in common with, the other excepting the mutual love of gain, and where this intercourse has been maintained at the point of the bayonet, we can expect to find but little sympathy between such extremes. The average foreigners in China, being wholly ignorant of everything connected with the history, social organization, and even the true character of the people, look down upon them from the lofty point of view which, during the past half century, has become the conventional stand-point. The more ignorant the foreigner, the more proudly he sees in himself the representative of the science, the intellectual refinement and material progress of the west. To this man the teeming population around him is simply a swarm of chattering animals, useful as producers of tea and consumers of opium. Even if they are human beings, they are only heathen, and, in the opinion of this man, who perhaps would not begin a journey on Friday, nor make a thirteenth at table, they are woefully superstitious. We cannot wonder at his treating them accordingly, when we find him either tacitly or directly encouraged by public opinion at home, and by the policy of his government. He has learned that a whole nation may be forced to consume a poison which at home can be bought only through the order of a physician. With this high assurance of the little value to be placed upon the moral and physical health of a nation, how can we wonder that our average representative of western civilization, acting on a smaller scale, should make the life and rights of a Chinaman subordinate to his own convenience.

I will give here one of the many instances which I saw illustrative of this line of conduct. A steam-boat which had been undergoing repairs, made a trial trip, crowded with most of the leading foreigners of Shanghai, all, like myself, invited for a pleasure excursion up the Wusung river. As we were steaming at full speed, we saw some distance ahead of us a large scow loaded so heavily with bricks as to be almost unmanageable by the oars of four Chinamen who were propelling it. They saw the steamer coming, and knowing well how narrow was the channel, worked with all their force to get out of it and let the boat pass. As we all stood watching the slow motion of the scow which we were rapidly approaching, I listened every instant for the order to stop the engine. The unwieldy craft still occupied half the channel, the coolies straining every muscle to increase her slow motion, and uttering cries which evidently begged for a few instants' grace. There was yet time to avoid collision, when the pilot called out, "Shall I stop her, sir?" "No," cried the captain, "go ahead." There was no help for it. Horrified at hearing this cold-blooded order, I waited breathlessly for the crash, which soon came. The scow striking under the port bow, veered around lengthwise and was almost instantly under the paddles. A shriek, a shock, and a staggering motion of our boat, and we were again steaming up the channel. Going to the stern I could see but one of the four Chinamen, and he was motionless in the water. Among the faces of the foreigners on the crowded decks there were few traces of the feelings which every new comer must experience after witnessing such a scene. The officers of the boat looked coolly over the side to see whether the bow and paddles had suffered any damage; and such remarks as were made upon the occurrence, were certainly not in favor of the victims.

I am aware that in thus describing an incident which I witnessed as an invited guest, I lay myself open to the charge of having committed a breach of courtesy, and I should certainly have passed this by in silence were it not so important an illustration of the condition to which our intercourse with the Chinese has been brought by long years of misguided policy on the part of the foreign and native governments.

The instance I have cited admitted of no excuse, as a few minutes' time could be of no importance on a pleasure excursion. It has long been the practice of foreign vessels to run into and sink any junks or boats that might be in their way, no matter how crowded with passengers these might be; and probably scarcely a day passed without a boat being thus sunk in Chinese waters.

After such an occurrence I was not surprised to see foreigners walking through crowded streets, and incessantly belaboring the heads of men, women, and children, with heavy walking sticks, to open a path, nor at the constant occurrence of similar abuses engendered and encouraged by the absence of any means of redress on the part of the natives.

I would not be understood as bringing a sweeping charge against all the foreign inhabitants of China. There are many noble exceptions, but as such they are powerless beyond the sphere of their own employés.

Having a strong desire to penetrate into the interior of the empire, I planned a journey to the upper Yangtz' and its tributaries. Before beginning the narrative of this trip it will be well to give as briefly as possible a sketch of the geography of the empire, and of the leading features which stand in close connection with the development of its history and civilization.

CHAPTER XVI.

GEOGRAPHICAL SKETCH OF CHINA.

THE eighteen provinces forming China proper, and occupying a circular area nearly equal to that of the United States east of the Mississippi, are bounded on the eastern semi-circle by the Pacific ocean, on the west by Thibet, the loftiest mass of mountain plateau on the globe, and on the north by the table-land of Mongolia, stretching from the plains of the Aral sea to the Amoor river.

The vertical escarpment of this table-land shuts in the empire on the north as with a wall, while two great mountain ranges with snowy peaks, the continuation of the Thibetan Kwenlun and Himalaya, extend from west to east nearly across the empire in the middle and the south. Excepting these two ranges, the conformation of the surface of China is entirely dependent upon the parallel ridges which cross the empire from southwest to northeast, members of the great mountain system which in another place I have called the Sinians, and which has determined the outlines and nearly all the physical features of the great continent, just as the Appalachians have determined those of the eastern part of North America.

Two great rivers, the Hwang Ho in the north, and Yangtz' in the middle, traverse the empire. While their general courses are determined by the east and west mountain systems, they are affected by the Sinian ridges, now following the northeasterly course of these, and now traversing them through deep gorges.

By the intersection of mountain ranges belonging to the different systems, large basins are formed, which are drained by important streams, tributaries of the two great rivers. While these feeders, which form nearly the whole water system of the country are in themselves sufficient to form a great main trunk, the upper courses of the Hwang Ho, and especially of the Yangtz', draining for a great distance the extensive snow-fields of the lofty Kwen lun, supply the vast floods which every summer overflow and fertilize the lower valleys.

In the south a third large and navigable river, the Si Kiang, taking its rise on the table-land of Yunnan, flows eastward to Canton. In the extreme southwest, the province of Yunnan is crossed by the middle course of the Cambodia, the sources of which are supposed to lie among the snow-fields of Thibet. North of the gulf of Pechele and the Yellow sea, there lies a broad depression running northeast and southwest between the mountains of Corea and Manchuria on the east, and the table-lands of Mongolia on the west. The northern part of this is drained by the Songari branch of the Amoor, while the southern part, comprising Shing-king, the newest province of China, is watered by the Liau river, which empties into the gulf of Pechele.

An extensive lowland half encircles the mountainous promontory of Shan-tung. With a breadth varying from one hundred and fifty to three hundred miles, it extends six hundred miles from Peking in the north to Hang-chau in the south. Its southern half is the common delta-plain of the Yangtz' and the Hwang Ho, while the northern portion is that of the latter river only.

Leaving out of consideration the rich provinces drained by the Si Kiang, and the smaller streams on the southeast coast, China proper is opened from its remotest corners by a wide-spreading network of navigable streams tributary to two of the largest rivers of the world, the lower courses of which are united by a ship canal, which, crossing them, extends the whole length of the great plain. These great river systems, the one draining the semi-tropical region of the middle, the other the temperate belt of the north, are the arteries to which first of all the superabundant life of the empire is due. Countless fertile and well-watered valleys, enjoying the most favorable climates, and the adjoining mountains, produce a list of vegetable and mineral material so inexhaustible in every direction, and giving rise to such a widely-branching manufacturing industry as to make of China a self-dependent world. To the unsurpassed system of inter-communication presented by its great rivers, the empire owes the homogeneous character of its population, and largely also its long-continued political unity.

The greatest source of wealth to this country lies in the fertile soil of its great plain, of its river bottoms, and of the foot-hills of the middle and southern mountains. The higher portions of the hilly country, generally either hard granitic rock or compact limestone, seem to be unproductive. This region, which must cover by far the larger part of the empire, seems to have been cleared at an early period of the forests which had probably covered it.

The climate of China, even along the coast, is everywhere from 1 to 3 degrees below that which belongs to its latitudes. At Peking, in latitude 40 degrees north, the mean temperature of the year is about 53 degrees F., while that of the different seasons is about as follows: winter, 29 degrees F.; spring, 55½ degrees; summer, 76 degrees; autumn, 54 degrees.

At Shanghai, in 34 degrees north, the average for the year is about 62 degrees F., with occasional extremes ranging from 24 degrees in winter to 104 degrees in summer. Snow falls here occasionally, and during the winter of 1845-6 there were ten days of skating on the Wusung river.

At Canton, in 23 degrees 12 minutes N. L., the annual mean is 70 degrees, with extremes ranging from 52 to 85 degrees.* This place has the reputation of being the coldest city near sea-level in the tropics.

This variety of climate is accompanied by a corresponding diversity of plant life. On the coast, in the tropical belt, south of the Nanling mountains, there grow palms, sugar cane, bananas, sweet potatoes, yams, etc. "It is remarkable † that here the violet blooms in the shade of the Melostoma; bamboos and conifers mix in the same groves, as well as pines and oaks, while potatoes and sugar cane are cultivated in the same field." On the northern declivity of the Nanling, the southern lip of the basin of the Yangtz', there appear the more hardy chestnuts, poplars, conifers, and a carpinus.

Between the northern and southern edges of the great basin of the eastern course of the Yangtz', a region nearly six hundred miles wide, the low hills and plains are cultivated to their utmost capacity, and the variety of products is as great as the range in latitude. Here the low lands are an unbroken succession of rice, cotton, and sugar plantations, while the low hills are covered with tea fields in the south and middle, and with wheat and mil-

* Stein und Horschelmann. Handbuch d. Geogr. und Statistik. Asien. † Ibid.

let in the north. The few trees seen are generally about the farm houses, and are always of useful kinds, as the bamboo, the mulberry and camphor tree, the orange, peach, apricot, and pomegranate, the walnut and the chestnut, and we may add the grape-vine. It is said that all the European fruits and vegetables, as well as many that are unknown to us, are cultivated in China.

In the extreme north, on the great plain in Chihli, and in the highlands south of the great wall, we find rice almost entirely replaced by millet and a species of sorghum. Even here, in latitude 39 degrees 30 minutes, there is raised a large quantity of cotton; but aside from this, great fields of barley, wheat, buckwheat and oats, and of beans, appear more in harmony with this northern climate. Here also are raised the castor bean, grapes, peaches, pears, apples, and what is with us called the Siberian crab-apple, persimmon, and jujube. Almost the only trees seen in this region are the willow in long fence rows, planted for charcoal, the funereal groves of cypress, and a few ornamental trees, generally the silver pine and the salisburia in the temple grounds.

The dense population of China leaves slight foothold for wild animals in the cultivable regions, and the necessity of cultivating every inch of available ground is the reason why one sees no more large quadrupeds than are needed to aid in tilling. All the tame and wild animals of the country belong to families which have a wide range on the continent, unless we may except the silk-worm and the Cicada limbata, which works the pith of the Ligustrum lucidum into white wax. Butterflies and beetles with brilliant colors abound; even these are turned to account, being sent to the cities in large quantities as ephemeral ornaments for the hair of ladies.

Even in China there are large districts which are but thinly inhabited, owing to the proximity of fierce frontier tribes, or to their uncultivable character. In the far southwest the jungles and wilds of Yunnan are inhabited by the animals common to Further India; among these are the rhinoceros and the Bengal tiger, the latter of which probably ranges through the mountains of the west and north, as it is found in large numbers in the forests of Manchuria and Corea.

The antelope and the deer of the plains of Tartary, and the

argali of the Altai mountains, are found in the alpine region of the northern provinces of Kansuh, Shensi, and Shansi.

The mineral productions of China are as numerous as those of the most favored countries. In the extent, variety, and quality of its coal beds, which are distributed through every province, it ranks second only to the United States. The number of localities where iron ores are found is very great. Through the western provinces there extend immense deposits of salt, from which during centuries past the saline waters have been obtained by artesian wells of great depth. Gold, silver, copper, tin, lead, quicksilver, and zinc are mentioned by Chinese geographical authorities as occurring and being worked at many points throughout the empire. Every province has an inexhaustible supply of marbles and other ornamental rocks, while at several points large mountains of decomposed granite furnish kaolin the basis of the porcelain manufacture.

In the mountains of the southwest we enter already upon the East Indian district of precious stones.

Before closing this very brief sketch of the physical geography of the country, I may be pardoned for glancing at the highways which form the principal routes of travel and commerce between the different provinces. Chief among these are the three great rivers, the Hwang Ho, the Yangtz' Kiang, and the Si Ho. Upon these and many of their tributaries commerce is carried on by countless flat-bottomed vessels, between one hundred and three hundred tons burthen. Smaller boats drain the trade of the country almost from the head waters of all the smaller tributaries. All these craft are propelled by the large butterfly sail, which admits of running very close to the wind. In addition to this they are moved by sculls, by poling, and especially by tracking along the shore. Thus nature has provided the means of bringing the productions of the three great basins of the north, the middle, and the south, to the ocean, the great highway of the world. But the seas of the China coast are dangerous by reason of their storms, rocks, and pirates, a circumstance which has led to an extensive use of more tedious but safer inland routes of communication between the north and the south. Thus trade has long been carried on between Canton and the valley of Yangtz' by ascending the Peh Kiang to the Nanling mountains, and, after portaging across these, descending either the Siang river through Hunan, or the Kan river through Kiangsi.

The products of the extreme south, as well as those of the upper and middle Yangtz', find their way to the far north through the great central market of Hankau, by ascending the Han river through Hupeh, portaging into the system of the Hwang Ho, ascending this and its tributary, the Fan river, through Shansi, and thence being packed on animals to the market of Kalgan, a gate of the great wall, and the chief distributing point for central Asia, Siberia, and Russia. This is the route taken by the famous caravan teas.

But the most important highway connecting the north with the south was until lately the imperial canal. This connected the waters of the Peiho, and through these the capital, Peking, with the waters of the Yellow river, the Yangtz,' and the streams of the province of Cheh-Kiang. Running more than six hundred miles, the whole length of the great plain, it served the double purpose of offering a safe route for large ships, and of draining the products of the most densely peopled area in the world.

These are the great highways of trade, which have long served the commercial wants of this productive and populous land. It becomes a question of very high importance, as to how far steamboats can be substituted for the present sailing craft, and to what extent the configuration of the country is adapted to the construction of great trunk lines of railway.

For several years river steamers of the largest class have run regularly upon the Yangtz' as far as Hankau, over seven hundred miles from the sea.

With the exception of the rapids between Hupeh and Sz'chüen, there is nothing to prevent the carrying of steam navigation to the extreme west of the empire. These rapids are all short, with great depth of water, and could without much difficulty be overcome. It is probable that the larger tributaries of the Yangtz' could be navigated by steamboats similar to those plying on our western waters.

With regard to the Yellow river, we know little beyond the fact that it is a large and turbulent stream, second only to the Yangtz' in size, and that it probably has a more rapid descent in its middle course than the latter. Still there can hardly be a question that its entire course across the great plain, and possibly as far as the province of Kansuh, is navigable for steamboats.

The valleys of the great rivers offer the most perfect routes for opening railway communication between the west and the east. The cities of Peking in the north, and Canton in the south, could be connected by a remarkably direct line of railway. From Peking to the Yangtz' river this would be a perfectly level route, traversing the productive and densely peopled great plain. From the Yangtz' it would ascend the Kan river by an easy grade, and descend the Peh Kiang after overcoming the Nanling, the only watershed requiring to be passed throughout its length.

The amount of steam traffic by rail and water which China is capable of supporting is so great that estimates of its extent would seem fabulous. Indeed, this capacity is about that which a population of four hundred and fifty millions would induce upon that portion of the United States lying east of the Mississippi river.

The ocean is not the only great highway by which China is approached. From early times the "Middle Kingdom" has held intercourse with the remotest parts of Asia. Several land routes connect her with Corea and the Amoor river, and through this with eastern Siberia, Kamschatka, and the northern islands of Japan. By these routes the Chinese obtained the rich furs of the northeast in return for tea, tobacco, and textile fabrics. This intercourse is of very ancient date, and has made a trading people out of some of the nomad tribes of the Amoor, who are now the middle men between the civilized Chinese and the wild hunters and fishermen of Siberia and the northern Pacific.

Further west, two great caravan routes connect the markets of China with those of Siberia. One of these, leaving Kweihwa, supplies all central and western Mongolia. The other, starting from the great market town Changkiakau, or Kalgan, crosses the plateau of Tartary to Maimaichin and Kiachta, where it connects with the postal and commercial highway which extends through the principal cities of Siberia to the great market towns of Tiumen in Tobolsk, and of Nijni-novgorod, the seat of the annual fair, and the eastern terminus of the European railroad system. This is the route followed by the caravan teas which are transported across Tartary on camels and through Siberia on sleighs. It is a remarkable fact that, although the Russians pay for their tea chiefly in silver, it can be delivered at St. Petersburg by this overland route from Hankau on the Yangtz' at a less cost than the same tea shipped at Hankau in a vessel which would take it by sea to the same destination.

Other great caravan routes, one extending north of the Celestial mountains through the province Ili, another south of the same range through Yarkand, connect northern China with the extreme west of Asia. Under the brilliant reign of the Han dynasty, nearly two thousand years ago, the latter of these two routes was safe for travel, and the greatest highway of commerce in the world; it connected the most powerful empires of the east and the west—China and Rome—and, between these, the then flourishing countries of central Asia.

In the west and southwest of China an extensive trade has always existed with Thibet and India, while the great rivers of Further India have been the avenues of commerce with Birmah and Siam.

During the reign of the Mongol dynasty, when all of continental Asia and much of Europe was under the rule of the descendants of Genghis Khan, these routes were all open, thronged with caravans and armies, and studded with relay houses for postal couriers. Where Marco Polo could then travel in safety, even a Chinaman could now pass only at the risk of life, while to a European the journey would be next to impossible. The advance of Russian arms in central Asia is fast opening up that region, and we may reasonably hope that in a few years those interesting countries will be accessible to exploration and commerce.

CHAPTER XVII.

JOURNEY UP THE YANGTZ'-KIANG.

A SUCCESSION of fine days in the beginning of May induced me to start upon a journey up the Yangtz'. Going on board the "Surprise," we steamed down the Wusung river, and out upon the broad estuary of the Yangtz'. The brown flood of this great river, the "Son of the Sea," empties into the ocean with a breadth of nearly fifty miles. It might be aptly called the "father of the land," as the immense quantity of silt rolled oceanward by its current is steadily adding to the continent, and filling up the Yellow sea.

During the first day of our journey the river was many miles wide, and where the shore was visible the land beyond was hidden by the levees. On the second day the tops of hills were seen in the distance rising gradually above the horizon, and promising a variety in the scenery for the coming day. This promise, however, was not to be fulfilled.

About midnight I was awakened by a loud noise under the window of my state-room, which was just astern of the starboard wheel-house. Looking out I found that the engine had stopped, and a number of Chinamen were trying to lower a boat from the davits. Just then the wheels began to move, and supposing that we had merely been aground, I returned to my berth and fell asleep, to be soon re-awakened. We were again standing still, and the Chinamen were making frantic efforts to loosen the boat, while a confused din of shouts and screams from the forward deck betokened some most unusual excitement. Knowing that we had on board a large number of Chinese passengers, it occurred to me that they might be merely a gang of rebels or pirates, who had mutinied in order to seize and rob the steamer. Such things had occurred before in Chinese waters, and the mere thought of it caused me to buckle on my revolver before going forward. The long saloon was empty, and filling with smoke.

Rushing over the forward deck, I nearly fell into a great hole, cut from the port side nearly half-way across the vessel. A man on the opposite side of this hole warned me to lose no time in saving anything I might have of value, adding that although our bow was grounded on a sand bank, there was fifty feet of water under the stern, and that she must soon break her back and go down. The crew and the Chinese passengers were in the boats, and the steamer was evidently on fire. I hurried to my state-room, and after dressing hastily, set about saving first the money, then my charts and instruments, fearing that each instant's delay might make me a second too late. Carrying all my property except some toilet articles and a box of cigars, I reached the bow and found the man who had warned me already in the boat and on the point of leaving. Learning that we had been run into by the "Huquang," a steamer which had been aground up the river for eight months, I rushed back to my state-room and saved my cigars. Such of my readers as are hard smokers will sympathize with me, when I confess that the risk incurred in saving this luxury seemed slight in comparison with the annoyance caused by the privation of it for two days. Before we had pushed off the steamer was in flames.

The collision had been caused by a misunderstanding of signals. Mr. Osborne, the captain of our boat, was knocked overboard by the shock, and although a good swimmer, was never again seen. The collision had actually occurred before I was awakened the first time, and when I had gone back to my berth the boat was fast sinking, and had I not awakened of my own accord I should probably have perished in it.

As soon as we had reached the "Huquang," the latter continued its course down the river, lighted on its way by the flames of the burning wreck.

After a delay of a day or two at Shanghai, I started again for the interior on the return trip of the "Huquang." This vessel was one of the finest and fastest river steamers in the world, and, like the other boats of the line, was built in the United States.

A little more than a day's journey brought us to the wreck of the "Surprise." The hull was burned to the water's edge, and little else was visible but the frame-work and warped rods of the machinery of this boat, which was once a favorite steamer on the California coast.

About four miles above the scene of the accident we passed the point where the Imperial canal crosses the Yangtz' and entered the treaty port of Chinkiang. This city had formerly great commercial importance from its position at the intersection of the two great routes of traffic. But during later years the silting up of the canal, and the destruction by the rebels of industry and trade throughout the productive neighboring country, had reduced it to a miserable condition.

In the middle of the river there rises a high and picturesque rock, called Silver Island, which forms a favorite subject for native artists.

Above Chinkiang we left the lowlands and entered the hilly district, which, surrounding Nanking with a radius of forty or fifty miles, rises like an island from the great plain. As we approached the ancient capital of the empire, its gray walls were seen winding across the tops and along the crests of the hills, but the city itself was mostly hidden by the inequalities of the surface. It was then in the ninth or tenth year of its siege, and few of the monuments of its former greatness had been spared by the hand of war, or the fanaticism of the rebels. Its grand pagodas and the porcelain town were so many heaps of ruins.

The progress of the rebels was everywhere marked by destruction, rapine, and murder. Nowhere did they attempt a reorganization of the industry and society which they had trampled down.

The rebellion seems to have begun among a clan in the mountains of Kwangsi, and to have been called into existence by the persecution of a small body of religious fanatics. A native who had learned something of the doctrines of Christianity and of the Old Testament had founded a new sect. Had the officials left them in peace, it is probable that the rebellion would never have had an existence; but persecution called forth resistance which, after a few easy successes, took the form of aggression, and the small religious sect became rapidly an army of insurgent fanatics. Appealing to the patriotism of the Chinese, they called upon the nation to cast out the foreign Manchu dynasty, and to place upon the throne the rebel leader, who claimed to be a descendant of the

Mings, and to possess the sacred banner of that dynasty. According to old prophecies the Mings should regain the empire in 1852, and the bearer of the sacred banner should be seated on the throne.*

In 1851 the movement had gained large proportions, the imperial armies being repeatedly beaten, each victory giving whole departments to the insurgents. At first the rebels seem to have killed only the Tartars, treating the people at large kindly, and destroying only the property of the Government, and the temples and priests of the various religions. Everywhere, however, they forced upon the people the ancient Chinese costume, and exacted the cutting off of the queus, the distinctive sign of allegiance to the Manchus.

The inefficiency of the successors of the Emperor Kienlung, during the present century, had told sadly upon the administration of government and justice throughout the empire. Theoretically, all the offices are given only to those who prove themselves in character and by competitive examination to be capable of honestly and intelligently performing their duties. During the brighter periods of Chinese history this rule has been followed, and has undoubtedly conduced to the great prosperity of the nation. But the war with England, following it is true after a long interval upon the protracted and costly expeditions of Kienlung against the Tartars, had so completely depleted the treasury that the Government resorted to the sale of offices, the most demoralizing means of recuperation. The first consequence of this course was the transformation of magistrates into extortioners. The sale for ten or twenty thousand dollars of offices nominally worth two thousand, was a direct authorization of dishonesty on the part of the official, and of the establishment around him of the terrible machinery by which the people of his district were robbed.

Every nook and corner of this vast empire, where population treads closely upon and often beyond the limits of production, had suffered for years the evils of this corruption. Thus the people had neither the power to resist the rebellion nor the love of the Government which was necessary to rouse them to extraordinary efforts. They either submitted passively to the insurgents, swelling their ranks, or fled in terror before them.

* MacFarlane's "Insurrection in China."

In 1852 the movement had grown to a gigantic size. The rebels overran the fertile province of Hunan, and captured three adjoining cities, Wuchang, Hanyang and Hankau. Here the leader, giving the executive power to a few followers, withdrew from the sight of his adherents, and, claiming divine attributes, directed their movements in accordance with revelations received directly from the Supreme Being. It was here, I believe, that he for the first time proclaimed his equality with Jesus Christ, whom he styled the Elder Brother. Here also he took to himself wives, who were assigned to him by revelation.

Using the Yangtz' river as a highway and base of operation, the rebels descended to Nanking, possessing themselves of the cities and provinces on their way, and leaving devastation in their track. Nor did the unhappy population of central China suffer less at the hands of the imperial troops, who followed or preceded the rebels. Their track was marked with equal destruction, and with the bodies of the murdered or starved inhabitants. Nanking being taken, it became the rebel capital, and the base of further operations.

The city of Suchau—"the Paris of China"—and nearly all of the fertile province of Kiangsuh, soon fell into the hands of the rebels. This, the most populous of the eighteen provinces, is also the principal seat of silk culture, and of all the arts and manufactures.

Crossing the Yangtz', the destructive horde overran nearly every part of the great plain, entering the province of Chihli, and threatening Peking. Had this movement been better organized, and less remote from the base of operations, the reign of the Manchus would have been brought to an end.

As it was, the rebels left an awful track of desolation. The Hwang Ho (Yellow river), which had for centuries been confined to one course by a system of levees, had gradually raised its bed until the stream was high above the surrounding country. Only by the annual expenditure of many millions of dollars, and the constantly applied labor of an immense force of men, was this turbulent river kept from bursting its barriers. The exhaustion of the imperial treasury by foreign and internal wars, and the official corruption reigning throughout the empire, had occasioned an almost total neglect of this, the most important public work.

On the arrival of the rebels, their ranks were swelled by the disaffected and starving guardians of the river. The complete neglect of the embankments was followed by a breach in these near the city of Ifung. For several hundred years the Hwang Ho had flowed in an east-southeasterly course into the Yellow sea; but at different times during Chinese history it had traversed almost every portion of the great plain. Bursting its northern barrier, this stream, one of the largest in the world, now poured with its whole volume over the plain of Chihli and Shantung, submerging immense areas, and finding outlets in the gulf of Pechele, several hundred miles north of its former mouth in the Yellow sea. When we consider that the average population of these two northeastern provinces is about four hundred and fifty souls to the square mile, and that the region overflowed was by far the most populous, some idea can be formed of the magnitude of the suffering which must have obtained.

In addition to the great direct loss of life, there came the misery entailed by the destruction of crops, and the plunging into beggary of immense populations. These starving millions, pressing in among their more fortunate neighbors, soon reduced the whole country to a condition of famine and anarchy. A necessary result of this state of things was the organization of numerous and large bands of robbers. This I believe to have been the origin of the Nien-fei bands, who have given the Imperial Government much trouble, and have generally been confounded with the Taiping rebels.

During the period between 1850 and 1864, every province of China, with three or four exceptions, had suffered fearfully from rebellions, having more or less connection with the Taiping movement.

Destroying industry wherever they went, the rebels relied upon obtaining possession of the seaports, and collecting the customs of foreign trade as a means of securing foreign recognition, and of continuing the war till the overthrow of the Manchu Government. But at the larger seaports they were met by English and French forces, and they failed to obtain the benefits of this commerce.

In 1860 a new element entered into this long contest. An American by the name of Ward, acting under a commission from the Imperial Government, and assisted by a few daring foreigners, organized and disciplined a force of native soldiers. Thoroughly practised in the Western drill, kept under the strictest discipline, and led into action by the bravest of officers, these native troops entirely disproved all Western ideas concerning the efficiency of Chinese soldiers. Inspired by the reckless daring of Ward, who was always first in the breach, these men showed themselves unflinchingly brave; and as they wrested city after city from the rebels by storm, they won the name of the "Ever Victorious Braves." General Ward was killed at the taking of Tsekie, and the command was transferred to Burgevine, one of his assistants, and like him an American. Continuing in their successful career, the "Ever Victorious Braves" increased the number of imperial victories, until finally, under the command of Major Gordon, a distinguished officer of the English army, they captured the city of Suchau, which next to Nanking was the chief rebel stronghold. The backbone of the rebellion was now broken, and the taking of Suchau was followed in a few months by the fall of Nanking, after a siege of nearly eleven years.

The hope entertained by many missionaries, and Europeans at home, that the Taiping movement would result in a change of dynasty, the christianizing of China, and the introduction of European civilization, was sadly disappointed. Throughout the whole course of the rebellion the insurgents failed to show the slightest power of organization. Their career was everywhere destructive of life, property, and industry.*

But let us return to the narrative, from which the sight of the beleaguered city has drawn us into a digression. Neither Suchau nor Nanking had yet fallen, although one of the longest sieges in history was drawing toward its close.

The walls of Chinese cities generally enclose a large area of arable land, but no amount of food thus obtainable could long support a large population. I confess that it has always been to me a source of wonderment how the inhabitants were kept alive during the long sieges of history. Perhaps the practice at Nanking may offer a solution of the problem. It is said that every morning, between certain hours, there was a cessation of hostili-

* The reader is referred to the Appendix, for several interesting extracts relating to the character of the rebellion.

ties, during which time an immense market was opened in the besieging camp, where the rebel garrison could purchase all the necessaries of life.

Passing out of the imperial lines, we steamed up the river, now through a broad valley with isolated hills rising from the plain, now approaching near to mountain ranges two and three thousand feet high. For many miles below Kiukiang the east bank of the river is determined by a range of barren hills, outliers of the Kingteh group, famous for its kaolin and porcelain manufactures. A high island rock, picturesque in form, and with precipitous sides, rises in the middle of the river. This is the Siau-ku-shan, or Little Orphan island, and the quaint buildings which crown its cliffs have a historical and legendary interest among the Chinese. Above this island, the high hills forming the east bank are cleft to their base, opening to the traveller a view to the outlet of the Poyang lake through a long gorge, with high limestone cliffs, and islands with broken outlines. This gorge is the gateway for the commerce of the fertile province of Kiangsi, and for the great routes of trade connecting the Yangtz' river with Canton, with Fuhkien, and with Chehkiang. The Poyang lake is connected with one of the largest tea districts by an intricate system of river and canal navigation. The cities on its banks have long been the seat of refinement, and its picturesque shores are the scene in which are placed many of the popular romances, and form the theme of innumerable songs. In the wild recesses of the neighboring Liu mountains there are sacred caverns and famous monasteries. It was near this lake that Abbé Huc had the illness which he has described with so much humor. One can hardly regret the Abbé's sickness, since it has supplied us with two such charming descriptions as his own, and that of the author of "John Chinaman, M.D.," in a recent number of the "Atlantic Monthly."

There were at Kiukiang many refugees fleeing before the rebels, and seeking protection in the city, which was now defended by foreign powers. A large proportion of these unfortunates had been well-to-do families, but now, reduced in numbers by violence or starvation, and plundered of everything they had possessed, they were indeed pitiful objects. Mothers, whose husbands had been killed or impressed by the rebels, brought their children to foreigners, begging them to adopt them, and praying in return only that their little ones might be insured against starvation.

Above Kiu-Kiang the river breaks through several ranges of limestone hills, the rugged cliffs and outlines of which render this portion of its course extremely picturesque. Indeed, the journey from Chinkiang to Hankau is one not easily to be forgotten. The river runs for long distances parallel to high mountain ranges, now hugging them close and undermining their cliffs, now bending away and separated from them by gently-sloping terraces, again bursting through these lofty barriers in wild gorges. In other portions of its course it wanders through broad plains, skirting here and there low hills and terrace bluffs, the predominating color in these and in the banks generally being a bright red, from which the water obtains its brownish tint. The hills are barren; even a tree is rarely seen. But the signs of life are everywhere. The gray walls of innumerable cities are constantly disappearing behind the steamer, and others as constantly coming into view before it, on the banks of the river and inland from it, spreading out over the lowlands, built upon slopes of hills, or extending over the crests, or again entirely enclosing isolated elevations. Look where the traveller will, he is sure to see the same gray walls, as dismally monotonous in color and form as are their inhabitants in appearance and in daily life.

At the time of my journey, a depressing air of decay seemed to envelop the country and cities of the entire lower course of the Yangtz'. Dilapidated walls and ruined houses, and an almost complete absence of the shipping which once thronged the river, were everywhere painfully apparent. But this paralysis was easy of explanation, as the causes were still at work. For more than ten years this portion of the Yangtz' had been the highway of the war, along and on either side of which rebels and imperial ists had vied with each other in the work of plunder and carnage. The countless vessels which had once served the trade of the river, had been impressed as transports. Nearly all legitimate trade was destroyed by the war. Small craft, often alternately pirates and smugglers, sailing under the protection of a foreign flag, and commanded by European desperadoes, preyed upon the little trade that remained. It was this state of things, especially the total destruction of the native carrying interests, that enabled steam navigation to be introduced upon this river without meeting with strong opposition. Once inaugurated, it became extremely popular among the natives, whose capitalists became part-owners in the boats, while the travelling Chinaman paid readily the high rates of passage.

At Hankau Mr. Breck, the American consul, and agent of Messrs. Russel & Co., kindly offered me the hospitality of his house, which I enjoyed while preparing to continue my journey.

The cities of Hankau, Wuchang, and Hanyang, situated at the junction of the Yangtz' and Han rivers, were estimated by Abbé Huc to contain an aggregate population of eight millions. Although this estimate was probably much exaggerated, it is still probable that these three cities, comprising a provincial capital, a departmental centre, and a chief market town of the empire, formed one of the largest assemblages of population in the world. Hankau, almost exactly in the centre of the empire, is the focus of commerce for all that immense region which is drained by the waters of the upper Yangtz'. It is also the point of trans-shipment into steamers and sailing vessels for the trade of this region with eastern China and the foreign world. Here I saw clipper ships taking in cargoes of tea for a direct voyage to England. Moreover, it is the starting-point for the large overland trade with Russia.

These cities had been twice taken and nearly destroyed by the rebels, and during the whole rebellion were constantly threatened with fresh attacks. A panic which followed one of these alarms is well described by Sir Harry Parkes, who witnessed it while accompanying the British expedition made in 1861, for the purpose of opening the river in accordance with the treaty.

"On the 18th, rumors were current in Hankau that a body of rebels had appeared in the vicinity of Hwang-chau, fifty miles east of Hankau. * * * These rumors became more alarming during the night of the 18th, and when it was known on the following morning that Hwang-chau had fallen, we witnessed a signal example of that intense bewilderment and alarm to which the Chinese people so readily fall victims. It was generally reported that rebel emissaries had passed through the streets at dead of night, knocking at the door of each house, and warning the inhabitants to take to flight; and though this, if it occurred at all, may only have been the work of local marauders, who have their own objects in promoting confusion, it was faithfully acted upon by all the people. As the alarm spread and it became difficult to procure the means of conveyance, they soon abandoned all care for their property, and sought only to secure their personal safety. The consternation was as great on the Wuchang as on the Hankau side: in both cases the population rushed frantically down to the water-side; and several instances of suffocation in the narrow streets, and in the struggle to gain the boats, are reported to have occurred. Scenes of great distress were observed by those among us who landed to inform ourselves of the state of affairs. We were asked on all sides by the people themselves, for the intelligence we ourselves were in quest of, while others who had made our acquaintance begged us to protect their property, or to aid them in getting away from the place. Darkness fell upon crowds of the people lying with their weeping families and the debris of their property under the walls of Wuchang, anxious only to escape from defences that should have proved their protection, and which, as they are of considerable strength, would, if properly defended, be proof against any ordinary Chinese attack. The noise and cries attending their embarkation continued throughout the night, but daylight brought with it a stillness that was not less impressive than the previous commotion; by that time all the fugitives had left the shore; and the river, as far as the eye could reach, was covered with junks and boats of every description, bearing slowly away up stream the bulk of the population of three cities, which a few days before we had computed at one million of souls. From such a spectacle we could only draw two painful conclusions: the one, that the rebels were held in detestation by the people who thus fled from them; the other, that the people had abandoned all hope in the power of the Government to protect them."

It was just two years after the occurrence of this panic that I visited these cities. Hankau, always an important centre, under the protection of foreign flags and the impetus given by foreign trade, was rapidly becoming one of the most populous cities in the empire.

Crossing over to Wuchang, the provincial capital, I was struck with the fact that while Hankau had far outgrown its former limits, the population of its neighbor had shrunken to a fraction of its recent size. Under the guidance of some ragged soldiers, I took a long ramble along the top of the city wall, which is said to extend fourteen miles around the city. It had suffered very much during the rebellion, and had recently been repaired at an enormous expense. Chinese cities, especially the more important ones, contain within their defences extensive areas of cultivable land, intended to supply the population during long sieges. But the great extent of wall which is thus made necessary, must render the greater number of towns indefensible, and prove a source of weakness during civil wars.

Excepting along a few of the principal streets, the city was in ruins. Grass was springing up on the top of the wall, and among it there was growing the wild strawberry; but it had a sickening taste, which was common to this fruit wherever I found it in Asia. Descending from the wall, I started upon a stroll through the ruined part of the city; but, overcome by the accumulated filth, I was soon forced to abandon the attempt in disgust. Returning to the inhabited streets, these were found to be but little better. They were indeed paved, but being scarcely more than from eight to twelve feet wide, enclosed between two-story buildings, and overhung by awnings, they were rarely penetrated by the rays of the sun. The atmosphere was reeking with the horrible stench rising from foul gutters. It was partly to the walk through these streets that I owed a long illness during the following summer.

Hastening out of this pestilential atmosphere, I crossed over to Hanyang. This city was a complete ruin. Only here and there appeared an inhabited house, while from the top of a high ridge which traverses the town, the ruined walls and dwellings were visible on all sides. This narrow ridge is continued on the opposite side of the river, through the centre of Wuchang, where several streets are said to pass through it in tunnels.

In making the preparations for the continuation of my journey I was largely indebted to the kind assistance of Mr. Dick, of the Imperial Maritime Customs. While I was fearing lest I should have to make the journey alone, I found in the Rev.

Josiah Cox a companion without whom I could hardly have made the trip.

My plan was to penetrate the coal fields of southern Hunan, and thence returning to the Yangtz' river to ascend this to Sz'chuen. But from every side we were warned against entering Hu-nan, as the population of that province was infuriated against foreigners. Several months previously some lawless soldiers had descended the river in boats which they had impressed in Hunan. While at Hankau this rabble had kidnapped an Englishman, and had nearly murdered him on one of their boats. In accordance with the retaliatory policy then ruling in China, the English gun-boats stationed at Hankau had burned the junk on which the outrage had been ommitted. This, instead of being a punishment visited upon the offenders, was an injury inflicted upon the innocent owners of the vessel.

The inhabitants of Hunan, who from their frequent intercourse with Canton had conceived a deeply-rooted hatred toward foreigners, made common cause in resenting what they considered to be an act of injustice. The Catholic missions were attacked, their chapels burned, and the native Christians persecuted, while the bishop and his priests owed their escape only to the devotion of their converts. Although this had happened sometime previous to my visit, the hatred of foreigners was said to be still in full force. The bishop and other missionaries of Hunan were at Hankau, not considering it possible for some time to re-enter their field. The presumption was that it would be impossible for us to travel in a region where men who were in the habit of courting martyrdom, rather than of shunning danger, hesitated to enter. Still we determined to make the attempt. The first necessity was a disguise. Unfortunately for the execution of this plan, nature had made us both decidedly un-Mongolian. Each of us stood nearly a head higher than the tallest Chinaman, and my light hair and blue eyes would have been very hard to disguise. The former could have been dyed, and the color of the latter hidden under a pair of blue Chinese goggles; but an insurmountable difficulty presented itself—I had thoughtlessly had my hair cut close just before leaving Shanghai, and there was nothing to which a tail could be fastened. So we concluded to make a virtue of necessity, and to show that the proper way for foreigners to travel was as nature and the tailors at home had made them. I confess it was not without many misgivings as to the success of this plan that we hastened on our preparations.

Finally, after much searching, we succeeded in finding a passenger boat of about eighty tons burthen, commanded by a skipper who assured us that he was thoroughly acquainted with the waters of Hunan, and of the upper Yangtz'. A carefully worded contract was drawn up under the supervision of Mr. Dick and Mr. Cox, both of whom were well versed in the language and character of the Chinese. Almost the only provisions we laid in were rice, sardines, crackers, and ale.

CHAPTER XVIII.

BOAT JOURNEY ON THE UPPER YANGTZ'.

In order to get an early start, we went aboard at midnight on the 23d of May. The weather was very warm, and, moored as we were at the filthy bank of the river, we slept that night in an atmosphere which was foul enough to disease any one but a Chinaman. Instead of getting an early start we were detained nearly all the next day, quarreling over the terms of the contract; and when we finally cast loose, later in the afternoon, I was already prostrated by a low fever. During more than a week I was too ill to take any interest in the country we were passing through, and when, thanks to a vigorous use of quinine, I felt myself gradually recovering, we had almost reached the entrance to the Tung-ting lake.

Our boat was a flat-bottomed craft, with a house extending nearly two-thirds the length of the deck, and divided into four cabins communicating with each other. Giving one of these to our servants, and another to Mr. Cox's Chinese writer, we made ourselves quite comfortable in the remaining two. By means of sailing, sculling, poling, and tracking, with a crew of nine men, we managed to make about twenty miles a day against the current.

From Hankau to the Tung-ting lake the river runs parallel to a range of mountains, the rugged and barren crests of which, lying some miles distant to the east, form the boundary between Hunan and Kiangsi. Between these and the river the surface is broken with low hills, while these are fringed with broad and gently-sloping terrace-plains, which terminate abruptly near the river-bank in bluffs of a bright-red color. The opposite bank is flat, and with it begins the plain of Hupeh, an extensive lowland, the silted-up bed of a large inland sea of which the Tung-ting is only a remnant. The early historians speak of it as a swamp, but it is now cultivated to a great extent, while the countless lakes, creeks, and canals, forming a navigable network between the Han and the Yangtz', make every part of it accessible.

Passing the departmental city of Yochau we entered the Tungting lake with a favorable breeze. This water has the reputation of being visited by dangerous squalls. Therefore, as a propitiation of the elements, the discharge of fire-crackers and the beating of gongs were prosecuted with more than usual vigor on the morning before our entrance upon the treacherous water. Not trusting, however, to these preparations alone, our skipper kept quite close to the eastern shore. This is much indented with little bays, miniature fiords, shut in by high red cliffs of the terrace formation. In the background the country is mountainous; ridge after ridge, made up of pyramidal and uniformly grass-covered hills, rising away to the eastward, form a green highland extending to the high and rugged mountain range which forms the eastern boundary of the province.

Twenty-four hours of sailing and sculling brought us in sight of the southern shore of the lake. The season of high-water was approaching, and the level of the lake was gradually rising. A lofty pagoda, whose base was washed by the increasing waters, served as a landmark to guide us toward the mouth of the Siang river. This pagoda was one of the few left standing by the rebels in their destructive course. These beautiful towers, which form the most characteristic feature of Chinese landscape, are always polygonal, and built with an odd number of stories, and are sometimes nearly two hundred feet high. The exterior is often highly ornamented and built with glazed tiles. The famous tower at Nanking was faced with blocks of fine porcelain. The walls, always of great thickness, are built to last for ages. Standing in close connection with the Fung-shui doctrine, the strongest of the Chinese superstitions, they exert as the people believe a most powerful influence in controlling certain supposed currents in earth and air, which are believed to be important agents in modifying, for better or worse, climate, crops, health, and even the ordinary actions of man. Strangely enough, one of the strongest objections raised by the Chinese against the introduction of telegraphs and railroads, is that they would disturb the course of these currents and bring calamities upon the nation.

Soon after entering the Siang river we passed the village of Siang-in (hien). Prettily situated upon the bluffs, and abounding in shade trees, it was, as seen from a distance, one of the very few agreeable-looking villages which it was our lot to pass. It is celebrated for its manufacture of rough earthenware, for which the red terrace clay supplies the material. We felt half inclined to suspect that the presence of the trees was due to their value for making charcoal, rather than to any less utilitarian cause. Possibly, had we closely questioned the inhabitants concerning some of the largest and finest of these trees, we should have found that they were being spared till they were large enough to cut up into respectable coffins for some fat Chinamen.

The valley of the Siang lies between high hills, fringed with the same red terraces that we have seen bordering the lake.

Two days of tracking and poling brought us in sight of the walls of Changsha, (fu), the capital of Hunan.

During the past few days we had several times been seriously annoyed by attempts to impress our boat on the part of soldiers descending the river. Hitherto Mr. Cox had prevented them from boarding us by explaining the power of our passport. But as we were slowly moving up the river, along the bank opposite Changsha, a party of soldiers had come aboard and raised the imperial flag, before we were aware of their presence. In vain we urged the rights guaranteed by our passports; they insisted upon keeping the boat. Not wishing to resort to force we made a compromise, by which they agreed to remove the flag, while we promised to remain moored to the bank until they should return with an officer. It was clear that we should have to await their return from the city; and as the river, owing to the inundation, was a mile or a mile and a half wide, with a swift current, we could hardly expect them under two or three hours. We moored under a low bank, the bow of the boat being connected with the shore by a rope of braided bamboo.

A little before sunset several boats loaded with soldiers made their way across the river and landed just above us, and we saw immediately that they had brought no officer. Three of our former visitors immediately came on board and renewed their demand for the boat. Mr. Cox met them forward, and while refusing to give up the craft, first requested, and finally ordered them, to leave us; while at the same time, with the utmost coolness, he prevented any more soldiers from jumping on board at the only place where the boat touched the shore. In the meantime an excited crowd of one hundred and fifty or more villagers and soldiers, armed with swords and pikes, had collected on the bank, and were shouting out to those upon our boat to kill the foreign devils. One of the three, running aft along the platform which surrounded the boat, attempted to beat in the cabin door. Feeling that words would be no longer of use, I threw the door open from the inside, and giving the man a sudden blow as he started back, sent him headlong into the river. This was the signal for a general attack. The mob having neither fire-arms nor stones, opened upon us with a perfect storm of lumps of sun-burnt clay. They were more successful with these than with their pikes, which were too heavy to be conveniently managed across the twelve feet of water between us and the shore; still it was not always easy to dodge their thrusts, and not wishing either to be spitted on such a weapon, or to be beaten to a jelly by their missiles, I drew my revolver, which had served so well in Arizona, and opened fire upon the crowd. Unfortunately, in the confusion of the moment, I dropped the pistol overboard. In an instant, however, I got another from the cabin, and re-opened upon the mob, supported by my companion, who showed far more coolness than myself. Our bullets caused the assailing party to fall back, and before they could return to the attack a new actor, or rather actress, came upon the scene in the person of our skipper's wife. Flourishing an immense knife, she rushed to the bow of the boat, and began to hack away at the bamboo rope by which we were moored, at the same time pouring forth such a torrent of abuse as can only flow in Chinese accents from the tongue of a Chinese virago. In the meantime the crowd, although kept at a distance by our pistols, made her the focus of a volley of missiles. She stood the attack bravely, never flinching either from her work with her knife or from her torrent of invectives. Clearly the Chinaman was right who said that a woman gains in her tongue what she loses in her feet.

Suddenly the cable parted, and yielding to the current the boat whirled quickly into the stream. A new difficulty now arose; all the crew had jumped ashore and run off in the beginning of the fight, except the captain and one man, and these were found hidden away below the deck. We should hardly have discovered them had not the skipper's wife appeared dragging her lord and his companion by their tails. All we could now do was to guide our craft toward a small island which lay about a mile below us. It was already nearly dark, and heavy clouds betokened a coming storm. We could see the soldiers embark and make their way as rapidly as possible across the river, where we knew there was a large force of their lawless comrades, and from these we expected a more determined visit during the night. We had hardly moored to the island before the storm came on, and with such a fury that it was evident we should be safe from any attack while it lasted. It was almost morning before the waters were quieted enough for us to send a man in the small boat to Changsha, with a letter to the Lieutenant-Governor of the province. In this document we complained of the soldiers, and asked for an escort to accompany us up the river beyond the city.

Soon after daylight a boat was seen coming toward us from the town. We watched it rather anxiously through our glasses, not knowing whether it contained friends or enemies. We were, however, quite prepared for the latter event, having all our arms spread out, including even an old "Tower musket," loaded with revolver balls. The boat, which was a large one, contained some twenty or thirty soldiers, among whom we discovered to our relief three military officers.

As soon as these officials were seated in our cabin they informed us that they had been sent by the Lieutenant-Governor to offer any assistance we might need. His Excellency, they said, had already received instructions from the Viceroy to aid us on our journey, and His Excellency had heard with the most profound sorrow of the attack made by lawless soldiers upon the honorable members of the exalted American country, and of the exalted English country; the soldiers, then on their way to Nanking, were desperadoes, robbing and murdering wherever they went, and were utterly beyond the control of His Excellency, or even of their own officers. These visitors gave us to understand that they were instructed to escort us during the rest of our trip on the Siang river; but either having formed an unfavorable opinion of our commissariat, or for some other reason, they suddenly left us a few miles above the city, inviting us to visit them on our return.

During two days we continued our journey up-stream, gathering at every opportunity information concerning the coal districts. Many boats passed us loaded with coals from southern Hunan; but we observed that they were invariably smaller than our own craft. From the crews of these boats we learned that it would be necessary to change our means of conveyance, that even then we could hardly reach the mines in less than three weeks, and that the journey would be attended with much danger, owing to the existing excitement against foreigners. Finding these statements corroborated at every step, I determined to turn back at Siang-tan.

Siang-tan is another of the great market towns—the collecting and distributing point for a large tea district.

Our progress down stream was very rapid.

The hills, which approach the river, consisted of argillaceous slate, limestone, and sand-stone. The last two rocks are extensively quarried—the sandstone in large blocks for building material, while the limestone is burned.

Seeing a large number of kilns in operation at Ting-tan, below Siang-tan, we landed, for the purpose of examining the process. The decided coolness with which the people at first received us soon melted before the polite bearing and "Confucian quotations" of Mr. Cox, and we were soon being shown over the premises. The burning is carried on in circular kilns of from twenty to thirty feet in diameter, which are built up of alternate layers of limestone and coal, the enclosing wall being constructed at the same time with large blocks of the same stone. As the kiln increases in height the outer wall is secured by encircling ropes of braided bamboo.

Here, as everywhere else in the province, I was struck with the neatness and apparent prosperity of the people. It was almost impossible to believe that the horrors of the rebellion had recently swept backward and forward through this land, and that scarcely ten years had passed since army after army of imperialists and rebels had laid waste to complete ruin the fields and towns now so smiling and prosperous. What better argument could be brought forward against the repeated assertions of national decay, and of corruption, moral and physical, social and political, that are charged against this people? Surely the same laws of nature must apply as well to nations, as to the families and individuals of which they are formed; and, as in the human body, the rapidity with which a wound heals is a measure of the soundness of the body, so it should seem that the rapid recovery of Chinese provinces from the effects of gigantic political wounds is an indication of a most vigorous vitality, both national and individual.

The next day after leaving Siang-tan we came in sight of Changsha, and of the dense forest of masts lining the shore for two or three miles in front of the city.

Thinking to enter the town, we proceeded to look up the boat of the officer who had escorted us, and who, being in command of the river police, lived on his flag-ship. Having found this and moored our boat near by, we sent on board our cards and compliments, and soon received a visit in return. Our former guest was this time accompanied by the chief of police ot the city. The latter gentleman had just given orders to facilitate our visit to the Lieutenant-Governor, when we became aware of an increasing distant rumbling noise. Just then the attendants of our visitors rushed in, pale and excited, proclaiming the approach of a mob. Opening the door, our eyes were greeted with a sight which, once seen, cannot easily be forgotten. Some ten or twelve tiers of boats moored close together lay between us and the shore. Beyond these the whole space between the city wall and the river, as far as the eye could reach, was densely packed with human beings. Evidently the news of our coming had preceded us, and the report of the arrival of the foreign devils had spread like lightning. Apparently the whole male population of an immense city was pouring out of the gates. Surging and clashing like an endless and many-colored wave, it rolled down the sloping bank, and advanced over the intervening boats, which rocked and swayed, threatening to go down under the moving mass that was sweeping over them. From exclamations heard on every side, we saw that the intentions of the crowd were anything but friendly. They were not less than thirty thousand strong. Pale, and with chattering teeth, our visitors hurried into their boat, and, beseeching us to flee for our lives, shot across the river. The skipper had gone ashore, but without waiting for him we made quick work in casting loose, and in an instant were whirled into the current. We were none too soon, for already a half-dozen of the unwelcome visitors had sprung on board; and now to their great surprise found themselves prisoners. Now that we were safe, we could look back with a different kind of interest on the imposing scene presented by this yelling mass of humanity. Our involuntary guests protested that they, as well as most of the crowd, had been attracted simply by a desire to see the honorable foreigners. They said, however, that the soldiers were inciting the crowd to mob us.

Many lives must have been lost in the frantic rush of these thousands over the boats, and unquestionably the authorities trembled till they had news of our safety. There is nothing that the Chinese officials fear so much as mobs in large cities. These disturbances give full play to lawless characters, while the force of the police bears no proportion whatever to the necessities of such cases.

Seeking the island which had once before given us a shelter, we waited till the return of the skipper.

For some distance above the mouth of the Siang the west bank is bordered by a lowland, which forms the southern border of the lake, and is apparently a delta-plain, produced by the Siang, the Tsz', and Yuen rivers. This lowland is traversed by many channels, into one of which—the Lung-tan Ho—we entered, in order to reach the west end of the lake without being exposed to the full force of the wind sweeping across a broad sheet of water. The greater part of the lowland was already inundated, and many farm-houses and even villages were partially under water. The inhabitants were fearing serious injury to the crops, and it was with great difficulty that we could purchase from place to place a scanty supply of rice. In anticipation of a famine the authorities had forbidden the sale of provisions to non-residents in larger amounts than was absolutely necessary to keep them from starving. Two days' journey westward brought us again to the lake, and after waiting forty-eight hours for a fair wind, we crossed over to the mouth of a river which communicates through the Tai-ping canal with the Yangtz' Kiang. The river-course was not distinguishable, owing to the wide-spread inundation; but when we reached the canal we found the country on either side of this ten or fifteen feet above the water.

In this, as in most Chinese canals, it is hard to distinguish between the work of nature and the work of man. We were two days and a half with a fair wind in going from the lake to the Yangtz'. The canal was found generally to have over five fathoms of water in the middle, and from three to four fathoms within forty feet of the bank. The width of the stream flowing through it was two hundred and fifty or three hundred yards at the time of our visit, while at its junction with the Yangtz', its breadth was five hundred or six hundred yards. This was during high water; during the season of low water, in 1861, Captain Blakistone found it to be only one hundred yards broad at the entrance. The current from the Yangtz' to the Tung-ting lake was very strong.

We were again upon the broad, swift stream of the Yangtz', or, as it is called in this part of its course, the Kin-sha Kiang—the river of golden sand—a name derived from the gold washings which occur along its course through Sz'chuen and Yunnan. An incident occurred during our journey through the canal, which was followed by some little annoyance. We had arrived during the night at one of the many inland custom-houses at which duties and tonnage dues are collected on all shipping. Having to wait till daylight for the arrival of the officials, we found ourselves in the morning surrounded by a number of junks which had come in during the night. Among these was one which carried a flag with the inscription, "Great French Nation." Knowing that M. Simon, a French gentleman, who was studying the agriculture and horticulture of China, was at that moment travelling on the Yangtz', and thinking that a meeting would be not less agreeable to him than to us, I addressed a polite note to him, which we sent on board by Mr. Cox's Chinese writer. He soon returned, accompanied by a Chinaman, who informed us that M. Simon and his companion had taken another boat for their journey, and that the one which we had seen was then on the way to Changsha, carrying some wine. The man showed great trepidation, and betrayed throughout the fact that he was lying. After his return to the junk it weighed anchor instantly, and made off with all possible haste; but instead of steering toward Changsha, went in the direction of the Yangtz' river. After finishing our business with the custom-house, we thought little more of the occurrence of the morning till we approached the city of Taiping-kau, at the entrance to the Yangtz'. As we neared the shipping we observed the Frenchman's junk sailing some distance ahead of us, and that a large number of boats loaded with people were putting off from the shore to see the foreign devils; but we saw also that these boats invariably turned away from our predecessor and came toward us. Now, there is nothing in the world more trying to the nerves than to be over-run by a crowd of even friendly Chinamen; one must submit to being felt of, stared at, and having the texture of his hair and clothes tested; to having his hat and boots tried on and passed around the crowd, with the chance of their disappearing in the capacious pockets of some acquisitive visitor. And all this must be submitted to until the whole population of a large town has satisfied its curiosity. There is no other alternative than to submit or fight, and the less fighting that pioneer travellers do the better for themselves and for those who follow them. It had been our practice to avoid observation as much as possible in passing large cities, and it was therefore with a feeling of annoyance that we sat in our cabin awaiting the coming development. The boats soon began to arrive.

"Where are the western barbarians?" asked several of the new-comers.

"There are none here," answered our men with perfect composure; "why don't you go to the boat with the French flag?"

"So we did, but they told us there that that was only the baggage boat, and that the barbarians were in this one."

"Do you suppose," returned our men, "that they would be such fools as to use that fine boat for baggage, and travel in this miserable craft? I think I saw the barbarians on that large junk," pointing to a vessel a little distance down the canal. Our would-be visitors, completely deceived, started off on the false scent, while we passed the city, and moored for the night on the opposite bank of the Yangtz'. We ascertained afterward that Mr. Simon and his companions were really on board the junk which carried the flag.

The next day, with the help of a light breeze, we made the town of Tung-tse, twenty-seven miles up the river, where we moored for the night. It is customary for the river craft to congregate in large numbers at night, for the sake of mutual protection against pirates. Thus, along the rivers, certain places have become mooring stations, to reach which the crews of junks bend every effort. At such places there are night-watchmen always walking the river bank, on the lookout for thieves, when they come from either land or water. We generally avoided these congregations, but, reaching Tung-tse toward sunset, we moored on the outskirt of the boats already there, and were soon shut in on all sides by those which came after us. A man has need to be deaf, or born a Chinaman, to endure with composure the ordeal of a night in such an assemblage. The din of a Chinese crowd is always great, but here it is as varied as terrible. The shoutings and invectives of the sailors, during the confusion of mooring, is soon mingled with the shrill notes of female voices. If each sailor makes more noise than his skipper, the wife of the latter makes more than all together. There seems to be an incessant quarrel about food, between the crew and their mistress, who reigns as supremely as shrewdly over the commissariat. But for one word from a sailor, the virago gives twenty, and with a force of invective which forebodes rather a diminution than an increase of rice. Loudest, because nearest, were the deafening accents of the mistress of our boat; but on all sides the same incessant wrangling could be heard, with the woman's voice dominating. After about half-an-hour of this vocal exercise, and when it seemed to be just reaching a climax, there suddenly sounded a gong. Quick as lightning every boat responded. From one end to the other of the vast fleet of junks, from a thousand gongs there poured out a deafening din, tearing the night air with the quickly-growing and dying shrieks and groans of the accursed instrument. The reader, who has often been tempted to violate the eighth commandment by carrying off the morning gong of some hotel, will appreciate my feelings. Hardly had the gongs ceased when a new noise arose, occasioned by the explosion of thousands of packages of fire-crackers. It may be doubted whether the observance of this superstitious ceremony is followed from a belief in its power over evil spirits, or from an actual knowledge of its effect on the female tongue. Certainly the victory was complete. Gradually the air became slightly tainted with the sickening odor of burning opium, and a death-like silence reigned through the night. Opium pipes were burning on all sides.

The worst effects of opium-smoking are probably not proportionate to the prevalence of the habit. Were it otherwise, the increase of the practice must be threatening the vitality of the nation. This vice is one of the fruits of intercourse with European civilization. Little more than half a century ago, this drug was used only as a medicine; at present, the importation amounts to between 5,000 and 6,000 tons yearly, which does not represent, however, the amount consumed, since within recent years a rapidly-growing area in China is devoted to its production. The profit netted by the East India Company from the opium trade, after deducting all expenses, is estimated to have reached an aggregate of £67,851,853 sterling. Who can estimate the consequence of the system, adopted by a Christian government, to introduce this poison? As a violation of the laws of nature, this deliberate paralyzing of a part of the great body of mankind must surely re-act upon the rest of the world. China is adapted, by the formation of its surface, by its climate and resources, and by the industry of its teeming population, numbering one-third of the human race—by all these it is adapted to become, not only one of the most important exporting countries, but also one of the largest consuming markets for the products of other nations. By as much as we diminish the muscular power and energy of this population, by just so much do we injure our own interests, by diminishing their power of production, and their ability to become purchasers.

Above Tung-tse the river makes a great bend, and the character of its scenery changes. The traveller is here approaching the central mountain range of the Sinian system, which, though it probably rises not more than four or five thousand feet above the sea, extends through the heart of China, from the southwest to the northeast, and finds its prolongation in the mountains of Manchuria between the Amoor river and the Japan sea.

A journey of two days brought us around the river bend from Tung-tse to Itu (Hieu). Above this place the river runs in almost a straight course from Ichang (fu). For a few miles above

Itu it is bordered by low hills of red sandstone, but beyond these the mountains rise in towering masses, which grow higher and more rugged till they are lost in the highest range, whose broken outline is visible in the west over all the intervening country. Further up the river the sandstone is succeeded by conglomerate, the massive beds of which are cut through by the river at right angles to the plain of stratification. Here the river-bed is narrowed and deepened, while the current is perceptibly quickened. The shores rise abruptly, often in high cliffs, worn into fantastic shapes. As we approached Ichang the hills became higher and more broken.

A few miles above the city, at the place designated as Mussulman point on Blakestone's chart, the conglomerate is succeeded by limestone: the two rocks conformably stratified, the former upon the latter, and rising with a gentle inclination toward the north-west. Continuing up stream the river suddenly contracts, and the great Yangtz', which a few miles below was over a thousand yards wide, is here narrowed to two or three hundred.

Without previous warning the traveller enters here the Ichang gorge, and with it upon some of the grandest river scenery in the world. The walls rise eight hundred or a thousand feet, overhanging the water in immense perpendicular cliffs of yellow limestone, or forming steep declivities, covered with a luxuriant growth of semi-tropical plants. The river, confined to a deep and narrow bed, rushes with a strong current through this chasm.

Long and time-worn chains are clamped into the face of the precipitous walls. Catching these rusty links with hooks on long poles, the crew moved the vessel slowly against the current, the mast often rubbing against overhanging masses of rock. In other places flights of hewn steps, and narrow paths cut along natural ledges, offer a foothold from which the trackers can drag the vessel by long bamboo ropes.

Deep inaccessible dells, filled with the rich growth of a semi-tropical vegetation, break the face of the vertical walls. Streams flowing from the mouths of caverns high above the river cool the air in their descent, while huge clusters of stalactite which they have formed—the work of ages—show well the chemical power of the smallest drop, side by side with the mechanical force of the rolling river.

The Ichang gorge is nearly seven miles long. Between its rocky walls, the whole volume of the great river, narrowed to less than one-third of its usual width, flows in a rapid stream of great depth, while water-marks, eighty or more feet above the winter level, show how great the rise must be during the season of inundation.

In passing through the gorge we had crossed the whole thickness of the limestone strata from their youngest bed, at Ichang, to the metamorphic rocks which underlie them at the upper end of the defile. From measurements made by me at this point, I found this limestone formation to have a thickness, at right angles with the plane of stratification, of eleven thousand six hundred feet, or more than two statute miles.

Emerging from the northwest end of the gorge, we came into an open though undulating country; low and rounded hills of granite and gneiss bordering the river on either side, betrayed the fact that we had reached the anti-clinal axis of this important range of elevation. The lofty limestone cliffs recede abruptly from the river at the upper end of the defile, but away beyond the granite hills one can trace their bold outlines and castellated forms, as, after encircling the open valley, they again bend toward the river, once more to narrow its waters in the Lukan gorge.

We were now approaching the difficult rapids of San-tau-ping. Here for a distance of several miles the river rushes with a velocity of eighteen miles an hour. Standing on the bow of our boat, and looking at the awful exhibition of the cataract before us—at the great river rushing and tearing down its rapid descent, and dashing over hidden rocks, forming strong eddies and whirlpools, whose great circles sweeping rapidly by covered the whole surface of the river—it seemed impossible that our heavy boat could be made to climb this hill of water.

But the experience of ages has taught the Chinese to look lightly upon these obstacles to inland navigation, and large numbers of vessels, of from a hundred and fifty tons burthen down, are constantly making the passage. The inhabitants of a large village at the foot of the rapids obtain their livelihood by tracking boats past the cataract. Arrived at this place the sailors beat the gong, and the skipper, going ashore with a bag of copper coin, engaged one hundred and forty or fifty men. Great coils of rope were brought out of the hold and laid in readiness upon the deck. The long bamboo tracking-rope was passed ashore, attached to the belts of a long row of coolies, and the work began. At one moment an eddy would favor us a little way, as far as some point of rock, past the end of which the water rushed with fearful speed; then would come a tug. The vessel was connected with the shore by the strongest cables, fastened to the rocks fore and aft, to secure us in case the tracking-line should part. In this way, by the slowest warping, the craft was brought to stem the wild current, her head being kept in the right direction by a long sweep, worked over the bow by several men. Other coolies managing a long spar, on the land side, kept her clear of the rocks, while others armed with poles cleared her from the shore. Every now and then, in spite of all their precautions, violent shocks showed that we had struck on sunken rocks. Then all was excitement. The air echoed with the beating of the gong, accompanied by loud yells, signalling for the trackers to stop, and every compartment of the hold was quickly examined for signs of damage.

Twice our tracking-line parted, and then the labor of hours was lost, for the cables in each instance were badly fastened, and gave way. In an instant our junk was whirled into mid-stream and went spinning around like a top, while at the same time she swept with fearful speed down the rapids. With no little skill our men steadied her with the sweep, and having stopped her gyrations, worked the craft by means of the sculls into a shore-eddy, and so brought us to the shore. Such accidents are not infrequent, and during the headlong course which follows, if the boat strikes a hidden rock complete destruction follows.

It is not an uncommon thing on Chinese rivers to see human bodies floating down the current; but disgusting and painful as this occurrence is upon the smooth river, there was something indescribably awful in the sight of a swollen and discolored corpse, which, coming dashing and rolling down the foaming rapids, swept by us on its way to the ocean. The sands under the Yellow sea must bury large numbers of Chinamen, the victims of internal wars, and of overwhelming inundations. During the last rebellion the smaller rivers in the neighborhood of large cities were often choked with the dead bodies, resulting from the massacre of the inhabitants. At the time of the Manchu conquest three hundred thousand people were destroyed at Kai-fung (fu) alone, by the breaking of the embankments of the Yellow river. * The loss of life by sword and flood is proportionate to the immensity of the population; and of the victims a large part must have found their graves in the recent deposit on the coast.

A remarkable instance of the formation of a deposit of fine material in the swiftest part of the river is observable in these rapids. Granite rocks rising to the surface, near the shore, form an obstruction to the current, which is here from fifteen to eighteen miles an hour, causing eddies in their lee, in which a constant precipitation of sand takes place. Banks of quicksand are thus formed, their tops almost even with the surface of the river. Their sides, too steep to remain at rest, are constantly being washed away, and as constantly replaced by the freshly precipitated material. At low water these banks line the shores, and during the high water season I noticed one more than half a mile long, and twenty-five or thirty feet above the river—the result of some previous very high freshet.

For a distance of six or seven miles the river is more or less broken by rapids, caused by the granite core of the range. As soon as we had fairly passed this succession of cataracts we were near the entrance to the Lukan gorge. The lofty marble cliffs, after having described broad curves on either side of the river, converged suddenly, until they now stood before us two immense walls a thousand feet or more high, and separated only by the narrowed breadth of the river. The gorge is not a quarter as long as the one above Ichang. At the western end the valley widens a little, and the cliffs, again receding from the river, describe a small circle, to converge again a mile or two further up stream. Here they again produce a grand defile, called by Blakistone the Mi-tan gorge. At the west end of this chasm the limestone disappears beneath heavy beds of sandstone, and the traveller has crossed the principal anti-clinal axis of China. From the granite core, which occasions the rapids, the great limestone foundation dips southeastwardly toward Hu-peh, forming the long gorge; and northwestwardly toward Sz'chuen, forming the

* Williams' "Middle Kingdom," Volume I., p. 79.

Lukan and the Mi-tan defiles. This great body of limestone, which appears, from such data as I could gather, to be of Devonian age, exists throughout all China, capping and flanking all the principal ranges of elevation, and sinking far beneath the surface of the intervening areas. Wherever I encountered this formation, I found it to disappear under the rocks of the Chinese coal-measures; just as it does at the west end of the Mi-tan gorge.

As soon as we left the defile, the scenery changed completely: the high cliffs no longer encircled the valley with their lofty castellated forms; the formation to which they belong lay far below the surface; while its uplifted edge, forming a great mountain range, was behind us, stretching southwest toward India, and northeast toward the Amoor river. The wild and broken scenery, to which we had become accustomed, was now succeeded by low and symmetrical hills of the sandstones and argillites of the coal-measures.

A few miles above the city of Kwei (chau) we came into the coal-field of Kwei and Pah-tung. Here beds of soft anthracite are worked by the Chinese by means of galleries driven into the hillside. The seams are very thin, rarely attaining more than one foot in thickness.

We had been eight days in accomplishing the last forty miles of our journey, and the season was so far advanced that I felt obliged to turn back from this point, a step which I was the more unwilling to take that I was now rapidly recovering from a fever which had haunted me since leaving Hankau.

If the journey of the past week had been slow and tedious, the return was rapid enough. In a little more than one day we rushed through the Mi-tan and Lukan gorges, and in a few minutes jumped the long rapids, shooting at a fearful rate past places where we had spent days in ascending, and gliding between the walls of the long gorge at a rate we would gladly have lessened to enjoy its grand scenery.

As we approached Ichang we found the river covered with boats gayly decked with flags, and moving about amid the music of gongs and the firing of guns. Numbers of long slender boats, gayly painted, and representing the heads of dragons on the bows, were running a warmly-contested race. The good people of Ichang were celebrating a dragon-boat festival. This is said to be observed in memory of a much beloved statesman, Wuh-Yuen, who about 300 B.C. drowned himself in the Yangtz' Kiang, and the festival commemorates the rivalry of the people in searching for his body.*

We were seventeen days in descending from Ichang to Hankau. Strong head-winds detained us for days at a time, and these delays were unfortunately on the great plain of Hu-peh, where there was nothing whatever to interest us. The entire country, so far as I travelled in the valley of the Yangtz', is barren of trees, as is nearly all of the empire. The only timber we saw was in rafts, which had come down the Yuen river from the mountains of southwestern Hunan, where it is said to be cut and sold to the Chinese by the independent Miautsz' mountaineers. Here and there about a farm house one may see a few small trees, but rarely enough to break the terrible monotony. And the absence of animal life, other than men and dogs, with here and there a buffalo, is another feature which strikes the traveller. But man is everywhere. Draw your boat along the shore in the most secluded places, and land with the firm conviction that you have at last found a spot where, free from intrusion, you may relieve the monotony of boat-life by a stroll upon the grassy bank; you shall hardly go a rod before your ears will be greeted with the exclamation, Yang-kweidsz'! Yang-kweidsz'! and as if by magic you will be surrounded by the grinning faces and pig-tails of inquisitive Chinamen.

On the nineteenth of July we moored our craft to the wharf at Hankau, and ended our boat journey on the upper Yangtz'. Mr. Cox, to whose companionship I was indebted for the successful issue, and much of the pleasure of the journey, returned to his missionary work, while I prepared to leave for Shanghai by the first steamer.

* Williams' "Middle Kingdom."

CHAPTER XIX.

THE CHINESE AS EMIGRANTS AND COLONIZERS.

IF we Americans of to-day turn from the splendid sunrise of our national morning, to the misty veil that enshrouds the future, we shall see a giant spectre slowly defining its shadowy form against the western heavens.

Let us look and reflect; for it is the mirage of a distant empire, a looming of one-third of the human race. It is the foreshadowing of a problem which only time can solve; but which is none the less one of the most important in the world's history. Let us examine the elements of this problem. On the western shore of the Pacific there is a country, not much larger than the United States east of the Mississippi, in which a population of more than four hundred millions treads closely upon the capacity of the soil for supporting existence. So true is this, that those years in which the productiveness of the earth falls below the average, witness widespread famine and all the horrors that follow in its train.

By untiring patience and industry, by intelligence and the skill attained through ages of experience, by uniting all these qualities in wresting from Nature the last atom she can yield, and, finally, by returning to Mother Earth, with scrupulous care, all that has been taken from her, with interest drawn from sea and river, this race maintains its vitality unimpaired. But it is a struggle for life. So long as the throes of this tremendous struggle were confined to China by strong natural and political barriers, they found a remedy in decimation by famine and pestilence. But the past twenty years have effected as great breaches in the political barrier which the Chinese had raised about them, as twenty centuries have made in their ancient wall of brick and stone. The social and political restraints which have opposed emigration are disappearing, and the first consciousness of an expansive power is beginning to show itself in the maritime provinces of the empire.

A few years since, the confines of Asia and its archipelagoes were the horizon of the world to every Chinaman. The small fields therein opened to a peaceful race attracted many enterprising emigrants; but neither were the openings large enough, nor the facilities for reaching them great enough, to initiate any very important movement. The discovery of gold in California and Australia, and the demand for labor on the distant shores of the Pacific Ocean, gave the needed impulse. Timidly, at first, small numbers went abroad; then tens of thousands; until now there must be nearly two hundred thousand Chinamen on the American continents alone. During these years there has been, also, a continuous stream returning to Asia, and carrying home, in the aggregate, a large amount of money and information. Thus, the number of Chinamen who have seen the outside world cannot be far from one per cent. of the whole male population of the empire. These act as a leaven on ever-growing circles at home, spreading among hundreds of millions those stories of adventure in distant lands, of wonders, of boundless demand for labor, and of high wages, which make individuals think and become restless. Thoughts arise, which, when they become common to large numbers, are intensified to a degree proportionate to the size of the masses swayed by them, until the sympathetic attraction of remote countries produces the tidal wave and currents of emigration. The measure of this movement is the exact resultant of all the social and physical forces which operate in its action. These are, of course, intricate and obscure beyond computation; but they are resolvable, in general terms, into one set of favorable and opposing forces in China, and other sets, with different resultants, for each country outside of China.

In China we have one-third of the human race, suffering from an excessive death-rate and all the misery of an incessant struggle for life, with no remedy but the ability to overflow into other lands, until the population at home shall stand in a proper ratio to the means of support.

Leaving out all other questions, the capacity of America for receiving emigration is at present boundless, as compared with the capacity of all the world to supply it. An eminent English geographer has carefully calculated that the two Americas are capable of supporting thirty-six hundred millions of inhabitants.

Room and subsistence are not wanting. The capacity for absorption of labor is scarcely more limited. The end of the long-continued exodus from Europe cannot be far off; to think otherwise is to believe unjustifiably in a rapidly-approaching decay of the nations beyond the Atlantic. Social and political reforms, raising the condition of the people, especially that of the women of the lowest classes; the increase in industrial prosperity, and the continued drain of skilled labor to foreign countries; seem to be silently working throughout Europe toward the establishment of a proper balance between population and means of support.

The Chinaman in this country was for years excluded from all participation in the development of the national prosperity, and was grudgingly allowed to work only in those gold diggings which were considered worthless by the American. But when a pressing necessity arose for labor on the public works of California and Nevada, the Chinaman was found to answer every need; and now, having become identified with our internal improvements, he has obtained recognition as a necessary element of population—the execution of great enterprises is based on his co-operation. For weal or woe, the Pacific Railroad is uniting more distant extremes than the two shores of our continent.

The facilities for crossing the Pacific are yearly increasing; and so is also the knowledge of America in China. Unless obstacles be placed in the way, immigration will increase rapidly; with additional encouragement it will soon become enormous.

Having no rights, exposed to continued extortion, treated with contempt and indignity, branded as an idolator, and charged with every vice by his scrupulously just, religious, and virtuous neighbors, the Chinaman, feeling that he has no position here, seeks California, as the pearl-diver does the bottom of the sea, and returns as soon as possible to the free air of his native soil. Place these Chinamen on the same footing with other immigrants, and the result will be, that, while many will return to the home of their forefathers, a large portion will make this the home of their descendants. This was and is the case in the Dutch East Indies, where they were less oppressed than in California.

Under these circumstances, if this immigration should be proportionate to the necessity for relief that exists in China, or to the capacity for receiving it here; or, again, if it should bear the same relation to the parent population that the emigration from Ireland and Germany bears to the home population of those countries, the male adults of Mongolian origin on this continent would soon outnumber those of the European race.

When we consider that the prejudice of race is, with us, a part of the foundation of politics; that the moral characteristics of various nationalities become important parts of the framework on which parties are constructed; that the opposing armies which fight with the ballot, and at times threaten the sword, are, to a large extent, massed by races;—when we consider this, and then turn to the prospect of a homogeneous mass of people among us, their male adults outnumbering largely those of all other component parts of the population, and having no sympathetic bond with us in their language, traditions, or, so far as it goes for anything, their religion; then the social and political importance of this great problem dawns on the mind.

To the thinker who has come to look upon the Americas as the birthright of the European under the tutelage of the Anglo-Saxon; as presenting the prospect of a hemisphere peopled with a new race, built up from the best elements of the European, numbering more than twice the present population of the globe; a race which will be homogeneous, enjoying the most complete means of inter-communication by steam and electricity, having one language, one form of government, and one idea of God; to him the startling possibilities involved in the problem before us come as the discovery of neglected data, which may invalidate the results of years of calculation.

If the probabilities of the case bear any proximate relation to the possibilities, the teeming population of our hemisphere two or three centuries hence may have more Chings and Changs in their genealogical trees than Smiths and Browns; for, other things being equal, the predominant blood will be that of the race best able to maintain an undiminished rate of increase; and the vitality of the Chinese nation during a constant struggle for life seems to bespeak for it at least equally favorable prospects in less crowded homes.

With an emigration from China standing in the same ratio to

the home population that the drain from Germany holds to the population of that country, we should have an influx of more than one million Chinese yearly. Ten years of this rate would place upon our soil a preponderance of male adults of Mongolian blood over those of all the other families of man among us.

The perception of this possibility cannot but awaken in the mind of the true American the gravest thoughts. The social, political, and ethnological questions involved are of transcendant importance.

The question of the prohibition or the heavy taxation of Chinese immigration is almost sure to be one of the earliest and most bitterly fought political issues of the Far West. The hostility to the Chinese of the white laborers, especially of the Irish, is already beginning to show itself openly in the most violent acts of intimidation. But it is not difficult to foresee that any legislation which has for its object the suppression of any social element or force that has once shown itself to be a necessity, in rapidly carrying forward the system of internal improvements on which a large part of our material industry rests, must ultimately fail.

We may therefore assume that the recognition of the necessity of Chinese labor in the Far West insures an influx of Chinese proportionate at least to the extent of the great system of public works which will be needful for the growth of the western States and Territories. We shall see, further on, that these Asiatics are obtaining strong foothold in almost all other branches of labor, because they answer the requirements better than any other class of people. It is therefore not improbable that they will find their way, in large numbers, to this side of the Rocky Mountains.

Is it probable that the party warfare of the country will leave this enormous quantity of possible political force in the latent condition appertaining to aliens?

Gaining the right to vote means gaining citizenship, the removal of disqualifications, and the protection of their distinctive interests and customs to a degree proportionate to the number of their votes. Having obtained these, the Chinese emigrant will become, beyond a doubt, a permanent citizen.

With this prospect before us it may not be uninteresting to

glance at the characteristics of this race, both in countries to which they have emigrated, and in their own home.

Twenty years of contact between the two races in California have done little toward removing the prejudice against the Chinese. They have poured steadily into and out of the country; but, surrounded by barriers, they have been forced to form a world of their own. Within this some fifty thousand men have been thriving, while many of them have amassed large fortunes. Many an enterprise, too, has swamped in failure, which would have given brilliant returns but for the tyranny of white workmen who prevented the employment of cheap Chinese labor. This tyranny is met with at every step: from the court-room, where the Chinaman is denied the right of giving evidence in mixed cases, to the "gold diggings," where white rowdies, acting as self-appointed collectors, levy the mining tax, which is never assessed upon Americans. Recently, however, various manufacturers, farmers, and others, braving that wild beast, the Irish mob, have begun to employ Chinese labor, and with such success that capitalists see in it the sinew and muscle of the Far West.

A writer in the "Overland Monthly," March, 1869, says of the Chinamen: "What they want is employment and such pay as will support them and leave something over to send back to the father and mother, or to the wife and children, left at home. So accustomed have they always been to give a full and honest day's labor to those who have hired them, that they expect to give their employer the service of their muscle and their skill during all the hours of the day, only asking a reasonable time for meals, together with the stipulated wages when their work is done."

The owners of woollen factories praise them as the best of workmen. The officers and foremen of the Central Pacific railroad—on which some ten thousand Chinamen are said to be at work—speak no less highly of them. Their work is full and honest, no lagging and story-telling, no whisky drinking, and few fights. Overseers declare that they can drill more rock and move more dirt with Chinamen, than with an equal number of men who claim this kind of occupation as their speciality. What they lack in bodily vigor is made up in persistency and steadiness.

Indeed, California is just beginning to feel how suicidal her course toward Asiatic labor has been, and she is finding that her material prosperity is increasing apace with the innovation upon that policy. The Chinese are found now in woollen, paper, and powder mills; in the borax works; in the hop plantations, fruit orchards, and vineyards; following the reaping machines on farms, and working the salt-pits on the coast; doing almost universally the cooking, and engaged in hundreds of branches of industry that would be impossible without their cheap labor.

The sure result of this will be that, in a few years, the small savings of these workmen will, by accumulation, transform the coolie of to-day into the capitalist, contracting to build railroads, owning large farms or factories, and lines of ships, and making great commercial combinations. This is certain, for no people on the face of the earth advance so unswervingly in the accumulation of capital; and in its investment from childhood upward they combine the shrewdness of the Jew with the many-sidedness of the Yankee. What the Jews have been in banking, the Chinese may easily become in general commerce and industry on the Pacific coast.

On the island of Java, where they have long been tolerated, the Chinese number not far from 150,000, the greater part having more or less Javan blood. The oppression of the Dutch is the cause of the population not being larger. "They are obliged to pay a mulct for leave to enter, and a larger one for permission to quit," besides a poll-tax; none of which imposts are levied on other foreigners. During the last century they were so badly treated that they revolted, and in 1740 were attacked in their quarter in Batavia, when ten thousand of them are said to have been slaughtered. Sir Stamford Raffles, writing in 1817, says: "The most numerous and important class of foreigners in Java are the Chinese, who do not fall short of 100,000, and who, with a system of free trade and free cultivation, would soon accumulate tenfold by natural increase within the island and gradual accessions of new settlers from home. They arrive at Batavia to the amount of a thousand or more in junks, without money or resources; but by dint of industry soon acquire comparative opulence. There are no women in Java who came directly from China; but as the Chinese often marry the daughters of their countrymen by Javan women, there results a numerous mixed race which is often scarcely distinguishable from the native

Chinese. Many return to China annually in the junks, but by no means in the same numbers as they arrive. They are governed in matters of inheritance and minor affairs by their own laws, administered by their own officials appointed by the Dutch governor. They are distinct from the natives, and are in a high degree more intelligent, more laborious, and more luxurious. They are the life and soul of the commerce of the country. In the native provinces they are still the farmers of the revenue, having formerly been so throughout the island."

Beginning on their arrival as coolies and laborers, they soon accumulate enough to work independently, and many of them amass large fortunes. They have obtained nearly the monopoly of the native produce, and an uncontrolled command of their market for foreign commodities. Their industry embraces the whole system of commerce, from the greatest wholesale speculations to the most minute branches of the retail trade. In their hands are all the manufactories, distilleries, potteries, etc., and they have large coffee and sugar plantations. Their means are increased by their knowledge of business, their spirit of enterprise, and their mutual confidence. They are equally well adapted for trade or agriculture.

In the English colony of Singapore, 50,000, out of a population of 80,000, are Chinamen, chiefly from the island of Hainan. Here the Chinese have obtained a strong foothold, and, under the full protection of English law, are accumulating great fortunes. Nearly all the trade is under their control, and this represented, in 1867, $35,000,000 imports and $28,700,000 exports. Carrying with them and retaining their innate energy in a country where both the natives and Europeans succumb, morally if not physically, to the enervating climate, they are absorbing every department of labor. The writer was told some years since that the English owners of a large machine shop at Singapore were gradually removing their English workmen and replacing them with Chinamen, having found the latter more docile, sober, and enduring, and, with the same amount of instruction, equally skilful. So successful is their competition, that Parsees, Jews, and Europeans can retain no foothold in face of it.

The growth of Chinese population and industry in the East Indian Archipelago is already a matter of great significance. In it we may see the coming solution of an important problem. The vast areas of tropical lands, insular and continental, have hitherto been, comparatively speaking, a closed world. And yet "the warm regions yield larger returns of those plants they have in common with the temperate zones, and have peculiar plants which yield more nourishment from the same area. Thus maize, which yields forty-fold or fifty-fold in France, gives one hundred-and-fifty-fold, on an average, in Mexico." "Humboldt estimates that an *arpent* (five-sixths of an acre) which will barely support two men when sown in wheat, will feed fifty with bananas."

A good authority has given the following tabular statement of the relation between latitude and productiveness.

Latitude	0 deg.	15 deg.	30 deg.	45 deg.	60 deg.
Productiveness	100	90	65	35	12 1-2

It is this excessive bounty of tropical nature that feeds the Southern races without labor. And the absence, during ages, of the necessity for labor in these regions, has unfitted the natives for active participation in making their countries contribute their full share to the needs of mankind. But the time must come, sooner or later, when these vast forests and jungles will be the granaries from which the deficiencies in the production of other lands will be made good; when they will stand in the same relation to other countries that our prairies and the wheat-fields of Russia hold to manufacturing England, or that Siam is just beginning to hold to China; and when the great wealth of raw material—greater by far than we as yet appreciate—which is contained in the vegetable world of the tropics, will be a necessity to countless manufactories, supplying comforts and luxuries to largely increased populations over the whole world.

The Chinese alone, of all races, have shown themselves able to maintain vigorous moral and physical vitality in the unwholesome and enervating climates of the South. Wherever they go and are allowed a fair field, they turn their attention to the discovery and development of the resources of the land in every direction known to their experience, and with fully as much good judgment, energy, and success, as are shown by the European. Indeed, they possess, in an eminent degree, the qualities that are essential in colonizers, especially that strongly-marked national individuality which enables them to retain the best characteristics of their race in the midst of the effeminate customs of the inferior natives. The ability to thrive in the most extreme climates is a remarkable characteristic of this people. We have just seen how well they resist the enervating and unwholesome climate of the tropics. The writer has also seen them—collected together from different parts of the Chinese empire—pursuing, in considerable numbers, the different branches of their industry, on the confines of Tartary and Siberia, where the mean annual temperature is thirty-two degrees (Fahrenheit), and where the mercury sinks, every winter, to sixty degrees below zero.

Whatever may be the future of China proper, it is perhaps not too much to foresee in the mutual adaptation which exists between tropical regions and Chinese colonization, the germ of a growth in which the best elements of their own and the western civilizations will blend to raise the offshoots of China to the rank of great powers in the councils of the world.

But it is in their own home and in the record of their national growth that we must seek the most important data for estimating the Chinese character. The limited space at my disposal admits of only a superficial glance at the outlines of this record, and the principles on which the social and political organizations rest. For the practical worth and working of these principles, we have a measure in the present social and political condition of the empire.

The most striking features in the history of China are the persistency of its civilization and its national vitality, which seems still undiminished notwithstanding the great age of the empire. This civilization is native to the soil. At every step we find unmistakable proofs that in remote times the ancestors of the race lived under a patriarchal government. The earliest records describe them as entering China from the northwest, and we know that in that direction, upon the high table-lands of central Asia, between Thibet and the Tienshan, there existed a civilization which was partly pastoral, but acquainted also with many arts, and in which the use of iron was known at the remote period preceding the separation of the earlier branches of the Arian race. Our own ancestors, and those of the Chinese, were perhaps near neighbors at that epoch. In entering China the latter found it occupied by an aboriginal race of which remnants live, to this day unconquered, in the southern and western mountains. The earliest records and traditions, carrying us back far into the uncertain period of history, show us the founders of the empire gradually forming colonies through the land, and carrying on defensive wars against the northern hordes, at the same time that they conquered both the natives of the soil and the natural obstacles in the way of their expansion.

Already in the dawn of their written history, we find them carrying out a great enterprise, building works to control the waters of the Yellow river—one of the most ungovernable streams of the earth—by confining it between dykes several hundred miles in length, to prevent its destructive inundations; an undertaking the maintenance of which, even at the present day, forms a heavy tax on the whole empire. Thus, in the infancy of the nation, there existed the germs that were necessary to its wonderful growth.

Every essential feature of their civilization, moral, social, political, industrial, is the offspring of their own minds. More than this, from China there have radiated many of the fundamental features of Asiatic and even of European civilization. The mariner's compass, printing, and gunpowder, were early inventions of that country, and there is little doubt that they were directly or indirectly introduced into the West during the reign of the Mongol dynasty, when so many Europeans wandered freely through all Asia. It has been claimed that the first printed copy of the Bible was made in China. The observing traveller in that country will see at every step the prototypes of familiar objects in common use with us and in Europe.

It has often been made a reproach to the Chinese, that their inventions have remained unperfected. This is certainly a remarkable fact, when we consider the fertility of mind necessary to have originated, throughout, such a civilization; but it would seem that the perfecting of the results of thought and labor is, to a certain extent, dependent on their transplantation into other countries, and on the reaction upon each other of different kinds of civilizations. China has ever been too isolated to enjoy the benefits of this interchange, although there is reason to hope that such an era is now dawning. It must also be remembered that China has ever been a world within itself; sufficient to itself.

Having no competitors, their inventions stopped at the point where the desired end was attained; they were intended to be labor-aiding rather than labor-saving. It would seem that with this isolation, the very fact that the Chinese civilization is indigenous would go far toward explaining the persistency of its type.

The principles upon which the whole social and political fabric of the empire is based had already been established, and had taken a firm root in the national mind in early historical times; and so firmly were they fixed that every attempt to overthrow them has ended in the extinction of the aggressive dynasties. These principles are, *paternal and filial duty, and individual responsibility for the public welfare.* As the Emperor is the son of Heaven and the father of the people, he is responsible to heaven for the well-being of the nation; a portion only of his power is delegated to the officers of the government. So also, in the family, the parent is supreme, but also responsible for the conduct of the children. The entire population of a city is responsible for the citizens; each ward, for its families; each family, for its members. No crime is greater than the violation of filial duty in the family relation, and all crimes acting against the public good are brought to the doors of the public sponsors.

But the Chinese, always too material and practical a people to vest the control of the imperial will in heaven alone, established, so far as we know, first among mankind, the principle that the will of the people and the will of heaven are synonymous. In the Shu-King, compiled by Confucius, 500 B.C., from authorities much more ancient, we find the following axiom: "That which heaven sees and hears manifests itself in that which the people see and hear." "That which the people judge worthy of reward and of punishment indicates what heaven desires to reward and to punish." Again it is said in the Chung-King: "The wise emperors of ancient times used the eyes and ears of the empire to see and hear, for the wishes of the people were their wishes, since it is in the wishes of the people that the intentions of heaven are manifested." Believing thus firmly that "the voice of the people is the voice of God," a council of the wisest men of the empire, themselves raised from the people, has ever surrounded the throne, holding the position of censors, memorializing the Emperor on the state of the country, and generally not hesitating to risk their lives in criticising a wrong policy.

As the people are the children of the Emperor, they are all equal, as members of one family. There is no distinction of class. The descendants of Confucius have, indeed, by that title, certain privileges of nobility, and the members of the Imperial family form, during the existence of a dynasty, a class of nobles; but they enjoy only a few slight prerogatives, which end with the ninth remove. Whenever a citizen has rendered some signal service to the state, advancing the public good, he is ennobled, receiving certain titles and privileges, but these cease at his death, his descendants having no further share in them than the honor of being his offspring. As no man can be greater than his father, the whole line of ancestors is ennobled. Thus, an aristocracy is formed, indeed, but it is wisely perpetuated backward into the other world.

All being equal, competition for office is open for all. Education is universal, and proficiency in scholarship forms the basis of this competition. The government, it is true, appoints most of the officials, but they are chosen from those who, in the successive competitive examinations, take the highest honors.

That these principles have not merely been acknowledged, but that they have been the true mainspring, acting weakly at times it is true, the Chinese nation at this day is a standing proof. Among them alone, of all peoples, has the principle that forms the basis of our own government, the equality of man, existed through all history.

The early philosophers of China taught these doctrines, as a moral and political code, and as the only just basis of government. At that time the country was split up into numerous feudal kingdoms; but when, some time after the death of Confucius, the empire was consolidated, the doctrines of the great teacher became gradually the rule of action, and until the present time they have never lost ground in their hold upon the national mind. As a code of morals, it is not venturing too far to say that the writings of Confucius have been and still are as much respected as is the creed of any other people.

The universal esteem in which scholarship has ever been held has made education one of the chief aims of life to a greater degree in China than in most other nations. An aristocracy of intellect assumes here the position which in other countries is assigned to birth or wealth; schools are universal, and the proportion of the inhabitants who are unable to read and write is very small. The classics and history of their own country are very generally studied. That their ability to learn is not confined to the groove of their own system of study is shown by the instances of Chinese educated in the West. About twenty years ago two boys, children of very poor families, were sent to America to be instructed. After leaving the school at Munson, one went through Yale, and in graduating took the highest place in English composition; the other carried off the highest honors in surgery and botany in the University of Edinburgh. Since that time the first has carried the experience gained in the West into the conduct of his business in China, and the other is esteemed by the European residents of the English colony of Hong-Kong as one of the best surgeons in the East. The science of war is considered inferior to scholarship, and the Chinese are essentially a peaceable people, although they have carried on great wars during different periods of their history.

The power of the central government is felt but lightly throughout the empire. There is a practical decentralization which leaves a wide scope for free action to the provinces and their subdivisions; this is exemplified in the application of the revenues, excepting maritime customs, to the use of the districts in which they are raised. The government of China is really one type of democracy, as that of Japan is of despotism. In China the people are represented in the government, in that, though all the principal offices are filled by the Emperor, they are filled from the people by competitive examination. This is the theory; practically many offices are sold to raise money, as during the wars with England and the rebellion. The central government is felt chiefly when its appointees are corrupt; but the power of the people is generally great enough to cause removals in such cases. Their faculty of organization and self-government showed itself repeatedly during the late rebellion. The British consul at Ning-Po paid them a high tribute in this respect, in praising the perfect order and self-government which was shown for a long time at that place, when its population, greatly increased by the crowds fleeing from the rebels, was abandoned by its officials and left to take care of itself.

Having no fear of the future world, they meet death with great courage, dreading it less than continued pain. The family ties are very close, and family honor is the strongest check on their actions. Their sense of commercial honor is deep, and my own experience, in central and northern China, leads me to think that honesty is quite as general there as in other countries. The existence of hospitals, founded by private charity, for the sick and for foundlings, and for other purposes, proves that the Chinese are not negligent of social responsibilities. They are proverbially industrious; and could we measure the amount of productive manual labor performed throughout the world, without the aid of modern labor-saving machinery, we should probably find that this third of the human race accomplishes not less than from six-tenths to seven-tenths of the whole.

It is no slight tribute to say that during nearly 5,000 miles of travel, in this closely peopled land, the writer never saw a drunken Chinaman.

The Chinese have been charged with being, as a people, corrupt beyond measure, given over to every abomination, and practising infanticide to the extent of destroying one-quarter of the female children; but it is the opinion of Doctor Lockhart, an eminent medical missionary, who has studied the question many years in different parts of the empire, that the latter crime is (in proportion to the population) no more frequent, or perhaps less common, than it is in its various forms in England and America; and it should seem that the healthy and moral condition of society is proved by the vitality of the nation, the overflowing population, and the rapidity with which gigantic wounds in the national body are healed. Of course the aggregate of crime must be very large, especially in the great cities; but it is doubtful whether it is greater, in proportion to the population, than among the nations of the West.

With all the admiration a careful observer must have for China, it is certainly not a pleasant country for a foreigner to live in, unless he recognize and keep always before him the fact that organic matter, in decaying and giving nutriment to plants, loses every vestige of its former character. There is too much of the human element; go where you will, look where you will, it is there. In the more closely peopled parts the traveller is surrounded by a turbid stream of life, while he treads a soil, almost human, the ashes of the unnumbered millions of the past; the very dust which he breathes and swallows is that of a charnel house. The water of wells is everywhere impregnated with the products of organic decay, and the rivers are the sewers of countless cities.

On the densely-peopled plain all the organic and much of the mineral ingredients of the soil must have made many times the circuit of plant and animal life; in other words, everything that goes to make and maintain the human body has formed part of human bodies which have passed away.

Few foreigners have the courage to enter the larger southern towns in summer, so horrible is the air. In the neighborhood of great cities on the delta plain, where water is found just below the surface, one may ride for miles always in sight of coffins bursting in the scorching heat of the sun, and breeding the pestilence that yearly sweeps off the surplus population.

What I have attempted to make conspicuous, is the fact that the spirit of the Chinese, as shown in their enterprise and energy as colonizers, in their commercial character and faculty of organization, in the democratic idea of the political equality of man, in the practical decentralization of their government, and in the universality of education and the making of education a necessary qualification for office, is in harmony with the spirit of the present age. This is the strong armor of the race, its safeguard in the future struggle for existence, by which it is clearly distinguished from those inferior races whose social and political systems belong to periods long past, and differ so much from our own that they fall at the first contact with us.

We have seen that there exists in China a boundless source of emigration, and the necessity for emigration; that the capacity of America for receiving this emigration is comparatively unlimited; that the emigration will be at least proportionate to the encouragement offered; that the encouragement is springing into existence through the recognition of the Chinese as a necessary element for the development of the resources of the Far West; that the immense influx of these people will constitute a possible political power which cannot remain latent, and that the attainment of the privileges of citizenship will make of them a fixed instead of a floating population, which, so far as anything we know to the contrary, may at no distant date largely outnumber the European element. The first question which naturally rises, is, in what can this people contribute to our material prosperity? It is not difficult to answer to this that by reason of their many-sidedness, their adaptability to all branches of industry, they can contribute more than any other foreign element in the first generation. They can supply labor for the house and field, for building railroads, for working in mines and factories, for every need on sea and land. Within the really impassable limits set by nature, they alone can render productive vast tracts of land, the cultivation of which is essential to the prosperity of our mountain territories. They can contribute largely to our wealth and that of the world by their saving of material, and by forcing us, through competition, to become more economical in this respect. They can advance greatly our material prosperity, not only by the product of their labor in working for Americans, but by their independent enterprise as capitalists. Indeed, the lowering of the price of labor in America, through Chinese immigration, taken in connection with the almost certain rise in price in Europe, appears to offer the best solution of the vexed question of free trade, by placing us on an equal or superior footing with Europe in the manufacture of those things which now require protection. It should seem that Chinese emigration, organized on the most liberal plan, in conformity with the emigration laws of China, and under the responsible guidance of Chinese contractors, would rapidly raise our Southern States to a height of prosperity never yet reached by them, and render possible the completion and maintenance of great works, necessary to control the overflow of the Mississippi, and to drain unproductive and malarious regions.

Will the price at which these benefits shall be gained be too high? Every one will answer this according to his own way of measuring the future by the past. But he who sees in events the resultants of social and physical forces, the operation of great laws, progressive in their action and tending toward that millennium when every part of the earth, according to its natural endowment, shall justify its existence, by contributing its full share, as a part, to the welfare of the whole; toward the unification of mankind by the assimilation of the best parts of its different races into a new type—who believes that

Through the ages one increasing purpose runs,

will feel the least anxiety in contemplating the future. To the charge that they will largely outnumber the Americans, absorbing many branches of industry and competing in all, he will answer that they can do so only by being able to compete with the European element; in other words, by being really equally efficient, and thus justifying their right to citizenship. To the assertion that their use of opium threatens the addition of another national vice to those we have already, he will reply that the rapid spread of the use of this drug, a use of only some sixty years' standing in China, was induced by natural causes, acting in a country which had reached an abnormal condition, and that it can exist as a national habit only where it is a natural necessity. The long-continued generations of temperance of this people show their normal condition, and we have little reason to fear that half a century of opium smoking can destroy the deep-seated, inherited vitality of the race, or have fixed it as a constitutional vice upon those who will emigrate hither.

The political aspect of the question is that of the most immediate importance, for many obvious reasons. Nothing is more certain than the impossibility of a foreign race continuing to live and increase, in America, in other than two conditions, viz., either under the animal-breeding system of slavery, or (and probably only) by being equally strong with the European element, in the average of all things which constitute strength in this age. The ability of any people to prosper, multiply, and co-exist among us, proves them to possess an average equality with us when measured by our standard, deficiencies in some points being compensated in others—these differences being desirable in the same degree that individuality is desirable. If an inferior race, or large bodies of vicious and criminal people, prosper and multiply, it does not invalidate this rule, but rather shows that our actual measure, on certain points, is far below our theoretical standard. If the Chinese, having the exercise of equal rights in a fair field, should prove themselves undesirable citizens, it would be proof of inferiority, of inability to contribute their full share to the general good; and the inability to compete with their neighbors would inevitably result in their disappearance from the arena as important rivals.

In view of all the possibilities of the case before us, it becomes evident now, more than ever before, how important it is that we should turn our energies toward Americanizing the foreign elements of our population. A large Chinese emigration is the strongest argument against immediate and unqualified suffrage. With the prospect of an unparalleled influx of Chinese, it is of immediate importance that we insist upon their understanding our social and political organization before giving them a voice, and this can be done only by insisting upon a residence of several years in the country, and by an educational test, which should not be less than the ability to read and speak the English language. Indeed, this is only an additional illustration of the necessity for an educational qualification, in the matter of citizenship in general, and it should seem sufficiently clear to convince even the most confirmed advocates of unqualified suffrage.

The danger most to be guarded against, is the enactment or continuance of special legislation with regard to Mongolians. Everything which tends to exclude them from the rest of the community, and, in a greater degree, everything which denies to them—as do practically the laws of California—the common rights of humanity, not only affects seriously the character of the aliens and retards the growth of the region in question, but reacts most injuriously on the European element, producing those moral evils which were the worst results of slavery with us—a re-action which is the curse following everywhere intercourse between the European and non-European races. To suppose that a whole state or nation is able to rise above all prejudice of race, to look upon such a question from a cosmopolitan standpoint, is almost the same as supposing the average intellectual level of the people to be on an equality with that of its most liberal minds; but it should not be demanding too much to expect to find this quality in the lawgivers of a land which claims that "all men are created equal;" especially should we look for it in the consideration of a question which pre-supposes an influx of Chinese by millions.

CHAPTER XX.

PEKING AND ITS NEIGHBORHOOD.

AFTER a sojourn of half a month in Shanghai under the hospitable roof of Mr. Edward Cunningham, I embarked on a steamer for Tien-tsin, the port of Peking and in due time sighted the low coast of the gulf of Pechele and the mouth of the Pei-ho. As we entered this river we passed the mud flat which was the scene of the terrible slaughter of English troops that led to the war of 1860. The entrance to the river is guarded by two large forts, the walls of which are almost washed by the high tides, while at low water a broad mud flat is exposed for some distance from the shore. The English plenipotentiary arriving at the mouth of the river with the intention of ascending the stream to Tien-tsin and Peking for the purpose of ratifying the treaty of the previous year, found the entrance effectually barred by stakes. The attempt to pass these being met with resistance from the shore, a force of several hundred men was landed upon the flat at low-water to storm the fort; but before they could reach the walls these unfortunate men became helplessly entangled in the mud directly under the enemy's guns. Between this fire and the rising tide nearly the whole force perished in sight of the vessels, which were unable to give them assistance.

The Pei-ho is a narrow and winding stream, deep enough to admit, as far as Tien-tsin, any craft which can cross the bar at the mouth; vessels drawing more than eight feet can pass the straight reaches only at high water.*

At different times within Chinese history this channel below Tien-tsin has been the lower course of the turbulent and wandering Yellow river.

Tien-tsin (Heaven's Ford) is a city of about 400,000 inhabitants. Lying at the junction of the imperial canal with the Pei-ho, it was, until the destruction of the former, a place of impor-

* Williams' "Chinese Commercial Guide."

tance in the internal trade. The chief exports are pulse, fruit, deers' horns, furs, wools, wax, flint-steels, and rhubarb. Toward the end of the American war some cotton was also shipped from this port.

The most comfortable route to the capital is by boat, but as this involved a four days' journey, and the land route less than three, I joined M. Garnier, a French gentleman, who was going by the road. Our baggage went in two-wheeled carts drawn by mules, while we were mounted on strong Tartar ponies. The journey was not a very interesting one, as the road lay over the broad plain of Chih-li. It was already the beginning of September. The crops were just ready to be cut, and our way was hemmed in on either side by broad, cultivated fields, gilded by the drooping ears of millet, or reddened by the ripening kao-liang, a variety of sorghum which grows to the height of ten or twelve feet. While millet here takes the place of rice as food for the people, the grain of the kao-liang replaces rice, as a source from which the alcoholic drink of the Chinese is distilled, and is also used largely for fodder. Many fields were planted with buckwheat, and others with cotton.

Although we passed many large farm-houses, well built of brick and roofed with glazed tiles, and surrounded with large enclosures, the greater part of the villages and isolated houses bore the marks of poverty, being built of mud, and thatched with reeds and straw.

Where the crops had been removed, the surface was a sandy plain, dried by the summer's sun, and sending up clouds of dust with every gust of wind. The soil is impregnated with alkaline salts, which effloresce on the surface, and render the fine sand extremely irritating to the eyes. On this great plain, sand storms often rage with all the fierceness and destructive consequences which one is accustomed to look for only on deserts. Only a year or two before my visit to northern China, one of these storms had prevailed for several days, and with so much intensity that the air was darkened, boats were unable to move on the river, and many people died from losing their way even in this thickly peopled region. In Tien-tsin it fell many inches deep in the courts of houses, and fine particles were even filtered through the paper of windows.

A lofty pagoda, towering high over village and plain, showed us that we were nearing Tung-chau (fu), twelve miles from Peking. The Pei-ho here receives a canal, which connects its waters and those of the grand canal with the capital of the empire.

Here we came upon one of the granite causeways, or highways, which radiate from the capital. The road is perhaps eighteen feet wide, and is constructed of granite blocks about six feet long by two feet wide and one foot thick. This massive covering was laid upon a thick and perfectly graded bed of concrete and cement. These roads were constructed for durability, and exhibit a great degree of skill; for, although they have probably never been repaired, the stones have undergone no movement from their original position. But a defect in construction, combined with the wear of long use, has made them now almost worthless. The slabs were laid with the longest axis across the road, and in such a manner that the end joints formed by each two slabs fell half-way between the end joints of the neighboring stones. These end joints being the weakest points, have, through long exposure to the tires of cart wheels, been worn into deep ruts as long as the slabs are broad. It was driving over this very causeway in a Chinese carriage that hastened the death of one of the gentlemen who accompanied Mr. Ward in the embassy to Peking. Had these roads been built of slabs sufficiently long to leave the end joints always in the middle of the highway, they would certainly have been masterpieces of the art of road-making.

Suburban villages with innumerable hostelries concealed the walls of the city until we were almost under them.

A large gateway, surmounted by an imposing tower and protected by a semi-circular curtain wall, which in its turn is pierced by three portals, stood before us. Through this we were allowed to pass, after a close examination of our passports by the officer of the guard, and we rode into Khan-balu, the city of the Khans.

It is no easy undertaking for a stranger to find his way to any given point through a city so subdivided as is Peking by inner walls. It was to this very difficulty that a foreign minister owed a diplomatic success. The Danish Government, wishing to make a treaty with the Chinese, had sent Count Rasseloff as plenipotentiary. But the Government, not wishing to enter into any new treaties, declined to receive the minister. This gentleman, however, having reached Tien-tsin, determined to push on to the capital, where arriving some time before his retinue, he entered the gate alone, and not speaking the language, soon lost his way. After wandering about for a long time, and trying in vain by gestures to learn from the astonished natives the whereabouts of the foreign legations, he rode up to a well-dressed Chinaman who was just leaving a house. After several ineffectual attempts to establish an understanding, the Chinaman good-humoredly got out of his carriage, and led the foreigner into a room where he found several other Chinese gentlemen. An interpreter was soon found, and refreshments were brought in. After a good deal of sociable conversation the embassador found that his guide was one of the high officers of the empire, and that he was then present at a meeting of the Board for Foreign Affairs—the authorities who had declined making a treaty—and at the same time the officials discovered that they were entertaining the very man whose entrance into the city they had endeavored to prevent. The accident led to a hearty laugh all round, and to a good understanding, which resulted in the speedy consummation of a treaty.

After quartering ourselves in a Chinese inn, I made my way to the American legation, where I met with a kind reception from our minister, and received, both from him and from Mrs. Burlingame, a cordial invitation to make my home at their house during my visit. It is from this time on that I date my real travels in China, at least so far as travelling means a study of the people. During this visit, which was prolonged many months beyond my original intention, I learned to free myself from the prejudices which every traveller is apt to contract upon the China coast, and during my subsequent travels to look upon the people, with whom I was thrown much in contact, from an entirely different stand-point. For the ability to do this I have to acknowledge my deep indebtedness to Mr. Burlingame, and to the late Sir Frederick Bruce. The broad-minded policy of these two men, based upon justness, and freed from prejudice of race, has begun a new era in the history of Eastern diplomacy.

Peking was founded by Kublai-Khan, about A.D. 1282, as the seat of his court. It is said to have been built near the site of an important town which dated from the Chow dynasty (1122 to 256 B.C). The enclosure is about twenty miles in circumference, and is divided into two parts, the Chinese and Manchu cities. The walls of the latter, which are the larger and wider, are forty to fifty feet high, and about forty feet wide at the top. Tapering slightly from the base upward, they are built with an extremely solid core of earth, faced with massive brick masonry, resting on a solid foundation of stone upon concrete. The top is paved with tiles and defended by a crenulated parapet. The outer side is protected by bastions some fifty feet square, and built at intervals of a few hundred feet. Of the sixteen gates which pierce the walls, seven belong to the Chinese town, six to the Tartar, and three to the partition wall between the two cities. Each gateway is surmounted by an imposing tower several stories high, and rising, apparently more than a hundred feet from the ground. Within the Tartar city, and occupying the heart of it, there is a walled enclosure called the imperial city, and within this again, the forbidden city, containing the imperial palaces and pleasure grounds.

Unlike most other Chinese towns, Peking is traversed by broad avenues, crossing the city in both directions, in straight lines. A stream, entering near the northwest corner of the Tartar city, is divided into two branches, which, entering the imperial city, surround the forbidden enclosure with canals and lakes; and then, re-uniting, the waters pass through the southern part of the Tartar city and the Chinese town into the Tung-chau canal.

Upon the west bank of this stream, in the southern part of the Tartar city, are the American, English, and Russian legations.

As the top of the wall forms the principal promenade for the few foreign residents, let us make our first excursion thither, in order to get a general view over the city. Passing out of the gateway of the American legation, we come upon the esplanade bordering the nearly dry bed of what was once a beautiful canal, but its marble facing is now dilapidated and scattered in large white blocks over the mud. Beyond the street, on the other side, a high wall encloses the large pleasure-grounds and shady groves of a prince of the imperial blood. We may often see ladies of His Highness' harem peeping shyly over the broken parapet.

It would be interesting to know whether these life-long prisoners feel more of contempt or of envy for the lot of foreign ladies, when they see them walking in public, on the arms of gentlemen, or riding on horseback, with all the freedom which they are taught belongs only to men. But we shall not get near enough to this coy bevy to learn their feelings from their looks, for they have already shocked their own ideas of propriety by allowing themselves to be seen, and their fresh faces have suddenly disappeared. It is not often that a foreigner of the male sex gets a near sight of the ladies of this class, other than when they pass in carriages. Still, there was one instance in which a dashing young foreigner played the part of Don Juan in one of these harems, though without meeting the fate of Byron's hero. But to return to our walk. Crossing over a white marble bridge, and following the dirty street which borders the canal, we leave the water-course where it passes, by a low archway, through the wall of the city. Giving a small fee to a watchman, we are admitted to a long, inclined plane, and ascending this we reach the top of the wall. We are now upon the partition between the two cities. Looking north over the Tartar town, we see little more than a broad forest, above which rise on every side the lofty towers of the gates, and the high roofs of the palaces and temples. Excepting the houses just beneath us, the private dwellings are hidden in the dense foliage. Strolling westward over the beautiful promenade, now almost green with the grass springing up between the tiles, we find ourselves in the shadow of the great tower over the middle gate.

Beneath us lies the Meridian Avenue, which, running due south through the middle of both cities, connects the imperial precincts with the temples of Heaven and of Agriculture. Immediately below us a busy throng of Chinamen is pouring in and out of the gate, with all the motley variety of an oriental population. A large square, paved, and surrounded with an open marble fence, is bordered on the north by the red wall and lofty vermilion gateway through which the Meridian Avenue enters the imperial city. Colossal lions of white marble guard the entrance to this sombre gate. Beyond this a succession of high buildings rise, one behind the other, on the line of the avenue, the yellow tiles of the roofs shining like gold in the sunlight, and contrasting well with the dark green of the foliage out of which they spring. Several miles to the north, and conspicuous above the intervening palaces, we see the "golden mountain," a beautiful hill, having several summits, each crowned with a picturesque pavilion. This feature in the scenery is said to be artificial, and to contain a vast store of stone coal. History records that the last emperor of the Mings, finding his cause hopeless, and the capital falling into the hands of the rebel Li-tsz-ching, retired to this mountain, and there ended his dynasty by stabbing his daughter and hanging himself.

Further on, in the northern part of the city, a massive building stands high above the trees. This is the great watch-tower, in one of the upper stories of which is kept the giant drum of Peking. On our left, near the western wall of the Tartar city, there stands a massive monument, an Indian tope of white marble; while further west, in the suburbs, stands one of the loftiest and most beautiful pagodas in China.

Away to the west, over some ten or twelve miles of intervening country, arise the high and barren mountains which form the western limit of the great delta plain, and the transition from the lowlands of the coast to the elevated plateau of central Asia.

Turning our faces southward, we see the Meridian Avenue emerging from the gateway beneath us, and in its southerly course dividing the Chinese town into two equal parts. For the distance of a mile or so this broad street is bordered on either side by the principal shops and market-places of the city. Beyond these, entering a large open space, it passes between two great enclosures, one containing the temple of Agriculture, the other the altar to Heaven. Conspicuous above the trees, and over all the city, rises the triple roof of the temple of Heaven. This beautiful structure is very impressive, not less from the uniqueness of its form, than from the fact that it is the centre of the state worship of an empire including a third of the human race; a worship which, though now dead to the hearts of the people, and of the sovereign, dates from the gray time of antiquity, and has ever been the channel through which the monarch has tendered to Heaven, of which he is the Son, the expression of that obedience which he exacts from the people who are his children.

The circular tent-like roofs of this temple are covered with glazed tiles of the deepest azure, and surmounted with a golden ball. The rays of the afternoon sun, falling on this brilliant surface, produce a rich purple sheen, a beautiful play of light, the sight of which was in itself sufficient inducement for the daily walk upon the wall.

But the sun is just going down behind the ragged peaks of the west, the wall is darkened for half a mile by the lengthening shadow of the tower above us, and the flood of golden light is leaving the yellow roofs of the imperial palaces.

The life of a foreigner in Peking is relieved of much of its monotony by the many objects of interest situated within a day's journey on horseback. The Chinese use horses but little, preferring saddle mules, of which they have the finest in the world, or the two wheeled vehicles of the country drawn by the same animals. To most foreigners these carts without springs are almost useless, as it requires a life-long experience to be able to balance one's body, even in travelling through the streets of the city, without being bruised to soreness by the jolting. At many of the principle points in Peking there are regular stands, where a number of these carriages may be found waiting, but they are rarely used by the foreign residents, whose stables contain fine horses from India.

We, too, will make our excursions in the saddle. Following the canal for a short distance, and turning the corner at the Russian legation, we enter a broad street, leading to the Meridian Avenue. As we approach the Meridian Gate the bustle of street-life surrounds us on every side. The broad paved square is filled with the hurrying crowd. Private carriages, or common hacks, clatter over the granite flags; hundreds of itinerant peddlars, cooks, and tinkers trot in and out through the gate, their burdens hanging upon their shoulders at either end of an elastic pole; well-dressed and thrifty shop-keepers saunter along the sidewalk, fanning their contented faces; scores of beggars, the worst outgrowth of Chinese city life, horrible wretches, clothed with the dirtiest of dirt, or at best with fragments of cast-off mats, besiege relentlessly every passer-by. As we approach the gates a party of horsemen pass us, dressed in yellow robes and mounted on Tartar ponies: they are princes of the imperial blood. A long train of camels, carrying coal, is passing through the gate. Stepping with caution on the smooth stones, the long line of giant animals move slowly along, chewing lazily the cud, and swaying their long necks and horizontal heads first to one side and then to the other, and fixing their beautiful eyes upon every object they pass. But here is another group of animals, not less useful in their habits than they are disgusting in appearance: a dozen or more of the most mangy dogs, and worse looking pigs, are fighting over a heap of offal. These are the scavengers of China.

A large bazaar borders this square; in it are shops and stands, containing all kinds of manufactured articles, among them many of foreign make.

The gateway is a high and arched tunnel, from sixty to a hundred feet long, in which swing massive folding doors, which, amid much sounding of gongs, are closed at dark, and opened at daybreak. Leaving this portal we enter a large semi-circular space, surrounded by the curtain-wall which defends this entrance toward the Tartar city. Of the three gates leading out of this space, two are open to the public, while the middle one is unlocked only for the Emperor.

The Meridian Avenue in the Chinese city is paved with granite blocks, which have become smooth and rounded and filled with ruts through the long wear of cart wheels. On either side are the shops and booths which form the chief market-place of Peking. During the winter months this city has no rival in the world in the abundance and variety of the game and domestic meat with which its market is stocked. Being near Mongolia it receives large quantities of good beef, and of the broad-tailed and common sheep. During the winter, long camel trains are constantly arriving, loaded with antelopes, two or three kinds of deer, wild boars, and wild ducks. Bears, sturgeon, and blue fish are brought in from Manchuria, while the surrounding country furnishes an abundance of pheasants, partridges, and snipe. As the thermometer stands low during the whole winter, these things can be easily preserved for months. The variety of vegetables and fruits is also very respectable, and foreigners have no cause to complain either of the character or cost of food in this part of China.

A ride of a mile or more brings us to a marble bridge, over

which the Meridian Avenue crosses a creek to enter the open plain between the temples of Heaven and of Agriculture. Here leaving the avenue, we can canter over the turf to a gateway in the enclosure sacred to Heaven. Strictly speaking, no one is allowed to enter these precincts; but foreigners having done so immediately after the surrender of Peking, established a precedent, which, with the aid of a small fee, continues to them the privilege. The

TEMPLE OF HEAVEN.

outer wall is some three or four miles in circumference. Within this a broad belt of groves and lawns, with shaded avenues, surrounds an inner wall. At the gate of this inner enclosure we leave our horses and proceed on foot. On either side, the avenue is bordered by a park, with clusters of fine trees scattered over broad lawns. And now the great temple rises before us. There high above the trees is the azure triple roof, brilliant as a sapphire in the sunlight. The structure stands upon three terraced stages, each one ten feet high, respectively one hundred and twenty, ninety, and sixty feet in diameter.* The form of these terraces is polygonal, and each one is surrounded by a balustrade; on them stand many large and beautiful bronze vases for burning incense. The whole is built of pure white marble, highly sculptured, and covered with bas-reliefs, representing the dragons and other animals of the early Chinese mythology. From each of the four points of

THE ROOFS OF THE TEMPLE OF HEAVEN.

the compass the terraces are ascended by broad inclined planes, constructed with massive and sculptured slabs of marble. Upon this really grand sub-structure stands the temple, a large circular building, painted vermilion and pierced with lofty windows. These openings are curtained with rolling screens, made of rods

* Article "Pekin," New American Encyclopedia.

of blue glass, which shut out all view of the interior. Over the main entrance is a tablet inscribed with the name of Shangte, the Most High Ruler.

A broad causeway leading southward, and passing through an arched gateway in a high red building, and under several elaborate arches, connects the temple with the altar to Heaven. This, like the terraced sub-structure of the temple, is built of white

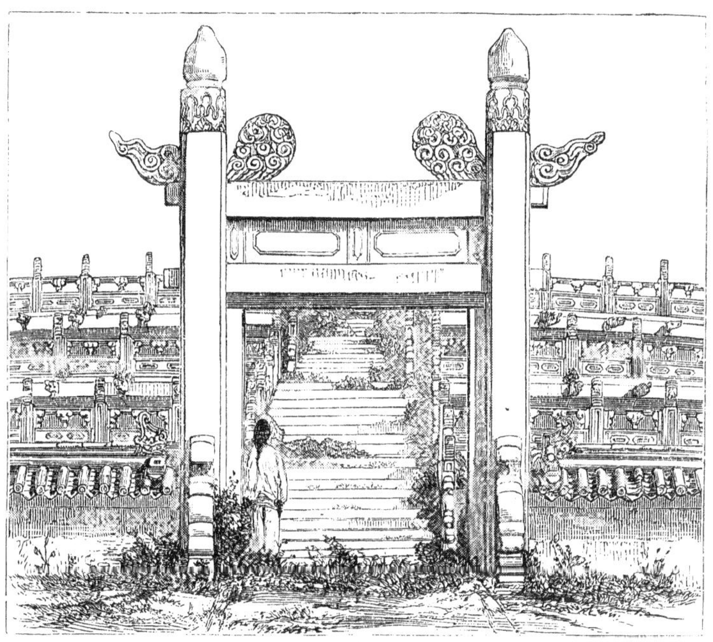

GATEWAYS BEFORE THE ALTAR TO HEAVEN.

marble, and has also three terraced stages, the upper one of which, judging from memory, is more than a hundred feet in diameter. It is covered with richly-sculptured figures of mythical animals, while the terraces are decorated with large incense vases of bronze, whose dark color and graceful outlines stand in beautiful relief against the white marble background. In the middle of the top platform three altars or small tripod tables are ranged in a line from east to west, while on one side a large iron basket seems intended for use in offering burnt sacrifices. On the south side stands a sacred gateway, also of white marble.

There can be but one temple of Heaven, and the Emperor, the High Priest—Son of Heaven—alone has the right to worship Shangte.

I never entered this spot without being impressed with a feeling akin to awe, or rather with the sentiment which ever attaches to the contemplation of those things which bear the stamp of great antiquity, and are hidden behind the veil of mystery. Under no other temple than the broad universe, this imposing altar—imposing in its simplicity—the only symbol of a religion which, unchanged by later corruptions, dates back far beyond the dawn of any history—is erected to a deity, or perhaps it were more proper to say, to an idea which has never been personified in the Chinese mind, and still less represented to the senses.

The worship of Shangte (Tien), the controlling power of the universe, was associated, in the earliest times enlightened by history, with the worship of the spirits of the hills and rivers. This belief in a governing power in Heaven, whether it exists now or is discarded, pervaded the early writings of China.* It is recorded that music was invented for the praise of Shangte. Rival claimants to the throne appealed to Shangte. He is the arbiter of nations. He is both benevolent and capable of being moved to wrath. In the "Book of Odes," composed mostly from 800–1000 B.C., and in part much earlier, Shangte is spoken of as seated on a lofty throne, while the spirits of the good "walk up and down on his right and left." Shangte is said to have "no voice or odor"—to be *le*—*i. e.*, a principle of nature. Dr. Martin observes that there is less anthropomorphism in the representations of Shangte than in those of Jehovah in the Hebrew Scriptures. The source of this worship is probably the same as that of the worship of Ancestors, which is so deeply rooted that the lapse of ages, national and family vicissitudes, and exotic religions have been powerless to impair its vitality. Indeed, so closely is this popular faith bound up with everything that is best in the morals and customs of the nation and of indi-

* Rev. Dr. Martin, "San Kiau: the Three Religions of China." New Englander, April, 1869.

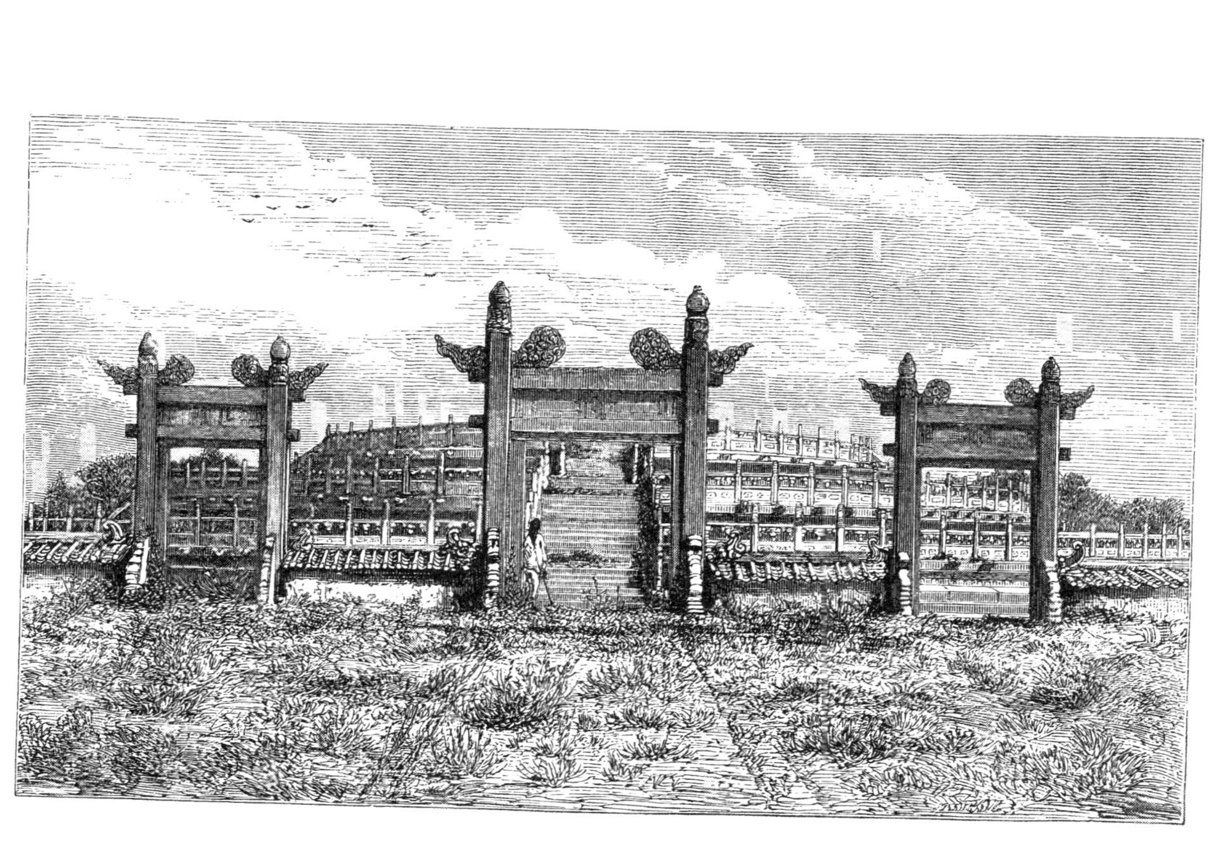

THE ALTAR TO HEAVEN.

viduals, that it should seem that its abolition must be accompanied by moral anarchy.

On the other side of the Meridian Avenue there is the temple of Agriculture, surrounded by extensive grounds. Here, in the spring, the Emperor performs the ceremony of ploughing the ground with a golden plough—a ceremony said to have been performed also by the Incas of Peru.

One of the most fertile sources of amusement to the stranger, in Peking, is the walk through the streets in which are collected the curiosity stores and lapidary shops. The latter occupy entirely a long street parallel to the Meridian Avenue in the Chinese city. Here I was in the habit of passing hours in examining the countless variety of carvings in precious and semi-precious stones. The most common articles are snuff-vials, and mouth-pieces for pipes, carved chiefly out of green and white jade and fei-tsui, a stone precious among the Chinese, and recently named jadeite by a French chemist. The ingenuity and patience which the workmen exhibit are truly wonderful. The snuff-bottles are generally oval and about two inches long, by an inch and a half wide, and two-thirds of an inch thick. The mouth is a little over an eighth of an inch in diameter, and retains this size to the depth of about half an inch. Below this the bottle is hollowed out, leaving to the walls everywhere an equal thickness of one eighth to one quarter of an inch. The whole is polished inside and out. The patience of the workmen will be appreciated when I say that I have seen bottles thus executed in the hardest materials, in rock-crystal, aqua marine, topaz, and even in rough sapphire, a stone next to the diamond in hardness.

The show-cases in these shops are filled with ornaments, in which all the precious stones known to us are represented, excepting only the diamond, emerald, and opal. The emerald is well known to the Chinese under the name of lieu-pau-shi (green precious stone), but they also call it tsu-ma-lu. The Chinese simply polish the natural surface of a precious stone, the art of cutting them into symmetrical shapes with facets seems never to have been practised by them.

Among the larger ornamental works in stone, vases in jade-stone, jasper, and rock-crystal, are the most prominent. But the finer specimens of these large productions are very rare. Choice pearls, and fine rose coral, are also found in these shops. Nor must we forget to mention a kind of jewelry peculiar to the Chinese, in which the most delicate part of the plumage of the kingfisher is so laid upon gold, as to produce the effect of a brilliant enamel, even under close examination.

Not far from this street is that which contains the principal curiosity shops. Here the collector wanders bewildered among the profusion of treasures. Piles of porcelain vases of every shape, and dating mostly from the present, and from the Ming dynasty, surround him. Objects in bronze, and beautiful cloissonee vases, the spoils of ruined temples and palaces, étageres of heavily-carved vermilion lacquer ware, loaded with vases, and ornamental carvings in jade, agate, and coral; piles of swords, in the ornamentation of which the antiquarian would read many an interesting history; these are some of the treasures which tempt even the most economical travellers to extravagance. Nor are their prices at all modest; five hundred to two thousand dollars is by no means an uncommon price for porcelain and cloissonee vases, in which beauty and moderate age are combined; it is only the productions of the present day that are cheap.

If we continue our walk a half mile or so through this street, we shall find ourselves in the booksellers' quarter, the paradise of the Chinese scholar, and of the foreign sinologue. The extent of Chinese literature is very great, and the number of works which are really monumental is large. Among these we may mention the dictionary of the Chinese language, in one hundred and thirty thick volumes, which was compiled during eight years' labor, by seventy-six scholars, with the assistance of literati in all parts of the empire, and under the supervision of the Emperor Kang-hi; * the Statutes of the reigning dynasty in more than one thousand volumes, and many other works historical and scientific, containing each several hundred volumes. The "General Geography of the Chinese Empire," under the present dynasty, contains two hundred and sixty volumes, descriptive and statistical, with a valuable collection of maps covering the whole empire. In compiling tables of the mineral productions of China, I had occasion to consult, through a native scholar, a large number of authorities, and, in doing this, I found the range of native litera-

* Williams' "Middle Kingdom," vol. I., p. 540.

ture on the geography of China, overwhelming. Under different dynasties during the past two thousand years, several immense general treatises on the subject have been produced. Not only this, but almost every province, department, and district, has its special and voluminous geography.

In this street there is a small confectionery shop, which the foreigner rarely passes without entering. Here, after running the gauntlet of curiosity stores and lapidaries' show-cases, one is tempted with candied fruits and jujubes dried in honey, and with Siberian crab-apples encrusted with a transparent coating of sugar.

CHAPTER XXI.

THE CAVERN NEAR FANGSHAN.

Among the remarkable places in the neighborhood of Peking, there is a cave celebrated for its extent, and for the wildness of the scenery in which it is situated. It lies in the limestone mountains, about two days' ride southwest from Peking. On a fine September morning, a party, consisting of Dr. S. W. Williams, Rev. Mr. Blodgett, and myself, started on an excursion to this interesting place. Leaving the city by one of the southwestern gates, and passing the suburbs, we came into the open country on a broad, cultivated plain. The tall kao-liang had been harvested, leaving the view open as far as the eye could reach. Groups of houses, barns, and villages were everywhere in sight. Here and there the eye could detect, in the distance, the gray outlines of walled towns, while, rising above all, the most conspicuous and picturesque, were lofty pagodas, the silent and ancient guardians of the mysterious currents of air and earth, which are supposed to exercise a potent influence upon the well-being of the country. Away to the south, two of these towns, standing in close proximity, rise above the horizon from the city of Tso (chau).

This portion of China, lying in the region of prevailing westerly winds, which deposit their moisture on the higher parts of the continent, is favored with an atmosphere so dry and clear that distant objects are defined with a distinctness of outline and detail rarely found in regions so near to the sea. Through this transparent air we could see with wonderful clearness all the details of gorges and cliffs, of spurs and peaks, and of range rising behind range of the great mountain region which, trending away to the southwest and the northeast, borders the great plain, and forms, through its valleys, the stairway to the high table-lands of central Asia.

The road we were following is one of the chief and most

ancient highways of the empire. Passing through Shansi and Sz'chuen, it forms the land route to Thibet and India. In its course it passes over lofty mountains, spanning deep gorges with suspension bridges, or with arched structures, and winding along precipices where the roadway had to be cut through the solid rock. It was along this route that Marco Polo travelled on one of his journeys when sent as embassador by Kublai-Khan. Before reaching our resting-place for the night we passed the first object mentioned by the Venetian traveller—the bridge of Liu-kiu-chao, over the Huen river—or, as he calls it, the Puli-sangan. This structure is built with many arches, and entirely of marble and hewn granite. It has undergone many changes during the six centuries which have passed since Marco Polo rode over it; but the marble parapet, with its posts surmounted by lions, still remains as a voucher for his story.

This highway, leading from Peking to the west, like the one approaching the city from Tung-chau (fu), is paved with granite slabs. Worn smooth, and cut up with deep ruts, it has long since sunk into disuse, and in places lies buried beneath drifts of sand.

During this excursion, as indeed everywhere in the neighborhood of Peking, I saw many private cemeteries of wealthy Chinese families. They consist generally of a sombre closed building, surrounded by groves of cypress. In the centre of the grove are grouped the tumuli, in which are buried the coffins. These mounds are from five to fifteen feet high, and are well covered with green turf. In many of them there is a profusion of marble monuments, often tall tablets eight or ten feet high, surmounted with the sculptured dragon, and supported on the back of the giant tortoise, indicating that they were erected by order of the Emperor in commemoration of some great services performed by the deceased. The imperial decree, with its date, is neatly inscribed upon the face of the tablet.

To these burial-places there is generally attached a certain amount of land, the revenue from which is devoted to the maintenance of the grounds. Some families have founded large Buddist monasteries, the monks of which hold their fee on condition of keeping the place in order. Hundreds of these cemeteries are scattered around the environs of the capital. In their various states of preservation are recorded the fortunes of many a family; for the first duty of a Chinaman, after that which he owes to living parents, is the respect which he is enjoined to show to the ashes of his ancestors. Undoubtedly the many ruined places of the dead, where nothing is now visible but fallen and half-buried monuments, exist still in the memories and traditions of scattered families whose wealth has long since departed. Some successful descendant of the neglected dead may be now reaping in California or Australia the fortune which will enable him to fulfil his family duty by restoring the ancestral hall and its monuments.

Toward sunset we passed through the gate of Leang-hiang (hien), and looking out for an inn, soon found ourselves in the court of the principal caravansary. This was a large square, approached through a high gateway, and surrounded by a one-story building. The kitchen, filled with busy cooks and hungry travellers, stood at the entrance to the court, and as we entered formed a centre of attraction to a group of ragged beggars. At the bottom of the square the building was raised a few feet higher from the ground than the rest of the inn, and contained the principal rooms. After a supper of cakes fried in oil, of boiled rice, of mutton and fried eggs, our servants unrolled our bedding, and we went to sleep.

The next day brought us to Fangshan (hien), a walled town at the foot of the mountains. Leaving this place after dinner, we crossed a granite ridge and passed through a region of low but rough hills. The road was paved with large blocks of stone, which had become so smooth that it was impossible to ride, and even difficult to walk and lead one's horse.

Passing through a small village, I knocked at the door of a miserable house, and asked for water to drink. The poor inmates brought me hot tea, not understanding how any one could wish to take into his stomach anything so insipid as cold water. When I offered a small amount in payment, they seemed almost offended, and I learned henceforth to credit even the poor mountaineers of utilitarian China with some of the delicate sentiments of Western life.

Toward evening we reached a small village, where we were obliged to leave our horses and hire donkeys to take us to the cave. The road being very bad, it was already dark when we stood knocking at the gate of the great monastery where we were to pass the night. The monks showed us to one of the best rooms, and our servants set out in search of the kitchen, where they were permitted to cook the fowls which we had taken the precaution to bring with us. This was a large monastery, full of rambling cloisters, surrounding courts and temples. When we went to sleep the distant sound of the low chant at vespers had not yet ceased, and the morning prayers greeted our ears indistinctly when we awoke.

After an early breakfast we set out on foot, and a long walk brought us to the entrance of the cavern. This is on the side of a precipitous hill, and high above the bottom of the valley. Near the mouth there stands a shrine and a marble tablet, erected by the Emperor Kang-hi, the second of the present dynasty.

Taking guides and torches we entered a long tunnel-like passage, and proceeding a short distance came to a large bas-relief of Budda, sculptured in the wall. It represents the great sage, either in the state of meditation or of absorption in the Nirvana. In all Buddist countries, many, if not all, caves are held sacred, and in many the shadow of Budda is supposed to be visible to those who, by leading holy lives, have so mortified the flesh as to be able to see things spiritual. We soon entered an immense chamber, the further end of which communicated by a low passage with the next in the series. Entering at first on our hands and knees, we came to a place where the passage was so small that the only way to pass was by lying flat and straight, and being pushed at the feet by one guide, and pulled by the hands by another. The most portly member of our party very fortunately took his turn last. Unhappily for him, although a pious man, he had not sufficiently mortified the flesh to be able to penetrate to the inner mysteries of this holy place. After vain efforts we were forced to leave him wedged tight, literally stuck, with a guide tugging at each end to back him out.

The second chamber is very large, and ornamented with stalactites to an extent which well repaid the trouble we had passed through. In the centre there arises a large dome, upon which stand immense stalagmite pillars, in the grotesque outlines of which devout pilgrims are taught to trace human resemblances; they are called the ro-han, or saints.

The once brilliant incrustations of this chamber are now blackened with the smoke of torches. A long series of chambers is said to continue far into the mountain; but the exit at the further end of this room had been walled up by command of one of the Emperors, because a party of pilgrims, having strayed beyond the explored regions, had never again been seen.

Retracing our steps we again went through the wire-drawing process and rejoined Mr. Blodgett in the outer chamber. The connecting passage between the two rooms had been polished to the smoothness of glass by the friction of countless pilgrims who had passed through it.

Taking a more round-about way on our return, we ascended to the head of the valley, and, crossing the water-shed, came into an exceedingly wild and broken region. The limestone mountains are here cleft to their base by deep gorges, with dashing torrents broken by waterfalls. Along the precipitous walls paths are hewn in the rock, now protected by parapets, now descending from ledge to ledge by long flights of steps cut into the cliffs. This seems to be the very paradise of monks. Monasteries and shrines, apparently centuries old, are scattered in profusion through these wild mountain recesses. They are perched in places seemingly the most inaccessible, crowning overhanging cliffs hundreds of feet high, their walls built up flush with the edge of the precipice, and in situations accessible only by steps hewn in the living rock. However practical the Chinese in general may be, there is certainly a love of the poetic in nature among the devotees of Buddism. It is perhaps from the comparatively limited number of imaginative Chinamen that Buddism recruits its monks. We visited several of these eyrie-like retreats, and were everywhere hospitably received, and invited to drink from that unfailing fountain, the everflowing tea-pot. Returning to the monastery where we had passed the night, we set out upon the road to Pekin, well pleased with all we had seen and experienced.

CHAPTER XXII.

VISIT TO THE COAL MINES.

I HAD nearly finished the necessary preparations for a journey homeward through Tartary and Siberia, when, at the instance of Mr. Burlingame and Sir Frederick Bruce, the Chinese Government requested that I should undertake the examination of some of their principal coal fields. In order to suppress piracy and smuggling, the Government had instructed Mr. Lay, their Inspector-General of Maritime Customs, who was then in England, to purchase and send out a fleet of gun-boats, officered and manned by Englishmen. A flotilla of eight steamers had accordingly arrived, under the command of Captain Sherard Osburn. Alarmed at the idea of having to pay from fifteen to twenty dollars a ton for English coal, and knowing that they had themselves large deposits of this mineral, they decided to search for desirable fuel among their own mines.

The arrangements were made over a lunch at the Tsung-li-yamun with the officers of the Board of Foreign Affairs. The interview, which was very friendly, brought out some curious ideas with regard to geology; among these was the belief in the growth of coal in abandoned mines: everything was produced by the co-action of *yin* and *yang*, force and matter, the active and passive, the male and female principles in nature; and where surrounding conditions had once favored the production of coal, why should they not always favor it? But at the same time they objected to extensive mining, on the ground that it would exhaust the store on which future generations would be dependent: an inconsistency in reasoning which they got over by saying that the rate of growth of new coal is not known. Another objection to extensive mining was the danger of litigation from trespass, and one of the officers immediately proceeded to give a long and romantic story of a desperate subterranean battle which had raged for days underground between the forces of two mines which had suddenly become connected underground, an encounter in which the participants were mutually exterminated.

It was agreed that three mandarins, two civil and one military, should go with me. The question having arisen as to how my name could be intelligibly written in Chinese, Tung Ta-jin selected for the first syllable the word Pang as the nearest approach offered by the language, and wrote it for me on a card in a character in which the principal element was the sign for a dragon. Did they think there might be some connection between the intended approach to foreign innovations, and the clutches of this terrific monster?

Through the kindness of Sir Frederick Bruce, Mr. Murray, of the English legation, was permitted to accompany me, and I will say in advance that much of the success which attended the excursion was due to his excellent knowledge of the Chinese language, as much of the pleasure was due to his genial companionship.

Our first day's journey led us to Yang-fang, a little west of north from Peking, and lying at the foot of the mountains. A few miles before reaching this place we crossed the Sha-ho river, near the city of Chang-ping (chau), by a long bridge of white marble. This is still in good preservation, if we except the deep ruts, which here, as everywhere else, have ruined the granite pavements.

At Yang-fang a bold granite spur juts like a headland into the plain. Some ten or fifteen miles beyond, the mountain is cleft by the Nan-kau gorge, commanded by the ancient watch-towers and forts, which form the outposts of the great wall of China.

The next morning, leaving the plain, we began the ascent into the mountains through a valley. Murray and myself, as well as Ma, the military mandarin, were mounted on strong Tartar horses, while Wang and Too, the civilians, being more effeminate, were carried in open chairs. Ma was a Mohammedan, and a type of the better class of Chinese soldiers; easy-going and tolerably frank, he did not hesitate to express his contempt for the effeminacy of the civil mandarins in general, and for those of our party in particular. Of these latter, Wang, the elder of the two, was a tall and well-conditioned man of about fifty, well informed after the Chinese fashion, and with a uniformly pleasant expression, which betokened a really kind heart. On the other hand, Too was a type of the too frequent class of overbearing and "squeezing" mandarin. His voice and manner, always harsh, became positively disagreeable upon the slightest provocation from an inferior.

The valley we were ascending is cut deep into the Devonian limestone, and shut in by high and ragged cliffs. A tolerably good road, leading over a low pass, brought us into another valley tributary to the Huen-ho, and after a short descent we drew up at an inn in the mountain hamlet of Tien-kia-kwan.

Before entering the house Too called the landlord to him and treated us to a characteristic scene.

"What have you to eat?" demanded Too.

"Boiled millet and eggs," replied the landlord.

"What do you charge for your eggs?"

"Very little—almost nothing, only six cash apiece," was the reply.

"How dare you call that cheap? You must know that we are no ordinary travellers. The Emperor has bought foreign steamers, and Prince Kung has sent this gentleman to find coal for them; therefore you should let us have the eggs for three cash."

By this time Too had worked himself into a passion, and fairly shrieked his argument into the ears of the host and of the gathered crowd. By his appeal to patriotism he finally succeeded in reducing the price by, in our money, about one-tenth of a cent per egg, making a gain of about two cents on our bill, to be divided among the pockets of our escort.

Although within fifty miles of one of the largest cities of the world, we were in a region where money is little used, nearly all the small transactions of the people being effected by barter of the necessaries of life. The currency of China is very clumsy, the copper coin being so bulky as to render its transportation costly, while the uncoined silver is extremely inconvenient, from the fact that it has to be weighed at every payment, while the scales of sellers and buyers rarely agree, and the legal standards of weight differ several times in the course of a few days' journey. In Peking, besides the ordinary cash, there is a copper coin of which the actual value is many times less than that which is stamped upon it; this is useless beyond the walls of the city. Peking also enjoys an institution which I had supposed was peculiar to the United States, namely, an endless number of wild-cat banks issuing paper currency; their notes are useless out of town, as no one will take them for fear the bank may have already failed, or that it may suspend before its notes can be presented for payment.

We found in the inhabitants of these mountains a simple-hearted and civil people, who were quite free from the dislike to foreigners which prevails among the inhabitants of the south, and for which Europeans and Americans have chiefly themselves to blame. Although every ounce of food that is gained from these barren hills is won by the hardest labor, I saw few signs of suffering among the inhabitants. They are contented with the boiled yellow millet, and a few vegetables, with now and then a dish of fried eggs, or a chicken which has passed the prime of life, whatever that period may be in the time allotted to a fowl.

The next day we continued our journey southward, through a deep and narrow valley in the limestone. The high and precipitous walls frequently approached each other so closely that the valley became a gorge. Finally we emerged into the more open country of the Huen-ho. Crossing a high spur, around which the river bends, we began our initiation into Chinese mountain-paths. Here the limestone has been traversed and dislocated by large dykes of porphyry, enclosing fragments of the slate which belong between upper and lower beds of the traversed rock. After passing this spur, our road lay for several miles along the steep face of the mountain, and high above the rushing river. The road, paved with porphyry boulders, was almost impassable; the rounded surfaces of the stones had been worn smooth as glass by the daily passage for centuries of long trains of mules loaded with coal. On such a road a false step might plunge both horse and rider into the roaring torrent below.

At Ching-pai-kau we were ferried across the river, and entered the valley of the Chai-tang creek. Here passing a little mill worked by an overshot wheel, we continued our route under the shade of the willows along the edge of the sluice, till the valley narrowed and we entered a wild gorge. The limestone cliffs, which at first formed the walls, were succeeded as we went south by the towering peaks and steep declivities and side ravines of the great mass of conglomerate, which, overlying the limestone, forms itself the foundation of the coal measures. Soon this was succeeded by overlying beds of the softer sandstones and slates of the coal series, and we emerged from the narrow gorge into the broad and open valley of Chai-tang, a region of low hills with soft outlines, such as are characteristic of most coal basins. A few miles' journey brought us in sight of the walls of Chai-tang on one side of the creek, while on the other rose a high, flat-topped hill, with a lofty watch-tower at each end, ancient guardians of the valley.

Soon after our arrival at the inn we were waited upon by the magistrate of the district, from whom we obtained a complete list of the coal mines in the neighborhood.

Referring the reader elsewhere * for a detailed account of the mines of this district, I confine myself here to the remark that there is within a radius of four miles from Chai-tang a large number of openings upon the coal seams. Within this area the coal varies from caking bituminous to pure anthracite. The seam containing the Fu-tau mine averages about seven feet in thickness, and produces a steam coal equal, if not superior, to the best Welsh variety.† The Ta-tsau or "great seam," about three miles south of the Fu-tau consisting of two beds, separated by about eight feet of sandstone, and containing an aggregate thickness of forty-eight feet of coal, is a deposit of remarkably fine anthracite.

The other mines contain coal of a more bituminous character. Each variety has its distinctive Chinese name, and is mined for some special purpose in the domestic and manufacturing arts. The coking varieties are burned to coke, and at every mine the dust, which with us is thrown away, is mixed with a little clay and moulded into cakes of artificial fuel. For many purposes, especially for use in the kitchen, this artificial product is esteemed more highly than when in the natural shape, as the globular form of the cakes admits a ready draught, while their composition is said to enable the consumer to control the rate of burning much better than with any other fuel.

* Pumpelly's "Geological Researches in China, Mongolia, and Japan." Published by the Smithsonian Institution. 1867.

† For analyses of Chinese coals, see Appendix.

In large cities situated at a distance from the mines the dust and cinders of coal are mixed with the dung of cows and horses, and with clay.

The absence of machinery for draining has prevented the Chinese miners from working more than a few feet below water-level, and as the seams of the Chai-tang district are highly inclined, this point is soon reached. Aside from this, their whole system is so defective that the utmost capacity of production of any one mine in this district is less than two thousand tons a year. The works are entered by an inclined plane, which descends in the coal to less than a hundred feet below water-level, when it communicates with a nearly horizontal gallery, which, extending to the furthest limits of the property, forms the main thoroughfare of the mine. Though unable to work below this level, the Chinese miner literally exhausts the fuel lying above it. By means of using inclined planes connected by levels, he subdivides the seam into pillars. Ventilation is effected either by air-shafts or by a blowing machine, constructed much upon the same principle as our fanning mill for grain. The timbering, which is almost confined to the main level, is very costly, owing to the almost entire absence of wood. The accumulating water of the mine runs along the bottom level to the foot of the inclined plane. One-half the width of this slope is cut out into hollow steps, four or five feet high, in each one of which stands a man armed with a bucket; by these the water is bailed from step to step, until it reaches the surface. In some mines this work is done entirely by blind men. The manner of raising the coal is not less primitive than the drainage, the bottom level and the inclined plane being covered with smooth round sticks, over which the coal is dragged in sleds by coolies. The passages are generally so low that these men are forced to go on hands and knees, dragging the sled by means of a cord passed around the neck and between the legs. The fuel sells at the different mines of this district at prices ranging from $1,70 to $2 per ton—2,000 lbs.

The coal field of Chai-tang is cut off at the west by a high escarpment, the edge of a large area of intrusive porphyries. In this region, some five or six miles west of Chai-tang, there occurs a small patch of coal, which is cut up into small dislocated fragments by dykes of porphyry, which in places traverse the seams, and in some instances are spread out parallel to these, forming for a greater or less distance the roof or the floor of the bed.

Near this place, which is called Ching-shui, there are the ruins of an old furnace, where some years since there were cast large quantities of iron currency. This expedient was adopted by the Government during its financial straits, with the view of making the iron *cash* pass for the same value as those of copper, than which latter, if anything, they were a little smaller. This attempt was a complete failure, and to this day this iron currency lies stored in immense quantities in one of the old palaces of the Tartar city.

After having finished the examination of the Chai-tang district, I determined to visit the coal fields lying at the edge of the great plain on the eastern slope of the mountain. When the question was raised as to what route we should take, Too instantly informed us that he had made careful enquiries into the geography of the region, and had found that there was actually only one road leading out of it, namely, the one by which we had come. I had wished to descend the valley of the Huen-ho to the point where it enters the plain, and in spite of Too's geographical investigations I felt confident that there must be a road of some kind following the course of the river. Calling in the magistrate of the district, and several men who were said to be thoroughly acquainted with the country, I held a council, which I had no doubt would confirm my belief in the existence of the desired road. But no; Too led off with an argument, giving physical and political reasons why no road could either now be or ever have been built in the valley; and he was unanimously sustained by the others. Murray, after a severe cross-examination, elicited the fact that a road had existed some time during the Han dynasty, or later, but that in many places the precipices, in the sides of which it had been dug, had fallen. But there was no road now; this they were all agreed upon. Close questioning, however, brought out an additional fact, namely, that there was a path, impassable, however, for animals, and attended with the greatest danger even for foot passengers. Good, I said, we will take this road to-morrow. But we had not yet vanquished all the lions that seemed to stand guard over the valley of the Yang-ho. The path, they said, if such it could be called, was very winding, crossing the river from shore to shore, and in places where the bed contained fathomless quicksands. This lion being defeated, a host of fresh ones came to the rescue. There were no inhabitants, and we could get nothing to eat; in places the water was poisonous; there were caverns which hurled out terrific blasts of wind; the river was subject to unaccountable freshets which were liable at any time to fill the gorges, carrying everything before them. When we asked one of the mountaineers how he had gained all this information about a valley which no one could visit, he replied that he knew it from two men who, in going through, had experienced all these horrors; but unfortunately for his testimony he added that they were both swallowed up by quicksands. I must give credit to Wang and Ma for having taken no part in the argument.

The next morning we returned to the valley of the Huen-ho, which we descended to the point at which we had previously entered it. Here the road forked, and the one which descended the river was certainly larger than the other one, by which we had come into the valley from the north. To the intense disgust of Too, I turned into the river road. We soon found that this was in constant use. After going a few miles we came to a point where the river narrowed, and the valley contracted to a gloomy gorge, enclosed between lofty cliffs of limestone. In the face of the wall the road was hewn into steps, by which it ascended to a point high above the river, from which it again descended by another steep stairway. The route was less than three feet wide, with a vertical cliff on one side, while toward the river it was protected by a parapet about one foot and a half high. It was an ugly place for man or beast; long use had polished the rock till it was as smooth as glass. Having begun the passage on horseback, neither Murray nor myself ventured to dismount, fearing to disturb the horse's balance on the smooth and narrow place. In making the descent my horse went down on his haunches, and I confidently expected that in his struggle to rise he would plunge us both over the parapet and down to the dark mass of waters which were rolling and dashing far beneath us. The strong animal with great caution regained his feet, trembling like a leaf.

I was not surprised when we found a considerable village a

little further down, and better yet a comfortable dinner and bed, in a region where we had been warned of the absence of people and food. If anything astonished me it was the long trains of hundreds of mules, heavily laden with coal, which we passed the next day, for it seemed to me impossible that they could go up and down the smooth stairways which we had passed.

During this day's journey we crossed the river once, fording over a bed of beautiful gravel; but although there were neither quicksands, nor terrific winds howling from the bowels of the earth, the road was certainly horrible enough to have been built in the time of the Han, and used ever since without being repaired. The river here keeps near the contact between the limestone and the overlying porphyry conglomerates. In each of these formations the aspect of the valley differs, but in both the scenery is extremely wild.

At the little village of Wang-ping-tsun, where we stopped for the night, Murray and myself paid a friendly visit to Wang. Behind all the politeness of the old man, we could perceive that our visit was not well timed. An opium pipe and lamp lying on the table were sufficient explanation of our friend's uneasiness. We had long known that he smoked opium, but the old man had supposed his habit unknown to all but himself. Seeing my looks involuntarily directed to the pipe, he made the common excuse, saying that he sometimes used the drug for relief from pain, but that he neither had contracted the habit, nor should he do so.

When we were seated, Wang told us how a former friend of his, who had once been a magistrate of the place where we then were, had fallen into the habit of using opium; how this habit, gaining on him, had caused him to neglect his official duties, and had transformed a kind-hearted and beloved magistrate into a hated tyrant, extorting from the poor villagers the means to meet the then high price of the drug; how, after being mobbed and driven from his office, he became an outcast, and his family beggars. When Wang finished the story of his friend, by saying that in an attack of remorse and despair he had ended life by an over-dose of opium, there were tears in the old man's eyes, and I could not help thinking that he was unfolding his own future, so true was his story to the career of almost all who become addicted to this vice.

The next day our road passed over three high ridges, by crossing one of which, the Niu-chau-ling, we saved a very great bend in the river. Having reached the climax of the horrible, in describing roads already mentioned, I have no words left to do justice to this. For a distance of several miles the way over this hill is paved with large irregular blocks of porphyry, the surfaces of which are everywhere rounded and polished. In many places the formerly slight depressions at the point of contact between three or four blocks have been worn into holes several inches deep by the shoes of countless mules, which during centuries have daily packed their heavy loads over this tedious pass.

At San-kia-tien we came upon an arm of the great plain, finishing safely our journey through what Too had caused to be described as the very valley of the shadow of death. The real object of dread on the part of Too was the shortening of the journey, thereby depriving him of the chance to "squeeze" perhaps ten dollars in his accounts.

Rounding a mountain spur, we entered the coal field of Mun-ta-kau, which lies in another arm or bay of the great plain. Here we found that a temple had been prepared for our reception, and that many little things had been done to make our stay comfortable.

The coal of this region is altogether anthracite, and many openings have been made upon the several beds. One mine which I visited has been worked to a horizontal distance of 8,500 feet. The seam is very irregular in thickness, varying from a few inches to six or seven feet. In this mine one man can bring to the surface only about one hundred and thirty-three pounds daily, owing to the great loss of time experienced in dragging the sled one mile and a half on hands and knees. The ventilation is assisted in this mine by a very large fan-blower.

After staying a few days at Mun-ta-kau, I determined to skirt along the edge of the plain to the coal district of Fang-shan (hien). To do this, both mules for the transportation of the baggage, and carriers for the chairs of Wang and Too, were needed. For these a requisition was sent in to the local magistrate, with a request that they might be ready by daylight the next morning. The next day, seeing no signs of the animals, the magistrate was sent for, but we received word that he was so drunk with opium that it would be some time before he could come. After several hours the officer arrived. He was a young man, a native of Sz'chuen, with a very effeminate and finely chiseled face. Dressed with the most scrupulous care, he was a type of the Chinese exquisite.

He had made arrangements for men and mules the night before, and now sent off his attendants to find out why they had not appeared. These arms of justice soon returned with the delinquents. The latter pleaded that their animals were employed on permanent contracts, from which they could not remove them without suffering much loss. "But you must fulfil the demands of the Government," replied the officer. "We cannot," answered the men sullenly. "Halloa there, beat these fellows," cried the enraged mandarin. Two executioners with peaked hats immediately stepped forward and forced the men to their knees, while others proceeded to apply a few blows with bamboo rods. In the meantime a considerable crowd had gathered in the temple court, and were beginning to force their way into the temporary hall of justice. "How dare you intrude here?" cried the mandarin. "Drive them out! drive them out!" But the people caring as little for the executioners as for their magistrate, and heeding the words of neither, continued to press in. The crowd grew larger, and it seemed probable that a long-growing dislike of their mandarin was about to find vent in a riot.

Just at this moment the crowd opened in the court, making way for Wang, who approached from our quarters on the other side. Wang had formerly been the magistrate at this very place, and the silence which came over the crowd, as well as the deference shown him as he passed, proved that the old man had ruled kindly and well, and that his memory was still held in respect. A few words from Wang put an end to our trouble, and men and animals were immediately forthcoming.

The small valley of Mun-ta-kau opens into a larger area of the great plain, and in the middle of this, a rugged hill, rising abruptly from the banks of the Huen-ho, is crowned with the picturesque ruins of the temple of Shi-ching-miao. As in some of the ruined castles of Europe, so here the broken sides and tops of cliffs are filled out with heavy masonry to make a foundation for the building upon the most picturesque and commanding point. Passages and rooms are hewn out of the sandstone rock. Ponderous doors of stone guarded the entrance to these rooms. The lands belonging to the temple are tilled by people who inhabit less ruined buildings, but probably a small part of the proceeds is devoted to repairs. I was told that this was the dwelling and temple of a formerly wealthy family.

Proceeding southward, we skirted the foot of the mountains. On our left the great plain stretched away to the eastward. From slight eminences in the road we could see the gate-towers and pagodas of Peking, and the triple roof of the temple of Heaven. On our right were the rounded spurs and knobs of the sandstone hills of the Mun-ta-kau coal field, while over these towered an immense peak of limestone with ragged sides and lofty cliffs. Here on the summit, almost inaccessible, except for stairways hewn in the rock, and perched 1,500 or more feet above the plain, are the cloisters and temples of a Buddist monastery. The mountain is said to be honey-combed with caves.

Our road now crosses a long, low spur which juts out into the plain. On the southern side of this ridge there are immense quarries of limestone. These have been worked for a great length of time, and over a large area; and the valley in the sides of which they occur is filled to the depth often of forty or fifty feet, with layers of half-burnt limestone, chert, fragments of coal and ashes—the remains of former kilns. Through this deposit, which is now cemented to a hard concrete, the mountain brook has cut its channel to the limestone below.

Passing out of this small valley, we came to a town of considerable size, called Ta-hwei-chang, or great lime depot. The walls had long been crumbling, till little was now left standing. But dilapidated walls in China are not necessarily a sign of decay in population or industry. As we proposed to dine at this place, we rode up to the principal eating-house. This was open to the street, and long before our dinner was served up the room was crowded with the curious of all ages, anxious to see, for the first time, and not only to see but to feel of, the queer barbarians of the western seas.

"Go out, boys," said Ma.

Upon this the largest lad in the crowd turned to one a little smaller, and exclaimed:

"Go out, boy—go out. Don't you hear that the lo-yé does not want any boys here?"

But this one passing the injunction to a still smaller neighbor, it was repeated in a descending scale, till a little fellow about two feet high picked up the smallest child in the room and thrust him into the street. This turned the joke against us—always a disadvantage to a foreigner in a Chinese crowd. A traveller who has command of the language, together with patience and sufficient wit to put the more demonstrative members of even a Chinese mob in a ridiculous light, has little to fear, provided the crowd is swayed by no stronger motives than mere curiosity. If, however, he resent the great personal annoyance by blows, he places himself in a position of great danger. An instance somewhat illustrative of this occurred to us in leaving Ta-hwei-chang. The whole population of men and boys followed us through the streets. From laughing at each other's jokes made at our expense, they proceeded to open ridicule of us, and, regardless of our official escort, began to hoot, and finally to throw missiles. When they had reached this point, Murray stopped his horse, and, turning to face the crowd, raised his hand to motion silence.

"O, people of Ta-hwei-chang!" exclaimed Murray in excellent Chinese, "is this your hospitality? Do ye thus observe the injunctions of your sages, that ye shall treat kindly the stranger that is within your gates? Have ye forgotten that your great teacher, Confucius, hath said: 'What I would not that men should do to me, that would I not also do to men?'"

The effect of this exhortation was as remarkable as it was unexpected by me. In an instant the character of the crowd was changed: the hooting and pelting had stopped to hear the barbarian talking in the familiar words of Confucius, the old men bowed approvingly, and a number of boys jumped forward to show us the way. This scene will appear more impressive by contrast, if we suppose a couple of Chinamen, followed by a crowd of a few thousand American men and boys, and if we suppose the two strangers to turn and quote in good English the similar passage of our Lord's sermon on the mount. The reader may form his own opinion as to the success of such an experiment.

Before sunset I found myself again in Fang-shan, but this time in quarters which had been prepared for us.

Among the principal mines which we visited in this neighborhood were those of Chang-kau-yü, in the mountains, about eight miles west of Fang-shan. They belong to the family, Chang, one of whose members is decorated with a blue button. We reached this place about noon. As these mines had been worked for a great length of time, I determined to enter them. It was no slight undertaking. After reaching the foot of the inclined plane, I found the galley so low as to be passable only on hands and knees for a great part of the distance. After creeping for more than half a mile, the proprietor, who I believe had never been so far before in his own mine, gave out completely, and I continued my way to the end, accompanied only by the head miner. After penetrating to a distance of six thousand feet, I had little strength left to use in examining the workings, which are conducted in the same manner as those already described. Much timbering is used, though chiefly the wood of fruit trees, etc., which costs at the mine twenty-nine cents per hundred pounds. When I again reached daylight, with the skin nearly gone from my knees, I learned that the miners protect these joints, as well as the hands, with pads. This was not very consoling information for one who had crept nearly two miles and a half without such protection.

It was a source of great wonder to the Chinese, as it was also to the Japanese, that a person holding my rank, and acting under an imperial commission, with authority to demand the presence of all officials on my route, should subject himself to the hardships which attend a personal examination of a mine.

The sun was setting behind the mountain cliffs when I reached the open air. The owner had prepared an extensive dinner in honor of the occasion. It would perhaps be uncharitable to say that this hospitality was in any way suggested by a desire to have the coal of this mine recommended for the new fleet; but I always had a suspicion that our friend Too, who was very fond of the good things of the world, had suggested the policy of appealing to my good will through the stomach. In vain I urged the lateness of the hour, and the danger of riding over the mountain road by night. Our host insisted that we should stay, and promised a procession of torch-bearers to light the way on our return. The dinner was good, as was also the rice wine, and we talked and laughed and ate and drank until I began to doubt even the ability of the torch-bearers to guide our merry party safely over eight miles of dangerous road.

It was nine or ten o'clock before we mounted our horses, and I think that with the prospect before us, even Ma envied Wang and Too the chairs, for using which he despised them. With a large number of torchmen we left the mine and started upon our perilous journey. I have given so many descriptions of bad roads that it is only necessary to say of this that it was nearly equal to the worst. Paved with large and polished blocks, it wound along the side of a rocky ravine, and the danger was increased by frequent stair-like descents. We must have presented a remarkable sight, as our party wound along this road, with flaming torches, which lighted up at every instant some new feature in the wild scenery, now a frowning crag towering above our heads, or again the yawning gorge beneath us, and the rushing torrent and waterfalls at its bottom. A wild sight it was, no doubt, and so too thought the inhabitants of the small hamlets which we passed in the dead of night, for we heard the barricading of doors. So thought also a lone and frightened Chinaman, whom we found shaking with fear, and hidden among some boulders, holding a pig which had betrayed him by its grunting. Everywhere we passed for a band of Ming-hwo, a class of robbers who in town and country make rapid raids in large numbers, and by torchlight.

In the small hours of the morning our remarkable procession reached one of the gates of Fang-shan. The gates of Chinese cities are locked at dark, and the keys deposited with the magistrate, and the law prohibits their being opened before daybreak. It required a long parley through the closed portal with the guard on the inside before they could be induced to send word to the Ya-mun that we wished to enter, and it was nothing but the fact that I was travelling under an imperial commission that caused the gates finally to swing open and admit our weary party.

The next day we received invitations to dine with the magistrate of the city. As we traversed the court of the Ya-mun, at the appointed time our ears were greeted with a sound of suppressed chattering, and we could see that all the chinks of the surrounding windows were occupied by the ladies of the household. Our host led us into a room where the table was spread. In accordance with Chinese etiquette, he spent some time in persuading each of the guests to take the head of the table, a distinction which each one was bound by the laws of politeness to decline. The host, then standing in that place himself, insisted upon each and all sitting down before him, which of course was persistently declined, as it would have been a breach of politeness for a guest to take his seat first. The dinner began with a cup of hot rice wine. The table was loaded with dishes, which were placed one upon another in tiers, forming a pyramid of Chinese delicacies. There were soups made of birds' nests, of the haliotis, and of sharks' fins; there was beche-de-mer; there were stews and patés; there were roots of the water-lily; but it would take too long to enumerate all the dishes spread before us, of each of which one was expected to taste. Great as is the variety of articles of food in the Chinese cuisine, some things which in other countries are considered most essential are missed by the traveller, and of these none more than butter, bread, and milk. There is a kind of bread which is cooked by steam, and there are flour-cakes fried in oil: they are poor substitutes. A little milk is sold, and women's milk is peddled round the cities mostly for the use of invalids. Foreigners are shy of patronizing the Chinese milkmen. There is an old story on the coast that at a dinner given by a foreigner, the host took a servant to task for serving no milk for the coffee.

"Boy go catchee milk," said the gentleman. The servant disappearing, soon returned with the answer: "No have got."

"What for no have got?"

"That sow have got too muchee piecee chilo; that woman have die," replied the boy. By this the servant informed the gentleman and his guests that they had been saved from drinking the milk of either a sow or a woman only by the death of the latter, and by the birth of a litter to the former.

The only unpleasant feature about our dinner was the custom of every one helping everybody else, so that I could eat nothing which had not made acquaintance with my neighbor's chopsticks. The intervals between the courses were occupied in eating the kernels of pumpkin seeds, which are so much used in China that they form an important item in the trade of certain provinces. In peeling these seeds, if in no other way, the long nails of a Chinese exquisite certainly do good service.

The next day we started on our return to Pekin. The crops were all harvested, and the tall stalks of the sorghum no longer obstructed the view. Hamlets and farm-houses were scattered far and near; the plain seemed like one vast field, broken only here and there by rows of willow trees, raised for the manufacture of charcoal. At every farm-house the hard threshing-floor of pounded earth presented a busy scene: laughing groups of men, women, and children were threshing grain, or tossing it in the air to be winnowed; while others, pushing a long lever, worked the mill which ground it to flour.

As soon as I reached the American legation I learned that the Government, abandoning the idea of organizing a steam navy, had decided to send the flotilla back to England to be sold. This unwelcome news put an end to my hopes of being able to study the coal fields of the more distant parts of the empire.

About this time there arrived at Pekin the Corean embassy,

THE COREAN EMBASSADOR.

bringing the annual tribute to the Emperor of China. I had hoped to get from them a great deal of information about their country, and its relations with China and Japan; but before I was able to do this, a severe attack of the small-pox put an end to my plans for the winter.

Dr. Pogojeff, of the Russian legation, succeeded in taking the photographs of several members of the embassy, including the chief embassador, whose state costume resembles that of the Chinese court under the Mings.

The attendants were dressed in white cotton clothes, padded throughout with cotton batting, and quilted. Their hair was arranged in a knot, secured under a cotton covering; over this they wore broad-brimmed hats of very open horse-hair work.

ATTENDANTS OF THE COREAN AMBASSADOR.

CHAPTER XXIII.

JOURNEY ALONG THE GREAT WALL.

THE month of April had now arrived. Two months of confinement with a severe attack of small-pox had passed, and now returning strength and the warming days of spring roused me to impatience for action. A journey made in the beginning of winter to the great wall and the confines of Tartary had only served to excite in me a wish to penetrate further into that mysterious and almost unknown region which occupies the great table-land of central Asia. My wish was, first to travel as far west as possible upon the plateau, in order to gain some knowledge of the nature of the country, and of the character and habits of the people; and then, after studying the language, to endeavor to reach the plains and valleys, which, lying between the Celestial mountains and the Himalaya, were in the dawn of human antiquity the cradle-land of our race.

I was fortunate in finding in Dr. Pogojeff, of the Russian legation, a companion for the journey. On the morning of the 5th of April we left the northwestern gate of the city. Nearly the whole of our first day's journey lay over the road by which I had begun my trip to the coal fields.

At Chang-ping-chau a road branches off, leading to the tombs of the Ming emperors, which I had visited on a previous excursion. These monuments of one of the most brilliant dynasties of China lie in a large circular valley, which, opening out from the great plain, is surrounded on all sides by limestone peaks and granite domes, a barren and waste amphitheatre. Grand in its dimensions, and almost awful in its desolation, it is a fitting place for the imperial dead of the last native dynasty.

Soon after entering the valley the road passes under an imposing gateway of sculptured marble, and after this beneath two large arched buildings. Some distance beyond these we come to the first of a long series of colossal forms of animals, in marble, which, standing on either side of the road, form an avenue of half a mile or more in length. Of these there are on either side: 1. Two lions standing. 2. Two lions sitting. 3. One camel standing. 4. One camel kneeling. 5. One elephant standing. 6. One elephant kneeling. 7. One griffin standing. 8. One griffin sitting. 9. Two horses standing. 10. Six warriors, courtiers, etc.

These pieces, thirty-six in number, are all colossal, and each is a monolith. In this remarkable avenue the figures face each other, and in passing between them my wild Tartar horse reared and pitched with something of the terror felt by my mustang in passing through a more horrible avenue of standing carcasses on the American desert.*

From here the road leads directly across the valley, passing over several marble bridges, now more than half buried under sand and gravel, and enters the grounds surrounding the central tomb.

At regular intervals, along a curve of a mile or more in length, upon the mountain side, are thirteen great halls, each consecrated to the memory of a Ming emperor. Passing through the grounds of the central one we come to an imposing building, and, ascending the flight of long steps by which it is approached, we enter a hall, of the size of which I remember only that its width is more than ninety feet, while its length is, I think, about two hundred. The ceiling, from forty-five to sixty feet high, is supported by a great number of pillars, distributed in several rows. Each of these columns is a single stick of teak timber eleven feet in circumference; these were brought for the purpose from the south, and with a land journey of more than thirty miles from Peking.

Behind this memorial hall there rises an artificial tumulus perhaps fifty or sixty feet high, through which there is built a rapidly rising and arched passage of white marble, leading to the summit, which is crowned by an inposing marble structure, a double arch, beneath which stands the imperial tablet. This is a large slab, sculptured at the top with the dragon, and standing upright upon the back of a gigantic tortoise. Somewhere in this tumulus lie the remains of the Emperor, but the entrance to the tomb is nowhere marked.

* See page. 58

The twelve other imperial sepulchres are said to resemble this one in every respect.

But let us return to the narration of the present journey. Long before we reached the mountains we could see the dark line of the defile which leads to the Nan-kau pass, and the watch-towers and fortresses and walls, winding from plain to peak, which formed the innermost defences of this important approach to the capital. After a ride of seven hours and a half we reached Nan-kau, our first resting-place, thirty miles from Peking. The next morning, leaving the plain, we entered the narrow valley, winding

MARBLE ARCH IN THE NAN-KAU PASS.

for several miles through a desolate gorge, enclosed by lofty walls and yellow cliffs of limestone. The mountain torrent, which at certain seasons dashes wildly through the valley, makes the construction of a durable road almost impossible, and it was only with difficulty, and with faith in the sure feet of our horses, that we managed slowly to pick our way through the long and narrow field of sharp-edged boulders and masses of fallen rock. After several miles of this work we came to a point where the remains of an ancient road rising some distance above the bed of the valley was preserved along the mountain side. Ascending this by a long flight of steps, of highly-polished blocks of limestone, granite, and porphyry, we passed through a gateway in an inner branch of the great wall, and came soon after to a beautiful white-marble arch built during the Chin dynasty. This structure is remarkable from the fact that while its blocks are cut for a circular arch, the inner surfaces are hewn to produce a ceiling of semi-hexagonal form. It is interesting also to the student of the Chinese language, from the fact that the interior contains inscriptions in an ancient Chinese character. As Dr. Pogojeff wished to photograph this monument, we remained here till the next day, quartered upon a poor family who could offer us nothing but their good will and hot water for our tea. The next day, continuing the ascent of the valley, we left the limestone and came into the granite heart of the mountain. Here, at a point where a bold cliff overhangs the valley, there is a Buddist shrine hewn into the face of the rock high above the path.

At many points in this mountain pass I observed the ruins of an ancient road, which, in its time, must have been built with a great expenditure of labor and treasure. But the mountain torrent and the frosts of centuries have left but small traces even of the ruins. Here and there a fragment of a massive arch, or a few rods of roadway paved with large hewn blocks of granite, have been left standing. After traversing about two-thirds of the pass, the way leaves the valley. Here ascending by a frightful road through the wildest of mountain scenery—a desolate region of barren and shattered masses of granite, cleft to their base by deep and gloomy chasms—we reached the summit, and stood in full view of the inner branch of the great wall of China.

The importance of this position led to its being well defended. The wall is built here of hewn rock, from twenty to thirty feet high, parapeted and well paved on the top, and defended by towers at regular intervals of a few hundred feet. This structure, now almost as perfect as the day when it was raised two thousand years ago, winds along the mountain crest, climbing every peak, descending steep declivities, and supported at the edge of precipices on bold masses of masonry; look where one will, its crenulated parapet and gray towers are visible in lines which apparently double and re-double on each other, now standing out against the sky on the peaks above us, or again winding along

the lower spurs, and crossing the valley beneath our feet. Only the parapet is of brick. Wherever the wall ascends the mountain side its top is built in steps to aid the ascent of soldiers. Many of the towers are several stories high, and are provided with loop-holes, and with arched windows.

A terrific wind was blowing when we reached the summit, and so strong was the blast which whirled through the arched gate of the wall that our horses could barely keep their foothold on the smooth pavement. The descent to Cha-tau is extremely rough. This is an ancient fortress, commanding the northern approach to the pass, and is surrounded with ruins of massive towers and arched buildings.

Here we entered upon the first of a series of mountain plains, fringed with loam terraces, occupying the enlargements of the valleys of the Yang-ho and its tributaries. We shall see that these are the beds of a chain of lakes, which once extended for six hundred miles across northern China, and have since been drained, leaving only rivers and creeks to wind along their former bottoms.

Picking our way over the stony plain, we reached the walled town of Yu-lin. It was already sunset, and without stopping to choose more closely our quarters, we rode into the court-yard of the first inn we saw. I had hardly dismounted when I remembered that I had stayed one night at the same house on a former journey. At that time the landlord had brought to me his son, a boy about eight years old, begging that I would cure him. I could not make out what was the matter with him, and would not have known had I been told. In vain I insisted that I knew nothing of medicine. The landlord, believing all foreigners to be physicians and sorcerers, still urged that I should cure him. Finding all protestation useless, I had left some simple pills, with very wise instructions as to how they should be used. The incident had passed entirely from my mind, and now recurred for the first time when I found myself again in the same inn. Heavens protect us! I thought, if the child has by any chance died, for we shall have the whole town upon us in a mob. I thought the landlord looked very unhospitable as he showed us to our room at the head of the court. When he left I had begun to hope that he had not recognized his former guest. But before long the sound of many voices was heard, and the clattering of feet, which showed that the court-yard was filling.

Keeping my revolver near at hand I waited, not without some anxiety, for whatever might be coming. Soon the door flew open, and a crowd of men and women entered; but much to my satisfaction, they were preceded by the very boy in question, led between his father and mother. The child and his relatives immediately went down on their knees, and knocking the ground several times with their heads, expressed in warm terms their gratitude to the "honorable and wise physician" who had performed this wonderful cure.

Now we were besieged in earnest; the fame of the cure had gone far and wide, and it did not take long to spread the news of the arrival of two doctors through the pretty large circle of suffering inhabitants of Yu-lin. During a good part of the night, and until we left the next morning, our room was a hospital for the blind and the halt, the deaf and dumb, consumptives and epileptics, and many other kinds of suffering humanity. The doctor could of course do little or nothing, and left with fees in the shape of well-earned blessings.

The great wall with its countless towers is visible several miles off, winding along the crest and over the peaks of the high mountains which shut in this valley on the south. Where the Yang-ho, leaving the plain, enters the deep gorge by which it finds its way through the rocky range, a large fortress like a walled city is built upon the mountain side.

Our road, after passing over several miles of fertile bottom-land, approaches the city of Hwei-lai (hien), a place which in its day must have had considerable importance. A long and handsome bridge of white marble with many spans here crosses a tributary of the Yang-ho; but several of the arches are gone, rendering it useless.

Beyond Hwei-lai the road, rising to the summit of a terrace, skirts the edge of the mountains, and passes through several walled towns, and near one or two which are entirely deserted, their crumbling walls enclosing now only cultivated fields. Before us rises a high, sharp peak with ragged and precipitous sides and crowned with ruins. This is called the Ki-ming-shan or Cock-crowing mountain. A legend relates that two pious sisters vowed, the one to build a convent on the top of the mountain, the other to bridge the river below, between sunset and daylight. The sister on the summit fulfilled her vow, but the cock crowing before the other had finished the piers of her bridge, she drowned herself in despair in the river.

Before reaching the town of Ki-ming-i we skirted the foot of a long mountain called the Pa-pau-shan, or eight precious hills, near the base of which lime was being burned. Passing under the walls of Ki-ming we came to the Yang-ho, at the foot of the Ki-ming mountain. This peak consists of the limestone which, as we have seen, forms the floor of the coal formation, and which here, bending upward with a vertical dip, forms the eastern border of a narrow coal basin, which it overhangs. The western side of the mountain has been honey-combed by the miners, and probably the caving in of these works has done much to give the hill its broken appearance. Although this anthracite basin is here narrowed to very small dimensions, it is either an outlier or a continuation of the coal field of Ta-tung (fu), in Shansi, for the valley of the San-kang-ho is in a synclinal fold, at the east and west ends of which we find respectively the coal of Ki-ming and of Ta-tung. A few miles northwest of Ki-ming the road enters a gorge, by which the Yang-ho finds its way through mountains of limestone and schalstone. The route is quite picturesque, being cut into the rock along the edge of the rapid and foaming river. At the northwestern end of these narrows a small cluster of houses, called Hiang-shui-pu, is the usual resting-place for the middle of the day. Here caravans of camels and mules are rested, while their drivers collect in a large room, which is at the same time kitchen and eating house. Here also we entered, and, sitting down at a rough deal table, ordered our dinner of the Chang-kweite, or, as Abbé Huc calls him, "the Inspector of the chest." There were stewed mutton, and fried mutton, and beef and poultry, chi-tang-chau'er or fried eggs, lau-ping and man-tau, or fried cakes and steamed bread, and vermicelli. There was also pork in various shapes, but our knowledge of the Chinese pig and its habits disinclined us from partaking of its flesh. Excluding this we ordered a little of everything else, and the cooking of our dinner began under our eyes. We heard the chickens squeal, and in a few minutes they were thrown through the window to the cook, who had them dressed and broiling in an incredibly short time; the bread-maker put the lumps of man-tau into the steamer and then busied himself with the lau-ping. Taking a large piece of well-kneaded dough, and making it into a stick a yard long, he drew, threw, pulled and twisted it until it assumed the dimensions of a girl's skipping rope, and then doubling and twisting and pulling it again and again, producing a double stub and twist texture, he cut it into small pieces, which after a good deal of flapping and patting became respectable disks; as he finished each of these he uttered a shout, and with a well-directed aim tossed it some twenty or thirty feet across the room to the cook. In the meantime another man was manufacturing the vermicelli. Seated on a machine, some three or four feet above the cooking range, this man worked a long lever which moved a piston in a cylinder with a perforated bottom; at every stroke the long white strings descended into a boiling pot beneath, until the cook, judging that the quantity was equal to the demands of our appetite, cut off the material flush with the cylinder, giving the man on the lever time to curl up on the narrow board and smoke his pipe till another customer should need his services. While waiting for dinner the traveller passes his time in drinking large quantities of tea, but during the meal the beverage consists of the strong rice brandy, sometimes flavored with rose leaves, and always taken hot.

From this place the road, leaving the river, crosses a desolate region of low hills, and then descends into the plains, and after a few miles approaches Siuen-hwa (fu). This is a large city, once of considerable importance, and now interesting to the traveller from the fact that it has some very good inns.

Our stopping place was outside the gate, but wishing to present a letter to the head of the Roman Catholic mission we entered the city the next morning. Two broad avenues, intersecting each other at right angles in the centre of the town, connect the four chief gates. At the crossing of these ways there stands a large tower several stories high and highly ornamented; it is pierced at the bottom by a groined arch, coinciding with the crossing of the avenues.

At the mission building we found only Chinamen, one of whom informed us, in very fair Latin, that the father had gone beyond the wall to administer the sacrament.

The lowlands of the plain are fertile and well cultivated, but a few miles northwest of Siuen-hwa the road ascends a terrace slope where the surface is stony and sandy, and then enters a region of hills of trachytic porphyry and drifted sand. The rock is amygdaloidal and contains very beautiful varieties of chalcedony. Passing this low spur, the road continues over a sandy plain to Chang-kia-kau, called Kalgan by the Russians, one of the great market towns of the empire, and a fortress of the great wall. It is a long and narrow place, stretching several miles along the west bank of a tributary of the Yang-ho. The stream here breaks through a short and narrow gorge with vertical sides, forming a natural outlet for the great highway to northern Asia. Here too is a gate of the great wall, and on either side of the gorge the timeworn structure and its towers are visible, climbing the steep slopes, and winding along the uneven mountain crest. The long pull to the top of the mountain is well repaid by the wide view. Climbing to the top of a ruined tower I could see in the north the level outline of the table-land of central Asia; while to the south, beyond the broad valley of the Yang-ho, the country rises in ridges, one behind the other, the furthest and highest just visible as snow-capped domes.

The great wall was built about 200 years B.C., as a barrier against the hordes of Tartar cavalry. It was everywhere constructed of the materials found in the immediate neighborhood. On plains and terraces, which afforded clay and loam, it was constructed with an earthen core, built up in well-pounded layers, growing narrower toward the top, and faced with large tiles laid flat. The top also was paved with tiles, and defended with a parapet. On mountains of stratified rock the facing was made of masonry, and the interior filled with earth and cobble-stones. Here on the mountain of Kal-gan, where the rock is a trachytic porphyry, which breaks only into most irregular shapes, the wall is of solid masonry, the stones being laid in cement; its section is here an isosceles triangle, the crest being brought to a sharp edge. Everywhere throughout its length it is defended by towers, which rise from it at regular distances of a few hundred feet. In many places the northern side was defended by ditches and embankments, but I do not know whether these formerly existed along its whole length, or whether those places in which I saw them were the sites of ancient attacks, during which these were thrown up for local defence. Every mountain pass and every weak point was defended by a fortified town. The wall is now in very different states of preservation, according to the material used. In the valleys, the points where it was originally the most needed, it has crumbled into a mere line of rubbish, which is being rapidly graded down by the plow.

During the early periods of Chinese history, when the young nation was asserting its existence against natural obstacles and the aborigines of the country, as well as external foes, it seems to have been a common practice to defend the approaches to the more peopled districts by walls of greater or less length. Frequent mention is made to this effect in the earlier histories of the northern provinces. Thus, in the Fang-yu-chi-yau, it is said that Chang-Wang, of the Chow dynasty (1134 to 256 B.C.), built the wall of old Nan-pi, two miles and a half northeast of the present town of that name, as a defence against the San-Sung (ancient Tartars). Nan-pi is in southeastern Chih-li. Again there is an earthwork thirteen miles south of Tien-tsin, which is said to have been built by the chief of the kingdom of Shan-tung, for protection against the northern barbarians.

The home of the nomads, chiefly the Hiung-nu (the ancient Turks), was on the plains of the plateau of central Asia. Along the edge of this region the princes of Tsin, of Chow, and of Yau, had built defensive walls.* This was during a time when China was subdivided into petty feudal states. When Tsin-chi Hwang-ti, "the first universal emperor," had consolidated all these contending territories, he began the work of uniting all the northern defences. The result, after ten years of labor, was a continuous wall, extending from the gulf of Liau-tung, fifteen hundred miles west, to the mountains of Kan-suh. "It has been estimated that this monstrous monument of human labor contains material sufficient to surround the whole globe, on one of its largest circles, with a wall several feet in height."

Chang-kia-kau is the frontier town on the main highroad to northern Asia, and the point of union of two great channels of northern trade, coming from Han-kau on the Yangtz', and from Tien-tsin on the Pei-ho. This position has made it the starting

* See note by Klaproth, in "Timkowski's Travels," Vol. I., p. 309.

point of the caravans which carry the immense quantities of tea consumed by the eighty or one hundred millions of the inhabitants of Russia. It is also a distributing point for the more varied trade with central Asia, though in this respect it has a strong competitor in Kwei-hwa-chung, or Koko-hoton, a market town near the northern bend of the Yellow river.

Before leaving Peking we had endeavored to obtain passports for Chinese Tartary; but the Government had declined to assume any responsibility for our safety beyond the limits of the great wall. We now found that without such documents we could get no guides, either among the Tartars or the Chinese. This was however no great privation, as the prospect of being thrown upon our own resources, on a journey which had no definite point in view, added considerably to the romance of the adventure, which is the delight of the explorer. As no Tartars would accompany us, we were obliged to retain our Chinese muleteers. Besides these I had my Chinese servant, and the Doctor was accompanied by a Cossack, from the Russian legation, who was both a Mongol by birth, and a Buddist by religion.

Leaving Chang-kia-kau by the gate of the great wall, we ascended a narrow gorge between lofty cliffs of trachytic porphyry. Eight hundred or a thousand feet above us the precipice on our left was crowned by the black line and ruined towers of the great wall. For several miles the valley was bordered by lofty hills of porphyry and tufa, with steep slopes and castellated summits, the declivities, often ribbed with dykes of younger rock, projecting like walls above the surface. The tufa and porphyry are quarried at several places in slabs and blocks for building. About seven miles from Chang-kia-kau the character of the country changes, and we pass for a short distance between hills of metamorphic schists, rising in sharp-edged pyramids with grassy slopes.

The valley has a rapid and regular descent, and its bottom is a smooth, even surface of gravel. A little further on, the walls of the valley are formed of flat-topped hills of gravel, eighty to one hundred feet high.

Near Tutinza, a small village of Chinese mud huts, the road begins a more rapid ascent for a few miles. After overcoming this, the traveller stands upon the steppes of Tartary, and beyond the limits of China proper. Here also the great wall rises to the top of the plateau, after making a sharp bend to the north. From a crumbling tower, standing on the very edge of the escarpment of the table-land, I obtained one of the fine views which, among the many reminiscences of extensive journeys, stand pre-eminently impressed upon my memory. Stretching far away on either side there was the precipitous edge of the plateau, overhanging the lower country as the cliffs of a bold coast overhang the sea. To the north lay the boundless steppes of Tartary; to the south the mountains of China. We were here on one of the sharpest boundary lines drawn by nature on our planet. The change, geologically and topographically, from the broken and barren mountains of metamorphic rocks, Devonian limestone, and Triassic coal, to the high grass-clad plains, forming the surface of the comparatively recent volcanic rocks and marine deposits of Mongolia, is extremely abrupt. Climatically and socially the transition is not less sudden; the plains to the north receive winds which have been drained of their moisture by the broad belts of surrounding countries. Being thus scantily watered, and possessing no fuel but the dung of cattle, they are suited only to the subsistence of pastoral nomads, and their herds of sheep, camels, horses, and cows. The habits and status of these wanderers are fixed by nature; there can be no progress, no transition from the nomad life to a higher order of existence, since the very elements of such progress are excluded by the surrounding physical influences.

Nowhere is the influence of nature over the condition of man more marked than here. There is no apparent limit to the length of time that a nomad race might roam over these plains without advancing a step in the social or intellectual scale; but simple habits, life in the saddle, and a meat diet, have made of them a race of hardy warriors, needing in the past only a Gengis Khan or a Timour to make them shake the world.

South of this boundary all is different. When the early Chinese, themselves probably long a nomad people, first entered their present country, they entered also upon a new life. A country suited only to agriculture, it necessarily revolutionized the habits of its settlers. The varied gifts of nature, and the necessity of using them; the obstacles offered by man and nature, and the necessity of overcoming them—these were the seeds which were to ripen; and being planted in a land wonderfully adapted to their growth, out of them has arisen, step by step, a civilization which until recently towered above all others.

From one ruined tower we could see the winding courses of the great wall, the barrier raised by man twenty centuries ago between barbarism and refinement. Though not always sufficient, it has withstood more than one shock. Tempted by the wealth of the empire, in wave after wave the fierce hordes of the north have spent their fury and their strength against this wall, and, rolling back, have overwhelmed the less resisting nations, even of Europe.

I could see that while the general course of the plateau escarpment was north of east and south of west, it was as sinuous as a coast line, bending northward in deep bays, or jutting south in long peninsulas, terminating in bold promontories. The belt from ten to thirty miles wide, lying between its base and the mountains of northern Chili, is far below the level of the plateau, and has the appearance of a region of low flat-topped hills. The plateau at its edge consists of a black volcanic rock, the decomposition of which furnishes the soil and nutriment for the heavy growth of grass with which the plains are covered.

The elevation here above the sea is 5,400 feet,* and is probably not less than from 3,000 to 3,500 above Chang-kia-kau. From this southern edge the general elevation of the plateau drops off to the northward to the sand desert of Gobi.

Near the tower which has just been described is a small postal station called Hanoor.

The view inspired me with a wish to travel westward on the table-land, keeping near the edge. This plan seemed to promise both insight into the geological structure of the country and a greater variety of scenery. I knew that Hanoor was near a caravan route which, branching off from the post-road, took a westerly course; but the only information we could get from the people was, that the first place to the westward was called Borotsedji. As it was already afternoon we determined to make that point our stopping place for the night. Leaving Hanoor with the intention of following the first indications of a route to the west,

* Fuss und v. Bunge.

we passed a small lake with no outlet, covered with ice excepting around the edges. In the little open water thus left them were many ducks, pioneers of the annual migration northward. The surface of the country here is rolling, or rather the plateau is covered with knobs, eighty to one hundred and fifty feet high, with rounded tops and broad bases, the profile lines forming unbroken and gently sweeping convex and concave curves.

Seeing some antelopes in the distance, I left the road with the Doctor and the Cossack to get a shot. The unaccustomed excitement put us so far off our guard that when we had finished the fruitless chase we found ourselves lost. After trying for some time to find the route we had left, which was more an imaginary line than a beaten road, we struck out in a northwesterly course, determining to keep this till we should find some brook, by following which we should probably come upon a Mongol encampment. After ascending many knobs and crossing the intervening valleys without finding any signs of water, we came upon the top of a large hill, from which the Cossack called our attention to some objects on another summit which he pronounced to be sheep. We thought that we could see them move, and were so sure of the neighborhood of the Mongols that we instantly set out for the spot. On reaching the eminence we found to our great surprise that there were no animals, and that we had been misled by an optical illusion; a few small stones, not a quarter as large as a sheep, had been distorted by an atmospheric effect. After the result of this deviation we determined to adhere strictly to a northwest course. The sun was already sinking near the horizon when we reached the top of the next hill; and here an unexpected sight met us. The rays of the setting sun were brilliantly reflected from the gilded vanes and balls which decorated the roof of a temple about a quarter of a mile distant. It lay in a broad grassy valley, the slopes of which were so regular and gentle that it was impossible to tell where the meadow ended and hill-side began. A narrow brook meandered through the meadow, and toward this thousands of sheep and camels, horses and cows, were wandering over the grassy plain.

Around the temple there were a few houses of brick, and a small village of tents. Toward these we directed our course.

The inhabitants informed us that the caravan route crossed the creek half a mile further north, and thither we turned our steps. It was nearly dark before we reached the place, but we could distinguish the outlines of a large enclosure surrounding some buildings, and the loud barking of dogs served as a guide. Fighting our way into the court through an army of savage curs, we found that our pack-train had arrived there, and that we were in Borotsedji. This was a large establishment for the collecting of wool and hides. The nights were still cold, and the *kangs* or beds were heated. I believe I have not yet given a description of these peculiar Chinese couches. At the end of the room there is a raised platform, about two feet high and eight or ten feet wide, with a length equal to the breadth of the room. The whole is constructed of bricks, and has underneath it a large fire-place, with horizontal flues extending everywhere immediately under the surface. The top is covered with a coarse hard matting of split bamboo, and forms the bed of as many people as can be uncomfortably packed upon it. Every traveller carries his own bedding, unless he wishes to sleep without any. Now, the kang at Borotsedji, although unusually large, presented no more area than was needed by the Mongols and Chinamen, and when we added our party of six we were packed rather more closely than was comfortable. The top of the kang was hot, and as we made up our beds the head of the house added to the fire a liberal supply of dry dung. During the night the heat which collected under the blankets was unbearable; and from a dream, in which I had imagined myself being roasted alive, I awoke to find myself being really stewed. My clothes and blankets were drenched with perspiration, while the effluvia which steamed off from some ten or fifteen bed-fellows, to whom bathing was unknown, rendered the air insupportable. Not less suggestive was the incessant scratching, by which my neighbors kept up a constant fight in their sleep with the countless denizens of their sheep-skin clothing.

The next morning we ascended the grassy valley of a small tributary of Narin Gol. This small stream, rising at the very edge of the plateau, flows northeast by Urtai, and turning to the south descends from the table-land at Teutai, and passing through the gorge at Chang-kia-kau joins the Yang-ho.

The country in this part of the route is everywhere cut into by valleys, varying in depth from one hundred to several hundred feet. The hill-tops thus formed are flat, and in the same plane—that of the original surface of the plateau—excepting when the erosion has isolated small hills, in which case the present knobs are lower than the general plane. Throughout this region the valleys consist of large and small oval depressions, connected by narrow ravines, and containing either small lakes, or meadows occupying the filled-up beds of former ponds. The whole surface of hill and valley is clothed with grass.

This part of the table-land, from the southern escarpment northward, consists of an immense development of beds of volcanic rock, of basaltic and trachytic varieties, which forms a belt of irregular width, of at least a hundred and fifty miles in length, and defines the southern edge of the plateau. After ascending for ten or fifteen miles the valley of the Narin Gol, through a succession of meadows, we reached the summit of a ridge which terminated in the southwest in a distant peak. Several miles to the south I could distinguish a long line of towers, which marked the position of the great wall.

Continuing westward through a series of meadows, connected by the smallest possible brook, we came upon the banks of a little lake which was covered with thousands of ducks. There was, however, no cover, and before we could get within range the whole flock had taken the alarm.

The valley here turned to the north, and as our object was to keep the general westerly course, we crossed a hill and continued toward the setting sun. The country dropping off rapidly to the west, we found ourselves almost before we were aware at the entrance of a very narrow and winding defile, in which we descended rapidly. Two or three miles of this down-hill work brought us suddenly out upon a terrace, beneath which there was spread out before us a broad valley, the fields and villages of which showed us that we had unawares left Mongolia and had entered China. The whole aspect of the country below us was different from that which we had left. Behind us was an unbroken mantle of green, while the region before us was a mass of yellow sand, which was carried by the wind in columns and clouds across the surface. The prospect was certainly uninviting. We had started for a journey among the Tartars of the table-land, and here, almost at the outset, our course had brought us into the valleys of China.

Continuing the descent, we came through dusty roads and clouds of drifting sand to Tau-li-chuen, a village built of sun-burnt brick, where we passed the night. Here occurred the only instance of dishonesty that happened to me in northern China. While the animals were being packed in the morning we had all left the inn for a few minutes, and on returning had missed a bag containing all the silver we had brought for the journey. This was too serious a loss to pass unnoticed, and we instantly began a search into every nook and corner of the inn. Not a box or barrel escaped, no room or chest, even in the women's quarters, was too sacred. The fear of having an end put to our journey overcame all scruples of modesty, and amid torrents of abuse, such as only a Chinese woman is mistress of, we turned men and women out of bed to examine mattrasses. Finally the missing treasure was found, hidden behind some barrels. Nothing but the rapidity with which we had conducted the search, and the fact that the stolen property was really found in the inn, prevented us from being mobbed by the crowd, which the landlord had collected.

My experience in China, especially in the north, did not corroborate the accepted ideas concerning the dishonesty of the Chinese. In this connection I might as well relate an incident which happened in Peking. Walking one day on the banks of the large ponds of gold-fish, which cover many acres in the Chinese city, I called a ragged boy, the only person in sight, and giving him a Chinese bank-note, of the value of about two dollars and a half, told him to buy two cents worth of bread for me to throw to the fishes, and to bring back the change. The nearest houses were an eighth of a mile distant, and as the boy made his way toward these, the two gentlemen who were with me, and who had long been residents in China, laughingly assured me that I had seen the last of the money. Not unwilling to back my faith in the boy's honesty, I accepted a wager from each of my companions, and awaited the result. The boy belonged evidently to the lowest class, and knew perfectly well that we Could not recognize him among a hundred thousand like him in the city. Moreover the amount was to him what fifty dollars would be to one of the same class in New York or London; and yet he returned with his hands full of bread, and bringing the change.

In our journey of the day before we had made a little too much southing; on leaving the village we rode northwest across the fields toward the distant escarpment of the plateau. The farmers were planting, and plows and harrows of primitive forms were at work in the fields; among other implements I noticed a machine, something in the shape of a wheelbarrow, to which was attached a hopper, and which was intended for sowing grain in drills. Over the surface of one of the fields which we crossed were scattered small heaps of material which proved to be a mixture of manure and earth containing beans; by planting portions of this in holes a great economy of manure is effected.

Finding a trail leading northward we followed it into the low and rugged hills, which form the outliers of the plateau, till it entered a ravine, by which we gained the summit of the table-land. For a distance of a few miles we tried to keep near the edge of the highland, but finding it broken by deep and impassable chasms we were obliged to turn northward.

Here also we saw how sharp is the boundary which the escarpment draws between the two races. The yellow sandy fields of the Chinese come to the very foot of the precipice, while at the top the grassy plains furnish pasture for the flocks of the Mongol to the very edge. The Chinese in the valley were ignorant of the Mongol names, of places on the plateau, and even of their existence; while the nearest Tartars seemed never to have heard of Tau-li-chuen. Upon the plateau we frequently came into the broad tracks of caravan routes, but being ignorant of their destination we generally avoided them, laying out a course of our own. In doing this it was necessary to keep a kind of dead reckoning, which I did by using a dioptric compass for bearings, and by timeing the regular gait of my horse for distances. The results of these observations being transferred to a Mercator basis supplied us with a daily knowledge of our position.

Supposing that we should now have little trouble in remaining upon the plateau, we followed the general westerly direction of our journey. For a few miles our route lay over the level grassy plains characteristic of this part of the table-land. The decomposing volcanic rock here furnishes sustenance to an exceedingly rich growth of grass, which in the early summer reaches the height of several feet. Before noon it was clear that the country to the west of us was rapidly descending, and we soon came to the brow of a declivity from which we saw spread out beneath us a broad rolling region dotted with Chinese villages, and cultivated to the foot of the descent upon which we stood.

Here again the view was obscured by the clouds of dust which in the cultivated portions of northern China are constantly raised by the prevailing westerly winds, before the crops have reached a height sufficient to protect the surface. The country which we had passed through during the morning was apparently used neither by Chinese nor Mongols; to the former, like every other part of the plateau, it was forbidden ground; and to the Mongolian herdsmen, the close proximity to the Chinese dogs rendered it probably rather dangerous grazing country.

The escarpment of the plateau, here several hundred feet high above the cultivated country, stretched away to the north as far as the eye could see. Much as I wished to remain upon the plains of Tartary, I did not dare risk the delays which might shorten our journey westward by making a detour of indefinite length to the northward.

Regretfully casting, for aught we knew, a last look at the grassy plains, we descended once more to the dusty fields of China.

The immense mantle of volcanic rock which, spread out with an irregular thickness, varying from hundreds to thousands of feet, forms the southern part of the table-land, has here disappeared; and these depressions, into which we seemed forced to descend, represent the surface of the granitic and schistose rocks which form the foundation of the volcanic formation.

These depressions are bays of the valley system of the Yang-ho, and in them are the head-waters of tributaries of that stream.

Since the erosion of the volcanic mantle this whole valley system has been occupied by a wide-spread chain of lakes, in which were precipitated the thick deposits of sand and loam which constitute the terrace formation already mentioned.

The surface of these lakes seems nowhere to have risen within several hundred feet of the top of the plateau.

Following the Chinese road, we came toward evening into the valley of a stream, and to the small village of Murh-kwo-ching.

It was the first place we had seen without an inn, and we had much difficulty in finding quarters for the night.

After applying in vain at several places, we came to the most respectable-looking farm-house, where we were also refused admission. There being no other way, we determined to take possession.

The farm-house was surrounded by a large enclosure, with a gate-house having several rooms, and in one of these we established ourselves. Then came the efforts to dislodge us. First appeared the master of the house, who politely informed us that he had nothing for us to eat, nothing for our horses, that the room was occupied by others, and that his family were on the verge of starvation. His well-rounded person and smooth face added no force to this protest. Then came, successively, a number of men, who all protested and entreated, and finally departed with threats to rouse the population of the village against us.

Things began to look serious; but the worst was to come. The shrill tones of a troop of women were heard crossing the court. Headed by the lady of the house, they burst into the room and filled it not only with their persons but with invectives. My experience on the Yangtz' river had taught me that the hardest attack to resist would be a troop of Chinese viragos.

As our best and only ally in the fight with the soldiers at Chang-sha had been the wife of our skipper—the woman who had turned the day in our favor—I now concluded that as we could not fight women we should have to give up our quarters, unless we could make the women fight for us.

"Leave this house!" they said. "You are impertinent, red-haired foreign devils!" "You turtles' eggs!" "You cross between a drake and a toad!" "What right have you to come into people's houses when you are not wanted?"

It was certainly not easy to answer invocations made with so much earnestness. Opening our bag of silver, I rolled out the large, rough lumps of the metal, and, displaying them, said to her who seemed to be the mistress:

"Madam, we wish to take nothing by force. We want little, will pay liberally for what we get, and leave in the morning."

The sight of the money evidently had a soothing effect, and removed us from the suspicion of being lawless characters. The old woman then in a softer tone informed us that the room we were in belonged to her son, who was an "unfortunate."

"What is the matter with him?" I asked.

The answer was given by a by-stander, who informed us that the young man was an idiot, who spent all his time in wandering about the country gathering pieces of stones. I involuntarily shoved the geological specimens which I had collected that day under a blanket, to hide what might seem to the good people rather strong evidence of mental aberration on my own part.

Pointing to the doctor I said to the mother: "My good woman, this gentleman is a physician, and may be able to help your son."

The effect was immediate, the old woman bounded from the house, and soon returned, followed by a young man, a hopeless idiot.

The doctor told the mother that it was a case beyond his power, and that he could do nothing. He patted the unfortunate gently on the forehead, and from that moment the poor fellow insisted upon staying near his new acquaintance, every minute motioning to the doctor to put his hand again upon his head. This gentle treatment won the heart of the mother, and through her of every one in the house; our horses were stabled, and a bountiful supper soon appeared. The next morning we found ourselves besieged by all the suffering population of the surrounding country.

The quiet farm-house seemed suddenly transformed into a temporary hospital for every form of disease. The patients were accompanied by friends, and in the tenderness and sympathy shown by these I read a phase of the Chinese character for which foreigners have never given credit to this phlegmatic race. The doctor did what he could, by confining himself chiefly to diseases of the eye, for which he had brought remedies.

The people of the house showed their gratitude by steadily refusing pay, while others brought offerings in the form of oats or hay, which they forced us to accept.

As soon as we could get away we turned our steps northwestward, and soon came into a broken country, where small isolated hills of volcanic rock seemed to indicate the neighborhood of the plateau. Ascending an eminence, I could distinguish the long straight line by which the table-land was defined against the sky, while a few miles to the northeast there lay three small lakes.

Toward these we continued our journey; they proved to be the Gurban-noor—three lakes, now merely three ponds, surrounded by broad margins of clay, covered with a glistening efflorescence of soda. Here was a small Mongol encampment, at which we tried in vain to get a guide. The people, fearing the Chinese officials, steadily refused even to give us any information. Following a narrow trail running westward we rose to the surface of the plateau, and immediately descended into a shallow valley, formed by a series of circular plains, which were formerly lakes, but which were now rich meadows connected by a winding brook.

Riding along the little stream, we came before sunset upon Mongols driving their herds of sheep and cows, and further on, to the encampment of Hoyurtolo-gol.

Dismounting at the best looking yurt, and leaving my whip outside, in accordance with the custom of the country, I entered the dwelling, in which were a middle-aged woman, and a girl of about seventeen. To the former I gave immediately an empty bottle, and to the latter a red scarf, and our good reception was insured; the old woman was very good-natured, and the daughter was the most graceful, and I might say the most beautiful woman I had seen since leaving Japan. This girl showed a modest ease and grace in exercising the duties of hospitality which astonished me, as she had certainly never before seen a foreigner.

These Mongol yurts are circular, generally about fourteen feet in diameter, with a portable trellis-frame wall about four feet high. From the top of this frame springs the roof, in the form of a dome; the whole is covered with thick felt, leaving a circular opening at the top, through which the smoke escapes. The entrance is a small square opening, protected by a heavy curtain; and the only furniture is generally a chest, with a small Buddist shrine, and a ritual in Thibetan if one of the sons be a Lama. The ground is covered with felt mats, and the bedding, generally of sheep skins, is stowed away around the circumference. In the centre of the dwelling a small tripod supports the cauldron, which is the only cooking utensil.

From the frame work of the tent hang pieces of dried meat, and the few other articles of food. Perhaps it was the beauty of our young hostess which inspired us with confidence in the cleanliness of the place; but in this we were sadly deceived, for on leaving the next morning we felt that we had carried away with us some of the super-abundant inhabitants which infest alike the dwellings of Mongols and of the poorer Chinese.

Leaving this hospitable encampment we followed the brook in its southwesterly course.

On either side and before us were everywhere the same flat-topped hills of the table-land, but they are here only the remnants of a volcanic mantle, insignificant in thickness, compared with that further east. The valleys here have everywhere cut through this covering and into the sub-structure of schistose rocks.

It was now only the seventeenth of April, and yet the whole country was clothed in the full beauty of spring; while from higher points we could see far away to the south the mountains of Shan-si covered with snow; around us the flat-topped hills, their sides and the broad meadows between them forming an unbroken carpet of green, were mottled with the flowers of early spring.

Scattered over the country, herds of cows and sheep, horses and camels, were lazily grazing, while the Mongolian herdsmen, too heavily dressed in skins to walk, lounged listlessly in their saddles, or spurred their horses across the plain to meet and wonder at our cavalcade. The valley led us through a narrow defile between walls of chloritic granite, and out of this into another bay, from which the drainage finds an exit through the Si-ho into the Yang river. Soon after leaving the gorge the road crosses a lava-stream one or two thousand feet broad, and from sixty to eighty feet thick, through which the rivulet has cut its way. This rock has a beautiful columnar structure, and appears to have flowed down from a neighboring mountain, which has all the appearance of a half-destroyed crater.

The eruption must have been subsequent to the erosion of this part of the plateau. It was the only instance in which I observed traces of true volcanic action, more recent than that to which the volcanic formation of southern Mongolia owes its origin. Near this point there is a large Chinese cattle-ranche, at which we nooned.

After a long ride through a rocky country we came, toward sunset and in the midst of a drenching thunder-storm, to the Mongol encampment at Chaganoussu.

Applying for admission at the principal tent, we were peremptorily refused by the old woman, the wife of the chief.

We learned that the men of the place were mostly away on military duty, and that the women were frightened at the arrival of our strange party. The doctor and I entered the tent with the hope of conciliating the chieftainess by means of presents, but it was useless; she stormed, and insisted upon our leaving, and went so far as to strike the doctor in the face.

This act so exasperated my Russian friend that he involuntarily drew his revolver, at which the old woman gave a howl and bounded out of the tent. Fearing that there would be trouble, we formed our party in the open space among the yurts. We had not long to wait; in a few minutes the woman re-appeared, leading a motley crowd of Chinese and Mongols, armed with sickles and clubs, whom she inspirited with wild gesticulations and loud cries.

There was something half ludicrous and half serious in the appearance of this novel force, as it rushed down hill toward us, headed by an enraged woman, whose robes and dishevelled hair were streaming in the wind; and the effect was heightened by the loud peals of thunder and bright flashes of lightning which broke at once the silence and the coming darkness of night.

The enemy came on and surrounded us bravely enough, until they perceived that instead of being frightened and fleeing we quietly stood our ground and only laughed at them, and that moreover we wore revolvers in our belts.

Being somewhat cooled in their ardor they formed a large circle around us, evidently needing stronger inspiration before beginning an attack. The old woman danced with rage, calling us and her followers all sorts of bad names, but all to no purpose; we continued to walk quietly up and down, smoking our pipes, and the attacking force maintained its distance. This state of things might have lasted all night had not the arrival of a Lama, who was the son of the woman, brought us an ally. Understanding Chinese he soon learned the position of affairs, and pacified his mother sufficiently to gain for us the right of using the tent. The volunteers were disbanded, and the only bad result of the battle was a thorough drenching all round.

Chaganoussu, like most of the lakes of Mongolia, has no outlet.

Filling the large depressions of valleys, these small bodies of water receive the drainage of the surrounding country. At some former time, when the precipitation of moisture was probably greater, the valleys contained streams which formed the outlets of the lakes into tributaries of the larger rivers; but now the rain-fall is hardly equal to the evaporation, which keeps the water-level below the point of outlet.

Leaving this lake we passed the dry bed of another, the Hoy-urnoor, and before noon came to a gorge which leads into the valley of the Kir-noor. Before descending we climbed to the top of a neighboring hill to get a view of the country. We were here again on the edge of an escarpment of the plateau. Before us lay a valley seven or eight miles wide, running nearly north and south, lying many hundred feet below us, and nearly surrounded on all sides by the almost vertical wall of the plateau. It is a broad plain, sloping gently from all sides toward the centre, and covered, excepting near the middle, with a heavy growth of waving grass. We could see no water; but near the centre a large area of glistening white efflorescence reflected the noon rays of the sun with dazzling brilliancy.

Descending from our lookout we reached the plain, and soon came to the Mongol village of Hoyurbaishin, consisting of houses built in the Chinese manner; they were the first of the kind we had seen among this people. In return for the hospitable reception we received here, the doctor exercised his knowledge of photography in taking the portraits of the inhabitants. The most patient as well as most delighted sitter was the wife of our host, who made up for her lack of beauty by the gay color of her silk dress, and by the amount of silver ornaments braided into her hair.

Seen from the plain, the face of the enclosing plateau escarpment is everywhere marked by parallel, horizontal lines, which are continuous on the same level around the headlands and valleys of the wall, and are reproduced on the sides of a hill which rises from the plain; they are visible to the naked eye at a distance of ten or twelve miles, defined where the ascent is gentle by masses of large and small fragments of rock, and on the steeper declivities by a slight variation in the angle of slope.

They undoubtedly mark former levels of the lake surface, and the higher ones probably belong to a time when the great chain of ancient lakes existed through northern China on a scale second only to that of the North American lakes.

The only trees which we saw after leaving Chang-kia-kau were two about twenty feet high growing in the rocks at the foot of the plateau wall. The greater part of the plain is covered with grass, supporting large herds of sheep; but, as we approached the recent lake-bed, the surface was cut up by dry and shallow water-courses, with only tufts of grass, between which the ground is bare and cracked. The present lake is a mere pond, bordered by a large area covered with an efflorescence of soda. It is said to be drying up; and the Mongols assert that its waters have flowed into the Te-Hai further west—an apparently unfounded belief, as there is no surface communication between the two lakes, and the natives on the shore of the Te-Hai were not aware of any increase in its volume. Still it is evident that the waters of the Kir-noor are rapidly disappearing; and the cause, whether temporary, or a constantly operating change in the climate, has been acting at least for several years.

Among the lakes we have already noticed, the Chaganoussu is also disappearing, and the adjoining Hoyur-noor has for several years only been represented by its dry bed.

Crossing the plain we forded a small stream of fresh water, and, passing through a marshy tract, approached the western wall of the valley. Here leaving the plain to ascend to the plateau, we passed a deep and gloomy gorge, cut through the table-land to its very foundation. This chasm seems to connect the valley of the Kir-noor with that of the Karaoussu, a tributary of the Tourgen-gol, which flows into the Yellow river. After a gradual ascent of one or two hours we came again among the flat-topped hills and shallow valleys of the plateau, through which we wound for several miles. Quite unexpectedly we came upon the brow of a precipice, overlooking a broad circular valley several hundred feet beneath us, presenting an unbroken surface of grass, covered with thousands of grazing animals. In the distance the gilded vanes and balls of a Lama temple reflected the rays of the setting sun, and gave the place the appearance of an enchanted valley. The sun had set before we found a practicable route for descent through a long and narrow gorge.

The hills rising in the valley are of gneiss, overloaded with garnets. It was night when we reached the Lamassery. This is one of the many temples and small monasteries which are scattered through the valleys of Mongolia, subordinate to the few larger ones which are the seats of living Buddas.

They form the centres of pilgrimage for the immediate neighborhood, and are the schools in which the young Lamas get the elements of their religious education. They are well patronized, as it is the custom for almost every family to set apart in early childhood one of its sons for the priesthood.

This was the last of the Mongol settlements, for the next morning, after rising to the surface of the plateau, we found ourselves among cultivated fields, and soon came into a Chinese village. The fame of the doctor had already reached this place, and while we were at dinner the court of the inn was filled with people wishing to be cured by the magician from over the sea. Evidently there was no lack of faith to help the action of medicine. They were chiefly troubled by diseases of the eye, and we were surprised to see the fortitude with which men and boys bore the application of caustic agents to that sensitive organ.

We had gone but a short distance when we were overtaken by several of the patients bringing bags of oats, which they pressed upon the doctor in return for the services he had rendered.

During the afternoon we suddenly found ourselves again upon an escarpment of the plateau, and overlooking a broad plain sunk a thousand feet or more beneath us. About twelve miles broad and eighteen or twenty miles long, it is almost entirely surrounded by the lofty wall of the plateau, from the foot of which its surface everywhere slopes gently toward a beautiful lake covering several square miles in the centre.

This valley is in great part cultivated, and the young crops had already covered it with a green carpet. The end nearest us was divided into large farms, containing groups of buildings of a superior class, surrounded by enclosures.

A long and tedious descent brought us to the plain, and we then found that the buildings we had seen were, at least in part, Chinese Buddist monasteries. We were now in the valley of the Te-Hai, or Daikha-noor.

The next morning we made a detour to visit the lake, and

found its waters salt, but not bitter; it is surrounded by a broad margin covered with efflorescence of soda.

Along the northern edge of the valley arises a lofty mountain ridge, of which the barren peaks tower high above the table-land.

On the south, perched upon the highest points of the plateau, there are ancient and crumbling watch-towers, commanding a view of the whole plain, and from which signals could be made to the long line of towers of the great wall. They are silent monuments of a time when the shores of these lakes were the homes of an aggressive race, ever threatening a descent into the fertile regions of China.

In the southwest the valley is apparently open, or divided only by a very low water-shed from the plains of the Yellow river.

I have shown in another place * that this opening was probably the connecting channel between the large lake which occupied the valley of the Upper Yellow river and the chain of inland waters which filled the valley system of the Yang-ho and the San-kang-ho.

It was here that we first heard of the Mohammedan rebellion, which, after spreading through Kashgar and Yarkand, and through the western and northwestern provinces of China, had now approached to within two days' journey of the Te-Hai. This state of things rendered it useless for me to think of carrying out my journey to the Tien-shan, and I decided to return immediately to Peking.

Leaving the lake, we turned our steps toward the southeastern part of the valley, where a deep gorge cleft through the plateau forms the only place of exit to the east. This was another connecting link between the ancient lakes, and at a later period formed an outlet by which the waters of the Te-Hai drained into the San-kang-ho; but now, the evaporation being in excess of the rain fall, the level has sunk below the bottom of the gorge. This defile is cut through the whole thickness of the volcanic formation, of which the black walls rise nearly a thousand feet on either side, while at the bottom they are seen resting on upturned strata of granulite impregnated with garnets.

At Ma-an-miau the valley opens to form the broad swampy plain of Fung-ching. Here the high plateau wall leaves the road;

* "Geological Researches in China, Mongolia, and Japan." Smithsonian Institution, 1866.

the part which formed the southern side of the gorge trends away to the south-southwest, till the steep face of the level outline of its edge is lost in the distance; the northern wall of the gorge continues a few miles further, and then before reaching Fung-ching bears away to the northeast; but we have not yet reached the southern limit of the volcanic formation. At a level of perhaps a thousand feet below the surface of the higher table-land there begins a lower plateau, the flat surface of which is two hundred or three hundred feet above the surface of the valley, and spreads southward from the foot of the escarpment of the higher. Consisting of the same volcanic formation as the higher table-land, it was without doubt once the continuation of the latter, the difference of level being due to the occurrence of an immense "fault."

Toward evening the gray walls of the large town of Fung-ching appeared above the plain, reminding us that we had re-entered China. In the midst of a drenching rain we passed the ruined gate, and traversed in darkness the narrow and muddy streets of the city. In vain we applied at inn after inn; none would receive us. In spite of the storm a large rabble of men and boys collected around us, growing more and more insolent after every failure on our part to find a resting-place. Tired and exasperated, we determined to proceed to the ya-mun and demand assistance from the magistrate. After being several times misled, through the malice of pretended guides, we arrived at the court of justice, followed by an unwelcome retinue of a thousand or more vagabonds. Theoretically every magistrate in the empire, and even the Emperor himself, is obliged to give immediate audience to any one who may sound the great gong before the ya-mun or the palace, but at the present day few Chinamen would be foolish enough to expect an answer to such a summons.

Knowing that any intimation to the magistrate of the presence of foreigners would be placing him on a bed of thorns till he knew that we were housed, and beyond the possibility of involuntarily creating a mob, which might cause him the loss of his place, we proceeded to take the most effectual means of making him aware of our presence. Riding up to the great gong I seized the beater, and with vigorous strokes sent reverberating through the night air, through court and hall, such peals of barbarous tones, as should rouse his worship, even though he were deep in the sleep of opium. Immediately the great gate swung open, and the wire-capped executioners and retainers of the ya-mun hurried out to learn who was so daring as to intrude so summarily into the precincts of justice.

I demanded instant audience of the magistrate, and in a few minutes a secretary appeared, saying that his master was too ill to be seen.

Giving him our passports and telling him of our trouble, I demanded quarters for the night. This produced the desired result; the magistrate dispatched several bailiffs, who led the way to one of the inns at which we had been refused admission, and this time we had no trouble in obtaining the best rooms in the place.

Upon enquiry I found that the aversion to foreigners had originated in the bad conduct of two who had preceded us.

Fung-ching lies upon the head waters of the San-kang-ho. The highly cultivated valley is cut up by rows of willow trees, raised for charcoal; and the water of the creek is carried along canals to turn the wheels of mills. After descending the stream for a few miles we rose to the surface of the lower plateau, and came again under the shadow of the great wall of China. Even in its ruins this great structure impresses one deeply, both by its extent and its antiquity, as well as by the scenes it has passed through, and the long struggles it has witnessed, perhaps at this very point, between the barbarism of the north and the refinement of the south.

Climbing one of the ruined towers I had a wide view, extending over the fertile valley of Fung-ching, and across the broad and partially cultivated surface of the lower plateau. Six or seven miles to the north arose the lofty escarpment of the table-land, stretching like a vertical wall far away to the northeast and southwest, and indented with all the sinuosities of a coast line. In the southeast and east the high peaks of the serrated barrier range bounded the horizon, while the great wall could be seen trending away east and west, a line of crumbling towers and falling masonry, climbing steep declivities, winding along crooked edges of precipices, or striking in a straight line across the cultivated plains.

A ride of a few miles in an easterly course brought us to the eastern edge of the lower plateau. Descending this we bade farewell to the table-lands of central Asia and entered the sandy and partially cultivated plain of Kwan-tung-pu. In this quiet village of farmers we found comfortable quarters among people who were eager to show hospitality, and content to gratify their simple curiosity without subjecting us to the annoyance and insults to which the foreigner is always liable in large towns. Everywhere in China I found the country people civil and kindly disposed, contrasting strongly in this respect with the rabble in cities.

The plain of Kwan-tung-pu is occupied by a heavy deposit of loam, thrown down in the ancient lakes; in this deposit a tributary of the San-kang-ho has cut out its course to the depth of one hundred feet or more. From the valley thus formed, deep and narrow ravines extend on either side, the result of retrograding erosion. One of these chasms, more than seventy-five feet high, with a width of only four feet, between vertical walls of loam, was seen winding in a crooked course for more than a mile up the slope of the plain.

As we approached the high range of mountains which border the plain on the south we came to the ancient fortress of Chung-hwang-kau, one of the gates of the great wall, which here climbs the range to wind eastward along its crest. Immediately after passing the gate we entered a deep gorge, by which the mountain is here cleft to its base, and through which we travelled seven miles between walls of metamorphic schists. This narrow chasm formed another connecting channel in the chain of ancient lakes, and in places its sides still show remnants of the loam deposit.

Leaving this gorge we entered the valley of the Yang-ho, and soon reached the walled town of Yang-kau. Before entering the gate a large crowd had begun to follow us, and by the time we reached the court-yard of the inn we found it occupied by several thousand people, who, taking time by the forelock, had rushed thither to secure a good view of the "red-haired devils" of the "Western Ocean." While we were eating, the room was crowded with all that could get in, and the paper windows were perforated with innumerable finger-holes, through each one of which an inquisitive eye was visible.

Those in our room annoyed us by feeling our clothes, and hair, and beards, or trying on our hats and shoes, which they kindly passed outside to undergo the inspection and trial of too many swarming heads and dirty feet.

Those outside contented themselves with struggling for a place at the door or window, or cracking jokes at our expense, which kept the crowd apparently in good humor. Before sunset we succeeded in clearing the room, and as the crowd resented this we ordered our Cossack escort to clear the court-yard, but without the use of arms. The people, taken by surprise, retreated beyond the gate, which we instantly barred and nailed. Our late visitors, now transformed into a mob, furiously demanded admission, threatening to kill the foreign devils and the landlord.

Taking turns at guarding the gate, we threatened to shoot any one who should attempt to open it from the inside before we were ready to leave the next morning. Before daylight we let out our pack-train and re-fastened the gate; but we had not finished breakfast when a noisy mob had assembled in large force, and was trying to push a very small boy through the opening under the door, to undo the fastenings.

Hardly had the boy got well under when I pounced upon him and drew him in, carrying him in spite of kicks and screams to the kitchen, where I ordered the landlord to give him a good breakfast. The mob shouted that the boy was being killed, and the shrill tones of a woman's voice were soon heard demanding vengeance. When we had finished breakfast we unfastened the gate and rode out, though not without receiving a greeting of stones, sticks, and mud in quick succession; but we came off without further injury than some bruises.

During the whole of this day our route lay across the plains of the Yang-ho. To the north the plain, rising rapidly, abuts upon the flank of the high range of the mountains along which winds the great wall; while to the south, over a low range of hills, we could distinguish the snowy domes of the high mountains of Shan-si.

Leaving the valley and ascending to the surface of a broad plateau of the loam deposit of the ancient lakes, we slept at the village of Ta-kiau.

On the following day we found this plateau like the plain of Kwan-tung, cut up in every direction by deep and narrow ravines with vertical walls; some of these, of very recent origin, had extended across the roads, compelling us to make considerable detours.

In places the wagon-road, following the course of such a ravine, is sunk from fifty to a hundred feet below the surface of the country, between vertical walls which barely leave room for one cart.

Stopping for the night at Hwai-ngan (hien), we continued our journey the next day through a long narrow valley, passing the deserted town of Kiu-hwai-ngan.

The walls of this place were crumbling, and the enclosed area was under cultivation.

It is no uncommon occurrence in China to find a town deserted, and a new one built a few miles off, bearing the same name, with the prefix *kiu* or old.

Following the little creek we reached a point where the walls of the valley approached each other to form a short and narrow gorge, which opened beyond into the valley of the Yang-ho.

There is here a broad sandy plain with little cultivation. During the afternoon a violent wind raised the fine sand in clouds, which rendered it almost impossible to find our way, and it was not till night had fallen that we entered the streets of Chang-kia-kau (Kalgan).

Wishing to visit the Roman Catholic mission of Si-wan, we passed again beyond the great wall, and ascended the narrow valley of a creek. For eight or ten miles our road lay between the steep walls and castellated cliffs of the porphyry mountains of Kalgan, and beyond these, between pyramidal and grass-covered hills of chloritic slates. Everywhere the hill-sides carried terraces of the loam of the ancient lakes; and as we approached Si-wan the valley widened, and the terraces, assuming larger proportions, formed cliffs of loam rising almost vertically from two hundred to three hundred feet above the creek.

We received a hospitable welcome at Si-wan from the kind-hearted missionary, who seemed well pleased to meet travellers of his own race. Containing almost solely a population of Chinese Christians, Si-wan is one of the many monuments of the zeal of the Catholic missionaries, who are scattered not only through China but in every part of the Pagan world.

Situated some distance from the seat of the magistrate, this small colony attracts but little attention and persecution. Their internal troubles are adjusted by the priest, whose influence rarely clashes with that of the civil authorities, and is then, I believe, generally exerted for good.

Few new converts are made in any part of China, the native Christians being generally, like the few thousand souls around this mission, the descendants of the proselytes of the seventeenth century.

The mission is neatly built, and the church tastefully decorated. Most of the dwellings of the people are excavated in the loam deposit, each house having several rooms, divided by walls of loam left standing, and finished with cement. They are neat and comfortable, and have the merit of being warm in winter and cool in summer. The rows of doorways and windows, cut in the face of the cliff, reminded me of the pictures of cities in Arabia Petrea.

At Si-wan I found a man whose name figures in one of the favorite books of my boyhood, and whom I had certainly never expected to see; this was no less a person than Samdad Chiemba, the Lama cameleer of Abbé Huc, and the companion of that intrepid missionary in his long and dangerous journey through Tartary and Thibet. He was no longer the wayward boy over whose caprices the readers of Huc's charming narrative have often laughed.

I engaged him as a guide over the rough mountains to the south. To avoid the long detour by way of Kalgan, we struck due south, over the high mountains between Si-wan and the Yang-ho. On one of these ranges we crossed again the great wall, here defended on the north side by three parallel ditches, which may be the remains of local earthworks, thrown up during some ancient engagement. Descending into the valley of Chau-chuen, we passed several villages excavated in the face of loam terraces, and, on the following day, reached the Yang-ho at Ki-ming, and thence, following the route by which we had come, after an absence of six weeks, we re-entered Peking.

CHAPTER XXIV.

WESTERN POLICY IN CHINA.*

FROM time immemorial the Emperor of China has claimed to be the Son of Heaven, and, as such, the sovereign of the race. He recognized no equals, and he could be approached by the representatives of other countries only when they came as tribute-bearers and as suppliants.

The free intercourse which was formerly permitted to Western countries was abandoned when the rapid advance of European arms in Asia exposed both the designs and the strength of Spain, England, Portugal, and Holland. The Chinese Government, fearful for its own independence, adopted an exclusive policy; and restricting foreign commerce to the narrowest of limits in the part of the empire most distant from the capital, ignored the foreigner except as a trader seeking gain. That which is known as the Opium War of 1840 added largely to the field open to foreign commerce; but, as it did nothing toward establishing diplomatic intercourse with the Central Government, it merely rendered more active the policy of retaliation, by increasing the points of contact with a people among whom,not only the cause but,the manner of conducting this unjust war had raised a deep hatred of the foreigner. This would ultimately have led to annexation of parts at least of China by European powers, had not the events at Canton in 1856–1858 caused the British and French to carry the war into the neighborhood of the capital. This war led to results which mark a new era, not only in the history of the relations of China to the outer world, but also in the history of Chinese civilization. It may not be amiss to recall briefly the events which led to such a consummation.

The concessions which had been obtained from the Chinese by the treaties of 1842, 1843, 1844, and 1845, consisted chiefly in opening to trade the ports of Amoy, Foo-chow, Ningpo, and

* This chapter appeared in the North American Review, April, 1868.

Shanghai, besides Canton, and in the recognition of consuls established there; in the transfer of the island of Hong Kong to England, and an indemnification of $21,000,000 for the opium destroyed by order of the Emperor, and for the expenses of the war. In addition to these, the subjects of the treaty powers obtained the right to travel within certain limits, and to lease real estate at the open ports, and at these points the toleration of Christianity was assured.

These privileges obtained by force were to a great extent counterbalanced by the hostility shown by the Chinese, and the relations of the two races became daily more and more complicated.

Soon after the close of the Crimean war England turned her attention to the accumulating difficulties in China. The immediate cause of the war which soon followed was in itself a good illustration of the intercourse between the proudest and most powerful nations of the West and East. In October of 1856 the native authorities at Canton seized a Chinese boat manned by the natives, engaged in smuggling under the protection of a British flag. This act was considered by foreigners to be an outrage, and the British consul demanded instant satisfaction. Governor-General Yeh having refused to give an explanation, the British squadron bombarded Canton for three days, destroying the Government buildings. France, and for a short time even the United States, through the frigate Portsmouth, joined England in the aggressive.

Preparations for war were begun on both sides, but the English forces destined for China were diverted to aid in suppressing the rebellion in India. After eight months of suspense, interrupted only by occasional aggressive acts on both sides, Lord Elgin arrived at Hong Kong, and Canton was declared to be in a state of siege. On the 12th of September, 1857, the declaration of war against England by China put an end to the hopes that the Emperor would disavow the acts of Yeh. In the middle of December the allied British and French forces occupied an island opposite Canton, and bombarded the city, and, after taking its defences by storm, finally took possession of Canton on the 5th of January, 1858. Yeh was sent to Calcutta, where he died a prisoner.*

* In this *résumé* of events, down to the taking of Canton, we have followed the author of the article "China" in "The New American Cyclopedia."

After the taking of Canton the allied British and French forces turned toward Peking, as being the only point at which the Central Government of China was vulnerable. Arriving at the mouth of the Pei-ho, and receiving no answer to an ultimatum sent to the capital, the Allies took the forts, and advanced up the river to Tien-tsin, about ninety miles from Peking. This action resulted in the appointment of Chinese plenipotentiaries, and the conclusion of treaties, in immediate succession, with Russia, the United States, England, and France—creating four new ports, throwing open the Yangtz'-Kiang to foreign trade, recognizing ministers accredited to the Court of Peking, tolerating Christianity and protecting Christian missionaries, permitting foreigners to travel in the interior, and indemnifying England and France for the expenses of the war. Such a sudden change in the traditional policy of the great empire seemed the beginning of a new era for Asia, and a fit subject for the first dispatch through the Atlantic cable.

But a murderous fire was opened upon the English and French at Taku in June, 1859, while attempting to force their way to Tien-tsin in order to effect at the capital the exchange of the treaties which the Emperor wished to have consummated at Peh-tang on the coast. This appeared to be a disavowal of the engagements entered into the preceding year. Whatever may have been the moving spirit with the Imperial Government in this affair, it led to serious consequences, which, though humiliating to the Government, have been undoubtedly beneficial to the country. The American minister, conforming to the wish of the Chinese that he should visit Peking by way of Peh-tang, was conducted to the capital. Although he there met with a friendly reception, he was obliged to return to Peh-tang to effect the exchange of the treaties. This step made clear the determination of the Government neither to make nor exchange treaties under the walls of the capital, and more especially to prohibit all direct communication with the Central Government. There is no doubt that the same would have been the case with the other ministers, had they avoided the mouth of the Pei-ho, and gone overland from the neighboring village of Peh-tang. But the anti- foreign party was so powerful at Peking, that it is donbtful whether the ratifications would not have been the beginning of serious troubles; indeed, the treaties were avowedly granted in order to gain time for preparation to resent the force used in obtaining them.

The English and French ministers withdrew to Shanghai, and the court of Peking refusing an apology, their Governments, deciding to obtain it by force, made preparations for war on a scale which should be decisive.

An ultimatum, demanding, first, an apology for the attack on the allied forces at the Pei-ho; second, the ratification and execution of the treaty of Tien-tsin; and third, the payment of an indemnity for the expenses of the naval and military preparations; was rejected by the Emperor.

In the summer of 1860 the allied forces, accompanied by the Earl of Elgin and Baron Gros, captured the forts on the Pei-ho and advanced to Tien-tsin, of which they took possession, and thence to near Tung-chau, a city twelve miles from Peking. During these proceedings the anti-foreign party ruled the weak Emperor; and when negotiations seemed about to be satisfactorily concluded, the Chinese, by an act of treachery, tried to cut off the forces, and seized Mr. Parkes and several other persons, who were returning under a flag of truce from an interview with the imperial plenipotentiaries. All negotiations were now stopped, and, as the prisoners were not given up, it was decided to punish such a flagrant breach of faith. Peking was invested, and Yuen-ming-yuen, the summer palace, a few miles west of the city, was destroyed. In the meantime the Emperor Hien-fung had fled to Tartary, a step which aided much the political revolution that threw the reins of government into the hands of his brother, Prince Kung.

Prince Kung, although very young, exhibited considerable tact and ability; while the fact that with his first appearance began a new policy gave to him a position with the foreign ministers that would not easily have attached to names better known to them.

Those of the prisoners who had not died under the horrible treatment they experienced were given up. A gate of the city was surrendered, and the articles of the Tien-tsin convention were signed, embodying the demands of the ultimatum, the opening of the port of Tien-tsin, and the permanent establishment of the ministers at Peking.

The war was over; the anti-foreign party was thrown into the background, and for the first time the field was open for the action of wise diplomacy in bringing China into the circle of interdependent nations. The manner in which this short and decisive war was conducted tended far more than is generally known to facilitate the attainment of this object. When the use of force was first decided upon, the British minister, Sir Frederick Bruce, who had succeeded his brother, Lord Elgin, turned his efforts toward relieving the people from any participation in the sufferings of war, and aiming the blow solely at the Government. During the presence of the troops in the North, their behavior inspired the inhabitants with such confidence that no difficulty was experienced in obtaining supplies, which were scrupulously paid for. After the taking of Tientsin its population remained confidently at their occupations, and the native committee that had been organized to supply the Chinese army undertook to do the same for the allied forces. Indeed, during the journeys of the writer in the North, he met several wealthy dealers who spoke earnestly of the good times when the foreign troops offered a profitable market for their products. By refraining from a bombardment of Peking, and destroying instead the widely celebrated summer palace, a blow was struck which humbled the Emperor without the loss of a single innocent life, and without injury to private property. The effect of this humane course, so directly opposite to the Chinese method of warfare, and indeed to the previous action of foreign armies in the East, was immediately apparent in the treatment which the inhabitants of Peking and its environs extended without exception to unprotected foreigners. And at present there are few countries in the world where one can travel with more safety than in northern China.

If the attitude of the people during this war exhibited an indifference to the most important political questions, and to the interests of the Government, it showed not less a great degree of independence among themselves, as well as an absence of unfriendliness to Europeans, and proved that our efforts toward the improvement of our relations with China must be directed as well toward them as toward the Government.

The great advantages gained by the treaties, and by the war that insured their validity, were the permanent residence of foreign ministers at Peking, the opening of the Yangtz', the right of travel in the interior for business or pleasure, and, indirectly, the extension of the foreign customs system. To appreciate the full value of these results, it will be necessary to glance at the position held by foreigners before the war.

Confined to a few ports, and treating only with the local officials, they were practically ignored by the Central Government. Having no intercourse with the latter, and treated as barbarian traders by the provincial authorities, such a thing as legal redress for injuries was out of the question. Gunboats ready to act on the orders of consuls, or even without them, were at every port, and no time was lost in using force on the slightest provocation. The different provinces were treated as so many independent nations, and war was waged at one port while trade was continued uninterruptedly at others. In all these troubles, the Central Government shifted the responsibility to the shoulders of the provincial authorities—a policy the effect of which became yearly more evident in the arbitrary action of foreign consuls, and in the insolent weakness of the native officials.

Such a system could not exist without leading to terrible abuse of power by the stronger side, and establishing dangerous precedents, which could be used by either party whenever a favorable opportunity offered; and, worse yet, it formed a school in which foreign officials, merchants, and their clerks, shipmasters, and sailors, learned to exercise with impunity the law of might, and to hold the rights, property, and lives of Chinamen as of no value. Wholesale murder was committed almost daily at the ports, where it was a common occurrence for steamers and sailing vessels to run into and sink dilatory boats and junks, often crowded with passengers. Young clerks drove rapidly through crowded streets, without stopping to care for the women and children run over by their carriages, and men of position made their way through thronged thoroughfares by belaboring the heads of the populace with heavy walking-sticks. Such acts were the more cowardly because of the timid and peaceful character of the natives, and the fact that the removal of foreigners from Chinese jurisdiction to the dead law of the consular courts almost insured impunity for every kind of crime. Hatred of the foreigner caused by this state of things, spread through all the provinces that were in close communication with the open ports.

That such an intercourse must have led to frequent and costly wars, and ultimately to a disintegration of China, and its absorption by European powers, can hardly be doubted; and this danger would have been multiplied with the opening of every new port, and with the increasing influx of lawless adventurers attracted by the rebellion.

But the establishment of direct intercourse between the foreign ministers and the Imperial Government—an intercourse based on a revolution in the policy of the latter—substituted diplomacy for force, and, by causing disputed questions to be referred by both sides to Pekin, reduced the powers alike of consuls and of viceroys to their legitimate limits.

Arriving at Pekin at a time when the Imperial Government was reduced to its greatest straits by the rebellion, the ministers were able to give direct proofs of the sincerity of their professions of friendship and good-will, and immeasurable progress was rapidly made in breaking down the barrier of prejudice that had grown up between the two races. But although the just action of the representatives of western powers was soon appreciated at Peking, and was generally met in a similar spirit by Prince Kung and the Board of Foreign Affairs, obstacles to harmonious action were not wanting on both sides at the treaty ports. In many instances both the consular and the provincial authorities were men who had been educated in the school of the past, and, with them, the traditional method of settling disputes by force was at times resorted to. Too often irregularities committed, now by the foreigner, now by the natives, caused troubles which were not referred to Peking till the use of force had made diplomatic action almost impossible. Unfortunately, too, the disregard shown at times by consuls for the treaties, furnished the Government with a ready answer when its viceroys were charged with disobedience to instructions sent from the capital.

The control of their respective subordinates was easier to the embassadors than to Prince Kung and the Ministers for Foreign Affairs. The Central Government, possessing in theory almost unlimited power, was practically fettered in its action by the corrupt policy of selling its offices, or of paying nominal salaries and allowing the officials to enrich themselves at the expense of the people and of the revenue—a practice which could not fail to produce endless troubles, by affecting trade adversely, now to the spirit, now to the letter of the treaty.

The anti-foreign party was not, and perhaps is not yet, wholly crushed; and though apparently daily losing ground before the increasing confidence in western governments, and before the rapidly growing revenue brought into the imperial treasury by foreign trade, and by the honest administration of the foreign custom officers, it necessarily impeded the action of the Prince and his advisers. And even when, after the death of Hienfung, Prince Kung became Regent during the minority of the young Emperor, the fact that he soon might be held to answer with his head for the administration of the Regency, prevented the use of extreme measures toward dilatory provincial authorities.

Thus in 1863 an accumulation of unsettled disputes with the different treaty powers, arising out of persistent disregard of the treaties at the ports and in the interior, threatened to produce a rupture, and to undo by a new war what had been already accomplished. Fortunately, the West was represented at Peking by men of just and liberal views, free from the prejudice of nationality and race, who were unwilling to risk, by precipitate action, the future welfare of one-third of mankind and the interests of the world. At this time, when war seemed imminent, and when, considering the gigantic proportions of the Taiping and Mohammedan rebellions, a war might have indirectly overthrown the ruling dynasty, and resulted in long-continued anarchy, the foreign ministers framed a co-operative policy, the basis of a moral warfare. This policy, which was endorsed by the respective home governments, marks a new era in the history of the relations of the West and the East, and will surely be not less important in its results to us than to that immense nation with whom the nineteenth century is rapidly bringing us into a contact pregnant with much good or much evil. Originating in the necessity for united action on the part of foreign governments to obtain the observance of the treaties, it binds the ministers to consult together and act in concert on all material questions: thus bringing to bear the moral pressure of the whole western world in support of the just demands of each power.

As experience has shown that the source of the greatest dangers in the future lies in the weakness of the Central Government, as against its provincial officials, the co-operative policy binds the foreign powers to use every peaceful means of strengthening the former, both by encouragement and by moral pressure. One of the first steps in this direction was the guarantying the integrity of China proper, so far as concerned foreign nations, by their agreement neither to demand nor to accept concessions of territory from the Chinese Government. To strengthen the Government within, and to raise China to a military position commensurate with the rank she should hold in the world, the ministers agreed to encourage a thorough reorganization of her army, to assist her in adopting European discipline and arms, and to furnish the officers necessary to introduce these changes. The next and equally important step was, to insure the maintenance of an honest and efficient administration of the foreign customs service, as a means of insuring the revenue necessary to centralized strength. While observing a general neutrality in face of the internal war, the policy called for such defensive action at the treaty ports as might be necessary to maintain treaty rights.

Each of the treaties of 1858 contained a clause permitting the subjects of the respective governments to acquire land for building-sites at the open ports. For greater convenience the consuls of the different treaty powers chose a considerable area for subdivision among their countrymen. These tracts soon came to be regarded as concessions of territory, forming no longer parts of the Chinese empire. The security to life and property at the open ports soon attracted thousands of Chinese families flying from their homes before the scourge of the Taiping rebellion; and thus the foreign settlements, intended by the spirit of the treaties to furnish homes and places of business to foreign merchants, became cities containing vast numbers of natives, who rented dwellings from foreign speculators. At Shanghai, the area under the control of foreigners, and more or less occupied by them, covers nearly ten square miles, and is rapidly filling up with houses. In 1863 the population of this area was nearly one million. The exterritoriality clause, which transferred jurisdiction over foreigners in all civil and criminal cases to their respective consuls, would have been easily extended so as to cover the native population, had the idea that the foreign settlements were concessions of territory been sustained. The first result would have been, that the most flourishing cities of the empire, cities rivalling the largest in the world, would have sprung up on these concessions, concentrating Chinese capital, skill, and enterprise at points beyond the control of the legitimate government. After a few years there would have been British, French, and American cities on the coast and in the heart of China, according to the predominance of the nationalities at the different ports; or they would have become free cities, like those of the Hanseatic League. The immediate interests of speculators—and almost every foreigner speculated—was to have this concession principle carried out, although unauthorized by the treaties; and, in the weak condition of the Government, the action of the foreign authorities, and the necessity of a municipal organization, were rapidly rendering it an accomplished fact. But the principle was too unjust; it was sure to lead to serious complications among foreign powers and with the Chinese Government, and was also sure to increase the weakness of the Central Government. In face of a strong opposition from their countrymen, the foreign plenipotentiaries at Peking agreed neither to ask nor to accept concessions of territory.

One of the difficult questions in our intercourse with Oriental nations is that of the jurisdiction over the foreigners, especially in mixed cases. In the treaties with China, as in those with all Oriental countries, the exterritoriality clause confers authority on consuls in all legal cases over their respective countrymen. The systems of Oriental laws and punishments differ so widely from those of western nations, and there is such general corruption in their administration, that it would be out of the question to place the lives and property of Europeans under their control. Still some other system than the present is imperatively demanded; for the tendency of the present method is to impair seriously the power of the native authorities over their own subjects, and the increasing amount of crime committed by foreigners is growing beyond the proper limits of consular courts.

It is evidently an outrage upon the spirit of international law that a Chinaman or a Japanese should suffer death for a crime against a foreigner, where for the same acts the latter would be punished with a fine or a short imprisonment. This is a question which will solve itself before long; for China has only the alternative of gradual reorganization and progress in the track of the civilization with which she is coming every day more and more in contact, or of retrogression and disintegration. She can no longer remain stationary. There is great vitality in the people; but, unless it become active in them and in the Government, western intercourse will be to China a deadly evil. But there are weighty reasons for believing that the vitality of this people will carry the nation onward through the stages of reform that are needed to effect a transition to a higher political condition, and this reform would involve great changes for the better in many branches of its polity.

The Burgevine imbroglio * proved the danger that might attach to the employment of foreigners in the Chinese army, at the same time that the force organized by Ward and Burgevine demonstrated the possibility of making brave and efficient soldiers of Chinamen, when acting under proper officers and paid regularly. The foreign ministers urged strongly upon the Government the necessity of beginning a radical change in the army, by providing bodies of native soldiers with foreign weapons, and having them disciplined by foreign drill-sergeants, and already considerable progress has been made in this direction. Before any nation can make itself respected by others, it must be in a position to enforce internal order, and to maintain its rights against all comers. The present army of China is wholly unable to do either of these things, and is merely a gigantic drain on the resources of the country, a scourge to the inhabitants, and a source of official corruption. Favored as the empire is by its geographical position, a small standing army disciplined and armed after the manner of western troops would be sufficient for any emergency, and would remove the consciousness of weakness—one of the greatest obstacles to general improvement.

* A few years since, an American, named Ward, acting under a commission from the Imperial Government, disciplined a force of Chinamen to act against the rebels. The undaunted bravery of their commander inspired these troops with a courage that carried everything before them, and their success won for them the name of "The Ever-Victorious Braves." After the death of Ward, from a wound in the head, received while leading his men through a breach in the wall of a rebel city, the command was given to Burgevine, one of Ward's bravest officers. This gentleman, after receiving a serious wound, was made the victim of intrigues on the part both of Chinese and foreign officials; and finding it impossible to obtain satisfaction for his just demands, very ill-advisedly deserted to the rebel cause. Had Burgevine's injury not impaired his energy, this step would certainly have prolonged the rebellion, and might perhaps have led to the overthrow of the Manchu dynasty.

But the most important and most active innovation is the foreign customs organization, which collects the duties on all foreign exports and imports. Originating, in 1854, in the appointment at Shanghai, at the request of the local officials, of three inspectors chosen by the consuls of the three treaty powers, the unexpected increase of the customs revenue attracted the attention of the officers of other provinces, and led to the ultimate extension of the system to every open port. From being a foreign governmental aid to the Chinese, it has become an arm of the Chinese Government, and as much a national institution as the customs department in any western country. At each port there is a commissioner, having under his orders the necessary number of clerks, tidewaiters, etc., of different nationalities. Over all these is an inspector-general, appointed by the Board of Foreign Affairs, with which he corresponds, and through which he reports to the Board of Revenue. The Government has been fortunate in choosing for its inspector-generals men of great ability and well acquainted with the language and customs of the country; and the present incumbent, Mr. Robert Hart, is evidently alive to the importance of the institution as a means of improving every department of Chinese administration.

Every effort is made not only to maintain thorough honesty in the service, but to attract to it young men of high intellectual capacity, and to this end extremely liberal salaries are paid. The employés are now taken from among the best graduates of the English and American universities, the former after a severe competitive examination. After studying the language for two years at Peking, with a salary of £400, they enter active service as clerks, with salaries increasing with promotion from £600 to £1,200; and when advanced to the rank of commissioners, of whom there are thirteen, they receive, according to the port, £1,200 to £2,000.

It is hoped that in time the necessity for employing foreigners will disappear, and that the administration will pass gradually into the hands of efficient native officials. The Government fully appreciates the advantages of the institution. Indeed, it could scarcely be otherwise, considering the great increase in the revenue derived from foreign trade. According to Mr. Hart, they are also gradually learning the importance of paying salaries large enough to raise officials above the necessity of being dishonest; and they are realizing, too, the advantages of departmental division of labor, as compared with the long-established practice of uniting in one official the most varied duties—a practice that renders any check on fraud impossible. If the successful working of the customs organization should lead to reform in these two particulars (and there is much reason for believing that it will), the greatest barrier in the way of improvement in other respects will then be removed, and the road to judicial reform will be open.

Among the great changes that remain to be accomplished, the most needed are such as would affect the finances of the empire; for by insuring a proper collection and application of the revenue, the provincial authorities would be made dependent upon the Central Government, instead of the reverse as at present, and the largest source of official corruption would be removed. The accomplishment of these changes, and those connected with the judicial organization, is a question rather of reform than of revolution. They could be brought about without the overthrow of the existing religious or social organizations, and without any change in the established theory of government.

Such reforms must be the fruit of the grafting of western ideas on the Chinese stock, and their growth must necessarily be slow. They can flourish only under the patient forbearance of more powerful nations, whose duty and true interest it is to encourage, and not repress.

Until ten years ago the decrees issued from the imperial throne taught the people to look upon all foreign nations as barbarian tribute-bearers, and as trembling subjects of the mercy or wrath of the "Son of Heaven." Now this language has disappeared: the decrees published in the gazette and sent through the empire speak in becoming terms of Europeans, and generally give to foreign employés the credit they deserve. Recognizing no equals, and nominally merely tolerating the presence of foreigners, the Government always insisted that in all our intercourse with it we should assume the attitude of suppliants. This stumbling-block vanished after the last war; and in 1863, acting readily on the advice of Mr. Burlingame, they employed the American missionary, Dr. W. P. Martin, to translate "Wheaton's International Law."

Some of the best scholars in the empire were associated with Dr. Martin as assistants; and Tung, perhaps the leading scholar of China, a member of the Board of Foreign Affairs, gave constant attention and the finishing touches to this great work, which was published early in 1865.

That the Government does not look upon this as a mere piece of fancy-work is proved by the fact that copies are sent to officials in all parts of the empire, especially on the coast, as also by the following circumstance: During the late war between Prussia and Denmark, the Prussian fleet in Chinese waters seized two Danish vessels. One of these was captured while at anchor within three miles of the shore; in the other instance, the Prussian, while anchored within the three-mile limit, sent its boats to capture the Danish vessel outside these bounds. The translation of Wheaton was not yet published; but its principles seem to have become familiar to some of the high officials, for the Government instantly demanded the release of the vessels, on the ground that their capture was an infringement upon the neutrality of the Emperor. Much to the astonishment of the Prussian minister, the Government quoted in support of its position decisions exactly covering the cases, and which had been rendered against England, by English law officers, during the war with America.

The establishment by Government of a school in which foreign languages and other subjects are taught is another step forward; for from this school are to be taken interpreters and secretaries for envoys to the West, and for officials at the treaty ports.*

In looking over the history of affairs at Peking during the last six or seven years one hardly knows which most to admire, the unexpectedly high degree of intelligence and statesmanship of some of the leading officials, or the wise diplomacy of the foreign embassadors in turning these to account. But the same history exposes the weak points of Chinese administration, and the existence of a public opinion that demands to be consulted. For example, when Mr. Lay, having, by authority from the Government, organized a flotilla, entered into an agreement with the commander, Captain Osborne, that he should act only under orders from Peking, he transcended not only the limits of his own

* This school has lately been enlarged in its plan, and is now called the University of Peking. Its president is one of the highest and most learned of the Chinese ministers, while an able corps of professors from the West has been attached to it.

power, but likewise those of the Central Government. It may be well to review briefly this transaction, which threatened to lead to disagreeable results.

The increase of piracy and smuggling along the coast and on the rivers called for action on the part of the Government, unless it were willing to have the police duty of the Chinese waters exercised by foreign men-of-war. The Board of Foreign Affairs, therefore, authorized Mr. H. N. Lay, the Inspector-General of the Chinese Maritime Customs, to contract for the building in England of a flotilla of gunboats, which should form a portion of the naval force of the empire, and be officered and in part manned by Englishmen. A fine fleet of eight steamers was accordingly built and sent out to China, and the command, with the rank of admiral, given to Captain Sherard Osborne, one of the best officers of the British navy.

The agreement between Lay and Osborne contained a pledge to the latter that he should be responsible only to the Central Government at Peking, at the same time binding him to act upon no orders, even from the Emperor, unless they had first received the sanction of Lay. This agreement the Government refused to recognize, not only because it had no wish to put supreme power into the hands of its chief of the customs service, but also because the theory and practice of Government in China required that the authority over the navy should be vested in the viceroys of the provinces in which its services might be needed. Thereupon Captain Osborne, declining to be placed in subjection to provincial officials, resigned his position; Mr. Lay was dismissed from service; and the vessels were sent back to England, where they were sold on account of the Imperial Government.

Thus was this costly and much-needed squadron lost to China, not simply because Mr. Lay had assumed to make himself the arbitrating medium through which the admiral should receive the imperial orders, but quite as much because of the fear of the Regency to assume a responsibility which by custom belonged to the provincial authorities.

How much greater the powers of the Emperor may be than those of the Regency, which will end when the Emperor decides to take the reins into his own hands, is a difficult question; but the strong language of censors in memorials to the throne reveals the existence of checks on the imperial will that have their origin in public opinion, whether this be the sentiment of the people generally, as is most likely, or of the large class of literati, or simply of the great body of officials.

The existence of such a powerful public influence should admonish us that the field of our labor is not confined to Peking and the Government alone. Great as is the advance already made, we have on our part to show the people throughout the empire that a treaty is not a mere concession obtained by force, and binding only the conquered.

How easily public opinion concerning us is formed was well shown in the province of Hunan in 1862. An English gunboat at Hankau burned a junk which was conveying soldiers to Nanking. The soldiers had brutally assaulted an Englishman, and with a precipitation in keeping with the old retaliation policy the junk was burned. But the vessel was private property, having been impressed in Hunan by the braves; and its destruction, instead of being a punishment of the offenders, incensed the whole population of eastern Hunan. Knowing no difference among foreigners, the inhabitants of that province visited on the heads of the Catholic missionaries the offence of the English gunboat, destroying the missions, and barely allowing the priests to escape alive. So strong was the hatred toward the foreigner—a feeling first communicated along the great transit route from Canton, and increased by this blind act of retaliation—that in 1863 the writer found it impossible to penetrate to southern Hunan with safety.

In strong contrast to this stands the treatment shown to foreigners through northern China: all who have travelled in that part of the empire will bear witness to the friendliness of the people.

It is not enough that the Government at Peking understands the whole meaning of the treaties, the privileges and obligations mutually conferred and exacted, and that it appreciates the importance to China of the plans followed and recommended by the foreign ministers: it is absolutely necessary that this knowledge should extend to the whole wide-spread body of officials, and further yet to the people at large. The treaties have been published throughout the empire, and the mandarins ordered to abide by them; but it requires time for the officials to learn the meaning of such innovations. Then, too, aside from the weakness of the Central Government, the local authorities have really little power over the people. An official would gladly pay a considerable sum to any foreigner to bribe him to avoid the limits of his authority, so much do they fear popular disturbances, which they are powerless to quell. The authority of the mandarin is, indeed, in great measure dependent on the forbearance of the people, and is proportionate to his popularity. Few officials, even in sight of Peking, venture to resort to extreme measures.

From these considerations it appears how much the extension of our intercourse with this race into fields not yet opened by treaties will depend on the manner in which we meet the people, or rather upon the policy by which western powers shall regulate the actions of their subjects. In China, the axiom, that the will of the people is the will of Heaven, and must be observed by the Emperor, the Son of Heaven, has during thousands of years been accepted as a fundamental principle of governmental science, and continued disregard of it has always caused the overthrow of the aggressive dynasty. This axiom is as powerful to-day as ever, and it is probable that the Emperor would not dare to make a concession antagonistic to the wishes of the people, and there is hardly a concession which we could now ask for that would not call forth a widespread opposition.

The foreign trade of China is as nothing compared with the increase which we have a right to hope for; but this increase will require the introduction of steamers throughout the immense network of inland waters, the construction of long lines of railways and telegraphs, and the development of a great mechanical industry, on the basis of the boundless resources of the empire in coal, iron, raw materials, labor, and capital.

We have no right to expect that the dense population of China will readily welcome these innovations. The Government cannot force them on the people; their introduction can only follow a general conviction of the advantages to be derived from them. From the Government we may ultimately get the right to reside in the interior, and to treat with its subjects for the purchase of property, right of way, etc.; but even this must be based on the strict observance of the treaties by foreigners.

There is little doubt that by exercising patience the prejudices that arise from ignorance of the principles of political economy will be gradually overcome. The Chinese are so essentially practical, and they are from childhood such adepts in the art of making commercial combinations, that we may reasonably expect a rapid introduction of the great modern instruments of material prosperity. The opening of the lower Yangtz' to foreign steamers—a step rendered easy by the destruction of native shipping by the rebels—is instructing the native capitalists and the people generally in the advantages of steam transit, and many steamers are now owned by the former, while native passengers willingly pay higher fares for the privilege of being carried more quickly than by junks.

Many, if not all, of the wealthy Chinese merchants at the open ports appreciate already the advantages to be derived from the introduction of modern improvements, and are ready to advance capital for that purpose, and the opposition of special interests will probably be overcome by driving the wedge gradually. But both the people and the Government must first learn that foreign ideas and improvements are not intended to overthrow the national independence and the imperial authority.

Thus far nothing has been said concerning the missionary problem, for it should not enter into the question of foreign policy. The zeal which urges the Catholic enthusiast to seek a martyr's crown in the interior is a fruitful source of trouble to France, the champion of the Church. As a religious movement, the Chinese Government views the missionary enterprise with perfect indifference, but it fears its political bearings. The authority of the priest too often impairs that of the mandarin, though frequently in favor of justice. Were there danger of more general proselyting, the fear of the extension of priestly power would probably raise an active opposition to the missionaries, but at present the labors of the latter are mostly confined to the small cures that have descended from the past. Few new converts are made beyond the children saved from death or bought from poor parents.

The work of the Protestant missionaries has thus far done little toward complicating our relations with China. Confined mostly to the immediate neighborhood of the treaty ports, they interfere little with the local authorities, and their success is so slight, and even so doubtful, that the Government now offers no opposition to their teaching.

In a conversation with Mr. Burlingame, one of the members of the Board of Foreign Affairs thus stated the views of the Government in regard to religion: "Our sentiments are identical with yours, though they are expressed by different signs; and our religious principles are the same as yours, though they are clothed in different forms: that is to say, what you mean by 'Lord' we call 'Heaven.' It is not a firmament of stone or vapor that we worship, but the Spirit who dwells in Heaven. In the popular idolatry we put no faith whatever, but the Emperor makes use of it as an auxiliary power in governing the people. The teachers of every creed agree as to the principles of virtue; any one of these systems will suffice to deter men from the perpetration of secret crimes, which the law of the land would be powerless to prevent. . . . . . As a proof of our liberality, I may mention that we are even now inviting Christian missionaries to become the teachers of our children; and if Christian churches ever produce better citizens than Buddhist, or Christian schools better scholars than the Confucianist, we shall gladly acknowledge their work."

It is well for China that the western powers have been represented at Peking by statesmen who had the wisdom to inaugurate a new policy of this broad character, and the patience to carry it out through all the opposition they encountered. The co-operative policy, framed chiefly by Mr. Burlingame and Sir Frederick Bruce, with the approval of their colleagues, at the same time that it acts as a wholesome check on individual judgment, insures as far as possible the observance of the treaties by all parties; and while it exerts a strong pressure on the Chinese Government, there is just enough diversity in the interests of the treaty powers, and enough of national jealousy, to guarantee that this pressure shall not be used unjustly.

Of the ministers who worked hand in hand in inaugurating the new policy, none are now in Peking. Sir Frederick Bruce, a true friend of America during its troubles, left China to represent his country at Washington. His death, last year, came at a time when his dispassionate judgment could not well be spared on either side of the Atlantic. How deeply interested he felt in the welfare of China will appear from the following extract from a letter addressed by him, a few weeks before his death, to the writer of this article:

"I have lost none of my interest in those countries [China and Japan], and sober reflection has only confirmed me in my high appreciation of the qualities of the people and of the statesmen of China. The great fact remains, that since 1860 they have pulled through their foreign difficulties, and have done much to improve their internal condition, without impairing their authority or their rights. We can claim for the 'co-operative policy,' that it contributed largely to that end; that the moderation impressed upon foreign ministers, by their agreement to act together, kept the individual representatives within bounds; and that the support given to the custom-house system affords the best, and, indeed, the only hope of assimilating pacifically the Chinese administration to the emergencies of western intercourse and ideas. I believe that if the policy then sketched out is steadily adhered to, and the Chinese are brought to rely on our friendship and good faith, we shall have little cause to complain, and the march of progress will be soon accelerated. The speed with which changes are effected bears some ratio to the size of the area where the changes are to be introduced, and to the numbers of the nation which it is sought to impress—a truth we are very apt to forget."

M. Berthémy, also an earnest worker in the framing of the co-operative policy, now represents his country at Washington.

Mr. Burlingame, after a short visit home in 1865, returned to Peking, where his position as senior member of the diplomatic corps, as well as his strong personal influence, enabled him to continue the harmonious action among the more newly-arrived ministers, and between them and the Board of Foreign Affairs. The brilliant appointment which he has lately received from the Chinese Government is an evidence both of the high estimation in which he is personally held, and of the successful working of the policy of which he was the most active framer.

CHAPTER XXV.

FROM PEKING TO NAGASAKI.

It was now the middle of May, and the season was already advancing beyond the period of comfortable travelling through the Indian ocean and Egypt. This was the route I had chosen, after failing to find a companion for a journey through Siberia. Taking leave of my many kind friends at Peking, I set out on horseback for Tung-chau (fu) on the Pei-Ho. The distance is only about twelve miles over the granite causeway that connects this port with the capital; but I lengthened the time of the ride by lingering at the bridge of Pa-li-kiao, the site of one of the battles of the last war, where the Tartar cavalry with miserable weapons made a most desperate resistance against the allied forces.

At Tung-chau I found my baggage already on board the boat, which had been engaged by my temporary companion, a young missionary.

It may not be uninteresting to the reader to have a slight sketch of the strange career of this person, whom, though in no unfriendly spirit, I must call a religious adventurer.

While yet a boy, feeling himself called upon to become a missionary, he started without any credentials and without having been ordained.

Enlisting as a marine, he went with the United States squadron to Japan, and there leaving the service began studying the language. Having no means of support he opened a tailor shop, and managed to eke out a subsistence, although, as I know by sad experience, he was apt to make one leg of a pair of trousers a couple of inches shorter than the other.

Failing in his attempt to convert the Japanese he became a merchant, in which he also failed, owing a large amount, in an attempt to overstock the China market with lumber.

Determined again to become a missionary in a new field, he went to Shanghai, and failing here to get a passport for the interior proceeded to Peking.

During this time he had learned a little Chinese, and had determined to preach the gospel in the most inaccessible provinces of the west. He had obtained his passport, and was now on the way to Tien-tsin, the starting point of his journey. He complained bitterly that he had been snubbed by all the missionaries at Peking, who had even refused to allow him to pray in their evening meetings. During our boat journey, whether asleep or awake, he talked constantly and always in Scriptural quotations, whether denouncing the missionaries as "sons of Belial," or complaining of his financial losses, or yet calling down vengeance upon the Chinese, if they should hesitate to receive his "glad tidings joyfully."

A monomaniac, he was about to undertake one of the most difficult journeys on the globe, entirely alone, and was going undisguised through regions where even the Catholic missionaries could hardly penetrate, though perfectly disguised, and always surrounded by their converts. I left him at Tien-tsin, after giving him my camp outfit, confidently expecting that he would never again be heard from. His subsequent career was remarkable: starting with a cart-load of Bibles, he travelled across Chih-li and Shan-si to the Yellow river.

Here, coming upon the line of engagement between the Imperialist troops and the Mohammedan rebels, he was arrested by the former, and sent in a boat down the river to the sea-coast. Not daunted by this rebuff, he started from Canton with another load of Bibles, and travelling through the southern provinces of China penetrated into the almost inaccessible region of Yun-nan, where he barely escaped death in several attacks of banditti. The last time that I heard of him he was circulating petitions through the United States for the pardon of Jefferson Davis, having accomplished his missionary work in China, by having, as he characteristically asserted, circulated so many Bibles in every part of China that the inhabitants of that country can show, at the Last Day, no good reason why they should not be damned.

The condition of the Protestant Christian missions in China is certainly not promising; during nearly half a century a constantly increasing force of zealous men has been actively at work at all the open ports. They have indeed established schools and churches, and formed congregations which, in the aggregate, may number some thousands of communicants; they have many native preachers, and distribute countless tracts and Bibles printed in Chinese; but with all this it is extremely doubtful whether the number of true converts is in any other than an insignificant proportion to that of the communicants. These remarks are made in no unfriendly spirit toward the earnest men who are giving up their lives to a labor which some of them at least feel to be almost useless. One of the most zealous of these men informed me that during an experience of more than twelve years, in which he had been applied to by thousands of natives to administer baptism, he had never yet felt sufficiently convinced of the sincerity of an applicant to perform the ceremony.

The reasons for hypocrisy among the natives are numerous. In China a population of more than four hundred millions is confined to an area about as large as the United States east of the Mississippi river, and the population treads so closely upon the limits of productivity that widespread famine always follows a year in which the production falls below the average. In such a country, and especially in its cities, the whole course of life is a constant struggle for existence—a struggle in which the need of getting daily food drowns all other considerations. It is therefore not surprising that thousands should apply for admission to a church, when it is well known among the people that its members are not only never allowed to starve, but have also the preference over their Pagan brethren in obtaining employment. A well-to-do Chinaman who should become a Christian would be held in contempt by his countrymen; but among the poorer people, the necessities of life form a sufficient excuse for nominal conversion.

I think too well of the Chinese, as a people, to consider them generally capable of hypocrisy; but when a native has once decided upon this course he goes patiently through a long career of deceit, which is well calculated to hoodwink the missionary.

By birth and education a thinker, learning to read his own language in committing to memory the philosophical writings of his own sages, the Chinaman finds no difficulty in understanding and remembering the doctrines of the Bible, and even the sectarian tracts which fall into his hands. After mastering these he comes to the missionary, often with a better knowledge of the questions involved in our religion than is shown by many converts at home. What wonder, then, if this knowledge is taken for sincere belief by men who are perhaps poorer judges of human nature than any other class. For years a native Christian, or even a whole congregation, will persevere in a career of successful deceit, until some internal dispute brings to light acts of hypocrisy and fraud, involving sometimes even the native preachers, and disheartening the missionary. How many millions of money and how many earnestly devoted lives have been thus misspent. The truth is that the Chinese, though superstitious, have no religion; at least none which stands in any relation to a future existence. In early times, before the density of population had rendered them a strictly utilitarian people, and before the religious idea had become almost entirely extinct, the Buddist missionaries, travelling from India, like the early spreaders of the Christian faith, with scrip and staff, and undergoing every hardship, found little difficulty in spreading their humane religion over the whole country.

A few centuries later, the intrepid Nestorian missionaries penetrated through central Asia into China, and we have the evidence of the inscription at Si-ngan (fu) that in the sixth century the Christian church had obtained a foothold in many parts of the empire. At present, although the country is full of Buddist temples and Buddist monasteries, they hold no other place among the Chinese than that of supplying the people with priests to perform funeral ceremonies, and to attend to the rites and homes of the dead, and to satisfy the wants of an active superstition no more connected with religion than is fortune-telling. The numerous monasteries, which are generally richly endowed, also offer places for retreat to persons who wish to leave the world.

Of Christian descendants of the Nestorian converts, no trace was found by the Roman missionaries who entered China during the reign of the Ming dynasty, and the converts made by these latter do not seem to have perpetuated the new faith beyond the circle of their immediate descendants.

A national religious change must pre-suppose that the supplanting faith meets some want generally felt among the people. The establishment of any religion pre-supposes a well defined belief in a future existence, and a feeling of utter dependence upon a Deity. That the Chinese had something of this religious sentiment in times which ante-date their written history, seems to be shown in their State religion, now sunken into a mere form. But the principle which the early philosophers established as the corner-stone of government, that the will of the people is the will of Heaven, has been carried to its natural consequence—the elevation of public welfare to the position of being the highest aim of monarch and citizen. The Chinaman has no God, and having no belief in a system of future rewards and punishments, has no fear of death, and consequently feels none of those wants which one must suppose to exist in a convert to Christianity. In this respect he differs from the Japanese and the Polynesian; the former, while strongly imbued with the religious sentiment, has outgrown in his intellectual progress the doctrines of a corrupted Buddism, while the latter is easily persuaded to exchange the bloody rites of his superstition for the humane doctrines of Christianity.

While Japan offers one of the best fields for proselytizing, China is certainly the worst.

One form of the missionary enterprise—the medical mission—has always commanded the respect and gratitude of the Chinese; the names of the excellent doctors, Parker and Lockhart, and others, who have spent years in alleviating suffering among the natives, are known far and wide in the empire, and will long be remembered for the good they have done.

When I arrived at Shanghai my friend Mr. Thomas Walsh agreed to make the journey homeward with me through Tartary and Siberia in the early autumn, a proposition which I eagerly accepted, as it was already late for the journey via India.

Therefore I accepted his invitation to pass the summer at the house of his brother, Mr. John G. Walsh, in Nagasaki.

Unfortunately, Japan was at this time shaken from north to south by its internal and foreign troubles, rendering it impossible for me to travel. But under the hospitable roof of my host the summer passed away pleasantly; its quiet was broken only by the news of distant battles, and the rumors of threatened attacks upon the foreign settlements.

The political troubles rendering it impossible for Mr. Walsh to leave his affairs, the time of our departure was delayed until well on in October.

In the meantime we made extensive preparations for a winter journey through a country of whose resources we knew nothing. I fear that my readers will accuse us of an undue regard to luxury in travelling, should I enumerate the quantities and varieties of provisions and drinkables which were boxed up for our journey, and stowed away on the brig which was to take us to Tien-tsin.

At the last moment, fearing lest the provisions already prepared, which were enough for forty instead of two, were not sufficient, Mr. Walsh sent on board an additional quantity and several cases of wines for the sea voyage.

CHAPTER XXVI.

THE TABLE-LAND OF CENTRAL ASIA.

At last we bid good-bye to Mr. J. G. Walsh and other good friends, and sailed out of the bay.

After several days of delightful weather we came in sight of the Corean island of Quelpart, and entered the Yellow sea.

During several days, nothing of interest occurred, excepting that the sea seemed alive with immense numbers of Medusae. The great discs of these animals, of two feet and more in diameter, were everywhere visible, floating like drab umbrellas near the surface, and as far as the eye could penetrate the clear blue waters. The vessel often cut a way through great masses of them, leaving hundreds of their broken forms in its wake.

During several days we passed through this immense shoal of jelly fish, which must have covered an area of thousands of square miles.

We were not deprived of an opportunity to study the habits of animal life within the walls of our vessel; the brig had been for a long time in the tropics, and had become thoroughly infested with cockroaches; they seemed to rival in numbers the Medusae outside; the floor, the ceiling, and the berths swarmed with them. After throwing several bushels of these unwelcome passengers into the sea, we were forced to conclude that, in so doing, we only made room for fresh and more hungry swarms from the hold. They were always first at table, turning up in every article of food, and sure to appear upon the most delicate morsels.

I had often heard that the favorite amusement of the animals was to gnaw off the toe-nails of sailors; and, indeed, after my experience on this journey, I am ready to believe anything of them, even the assertion that they form the principal ingredient in India soy, as they certainly were largely represented in our food.

A violent storm prevented our rounding the promontory of

Shan-tung, and drove us north between the coast of Corea and the peninsula of Shan-tung, where we lay for several days before we could enter the gulf of Pe-chele and reach the mouth of the Pei-Ho. Here we disembarked and forwarded our supplies by boat to Peking, making the journey ourselves on horseback.

At the capital we were so fortunate as to make an addition to our party in the person of Mr. St. John, Secretary of the English legation. While waiting for the preparations which our new companion had to make, we passed our time in getting carts, which we had enlarged to admit of sleeping, and in having our clothes lined with fur. Gen. Vlangali, the Russian minister, kindly placed a Cossack at our service for the journey, besides supplying us with numerous letters of introduction for Siberia.

On the morning of the twelfth of November we left the hospitable gates of Mr. Burlingame's house to set out upon our long journey across the table-land of central Asia, and through Siberia and Russia to the Atlantic ocean, through countries of which no one of our party spoke the languages.

As the gorge of Nan-kau is impassable for carts, we had ours taken to pieces and packed upon mules, as were all our supplies and baggage; it was quite a ride from the rear to the front of our long and straggling caravan. Stopping the first night at Sha-ho, we made an early start next morning; but before reaching Nan-kau Walsh's horse fell and sprained the ankle of his rider so badly that I feared we should have to give up the journey at its first stage, or take my friend back and leave him at Peking. But not daunted at the idea of making the longest land journey on the globe in a crippled condition, and disregarding present pain, Walsh insisted upon being carried in a chair to Kalgan, where our carts were to begin their work.

At Nan-kau we bought a wooden chair, which, slung between two poles and carried by strong men, formed a very convenient means of travelling.

Four days' journey from Peking brought us to Kalgan; here we were detained four days in perfecting a contract with the Mongols, who were to take us to Kiachta. As we were bearing dispatches, the Chinese Government had given us passports for Tartary, without which it would have been impossible to obtain either guides or camels. Finally, on the 21st of November, at four o'clock in the afternoon, we left Kalgan in a heavy snowstorm; the ascent to the summit of the plateau being too steep for camels to draw the carts, this work was done by horses as far as Borotsedji which we reached at daylight. Here we found our camels, twenty-six in number, including those taken as reserves in case of accident.

The first work was the organization of the caravan, the carts, of which there were four, one for each, including Peter the Cossack, were intended for sleeping-places, as it was our intention to travel seventeen hours out of the twenty-four, stopping only once to eat. The vehicles, mounted on two wheels and without springs, were covered with a housing of felt less than three feet wide and about seven in length; they were closed with a door on one side, and furnished with abundant blankets and furs, and fitted with pockets without number; the long shafts in front were slung in loops suspended from the saddle of the camel, and a guide mounted on another animal accompanied each cart. The baggage was packed on eight or ten other camels, each animal having its nose pierced and fastened by a cord to the saddle of the one before it, the foremost being led by a mounted cameleer.

The ascent to the summit of the plateau, here between five and six thousand feet above the sea, brought us into a region of intense cold, which was rendered almost insupportable by a strong north-northwest wind. The thermometer, which at Kalgan had been ranged near the freezing point, stood here at ten degrees below zero (F).

The wind, having a clear sweep over the plains lying between us and the Arctic region, blew with unbroken force, obliging us to take shelter in the carts, while the preparations were being made for starting. Finally, when all was ready, the cameleers, enveloped in immense masses of sheepskin robes, mounted their animals and formed into line. During the first two or three days our whole time was occupied in endeavoring to find the best means to keep from freezing to death, a fate against which I saw we had not taken sufficient precaution in our preparations. After being for hours in the carts there would be not more than three or four degrees difference between the inner and outer temperature.

Although the vehicles were an excellent defence against the wind, the temperature of every object on the inside equalized itself with that of the outer air. Woollen blankets and furs became so cold that it was impossible to touch them with the naked hand. Sometime during the first night our route emerged from the flat-topped hills of the volcanic region of the plateau, and entered a country of gravelly plains, crossed by low granitic ridges. It was not until the fourth day of our caravan journey that we were able to summon courage to face the fierce wind and clear cold outside. Feeling a necessity for exercise we mounted our Tartar horses, and, leaving the caravan, galloped in the direction of a small column of smoke rising from the neighboring hills. Reaching the top of a small eminence we saw in the valley beneath us a collection of yurts, from which herds were moving away to graze. A loud and fierce barking of dogs showed that we were already discovered, and as we approached the encampment a score of these savage brutes offered us battle, and we should certainly have been worsted had not their masters come to our assistance.

I had taken the precaution to bring an empty bottle, and a paper of needles, which we immediately presented to the good woman of the tent. We had not long to wait for her gratitude to show itself. Putting a large cauldron over the fire she threw in some tallow, and after this had melted, poured in a quantity of water, to which as soon as it had begun to boil was added a liberal quantity of brick tea with salt, and small pieces of the fat of a sheep's tail. When this was done and a handful of parched millet sprinkled over the surface, the good woman served it up in wooden cups, putting into each one a lump of cheese, about the size of an egg. We stood almost aghast, frightened at the hospitable offering which our presents had called forth; and, indeed, a decoction of tallow, tea, fat, salt, and cheese is certainly a formidable compound for a western palate. But notwithstanding the epithets with which we reviled the mixture, in a language fortunately unintelligible to our hostess, the cups were repeatedly filled, and as often emptied. Before we had left Mongolia this Tartar tea had really become a favorite beverage with all of us.

We were now in a rolling country, or rather the true plateau, cut up by water-courses and the beds of generally empty lakes. Riding to the top of a hill we could distinguish our caravan winding along the bottom of the great valley, and some two or three miles ahead of us. Descending into this depression, we soon cut the tracks of the camels and cart-wheels, which we had no difficulty in following. A great change had taken place in the weather, a light south wind keeping the mercury all day above freezing. Low hills of limestone and gypsum rose on all sides from the valley plain. The sides of these hillocks, covered with crystals of selenite from the gypsum beds, glistened in the sun-light as though encrusted with diamonds. In the distance a horizontal line marked the limit where the cliffs of the table-land shut in the broad valley.

On the morning of the 27th we awoke in a rough country, among the hills of Mingan, a mass of metamorphosed sandstone, quartzite, and limestone in highly-inclined beds. These hills, rising like an island from the table-land, and several hundred feet above its surface, are barren masses of rock interspersed with patches of grass-covered soil. The western base sinks into the broad valley of Olannoor, while to the northwest we descended to the great steppe of Tamchin Tala.

This broad plain, which has suffered but little from erosion, has a surface of gravel and sand, with scattered patches of grass. Pebbles of chalcedony, agate, and cornelian, are strown among the gravel. The table-land, at least along the whole line of our journey, is utterly destitute of trees, and the first and only perennial which I saw was a low thorny bush, which appears on the Tamchin Tala, and other equally barren soils. From the hill-tops one overlooks an immense area of plains or undulating country, as boundless and unbroken as the ocean. In the summer this is covered with a waving mass of tall grass, forming a green mantle, which toward the distant horizon becomes a deep blue. In the winter the scene is entirely changed: the plains and low hills, yellow from the color of the gravel and dead grass, have all the appearance of a boundless desert. But little snow falls on the table-land, and that little soon disappears, drifted into depressions, or evaporated by the intensely dry atmosphere. But the little snow that falls is one of the worst enemies of the traveller. Frozen into a fine, sharp sand, it is driven with cutting violence before the strong north wind, blinding for the time men and animals. Lifted by the whirlwind from the ground, it sweeps over the surface in eddying clouds, sinking or rising with the varying force of the blast, now covering, deeply, large areas, and soon leaving them again a barren surface. Seen during one of these *bourans*, the same plains, which in the summer resemble the smiling savannas of the tropics, have all the appearance of an ice-sea, lashed by the fierce snow-storms of an Arctic winter.

When we came up with our caravan we found it already encamped, and we began the process of cooking our single daily meal. We were in the habit of stopping about an hour before sunset, to give the animals a rest of six or seven hours out of the twenty-four.

One large tent answered for the whole party. In the middle the Mongols put up their tripod and cauldron, and another fire-place for our own cooking. We now spread over the country, one party in search of snow, the other to forage for argols. It was not always an easy matter to find enough of either of these articles, both of which were absolutely necessary for cooking.

Our great forte was in the production of soups; to this all our energies were directed, and it was made the subject of countless experiments.

Obtaining a kettle of water by melting snow, we first put into it such frozen vegetables as we had brought from Kalgan, and then such fresh meat as mutton, horse, or cow, as we could get from the Mongols, without being over-scrupulous as to the manner of its death; adding to these a pound or so of fat of the sheep's tail, and allowing the whole to cook, we put into the cauldron one tin each of the following canned provisions: peas, beans, ox-tail soup, mock-turtle soup, Frankfort sausages, salmon, and tomatoes. How this compound would taste in civilization it would be hard to say, but no dinner at the Trois Freres, or at Delmonico's, ever disappeared with greater relish than was shown at these four o'clock meals on the steppes of Tartary. And they were well-earned, for although we had to work hard in cooking them, we often had to work still harder to keep from freezing while eating them. The tent offered slight protection against the cold winds, and the argol fires gave no warmth at the distance of a few inches.

Consequently, in a strong wind, with the mercury at 20 or 30 degrees below zero, we were obliged after every few mouthfuls to jump up and run an eight of a mile or so to renew the circulation. Owing to these interruptions the evening was generally far advanced before we reached the bottom of the liberal cauldron. Even this ample dish was not always sufficient to satisfy appetites of twenty-four hours' growth, which had been whetted by the cold air and constant exercise. As it was only by rare accident that we were able to get a cup of Mongol tea in the morning, we studied various methods of keeping coffee in a fluid state during the night.

To effect this each one made a bottleful of boiling coffee, which was rolled carefully in a large blanket; after this had been heated and folded, and re-heated until it was scorching hot. Then thrusting the precious bundle under his fur cloak, each man rushed to his cart, and, diving under the bedclothes, carefully hugged his charge all night.

Even a baby could not have been treated more tenderly. In this way we generally succeeded in having a bottle of iced coffee on awakening in the morning; but woe to the unhappy man made restless by an over-hearty dinner; his neglected bottle, to which he looked for consolation, would be frozen, perhaps burst, or, at the very best, the coffee was a mass of needles.

On the morning of the 28th we were still traversing the Tamchin Tala. There was no wind, and the thermometer stood at 24 degrees. As the morning wore on we could see that we were approaching a change in the character of the surface.

Before noon we had reached the edge of a cliff which formed a perpendicular wall, 150 or 200 feet high, overlooking a large depression like the abandoned valley of a river or of a long lake. The exposure in the cliff showed the plateau here to consist of horizontal strata of coarse and fine sandstones with calcareous cement, containing many fragments of chalcedony and agate. On the bank of a small creek stood a small collection of yurts, which seemed more permanently established than are generally the habitations of this wandering people. After travelling several miles in this valley, which must be very beautiful in summer, we arose to the table-land on the opposite side. The country was here rolling, and evidently well covered with grass in summer. Hardly had we put up a tent before a number of women and children appeared with baskets of argols, which they gave to our cameleers. The children had several strings of agates, which they parted with for some pieces of brick tea. The gift of the argols was not prompted by pure hospitality, as I had supposed.

While our Mongols were cooking their mess, the new-comers sat with eager eyes just inside the door of the tent. Our cameleers had a cauldron filled with large pieces of beef, which I strongly suspected of having belonged to the frozen carcass of a cow we had passed that morning. Almost before the meat was warmed through, our guides seized enormous pieces, and began the meal by cramming into the mouth as much of one corner of the piece as they could get in, and then sawing off the rest just outside the lips. Their throats seemed made of india-rubber, so rapidly did one large piece disappear after another.

Indeed it is hard to understand why the Tartars are endowed with molars. Altogether carnivorous, they used their teeth, so far as I could discover, only for tearing their food. In cooking, no part of the animal is lost, and they are not over-careful as regards cleanliness in preparing their meat for the pot.

Every now and then our chief cameleer, taking a piece, generally one of the poorest, from the cauldron, tossed it across the tent to the ravenous assemblage of women and children.

Although most Mongols carry a pair of chop-sticks slung in their girdle, they can only be for ornament, as I certainly never saw them used.

Our chief cameleer was a Lama, and had travelled not only through Tartary and northern China, but had been to the shrine of Tsongkaba, and had knelt before the Grand Lama at Lhassa. Fat, and with as jolly a face as even a priest could wish, our good natured Lama, while telling the beads of his rosary, or repeating the monotonous Buddist formula, wore an expression of most perfect contentment—might have sat as model for a statue of Budda in the *Nirvana*.

The next morning was comparatively pleasant, with a southwest wind and the thermometer at 17 degrees. The road lay through an uneven country, among low granite hills. During the afternoon we crossed the boundary between Inner and Outer Mongolia. This limit is marked by rough piles of stones. Thus far we had been travelling through the land of the Sunite Tartars, while north of the boundary we would be in the country of the Kalkas, under the rule of the Khans of Tushetu and Tsetsen.

The Sunites are looked down upon by the Kalkas, who border them on the north and on the southwest. There may be some reason in this contempt, as I certainly saw no encampments among them which looked as prosperous as those I had passed through in my journey along the southern part of the plateau.

Thus far we had rarely seen encampments of more than five or six yurts, and the herds looked small, and their owners had the appearance of extreme poverty. Near our camp, which was a few miles north of the boundary, I picked up a piece of petrified wood, a thing apparently of not uncommon occurrence in this region. In Peking, several pieces of silicified wood were shown me under the name of han-hai-shi or gobi stone.

In looking for snow I came not far from our camp upon a well, at which large numbers of animals were being watered. It was dug in an isolated depression, was only a few feet deep, and walled with stone.

The morning of November 30th opened with a northwest wind and the thermometer at 15 degrees. On getting out of the cart we found ourselves in a hilly country, near the place marked on maps as Arshantyi; the hills consist mainly of clay slates. After traversing these for some time we came upon a broad, dry, gravelly water-course, which, descending to the west, below low granite cliffs, widens out in the valley of the Ulannoor. These granite hills are perfectly bare of soil, and devoid of any vegetation, with the remarkable exception of two or three stunted trees, growing in crevices of the rock. These were the first and only trees which we saw on the plateau.

On emerging from the valley we came into a country of high terraces of clay. Near this point we expected to find a large town, as nearly all maps have a place marked at this point with the name of Gashun; we consequently set out to explore for it on horseback.

After passing the first hill we saw a large herd of hwang-yang quietly grazing in the valley below us; but being to the windward of the herd they soon scented us, and a troop of several hundred dashed over the hills at a rapid rate, and were soon out of sight. After a further ride of two or three miles we came upon the object of our search, which, instead of being a large village, consisted of only two or three yurts. Still, we breakfasted luxuriously on Tartar tea and lumps of boiled fat of sheep's tails. This part of Tartar sheep is considered a great delicacy through all Asia, and is really almost equal to marrow. The tail of this animal in Tartary attains a weight of from thirty to fifty pounds of pure fat. Seen from behind, the animal is all tail; and, when the appendage attains its largest dimensions, it becomes necessary to attach a contrivance, by means of which the animal can conveniently carry his own tail without allowing it to drag. This is sometimes effected by suspending it upon a kind of wheelbarrow, or upon two sticks, which at one end are fastened to the sheep, and at the other dragged upon the ground behind him. This growth of fat seems to be peculiar to the table-land, for it is said that the same breed, when taken to India, soon loses this peculiarity. It may perhaps serve the same purpose as the hump of the camel, that of supplying in time of plenty an abundant store of fat, upon which the animal can subsist through a season of deep snow, when it would otherwise starve.

When the English troops occupied Afghanistan, the soldiers became so partial to the tails of these sheep that they discarded almost entirely the lean. The result was a congestion of fat in the intestines, which caused a great mortality in the army. Fortunately we had not heard of this fact when we travelled in Tartary.

At Gashun we bought of the good woman of the tent a liberal supply of cream, put up like immense sausages. As it was frozen it was easily carried, slung to the saddle, without danger of being churned into butter.

On the morning of the 1st of December the thermometer stood at 3 degrees below zero. All the morning our road lay over hills of metamorphic slates and limestone in vertical beds, striking N.E., S.W.

The beds of limestone, being least susceptible of disintegration, form ridges 100 to 150 feet above the intervening slate out-crops, thereby producing parallel valleys, containing in the season ponds or lakes. Descending from these hills we entered a large valley with broad, terraced slopes, gently inclining toward the centre, and, crossing this, we came on the northern declivity upon a line of conical hills of basaltic lava, between 100 and 200 feet high. They rose like isolated towers from the gently-sloping surface of the terrace, but detached from the plateau, the cliff line of which lies a few hundred yards further north.

We were obliged to go into camp several hours earlier than usual, in order to wait the return of our chief cameleer, who had gone to hunt for two camels which had strayed away.

Although secured by strings passed through the nose, the camel will sometimes tear out the flesh, and, once away from the caravan, will often give his pursuer a good chase. Still, the Tartar or Bactrian camel is far more docile than his brother of Egypt and southwestern Asia. Much larger than the southern camel, he is provided with a heavy coat of long hair, and with two humps, which, after a season of grazing, stand upon his back great cones of fat, forming the most comfortable of saddles.

Most people are accustomed to associate the camel only with tropical climates.

The Bactrian species is of little use during the hot season, while during the coldest winter it performs nearly all the labor of transportation in central Asia. In countless caravans these patient animals traverse, in every direction, the frozen deserts of the table-land, and descend into the region of deep snows and intense cold of southern Siberia.

Their broad, spongy feet, more pliable than the palm of the human hand, and armed with claw-shaped nails, are adapted only to walking over sand; rocky or gravelly surfaces soon wear out the thick skin of the foot; while on mud or ice they find no foothold.

The life of the camel in northern China, where large numbers are used in the transportation of coal, is one of torture. Toiling day after day over the rough rocks or smooth pavements of the mountain roads, and hardly fed at all, its feet worn to shreds, and its humps hanging in loose bags over the side, the Chinese coal camel is as much an object of pity as a Broadway stage-horse.

Even in many parts of Mongolia the caravan routes are gravelly, and wearing to the camels.

While waiting for the return of our Lama we witnessed the operation of re-soling or rather patching the soles of a camel's foot, where a hole about an inch in diameter had been worn through to the quick. The animal being thrown on his side, and all four feet bound tightly together, and his head tied back near the humps, was held motionless. After cleaning out the wound, a piece of raw cow-hide, perfectly fresh, was sewed to the skin of the foot, two or three stitches being taken on each side of the piece. The hind feet seemed to suffer most, and the operation has to be renewed every few days.

While roaming among the hills, not far from our camp, we came to a well, at which immense herds of camels, horses, oxen, sheep, and goats, were being watered. To us the most interesting and novel part of the assemblage were the young camels; even the smallest showed the staid and sober bearing of its race, and none of the exuberant friskiness common to young colts and calves.

The next morning opened with clear, quiet cold of 8 degrees below zero. During the day we crossed two broad valley depressions. From the highest ground the flat outline of the plateau was visible in every direction, excepting to the south of us, where the horizon was broken by the hills we had lately passed through, which rise perhaps 1,000 feet above the neighboring table-land.

Although the thermometer marked several degrees below zero, we experienced no inconvenience from the cold, partly owing to the absence of wind, and partly to the clear sun. I doubt whether any one, who has not wintered on the plains in the interior of a northern continent, can appreciate the feelings which led the early inhabitants of central Asia to love and worship the sun. In the intense cold of an elevated region, the plains of which, unprotected by forests, are open to the almost perpetual blast of the polar wind, life would be unbearable without the quickening influence of an unclouded sun. The atmosphere of central Asia is intensely dry, because the winds reach it from every direction only after having deposited their moisture on the broad belt of lowlands and the high mountain peaks which intervene between the table-lands and the oceans; thus, especially in winter, the sun rises, runs through its daily course, and sets, an unobscured orb, whose rays, suffering a minimum of refraction, arrive at the surface with a greater degree of warmth than would obtain in more moist regions in the same latitude.

Often in this journey, in travelling northward, facing the strong Arctic winds, with a thermometer at 10 and 20 degrees below zero, while almost ready to drop from the saddle, owing to stiffness from cold, I have turned my horse to face the sun, and have felt in a few minutes the warmth of its rays stealing gently through my veins, like an influx of new life and fresh vigor.

The heavy icicles formed by condensations of the breath upon the beard would gradually loosen, and the mask of ice, which sometimes formed a protection to the face, would slowly disappear. How often have I then felt that, had I been born a nomad, I should have fallen down to worship the great light-giving god of day, as he was adored by the earliest bards of our race, the authors of the Vedas.

During the night there fell two inches of snow, and when we mounted our horses in the morning we had to face a fearfully cold wind and the eddying clouds of snow, which, driven like sand, fairly cut the face with its sharp edges. It was a hard day for man and beast. The long train of camels faced reluctantly the blinding force of the storm, and we made but little progress.

During the afternoon the plain began gradually to descend, and finally ended among low ridges of granite.

During the night the storm increased in violence till it blew a very hurricane, rendering all thought of starting out of the question.

The cold also increased to such an extent that there was danger of freezing, even in the carts. When daylight came our blankets were covered with half an inch of snow, from the condensed moisture of the breath. For some time past our bedding had become frozen stiff as boards, from the same cause. During the 4th December the thermometer stood at 16 degrees below zero, but the continued force of the hurricane kept us encamped.

We were here at a small Mongol village called Buteryn Chelu, half-way between Kalgan and Kiachta. We passed the day in the Mongol yurts, endeavoring to thaw out and dry our blankets and furs over the argol fires. The next day, with the thermometer still at 16 degrees below zero, but with an abated wind, we continued our journey among low hills of granitic and metamorphic rocks, among which I observed beds of dolomitic limestone, impregnated with flakes of graphite.

In the afternoon we encamped at a place called Huri, among some hills of trachytic porphyry, identical in character with that of Kalgan.

For several days we had seen before us a mountain peak, which in the clear atmosphere of the plains seemed so near that we each day thought to pass it before night; but each morning it stood still beyond us, towering higher than on the previous day.

On the afternoon of the 6th we approached the base of this picturesque peak, which is called the Bogdo Oola, or sacred mountain. From a broad terrace, which forms the foot-slope of this peak, a large valley was visible in the southwest, threaded by a winding frozen river, the Russ Gol.

While crossing this plain an accident occurred which might in several ways have produced serious results. A cameleer in charge of the carts had fallen asleep in the saddle, and the animals, taking advantage of this, had strayed on to uneven ground, where they could browse, while lazily moving forward. In making a short descent one of the carts was upset, breaking one of the shafts. We all rushed to the spot, and while attempting to right the vehicle a violent altercation arose between the owner of the cart and the Mongol whose stupid negligence had caused the accident. The foreigner, finding that strong English produced no impression on the Mongol, endeavored to enforce his meaning, by well-directed lumps of ice, which fell harmlessly upon the quadruple thickness of sheep-skins which encased the cameleer; not so, however, when returned with increased force upon the simply woollen-clad foreigner. In self-defence the latter now drew his revolver. It happened that a considerable number of Mongols from a neighboring village were standing by, laughing at the unequal odds of the battle; but when these saw the pistol they drew their long knives, to use them on the side of their fellow-countryman. Our situation seemed to be growing very serious, when another matter called for the attention of all parties.

Frightened by the noise, the camel drawing St. John's cart had turned and fled. Dashing at full tilt over the rocky plain, we could see the cart, now swaying from side to side, now bounding high in the air. Soon the wheels left the body, and the contents of the cart were seen flying in all directions.

This turn of affairs was so ludicrous that even the owner of the cart could not help laughing lustily. But when it occurred to him that all his money, in gold, for the long journey through a strange land, was in one of the slender cloth pockets of the vehicle, the matter appeared in a more serious light. Twenty or thirty Mongols were already in advance of us picking up the scattered articles, and there seemed no likelihood of recovering the money. When we reached the cart we found the pocket torn and the treasure gone. It was of course natural to suspect our visitors of having appropriated the coin to their own use, and it was proposed that we should forcibly search them—certainly not a very easy thing to be accomplished with impunity by four foreigners, upon two score of Mongols, in the heart of central Asia.

While we were discussing the matter among ourselves a loud shout was heard from a strange Mongol, who was digging all alone some distance back in the track of the cart.

Hurrying to the spot, he pointed out a pile of shining sovereigns, which would have been an immense fortune to him, but which he had carefully gathered together out of the sand, in which they had been buried by the blankets dragging behind the cart, and which he triumphantly handed over to the owner. Not one was missing. St. John rewarded the man liberally; and from that time we all of us had a higher opinion of the honesty of this people. Theft, I believe, is a thing of rare occurrence among this simple people; they will over-reach in bargains, but the Buddist commandment —"Thou shalt not steal"—is, perhaps, more generally observed than is that of our own religion in more civilized countries.

The next day was passed in repairing the carts. Although the thermometer stood at 17 degrees, the absence of wind rendered the day not unpleasant; but owing to the bad road, and the weak condition of one of the carts, we made but little progress. Encamping early, we lay over till the next morning.

When I awoke in the morning the thermometer was at 20 degrees below zero, and the fierce blasts of wind which whistled around the carts, causing them to sway to and fro, bespoke a hard day's work. It was too cold to remain inactive in the carts, between the icy blankets; and the resistance offered by the north wind rendered it very difficult to walk for any considerable length of time. Our only resource in such places was to mount our horses, which were already much fatigued by travelling seventeen hours daily.

None but animals born on these plains could have endured the hardships of this journey; but the large Mongol ponies, covered with a long, shaggy coat of hair, followed patiently the carts, to which they were tied at night, and carried us during the greater part of the day.

For a whole week at a time getting no other water than the little snow that they could pick up when our route passed a drift, and, excepting a handful of barley, no other food than a little frozen grass, which they picked up during the hour before sunset, these patient brutes served us well through the whole of our journey to the Siberian frontier.

Toward evening we came suddenly to the brow of a hill, from which we overlooked the Lamasery town of Churin Chelu.

The light of the setting sun was reflected back from the gilded spires and balls of the temples, producing an effect as startling as it was unexpected in the middle of the Gobi desert. The place has perhaps a hundred houses, many large yurts, and several fine temples. The houses are built of wood, brought from Urga, beyond the northern edge of the plateau. As we passed the village the streets were filled with Lamas, in their colored dresses, and the evening air bore the sound of the chanted vespers from the temples. The next day was very cold—20 degrees below zero, and a strong north wind. It seemed as though we could not possibly reach Siberia without having some parts of our bodies frozen. Long and swinging icicles hung from the shaggy coats of camels and horses, producing a strange tinkling sound at every step. During this morning the ice accumulated on my whiskers and beard until it hung in a mass nearly a foot long and of no inconsiderable weight. Even the mouth-piece of my pipe became fixed in the ice formed on my moustache. Turning my back to the wind, a few minutes' exposure to the sun removed these icicles, which formed again after travelling a short distance.

During the day we passed through a small village, in which the yurts were very large, and had wooden vestibules. Entering one of these dwellings, we found it very roomy and warm. It was occupied by two Lamas, who gave us tea in return for tobacco. They were much interested with my pipe, which represented the head of a heavily bearded Zouave, and which they took to be a portrait of myself—a rather doubtful compliment. We had already passed the middle of the desert, and the country had now a general ascent toward the north. The great table-land of central Asia forms a shallow trough-like depression, beginning in the region between the Tienshan and the Kwen-lun mountains, and extending northeast to the Kin-gan mountains of western Manchuria and the Amoor river. Its northern and southern limits are respectively the Altai mountains and the bold escarpment with which it faces northern China.

From these edges, which have a general elevation of 5,000 and 6,000 feet above the sea, the surface has a general descent toward the centre, where the altitude of the plains is between 2,000 and 3,000 feet. The general width of the table-land is about 500 miles. The sandy plains, which through the whole length occupy the centre of this shallow trough with a width of 100 miles or more, form a dreary waste, called the Gobi desert. But as we leave this, going north or south, we traverse the great grassy plains which alone render this country habitable, and from which it gets its name—the land of grass. It is a continental basin, having no drainage to the sea, and few streams. In the far west the rivers, formed by the melting snows of the Tienshan and Kwen-lun, find their way into Lake Lop, which has no outlet except by evaporation into the dry atmosphere.

At no very remote geological time this region was the bed of an extensive sea, which during one period of its existence formed part of an ocean, extending over much of Siberia, Tartary, western Asia, and eastern Europe, connecting the Polar sea with the waters of the Caspian and Mediterranean. The elevation of the plateau was, perhaps, the first step in the series of natural causes by which the area of this great body of water was gradually diminished till it was replaced by dry land.

On the 10th we camped on the plain of Borudzurintala, over which we had travelled all day.

The surface was covered with abundant dead grass. The next morning we found ourselves in a hilly country. Flat-topped hills of volcanic rock seemed to indicate the existence on the northern edge of the plateau of a volcanic region, corresponding to that of the southern escarpment.

The next day the country had changed its character, and we found ourselves ascending a broad valley, with sweeping vertical and horizontal curves, bordered by round-topped hills of clay slate.

The surface of hill and valley was clothed with grass, which during the season must grow to a considerable height.

The soil of the valley and hill-slopes was a rich black earth, different from anything seen on the rest of the plateau. We were here in the Horteryn-Daban (Daban-mountain). During the following night we felt, from the motion of the carts, that we were going down hill, and morning found us descending a flat gravelly plain or valley, enclosed between hills from 300 to 500 feet high, which were remarkable for their pyramidal form.

The sides of some of these were clothed with pine forests, which, though a novel sight to us, gave an air of gloom to the country.

Among these hills, at the junction of the valley we were descending with that of the Tola river, lies the town of Urga, or Kuren, the seat of one of the four or five living Buddhas, who, subject to the Talai Lama, rule the inhabitants of Mongolia and Thibet.

There is a Russian consulate at Urga, and as we had letters of introduction to M. Chischmareff, the consul, we directed our steps toward his house. This was a large, two-story building, constructed of logs, hewn to a plain surface, outside and in, well painted without, and with a carefully furnished interior. Before reaching the consulate I was taken by surprise by our chief cameleer, who, rushing up to me, began to rub my face vigorously with snow, but I soon learned that my nose was frozen, and that the object of the washing was to thaw out the frost.

M. Chischmareff being absent, we were politely received by his wife, and the secretary, M. Borzakqsky. I soon began to feel the effects of having frozen my nose, and it was many days before I was freed from the pain and the swelling.

On the 13th we took a walk through the city, which has a population of 16,000, of which one-half are Lamas.

The present Grand Lama is as usual a Thibetan, and only sixteen years old.

The palace in which he lives has a roof highly ornamented with gilded spires and balls.

During our walk we saw many large buildings, most of them of unfamiliar shapes, and one built exactly like a yurt, but of great size, being, I should think, thirty or forty feet high, and sixty or seventy feet in diameter. Entering one large temple we saw an immense image of Budda apparently of wood, covered with sheets of gilded copper. The proportions are well preserved throughout the statue, and some idea of its size may be formed from that of the great toe, which was more than eighteen inches in length. This image, though well finished, does not compare, as a work of art, with the statue of Budda in repose at Kamakura, near Yeddo. In front of this, as well as of the other temples, there were many cylinders, or praying machines, which were easily set in motion by turning a crank, each revolution accomplishing in the way of prayer an amount of work which if done verbally would require some hours.

It has often been asserted, perhaps oftener now than formerly, that the ritualism of the European Church is a direct offshoot of Thibetan Lamaism. The resemblance is so strong in a majority of the details of both that Abbé Huc, a Roman missionary, well versed in the history and religion of Thibet, could find no better way of accounting for the similarity than by supposing it to be an artifice of satan, invented to bring disgrace upon the holy Church.

But these praying machines are a refinement which not even the extremists of the west have adopted. Even the simple crank motion has been improved upon by the ingenious Lamas, who attach the cylinders to wind-mills and water-wheels. The worshipper, setting one of these in motion, goes on his way with the assurance that every revolution of the cylinder completes a large number of prayers for his benefit. The advantages of this over the rosary, which they use also, are obvious.

The Buddist faith was introduced into Mongolia directly from Thibet, and probably at a time when the religion had already received those characteristics which distinguish the Thibetan form so widely from the Indian, Chinese, and Japanese. The engrafting of Brahminical doctrines upon the simple teachings of Budda was the earliest corruption of the faith, and to this were added in China many of the superstitions of that country; and finally, reaching Japan, this accumulated burden was further diversified by the dogmas of Sintuism. Under the control of no central head, the corruptions of these branches have multiplied many fold, and the church has split into many sects. But the early establishment in Thibet of a hierarchy, controlling church and state under the immediate rule of an incarnate Budda, insured a vitality which does not yet seem to be on the wane. Although in Mongolia the religion of Bndda has become corrupted by preexisting Shamanism, it still retains more of original purity than among the other branches. The observations of Abbé Huc show that in Thibet, even at the present day, the original teachings of Budda are followed by a large number of priests and monks with a zeal not found elsewhere. In the monasteries and hermit cells of the mountains of Thibet there exist to-day countless monks and hermits, who, living lives of the most rigid asceticism, seek crowns of glory through life-long mortification of the flesh. In principle we have here the exact counterpart of one of the earliest outgrowths of Christianity, in which was nurtured that zealous devotion to the Church which accomplished so much in spreading the faith, and which marked the period of its greatest vitality.

The influence of the humane doctrines of Budda, from a social point of view, is most marked among the Mongolians, whose character they seem to have moulded as much as Mohammedanism has that of the Kirgis tribes further west. To-day we would not recognize in the Mongols the race which, under the leadership of Gengis-Khan and his descendants, overthrew the dynasties of all Asia and of eastern Europe, sending terror even to the shores of the Atlantic. This people, once a scourge to humanity, is now perhaps the most peaceable upon the globe.

The Chinese court, mindful of their struggles with these northern neighbors, has craftily taken advantage of the influence of Buddism upon their character. During centuries it has fostered Lama Buddism, encouraging in every manner the multiplication of Lamaseries and monasteries; thus, by largely increasing the number of priests (who are not allowed to marry), it has, at the same time, diminished the population, and subdued the warlike character of the race.

At the same time it keeps up a constant drain upon the male population to supply the Chinese army with soldiers, who are decimated in rebellions and wars with foreigners. But the draft into the priesthood operates the most powerfully in keeping down population. At present, in every family, one and often several of the males become Lamas at an early age. This immense army of drones lives, of course, off of the substance of the remaining population. The Lamas pass their time in Lamaseries, or in roaming through Tartary and Thibet, serving the wants of the native superstitions, and practising all the arts of a crafty priesthood. The numerous festivals which take place at the monasteries attract immense crowds of the devout laity, who often return to their homes impoverished by the offerings of large herds and treasure which they have been called upon to make.

On the 14th of December we left Urga for Kiachta. The turn in the road brought us into a valley tributary to the Tola. Some distance before us two buildings of great size, one on each slope, commanded the valley. They are built on high terraces; and one of them, constructed in the Thibetan style of architecture, which was slightly inclining toward the top, was certainly the most sepulchral and gloomy structure I had ever seen.

From this valley we passed over a high and steep hill, where the carts had to be drawn by oxen led by women.

The next day, while riding in a temperature of 20 degrees below zero, we saw coming toward us a train of camels and carts, in front of which rode two Europeans. These proved to be Mr. Papoff, of the Russian legation of Peking, and his bride, a Russian lady, whom he was now taking to China. Mounted on a good horse, and thoroughly protected by furs, this lady assured us that she did not dread either the cold or the hardships of the long journey that lay before her.

Fortunately, by going south, they escaped facing the almost constant north wind, which is the most disagreeable part of the climate.

The next day, with the thermometer at 22 degrees, we passed through several fine valleys clothed with grass, and enclosed between rounded hills, whose northern slopes were covered with pine forests.

On the 17th we awoke in a country of plains and hills, the latter having the appearance of an archipelago of small rocky islands rising out of an extensive steppe. We encamped at Bain Gol, and were soon visited by a large number of Mongols. Considering the sameness of life, of climate, and pursuits, which exists throughout Mongolia, it is remarkable that this people should show the diversity of types of faces that we find among them.

Certain characteristics are common to them all. Of medium stature, rather above that of the northern Chinese, they had the almond eyes, prominent cheek-bones, the scanty beard, without side-whiskers, which are all marked points of the Mongolian race. There is, perhaps, more diversity in the nose than in any other feature.

Among the women at Bain Gol I noticed some with regular, and others with really aquiline noses, though in general the nose had so little prominence that, when looked for in the profile, it was entirely hidden by the prominent cheeks. If I were asked to define the difference between the Chinese and Mongolian face, I

MONGOL PRINCE.

MONGOL CAMELEER.

should say that the features were the same, though more delicately chiselled and softened down in the Chinaman; and in China this difference increases, until in the southern provinces we find the same features formed in a much more effeminate mould, while the people are also much smaller in stature.

While we were at Bain Gol several trains of small carts, drawn by oxen, passed us on their way south, carrying millet, which seems to be the only grain used by the Mongols.

During the summer the transportation is carried on almost entirely by oxen.

During the next two days the mountains bordering our route appeared to be higher; and in the forests, with which they were covered, there appeared an increasing number of deciduous trees, particularly the white birch.

The Mongol villages through which we now passed had a more permanent character than those of the plains, the houses being more generally built of logs, and surrounded with some cultivated land.

We were now crossing the eastern extension of the Altai mountains; and on the morning of the 21st, as we emerged from the forest on the northern slope, the Mongols called our attention to a group of houses and spires, which lay on the opposite side of a broad plain stretched out before us. This was the double city of Kiachta and Mai-mai-chin.

About noon we reached the latter town, which, lying on the Mongolian side of the frontier, is entirely Chinese in character, as it is also the principal frontier market-town of the empire. In traversing its narrow streets, between rows of Chinese houses, and threading our way among neatly-dressed Chinamen, we could almost imagine ourselves again south of the great wall.

Entering a large open place, we found several caravans, some encamped, others just coming or leaving. After some little delay, in having our passports examined by Chinese officials, we were permitted to pass the wall which separates the two towns. One can hardly imagine a sharper line than is here drawn. On the one side of the stockade-wall the houses, churches, and people are European, on the other Chinese; with one step the traveller passes really from Asia, and Asiatic customs and languages into a refined European society.

CHAPTER XXVII.

SIBERIA.

OUR first step after reaching Kiachta was to present our passports and letter to M. Pfaffius, commissioner of the frontier. From this gentleman and his wife we had a cordial reception, and an invitation to dinner the next day. The Russian minister to China had kindly written in advance of our coming, and we found that M. Garnier, with whom I had travelled the previous year to Peking, had prepared quarters for us at the town of Troitzkozavsk, about four miles distant, whither we immediately went. It was no easy task to transform ourselves into the semblance of decent Europeans; for nearly six weeks we had been unable to make any change of clothes, and our only ablutions had been an occasional wash of face and hands with greasy soup, as a preventive against chapping.

Our long exposure to the intense cold of the plateau rendered the heat of Russian houses almost insupportable. By opening the wind-wheel ventilators, which pass through the upper panes of the double-glazed windows, we reduced the temperature to 45 degrees, but even this was at first oppressive. Soon after our arrival we were told that the bath-house was heated; we were shown into an outer room, and after undressing, into another filled with steam. In one corner a large oven, containing a quantity of cobble stones, had been heated for several hours; into this a servant dashed a pailful of water, which immediately becoming steam, filled the room. This process of bathing, which was at first so disagreeable as to be almost painful, we soon learned to regard as a luxury, and there is certainly nothing more refreshing. The next day, after paying the Mongols, and discharging the Cossack, we drove over to Kiachta to dine with Mr. Pfaffius, and after dinner sat down to cards, the principal amusement of the country.

Among the company was Colonel Buthets, who was sent by his

Government in 1842 to the United States, to engage Mr. Whistler as chief engineer of the railroad between St. Petersburg and Moscow. Colonel Buthets, who was now working gold placers, informed me that 27-100ths of an ounce of gold to a ton of earth is considered rich.

His workings, which are in the district east of Kiachta, are in and near the beds of mountain creeks. The earth is here almost alway frozen, and the gold can be gained only by breaking up the ground in winter, and working it in summer, after the exposed heaps have thawed.

When associated with much clay, it is comminuted by passing it with a stream of water through a revolving drum, in which it remains a longer or shorter time, according to its consistency; from this it passes over tables of variable form, where the gold is collected. The valleys on the northern slope of the Yablonoi mountain seem to abound in auriferous localities. In the valley of the Olekma river, a tributary of the Lena, the water, confined under a heavy pressure every year by ice, bursts its covering, flows over and freezes upon the surrounding country, until toward the end of winter the accumulation of frozen overflows have a thickness of from ten to twenty feet. This covering, and the fact that the earth between it and the pay-dirt never thaws, render the working very difficult.

The thickness of the ice-bed is often diminished by keeping long, parallel trenches open over the ground which it is proposed to work in summer. Much of the water flows off through these ditches, which are alternately cleared of the constantly forming ice.

This tendency to form frozen inundations is very common among the Siberian rivers. Rising in the south, and flowing from warmer to colder latitudes, their lower and middle courses are frozen, while the head-waters are still open. The ice forms in shallow places clear down to the bottom of the stream, while, for a hundred miles or more above, the river, covered by a thick sheet of ice, is in the condition of a tube with its lower end closed. Under the enormous pressure thus brought to bear, the water bursts from its confinement, overflowing its banks where they are lowest, covering gradually the whole valley with accumulating thicknesses of ice. In this way I have seen a ravine gradually filled to the depth of twenty feet by the congealed waters of an insignificant rill. This, and the perpetually frozen character of the ground, form a great obstacle to the development of the rich gold fields of northeastern Siberia. Some of the gold of this region is said to have a fineness of 980-1000.

While at Troizkozavsk we visited the bazaar to buy furs for our journey through Siberia. The skin most generally used by gentlemen is that of the *genette*, or American raccoon. It is imported mostly from the United States. A superior robe of this costs about 200 roubles, which is equal to $150. The fur of the sable is worth from 25 roubles upward apiece; the finest qualities readily bring 50, 100, or even 200 roubles.

In this bazaar we saw English iron, which is much used, and costs about 23 per cent. more than Russian; it is brought from China through Mongolia. The average cost for freight from Tung-Chau, the head of boat navigation on the Pei-Ho river, to Kiachta, is about $60 per ton.

A considerable quantity of American tobacco, under the name of "Maryland," is imported for the manufacture of ladies' cigarettes, while the material for men's smoking is brought from Turkey, although a good deal of inferior tobacco is raised in different parts of Siberia.

On the Russian Christmas Day we drove over in the evening to dine with M. Pfaffius. As there is rarely enough snow for sleighing in this part of Siberia, south of Lake Baikal, the inhabitants rely altogether upon wheeled vehicles. This evening St. John and myself drove alone. We had hardly gone over half the road when a break in one of the wheels brought us to a stand-still. While we were trying to repair the damage, our attention was suddenly attracted toward a group which was approaching, and which evidently took a marked interest in us. The bright moonlight, which illuminated the open plains far and near, revealed to us several wolves, which were rapidly approaching. Suddenly they stopped on a small eminence close at hand, as if to take a good look at us. Their large, shaggy forms, clearly defined against the sky, were anything but a pleasant sight, considering that we had neither arms to fight, nor means of getting away. Instantly our memories recalled the long-forgotten stories of Russian wolves, including that of the mother who saved the lives of herself and one or two children by throwing out of the sleigh, one by one, the other members of her family. Dashing toward the group, we waved our hands, and shouted a duet, which took our visitors so completely by surprise that they turned tail, and trotted off at a quick pace, stopping, after the manner of wolves, every few rods, to look back.

The ease with which this victory was accomplished, surprised us quite as much as our chorus did the enemy. We lost a long-cherished respect for Russian wolves, as completely as Europe did a few years since for the Russian bear. I afterward took occasion many times to question into the authenticity of those Russian wolf stories which, with us, have passed almost into household words. At the risk of being classed among those unpoetic iconoclasts who would even leave Romulus and Remus unsuckled, I am compelled to say that I never found a Russian to whom these terrible tales were familiar.

At dinner we met, among others, a gentleman who was by birth a full-blooded Buriat Mongol, and whose face was marked by the extremest characteristics of his race; he was well educated, and struck me as in no respect inferior to the European gentlemen by whom he was surrounded. After dinner the whole party drove over to the club at Kiachta, a large building with rooms for dancing, conversation, reading, and billiards, and the inevitable buffet, which everywhere in Russia assumes an importance unknown elsewhere. The company, of both sexes, seemed to divide their time between dancing and playing at cards, with rather stronger inclinations to the latter. Among the dancers was an officer who had lost one leg in the Crimea, a circumstance which did not prevent his going gracefully with wooden-leg and crutch through a quadrille. During our stay at Kiachta we accepted an invitation from Major Muravieff, nephew of the former Governor-General, to accompany him to his head-quarters at Kudara. This officer, to whom we were indebted then, and subsequently, for many favors, was in command of the Cossacks, along 600 miles of the frontier. The distance was about forty miles, which we traversed in little over three hours. There being no snow on the ground, we travelled in a "tarantass," a four-wheeled vehicle, constructed on the principle of the buck-board wagon, being a box slung on long poles in lieu of springs, and drawn by as many horses harnessed abreast as the passenger chooses to pay for. We found a large village surrounding the well-built and elegantly-furnished quarters of our host. The inhabitants are all Cossacks, part of the frontier guard established by Peter the Great, for the double purpose of settling and defending the outskirts of the empire. Being at the same time soldiers and farmers, they enjoy with their families many privileges guaranteed to them by the edicts of their founder, and his successors. The number of this population under the command of Major Muravieff was about 17,000 souls.

We arrived at Kudara during a festival, and in the evening went with the Major through the village to see the amusements of the people. Hearing a sound of music and singing in one of the houses, we went in. In the unheated vestibule a shower of snow was falling, caused by the continuous condensation of the moisture which found its way through the cracks of the inner door from the crowded room within. Entering this latter, we passed at once from a temperature of 30 degrees below zero to more than 100 degrees above, and found ourselves in an assemblage of Cossack men and women, who gave a hearty greeting to their commander. A national dance was just beginning, and the three prettiest belles of the room were detailed to select us as partners. This dance begins with a slow promenade of the ladies, who then separate and choose partners, with whom they march up and down the room, each lady chanting the praises of her companion, winding up by kissing him on the forehead and each cheek, and singing at the same time: "Therefore I will kiss him thrice, in the name of the Father, Son, and Holy Ghost," an invocation rather adapted to take away from the individual emphasis of the salutation. They then separate, and the men in their turn choose their partners, and after praising their beauty and excellence, repeat the kissing, which seems to be the chief end of the ceremony. The music and songs of the Cossack are full of melody, though of a weird and barbaric kind.

While at Kudara, Major Muravieff organized for our amusement a white-hare battue, from which we brought back several good specimens of the fur of this arctic animal. The next day we returned to Troitzkozavsk.

The eve of the Russian New Year we spent at a ball, at the house of Mr. Sabasnikoff, the leading merchant of Kiachta.

Here we saw so much refinement and elegance, as well as beauty, among the ladies, that it was difficult to remember that we were in eastern Asia, and on the confines of Tartary. Here, too, we enjoyed the same dance which we had seen at Kùdara. While at Troitzkozavsk I passed much time in studying the collection of Mr. Nicholas Popoff, a gentleman to whom I am indebted for much interesting information concerning the mineralogy of eastern Siberia, and from whom I obtained a choice suite of the beautiful aqua-marines and topazes of Nertschinsk. Mr. Popoff has also a large and very complete cabinet of the insects of north-eastern Asia.

We had been detained for nearly a month at Troitzkozavsk, waiting for lake Baikal, 180 miles distant, to become permanently frozen. It is generally the middle of January before the ice forms to a thickness sufficient to prevent its being broken up by the winds. On the 15th we learned by telegraph that sleighs had already crossed the lake, and after bidding good-bye to our many hospitable friends we started for Irkutsk.

Henceforth our journey was to be made by post, and to facilitate our progress Mr. Pfaffius kindly furnished us with what are called crown passports, which are intended only for officials travelling on Government business. These papers insure the immediate furnishing of relays and horses, while travellers who have only the ordinary passport are subjected to constant delays and extortion, and are everywhere at the mercy of grasping post-masters.

M. Garnier, having business in Irkutsk, decided to accompany us, taking with him his Cossack cook. This region partakes to a great extent of the dryness of the atmosphere of central Asia. The mountains lying to the north condense the moisture brought from the Arctic ocean, leaving but little to be precipitated on the plateau and its northern declivity, and this in the intense cold falls in dry, flat crystals to a depth of only an inch or two. The first part of our journey had consequently to be made in wheeled vehicles. When we were ready to start we found the cook too drunk to keep his seat upon the baggage, and after he had rolled out once or twice, at the risk of being left on the road, we hit upon the expedient of tying him to his place.

The first stage of our journey brought us to the Selenga river, whose frozen surface enabled us to change our wagons for sleighs. The valley of the Selenga is broad, and bordered with high terraces, which seem to form a continuation of the northern edge of the plateau of Tartary, and to connect this with the plains of Siberia. There is considerable cultivation in this valley, notwithstanding the fact that the mean annual temperature is the freezing point of water. After two days and nights we came in sight of lake Baikal. This great inland sea, more than 400 miles in length, and enclosed between lofty walls, burst on our view at sunrise, a sheet of glistening ice, whose opposite cliffs, about thirty miles distant, seemed to be within cannon-shot, so deceptive is the clear atmosphere of this country. For several miles from the shore the surface was very rough. The ice of previous freezings, driven landward by the wind after each breaking-up, was piled in rugged masses of white and transparent green. Beyond this broad belt, which looked like the tumultuous waves of an angry sea, extended a clear expanse of fresh, dark ice, out of which the cliffs of the opposite shore appeared to rise, their base and the white rough border being hidden by the convexity of the earth.

This country was visited on the 31st of December, 1861, and January 1st and 2d of 1862, by a violent earthquake. A flat alluvial tract on the shore of the Baikal, near the mouth of the Selenga, was submerged, drowning the herds and population, and converting the land into a bay of the lake. The shock, which was felt severely at Irkutsk and Kiachta, was noticed south of Urga in Mongolia, and seems to have been perceptible over the distance of 700 miles from north to south.

After travelling a few miles along the brow of the bluff we came to the post-house at Posoloskoi Monasturi. This house is an ancient turreted building, erected in memory of an officer who was murdered by the Buraets about the middle of the 17th century.

The journey across the lake was the most exciting stage of our trip. At first we bounded at a rapid rate over the rough border, between great blocks of ice, whose transparent green gave them the appearance of immense crystals of aqua-marine. We came at last upon the smooth ice, the dark glassy surface of which stretched away as far as the eye could reach. Over this the horses bounded at a terrific pace. We seemed to be gliding in some mysterious manner along the surface of a calm sea, and the strangeness of our situation was occasionally heightened by loud reports, which echoed like thunder through the air. These were caused by cracks, which are repeatedly forming in cold weather, cleaving the icy surface for many miles. We were several times obliged to make detours to avoid these, where they were either too wide to jump with the sleigh, or where one side had been raised two or three feet higher than the other. In the middle of the lake an enterprising Russian had established a restaurant upon the ice, where we took a welcome dinner.

When we reached the opposite side we were detained for some time waiting for the moon to rise, as our road lay for several miles further along the shore of the lake, where travelling in the dark was not considered safe. By the time the moon rose a number of other travellers had collected at the station, and as we left terra firma we found a procession of five or six sleighs. The one occupied by St. John and myself, being the lightest, was allowed the rather doubtful honor of taking the lead, to test the strength of the surface. The route was by no means free from danger; the water of the lake having sunk, the ice in many places remained without other support than its own stiffness; and the hollow sound which reverberated beneath us, as we passed over these places, while it gave a timely warning to those behind us to profit by our experience if we should disappear, was by no means re-assuring to us. Two or three times the covering broke and horses and sleigh went through, bringing up, fortunately, however, in each case, on a second sheet of ice, which had formed two or three feet beneath. These accidents sometimes happen in places when an under sheet has not had time to form. Few years pass without some lives being lost in crossing the lake.

Daybreak found us travelling over the inhabited plains, on the eastern side of the Angara river. Here, for the first time, we witnessed one of the most beautiful phenomena in nature—a Siberian mist. A thick haze filled the atmosphere, and disappeared with almost the first rays of the rising sun. As it lifted like a dissolving veil, a feathery coating of ice crystals covered every object far and near; the surface of the endless fields of snow, our sleigh, the backs of our horses, the clothing of the driver, and the forest from the roots of the trees to the tips of the smallest twigs—everything that the eye fell upon was covered with a downy coating of these flat crystals, reflecting everywhere the rays of the sun, like a universal incrustation of diamonds. The telegraph wires over our heads had the appearance of a jewelled cord an inch thick. No description can convey an idea of the enchanting appearance of this scene, which was visible but a few minutes, and then vanished with almost magic suddenness before the first warmth of the sun. This phenomenon is apparently caused by the evaporation of the overflowing water of the Angara into an atmosphere of a far lower temperature.

Before noon we came in sight of Irkutsk, and soon entered the streets of this city, which is the capital of eastern Siberia. Here, also, we found that a letter written by General Vlangali, from Peking, had insured us a good reception. We were taken by our new friends to a large and elegantly furnished house, which we were told was entirely at our service.

Colonel ———, the chief of police, after accompanying us to our quarters, kindly placed his valet at our disposal during our stay.

On the day of our arrival we paid our respects to General Salaschnakoff, the acting governor-general, and afterward to his wife, who we found spoke English with remarkable fluency. We also formed immediately a circle of acquaintances in the society of Irkutsk, which made our sojourn in that city extremely pleasant, besides giving us the means of judging somewhat of the social condition of a country which is considered the frozen tomb alike of Russian criminals and political reformers.

At Irkutsk our party was compelled to break up. Mr. Walsh, having pressing business in St. Petersburg, left us about a week after our arrival, and made the journey with an officer of high rank who was travelling as courier. Mr. St. John left a few days later in company with our friend, Major Muravieff, who also travelled in the same manner. Not being pressed for time, and wishing to stop at several points on the route, I remained behind, prolonging my stay in Irkutsk to nearly three weeks.

The Russian conquests in northern Asia, begun by the daring robber Yermak Timofeyef, and continued partly by the advance of an adventurous population and partly by organized warfare, would form a chapter in history full of national romance, presenting many points of resemblance with the history of European conquest in America.

In 1579 the Russian family Stroganof, who had received from the Czar a large tract of land on both sides of the Ural mountains, applied to the robber Yermak for assistance against the Finnish Khan Chutschun, who ruled the country of Sibir, lying eastward on the Tobol and Irtisch rivers. Yermak, accepting the proposition, led his adventurous band of Cossacks of the Don into a war, which resulted in the subjection of the Khanate Siberia to the Czar in 1587. The cities, Tobolsk, Tiumen, Pelymsk, and Beresov, were founded and settled by Europeans. The spirit of conquest and adventure, once aroused, impelled the Cossacks ever further eastward, while hunters and traders, following quickly in the steps of the conquerors, established settlements, which confirmed Russia in possession of the territory. Already, in the beginning of the 17th century, the city of Tomsk had begun to exist as a frontier village. With an increased force the Cossacks pushed further and further toward the Pacific, founding Kuznetsk, Yeniseisk, Irkutsk, Selenginsk, and Nertschinsk, and never resting till they had reached the shores of Behrings straits.

At this period hunting, fishing, and trade in the valuable furs of the country, formed the basis of Siberian industry and wealth.

This immense region, with an area of more than 7,000,000 square miles, stretching from the Ural mountains to the Pacific, and from the Altai mountains to the Arctic ocean, is not everywhere the frozen and inhospitable region that it is generally supposed to be. In the western part the Barabinsky steppe traverses it from north to south, a broad tract of lowland extending from the Arctic ocean to the Aral and Caspian seas.

Within the limits of Siberia this plain is variable in character: grassy prairies alternate with reed marshes, fresh lakes with salt, and rich tracts of arable land with extensive forests of birch, ash, tillia, and conifers. Parts of this region are said in spring and summer to present the grandest of park scenery, where wooded hills rise from grassy plains covered with the most brilliant flowers. In these forests the birches often attain a diameter of four feet, and a height of a hundred and fifty, and the pine much greater dimensions. Large areas are covered to the depth of more than two feet with a fertile black soil resting on clay, and yielding from five to ten-fold. Grain ripens as far north as the 62d parallel of latitude, the southern boundary of Siberia being about 51 degrees N.

South and east of this steppe the terraces of the north flank of the Altai mountains border the plain, jutting far into it like the bold headlands of a sea-coast. Here the tributaries of the Yenessei, the Obi, and the Irtisch, rise among "great forests of birch, pine, and willow; and poplars, elms, and Tartarian maple" overhang their banks.

As we go north from the Arctic circle we pass from boundless forests of firs into a region of salt steppes and endless swamps, where the soil is perpetually frozen to the depth of hundreds of feet. Here "the surface itself, not thawed before the end of June, is again ice-bound by the middle of September, and deep snow covers the ground nine or ten months in the year." "Here endless snows and ice-covered rocks bound the horizon, nature lies shrouded in almost perpetual winter, life is a constant conflict with privation and with the terrors of cold and hunger—the grave of nature, which contains only the bones of another world. The people, and even the snow, smoke, and this evaporation is instantly changed into millions of needles of ice, which make a noise in the air like the sound of torn satin or thick silk.

"The reindeer take to the forest, or crowd together for heat, and the raven alone, the dark bird of winter, still cleaves the icy air with slow and heavy wing, leaving behind him a long line of thin vapor, marking the track of his solitary flight. The trunks of the thickest trees are rent with a loud noise, masses of rock are torn from their sites, the ground in the vallies is rent into yawning fissures, from which the waters that are underneath rise, giving off a cloud of vapor, and immediately become ice. The atmosphere becomes dense, and the glistening stars are dimmed. The dogs outside the huts of the Siberians burrow in the snow, and their howling at intervals of six or eight hours interrupts the general silence of winter." *

The climate of Siberia may be divided into winter and summer. In the far north the thermometer sinks in winter to 70 degrees

* Mrs. Somerville, quoting Admiral Wrangel.

and even 120 degrees below zero. Even in the neighborhood of Irkutsk, where the mean annual temperature is one-half a degree below the freezing point, the mean for the winter is zero, the thermometer at times sinking to below 70 degrees. The waters of the Lena are covered already, in the end of September, with two feet of ice, and the Tobol and Irtisch are generally frozen from the 20th of October to the 20th of April.

But with returning spring the rays of the sun traversing the clear atmosphere produce almost a magic change in the appearance of nature. The melting snow is rapidly followed by budding foliage and blooming flowers, the prairies are covered with grass, and the planted grain springs up and hastens to maturity; in an incredibly short time a vast ice-bound region is converted into a blooming garden. The summers are favored by a continued absence of frosts. Even at Yakutsk, in 62 degrees N. latitude, the thermometer stands often at 77 degrees in the shade, and wheat and rye produce from fifteen to forty-fold, while during the winter the mercury is constantly frozen during two to three months.*

It is a country where extremes of climate and of animal and plant life meet. In this connection Erman, in his "Travels in Siberia," says: "M. Turchaninov had discovered not less than 1,000 phanerogamous plants in the neighborhood (Irkutsk), many of them of unknown species. In spite of the climate, the flora of Irkutsk is richer than that of Berlin, exhibiting the plants of warmer countries intermixed with those of the Arctic regions.

"The wild peach of Nerchinsk is a true apricot (*Prunus Armeniaça*), and contains a very agreeable kernel in a fleshless envelopes, while in the very vicinity of these products of a more favored climate we find the Siberian stone-pine and the dwarf birch of the polar circle in the highlands. The same holds good with regard to the fauna of the Transbaikalian districts. We see the Tunguze mounted on his reindeer, pass the Buraet with his camel, and discover the tigers of China in the forests where the bear is taking his winter sleep. * * * * It would hardly be possible to point out any other country on the earth combining such remote extremes of physical character and condition."

The population of Siberia, estimated at 4,270,938 souls, consists

* Mrs. Somerville, "Physical Geography."

for the greater part of settlers and exiles of Russian origin. The remainder is made up of representatives of most of the fragments of tribes and races which, successively crowded off from the table-land, have sought refuge in the wilderness of northeastern Asia.

According to their capacity, these remnants of races are either sinking out of sight before the contact with European civilization, or are leaving their aboriginal habits and rising in the social scale under the tolerant government and fostering influence of their conquerors. Some of these tribes which have been long subject to Russian influence, especially the Mohammedans, are among the best elements of the population.

Russia, having no capital punishment, has long been in the habit of banishing its criminals of all kinds to Siberia, the distance of exile beyond the Ural mountains being generally proportionate to the degree of crime. Those offences which in Europe are punishable by death, are here expiated by labor in the mines of the far east. Thus, even treason is made to benefit the State, the offenders being compelled to perform the work of reclaiming an immense part of the empire, and of laying the foundation of a state which is destined to rise to a position of great commercial importance. Some crimes were made punishable by life-long labor in the mines, but the extent of the penalty in the greater number is limited to the restricting of the offender to a certain district, beyond which he is not allowed to wander, but within which he is free to labor in his own behalf, unhindered, but under the surveillance of an ever-active police. The absence of serfdom in Siberia has, perhaps, always nearly compensated for the lower standard of morality which must always exist among a population where the convict element predominates.

The political agitators of Russia, and of Poland, have long supplied Siberia with a superior element of involuntary population; and the refined society which the traveller meets with in the cities owes its existence in great part to this source. These exiles were often voluntarily accompanied by their wives and families, thus bringing with them the social cultivation of the highest circles in Europe. Instances of this devotion on the part of Polish women are of such common occurrence as scarcely to invite notice. During my stay at Irkutsk, when the Polish rebellion was furnishing exiles by tens of thousands, the wives and families of the wealthier prisoners frequently arrived, ready to sign papers by which they condemned themselves to undergo the same life and hardships and complete isolation from the rest of the world, indeed to submit themselves and their children to the same fate as their husbands, so long as these should live. A still more touching though rarer instance occurred in the case of two young ladies, who had been engaged to Polish officers condemned to life-long labor in the mines. They arrived at Irkutsk, and entreated for permission to be married to the officers, and to sign the papers which would for ever cut them off from the world, and condemn them also to perpetual prison-life. Their petition had to be submitted at St. Petersburg, and no decision had arrived when I left.

The descendants of these exiles become firmly attached to the country. When they can afford it they travel through Europe, many of them going thither several times. Whenever I questioned Siberian ladies as to their attachment to the country, they invariably replied that, although they were very fond of making long journeys to Paris and Italy, they would never choose for their home any other country than Siberia. And the attachment is even stronger with the peasant, who, next to his God and the Emperor, reverences the soil of his birth-place. I must confess that, having myself a strong partiality for climates where an intensely cold and clear atmosphere is rendered cheerful by an unclouded sun, I could appreciate this affection for a land where the snows of such a winter bury the germs of vegetation far below the surface, but not so deep as to prevent it from converting the country into a blooming garden in summer. Nor is the social life with all its gayety to be left out of consideration.

The long-continued influx of political offenders, and the large number of Government officials, form in every city an extensive circle of cultivated society, which manages to compensate for the severity of the climate by a continued round of amusement. In Irkutsk, masquerades, the theatre, dinners and balls at private houses and at the club-rooms, left little to wish for in the way of enjoyment.

I was struck with one peculiarity of Siberian society, which however did not extend below the merchant class—this was the apparently greater amount of care bestowed upon the education of women. They seemed to be generally much better trained, not merely in music, but in foreign languages, and in the general branches of education.

The bracing climate, and the great and varied resources of this sparsely-peopled country, have developed in its European population a spirit of enterprise which resembles in many respects that which is building up the States on our Pacific coast. Manufactories of cloth and linen, of glass and iron, have long been established, and numerous similar branches of industry are everywhere springing up. Mines of gold and silver, of copper, iron, and salt are worked by Government and by private enterprise. There are extensive fisheries in the rivers and lakes, and the area of cultivated land is yearly increasing. During the summer, steamboats ply on all the large streams and on lake Baikal, rendering it possible to go from St. Petersburg to the mouth of the Amoor by steam, across the entire breadth of the great continent, with less than a thousand miles of transit by wagon. During the winter the roads are covered with long trains of sledges, by which the internal commerce and the trade between China and European Russia is carried on. Some idea of the commerce of Siberia may be formed from the sales at the fair of Irbit, which in 1859 amounted to 42,628,200 silver roubles. At Petropaulowski, on the Ishim, the central point for the trade with central Asia and western China, the imports in 1843 amounted to 825,481 silver roubles, and the exports to 715,926. In 1858 the imports from Tashkend amounted to 602,319 roubles, and the exports to 485,400. In 1862 the imports at this place amounted to 2,741,000 roubles, and the exports to 1,787,691; the differences between the value of exports and imports being paid in Russian money. At Kiachta, in 1862, the value of imported tea amounted to more than eight and one-half million roubles.*

* The following table shows the imports and exports at Kiachta for 1862:

IMPORTS.	Roubles (silver).	EXPORTS.	Roubles (silver).
Tea,	7,851,445	Cloth,	1,951,767
Brick Tea,	897,371	Cotton fabrics,	1,485,976
Cattle,	128,950	Furs,	438,636
Sugar,	104,322	Tanned leather,	154,452
Leather,	49,118	Juchtn,	139.539
Cotton stuffs,	27,274	Metal wares,	58,097
Furs,	24,519	Grain,	56,569
		Woollen wares,	55,962
		Flax and Hemp fabrics,	26,674
		Coral ornaments,	19,524

It certainly is a remarkable fact, that of two shipments of the same tea from Han-kau, the one going by sailing vessel to England and St. Petersburg, and the other by the long land route—through China on boats and mules, through Tartary on camels, through Siberia on sleighs, and through Russia by railroad—that which has taken the land route costs the same, or less, in St. Petersburg as that which has gone by sea. This is owing in part to the excess of duty at the Atlantic port of Russia over that on the Siberian frontier, and partly, perhaps, to the fact that the tea which takes the ocean route requires more manipulation before shipment than the other.

The tea trade alone between China and Europe is very large, and seems, when taken in connection with many other reasons, to warrant the belief that the near future will see a railroad along this important route. It would be almost impossible to over-estimate from a national commercial point of view the benefits which would follow its construction. At its two ends would lie the most densely-peopled market-lands of the world, while hardly a hundred miles of its whole length would be in regions which are not already productive. Its easterly division would traverse the fertile and closely-occupied lowland of China and cross the Yangtz' and Yellow rivers, the chief commercial arteries of the empire, near their outlets to the sea. It would pass over the plateau of central Asia, a grazing land which from the most ancient times has supported immense herds of cattle. And the Siberian link would provide an inlet and outlet to a country which has all the resources, agricultural and mineral, necessary to the formation of a great state, and where these resources are already undergoing a rapid and healthy interior development. The distance from Shanghai to Kazan, the eastern terminus of the Russian railroad, is about 4,600 miles, and the total distance from Shanghai to St. Petersburg 5,600.

At the Chinese end an altitude of about 5,000 feet above the sea would have to be overcome in ascending to the summit of the plateau. This elevation is distributed over about 125 miles.

The plateau itself presents no engineering difficulties, and a gradual descent from the northern edge could be obtained through the valleys of the Tula and Orkhon to lake Baikal. Nor are there any important obstacles on the plains of Siberia and in the passes of the Ural mountains, unless such may exist in the tendency of the rivers to form extensive frozen overflows. Aside from international difficulties, the construction of such a road would, notwithstanding its greater length, seem to be a simpler problem than that of the now nearly finished Union Pacific line, for the European-Asiatic road, besides connecting the two greatest markets of the world, would be sure of an immediate and extensive way-traffic, because in the vast regions it would traverse all the elements necessary thereto already exist.

During the present century a spirit of enterprise, especially in the working of gold deposits, has caused the accumulation of large fortunes in many parts of the country. This has been attended to a certain extent by the extravagance and the vices which were for years prominent in California and Australia. The two great evils of the country, which run through all classes, are gambling and drinking to excess. I know of no nation in which drunkenness assumes such frightful proportions as in this eastern part of the Russian empire. During my stay in Irkutsk a gentleman told me, in illustration of this fact, that immediately after a reduction of the Government tax on spirits, thirty-five men and women in a village of 500 souls had killed themselves with drinking in one week. Another instance, related to me by a Siberian lady, was, that one of her female servants, having obtained leave of absence under pretence of visiting her dying mother, had gone directly to a drinking shop, where she lay four days in an incessant state of drunkenness. But another most absurd example was one which came under my own observation.

The reader will remember that on leaving Kiachta we were obliged to tie the cook fast in the carriage. M. Garnier, having decided to return to Troizkozavsk, had taken the precaution to send this man the day before with a note to the chief of police, requesting that the bearer might be put in prison until he should be sent for. When everything was ready for the journey, and M. Garnier had taken his place in the sleigh, the cook arrived under special charge of a policeman, and perfectly sober. My friend was delighted at the success of his manœuvre, but having forgotten some small article of baggage he sent the man into his room for it. Entering the house about a minute afterward, I found the rascal just putting down empty a decanter which a few minutes before had been nearly full of our choicest brandy. The fellow had made the best of his opportunity, and before the sleigh started was of course as drunk as when we left Kiachta.

I was told that in Kamtchatka the inhabitants are in the habit of using a fungus in their liquor, which not only increases the intoxicating effect, but has also the advantage that as soon as a man begins to get sober a glass of pure water will make him as drunk as before.

It is said that in delirium tremens the Russian, instead of being tormented with visions of snakes, and other animals, sees only little devils of the conventional type. "He has seen the little devils," is a common phrase in explaining that a man is in the last stages of drunkenness.

The vice of gambling seems to be even more widely spread than that I have just described, since it pervades not only all classes, but both sexes. The Siberian ladies are great adepts at cards, a fact which my companions and myself learned to our cost on the very threshold of the country. After dinner, soon after our arrival at Kiachta, we each of us, in the course of an evening, lost to our hostess at whist nearly the whole sum which, for the purpose of avoiding the appearance of singularity, we had calculated on devoting to play. During the whole game the lady kept up a constant fire of sparkling conversation, but was such an excellent player that, while our attention was constantly diverted, she kept the run of the cards perfectly, and had at the close every detail in her memory.

It is hardly considered proper for ladies before marriage to play for money, but they certainly make up for the privation immediately after. Many of them begin in the morning to make their calls, and drive from house to house till they happen at some friend's to find a gathering large enough to form a party at their favorite game of hazard *stut-kolka.* Even at balls the band plays to almost empty dancing-floors, the stronger excitement of the card-tables drawing away nearly all the guests. One lady told me that, although she was very fond of cards, she played them quite as much in self-defence as for the pleasure, "because," she added, "while my husband is losing at the club, I am just as likely to be winning from his opponent's wife."

In a country where gambling is so universal, one expects to

find every foreign and native device that has been invented for games of chance, but I was told of one for which I think none will dispute the honor of invention with the Siberians. In the prisons, where gaming is strictly forbidden, the inmates resort to the following curious means of indulging in their favorite propensity. Each man carries in a corked quill a select specimen of an insect, which he is never at a loss to find without going further than his own clothing. The game consists in putting these animals in the centre of a circle chalked on the table, and betting as to which will first reach the circumference. Each man knows his own racer, which he has trained with care, feeding it in certainly the most affectionate manner by holding the open end of the quill against his wrist or temple.

The habits of luxury in Siberia seem out of all proportion to the salaries of the official class, which are so absurdly small that they will scarcely buy the common necessaries of life. The official corruption which prevailed throughout the empire during the reign of Nicholas, and which still exists, is owing almost entirely to this insufficiency of pay.

During my journey I incurred a lasting debt to the Siberians for their hospitality. I could not help thinking that this was extended to me quite as much in my character of an American as individually. It was pleasant to meet everywhere with an expression of the most cordial feeling toward the United States, and I was often surprised to hear in this distant part of Asia a very just appreciation of the causes and probable results of the war which was then going on at home. Everywhere there existed the strongest sympathy for the North, and a general good feeling had become widely spread in every part of the empire by the accounts of the cordial reception which the Russian fleet had met with in the United States. The position occupied by the slavery question in our struggle had something to do in influenc ing the feelings of a nation in which the emancipation of serfs had recently become an accomplished fact; somewhat was due also to the many points of resemblance between the rebellion in America and the one then being crushed in Poland.

CHAPTER XXVIII.

SIBERIA.

My departure from Irkutsk was delayed several days, owing to the difficulty in obtaining a comfortable kibitka, or travelling sleigh. This vehicle is of all sizes, entirely open, or with a hood behind, or completely covered. It has only a single pair of long runners, and, to prevent upsetting, is provided with a guard-frame, which, starting from the body of the sleigh in front, spreads out some twelve or eighteen inches from the sides at the back end. As soon as the vehicle tips, this framework touches the ground, and must break before it can capsize.

Every part of the kibitka is thoroughly braced, in a manner to secure the greatest possible strength, as well as lightness, without too great rigidity; precautions which are absolutely necessary, since these sleighs are expected, before wearing out, to make several journeys of from two to four thousand miles, at the rate of ten and sometimes even of fourteen miles per hour, over roads that are anything but smooth.

Expecting to travel alone I waited until I found a very light sleigh, which was not much more than wide enough for one person.

The postal service in Russia is, in many respects, the most perfect in the world, considering the immense network of roads it covers on both continents. In some parts of the empire it is given under contract to private enterprise, but through Siberia it remains in the hands of Government. Relay-stations are established at distances of from eight to fifteen miles, under the charge of postmasters, whose duty it is to provide horses and attend to the mails.

There are three ways of travelling—by buying a ticket as passenger with the mail conveyance; by purchasing a common order for horses; or, finally (if travelling on Government business), by having a Government order, which cannot be bought. In the first of these methods, which is very cheap, costing only 1½ kopeks per werst, the traveller is obliged to go directly through, and is, moreover, likely to be associated with not over-pleasant company.* In the second, with the common permit, he is exposed to the extortion of postmasters, and to delays which may lengthen his journey by weeks, unless he satisfies the greed of these officials.

The much-coveted Government order admits of no delay, and requires the furnishing of horses in preference to everything but the imperial mail. The traveller is allowed as many horses as he is willing to pay for, at the rate of 1½ kopek each per werst east of Tiumen, and west of that point at 3 kopeks each. Through the kindness of the Governor-General of eastern Siberia I obtained a Government order, which relieved me from the anxiety I had felt at the prospect of a long journey through a country of whose language I knew nothing, and where at every station I would have been exposed to the most annoying delays and impositions.

Before taking final leave of Irkutsk, I would express my deep sense of obligation to the Governor-General of eastern Siberia, to the Chief of Police of Irkutsk, and to Count Paul Anosoff for their private hospitality, no less than for their official assistance, without which my journey would hardly have been possible, and also to Colonel Reingard and Mr. Andre Razguildieff. To Prince Krapotkin I am indebted for much valuable information concerning eastern Tartary and western Manchuria, countries through which he had travelled in disguise.

On the evening of the 6th of February I left Irkutsk, and started on my lonely journey westward. Following the Russian custom, I had my baggage spread out over the bottom of the sleigh and covered with a quantity of straw, and placing over this a Japanese mattrass and a number of fur robes, I secured a bed which was both soft and thick enough to deaden the shocks of rapid travelling over a rough road. A number of large pillows were placed at the back, to raise and support the shoulders and head, for the Russians have discovered that a half reclining posture is the most convenient in travelling, since every muscle is at

* The kopek being equal to two-thirds of a cent, and the werst to two-thirds of a mile, the fare by post is equal to 1⅙ cents per mile.

rest, and yet the elevation of the head permits a view of the surrounding scenery.

Having learned by our rough experience in Tartary how necessary it is to clothe one's self in the manner which the natives of the country have found to be the best, I had taken every Russian precaution against the cold, and had encased myself in an outfit which I can recommend to travellers as a sure protection in the most extreme climate.

Over a pair of thick and loose woollen trousers and a woollen shirt I put on the close-fitting robe worn by the peasants, reaching from the neck nearly to the ankles, and made of sheep-skin, with the wool inside, and over this a loose robe of the fur of the Arctic fox, with the hair also on the inner side. My feet were encased in very loose boots made of felt, and reaching nearly to the knee. A Chinese skull-cap of felt, with fur lappets, protected the head and ears, while a long knitted comforter, covering the whole face below the eyes, after being crossed behind the neck and tied under the chin, protected the nose, throat, and lungs. On getting into the sleigh the traveller puts on over all his other garments a wrapper of deer-skin, with the hair outside to break the force of the wind, and furnished with loose sleeves and a collar, which when raised envelops the head and face. Lying down and putting his feet and legs in a large wolf-skin bag, he pulls over him a fur sleigh-robe which reaches nearly to the chin. He is now ready to defy the greatest severities of even a Siberian winter.

The cold, which had been increasing every day, seemed on the first night out of Irkutsk to have reached a more intense degree than I had yet experienced, and before midnight my hands and feet were nearly frozen. At the first station I stuffed my boots with dry hay, and was fortunate enough to find a woman with an ample muff, which I bought for a few roubles, and found to be preferable to any gloves. After this, during the whole journey, I never for a minute suffered from cold. The nose is always the most difficult part of the body to protect; but by pulling the comforter about an inch forward, and holding it there till it stiffens with the frozen breath, the whole face is kept warm by the heat of the breath.

Finding myself thoroughly defended against the severity of the weather, I now began to enjoy the wonderful night-scene which surrounded me. Three bounding horses carried the sleigh at almost railway speed over the road, dashing in rapid succession through groves of trees, through fields and forests, and over the hills and valleys of an uneven country, whose face was covered with a deep mantle of snow, rounding and softening all its outlines, and illuminating the whole scene with the tender light reflected from its pure surface. Overhead the stars shone with flashing lustre through an atmosphere whose purity is equalled only on the higher and dryer parts of the earth. After a time I allowed myself to yield to the call of the system for sleep, feeling that protected as I was there was no danger.

On awakening I was not a little startled at being unable to open my eyes. Feeling of the lids I found them perfectly sensible, but the lashes were frozen together and to the edge of the comforter. After fruitless attempts to force them apart, I enveloped my head in the collar of the outer cloak, and gradually succeeded, by breathing, in raising the temperature sufficiently to thaw the icy chains. On looking at the thermometer I found the mercury frozen, and even the brandy in my bottle had assumed an oily consistency. At the station we reached before sunrise I got out for breakfast. Having been warned of the impossibility of getting any decent food outside of two or three large cities, I had taken an abundant supply of tea, coffee, and sugar, and dinners for twenty-four days in the shape of twenty-four plates of soup, each one frozen into a separate cake, and enough bread to last for several days. Almost every Russian house owns a samovar, or urn, for boiling water, which is heated by charcoal in a tube extending from top to bottom. This is the only thing, excepting plates and glasses, and other rough table-ware, that the traveller can count upon at Russian inns, or at least in Siberia. The samovar was heated, and in a few minutes from the time of my arrival I had made a sufficient breakfast on six or seven large glasses of tea and a couple of slices of dry bread, and I adhered to this bill-of-fare during the rest of the journey. There is nothing so refreshing and so sustaining in a cold climate as good black tea. Its stimulating effect is both gentler and far more lasting than that of spirits. On the way from Kiachta to Irkutsk we had stopped to make tea at every station, and the temptation was very strong for me to continue the habit; but an easy calculation showed that a delay of half an hour at every relay would lengthen my journey by more than a week, and I resolved to confine myself to three stoppages daily.

The spirit thermometer outside of the station marked 45 degrees, or about 70 degrees below zero of Fahrenheit, while within doors the heat could not have been less than 85 or 90 degrees (F.), involving a plunge from extreme to extreme which is not only uncomfortable but dangerous. In entering these station-houses it is necessary to leave in the sleigh the outer deer-skin robe, as the low temperature of the fur would cause it to be drenched with the condensing vapors of the hot rooms to an extent that would render it as stiff as a board on re-exposing it to the outside air. I was now entirely among strangers; my only companions, the drivers, changed at every relay with their horses; and understanding, as I did, nothing of the language, the long journey loomed up before me like an impracticable task, an endless succession of strange postmasters, and I resolved if possible to take in some Russian as a fellow-passenger.

During the morning of the second day, just after I had entered the court-yard of a station, the postmaster appeared, and to my delight addressed me in German.

"You are going through to Moscow?" he asked.

"Yes," I replied.

"Could you take a fellow-traveller?"

"I have every wish to be accommodating; still it depends upon who the traveller may be."

"Oh! I will guarantee her sociability."

"Her? the traveller is a woman, then!"

"Yes, sir," replied the postmaster, "a young lady who is travelling westward on very pressing business, but whose kibitka has broken down, and I am unable to give her another. The only alternative she has, if you will allow her an alternative, is between travelling in your sleigh or in that of a Russian priest who has just arrived."

"How is it possible," I asked, with astonishment, "that any lady could hesitate in choosing between a perfectly strange foreigner and a man of God?"

The postmaster disappeared to gain some further light on this strange proceeding.

Now, in making a resolution to take the first respectable traveller I could find, I had made an express reservation against lady passengers; but here was a prospect of being wedged into a narrow sleigh I did not know how many days and nights, with a woman of whose appearance or proportions I had not the slightest idea. It was certainly an alarming prospect for a bachelor. But before I had time for further meditation the postmaster re-appeared, and with a half-suppressed smile remarked that the lady preferred the stranger, as she was not partial to Russian priests. There was no getting out of it; and with the best grace possible, under the circumstances of my ignorance of her size, I sent the landlord to assure the lady that I should be delighted to have her share my sleigh. After her baggage had been carefully stowed with mine in the bottom of the kibitka, and her own bedding distributed over mine, my fellow-passenger appeared, but wrapped in such quantities of furs and so closely veiled that it was impossible to judge of either her age or appearance; but just before getting into the sleigh she raised her veil to salute me, and perhaps also to take a good look at her travelling companion, and in doing so exhibited a young and remarkably beautiful face. I inwardly congratulated myself upon not having adhered to a resolution which would have deprived me of so charming a companion. People may say what they will, but whether in Siberia or in a New York street-car, I have observed that a pretty face commands more willing attention than a plain one. After travelling for half a mile or more I broke the silence by some commonplace remark in German. My companion shook her head. "She speaks French," I thought; "all Russian ladies speak French;" so I repeated what I had said in that language. Again she shook her head. "Perhaps she understands Italian; the Russian ladies are great musicians, and generally study Italian;" so I reiterated my attempt in Tuscan, and then in English. But each time there came that ominous shake of the head. I was now in despair; the idea of travelling for days, or perhaps weeks, with a companion, but without having a single expression in common, was too aggravating to be borne. I knew one Russian word—that for horse. Leaning forward I pointed to the animals and called out "loshada! loshada!" The effect was electric. She saw that it was the only word between us, and the whole ridiculousness of our situation presented itself to her mind as it had to mine. After a hearty and musical laugh, she talked for some time in Russian, and the ice which had threatened to separate us was at last broken.

I think it was during this day, or the following one, that our road lay along the brow of one of the lofty terraces which flank the Altai mountains on the north. The country on every side was covered with a dense forest. On our right hand it was depressed far below us, and the eye ranged over the unbroken surface of the wilderness, which extended to the horizon, and as I knew continued like a boundless ocean ever further and further northward till it reached the limit of trees around the pole. These northern solitudes still inspire one with something of the mysterious fascination which we see in the ideas of the ancients concerning the Hyperboreans, and the Arimasps, who fought with the Griffons for golden sands in this land of perpetual night. From where we stood there was but a single transition between us and the pole, one vast and gloomy forest, giving way at its northern limit to perpetual ice. Although the forest disappeared under a distant horizon, I could trace in my mind its changes toward the north; birches and maples becoming ever fewer, their places supplied by lofty pines, and these dwindling in stature and at last giving way altogether to the more hardy firs of the Arctic swamps, and these in turn yielding to the polar tundras which cover the frozen tomb of the mammoth.

During the day we came to a long and steep descent from the terrace. Already, before we reached the brow, the driver whipped up his horses, and in going down the hill kept them on the run. The road was as smooth as glass, and our speed terrific; but as soon as the traces began to slacken, or the sleigh to swerve in the slightest, the driver again used the whip. This is unavoidable on hills, where the smooth surface is frozen so hard that the runners take no hold upon the snow, and is the only way of avoiding either being upset or going down hill backward, dragging the horses. I must confess that this coasting experience on the first long declivity fairly made my hair stand on end. When the sleigh struck in the deep cross-trough (with which every long descent ends in Siberia) it bounded two or three feet into the air, leaving my companion, myself, and all our baggage mixed up in an almost inextricable mass.

For many days the journey was devoid of remarkable incidents. Travelling uninterruptedly day and night, and leaving the sleigh only long enough to take our three slight meals, I kept few notes, and lost altogether the run of dates. The general appearance of the country, its succession of great forests, of hills and plains, of the valleys of great rivers where cultivated fields lay hidden under the white cloak of winter, its countless villages buried in snow up to the roofs of the houses, with excavated streets—all these remain impressed upon my memory rather like a vision of an enchanted land than as the real scenery upon an actual journey. I remember one or two terrible snow-storms which fell with blinding force and with a fierce wind.

The moon waxed full and waned, and still my companion occupied her place in my sleigh. When she would leave I had as yet no idea; I was not anxious that it should be soon. In the meantime I made progress in Russian. Every day added a few words or phrases to my vocabulary, until finally we were able to bring a little language to the aid of conversation, which was at first kept up only by signs. It was sometimes not easy to make out whether my companion was asleep or awake, especially in the early morning, nor was it an easy task to make preparations on my own part for finding this out. In the first place, there was the usual necessity of thawing out one's eyelashes; it was only after this, and pulling down the great collar of the outer robe, and rolling over on the left side, that I caught sight of my companion, or rather a mountain of shapeless furs towering beside and above me, and with a small spiral column of vapor issuing from the top like that which betrays the wintering-place of a bear. How was one to know whether sleep or wakefulness existed under these motionless robes. The mother of invention taught me a ready expedient: lighting a cigarette I puffed vigorously till I felt sure that every fold and crack was penetrated by the aroma. It was a sure test; for my companion, like all Russian ladies, was passionately fond of smoking, and never could resist the temptation. If she was awake, a gentle movement was soon perceptible, ending after a while in the appearance of a small hand with a cigarette, stretched out to be lighted. In this way the time passed smoothly enough, which is more than I can say of the road; the endless succession of cross-troughs sent us bounding every now and then into the air to come down with a shock that entirely destroyed the equilibrium of our arrangements, which required very delicate adjustment in a sleigh not more than three feet and a half wide at the back and two in front.

But it is now time that I should relieve my companion from the rather embarrassing position which she must hold in the reader's mind, when considered simply as the co-occupant of a strange gentleman's sleigh during so long a journey. Her strange history, which I learned in part from her, I will give as I afterward heard it more fully stated at St. Petersburg. This lady was the daughter of a noble family of Warsaw, of which she and a brother were the only children. The latter had become an officer in the Polish army, and had been made prisoner under circumstances which caused him to be convicted of high treason and sentenced to life-long labor in the frozen mines of eastern Siberia. This punishment, which seemed to the aged parents and sister more awful than death, was rendered more painful by the fact that no communication could be held with the exile, who might fall under the fatigues of the long and terrible journey across Asia. In order to give comfort and companionship to her brother during his journey, and to bring back news of his safe arrival, this girl, scarcely eighteen years old, formed the resolution to accompany him, a point which she carried against all opposition. In company with a large number of political exiles and convicts of every class, this young woman, who had hitherto seen nothing but the comforts of home and the gayeties of a brilliant capital, made the long and terrible journey, wading for months through the snows of Siberia, exposed daily and nightly to the hardships and filth of the prison stations, and surrounded by scenes of suffering. After seeing her brother arrive safely at his destination, without waiting to recover from the fatigues she had gone through, she started immediately on the long journey to Omsk on some business connected with the exile's condition, and it was on this trip that the breaking of her sleigh threw me into her company. This devotion, and the circumstances by which it was surrounded, cannot but recall to the reader the touching story of Elizabeth, whose life was in the same land, and whose journey was partly over the same road.

Wishing to rest for a few hours at Omsk, I drove to a hotel and ordered dinner. During the meal a soldier arrived and demanded my passport. To my horror I now remembered that I had left this behind, at a station some distance off. In its stead I handed over the Government order for horses, and told the officer that I was travelling from Peking to the United States on official business. With this information he departed. Before long he reappeared, stating that the chief of police had himself been in Peking, and would be happy to see me. Accompanying the policeman I proceeded through the city, and was brought into a large public building, and in this into a room which I instantly perceived to be a police court. About fifty men and women of the lowest class were standing in a circle, while at a table there were seated several clerks, and an officer in the uniform of a colonel. After informing me that this officer was the chief of police, my guide went up to him and whispered something in his ear. Very much to my surprise, the man who had invited me on the score of having been in Peking merely looked up, and after a long stare went on with the business in hand. Not having been asked to sit down, I walked to the nearest chair and seated myself, but was immediately forced by a Cossack to stand up. Being indignant at this treatment I went up to the chief of police, and finding that he understood neither English, French, nor German, told him in broken Russian that as he had been in Peking he probably spoke Chinese. In the best mandarin that I could muster I explained the loss of my passport, and demanded to know why he had brought me thither to be treated as a common criminal.

Not understanding a word of what I said, the official became furious, and ordered me into arrest. As the prison-keeper started to take me from the room I shook him off, and demanded of the clerks whether any of them spoke German. As one of them gave me a nod, which was intended not to be seen by his master, I turned to him and said, "Tell the chief of police that I am bearing dispatches from the United States minister at Peking to my Government at Washington, and that he will be held to account at St. Petersburg for every hour I am delayed." The old man after some hesitation interpreted my language. The chief of police answered that he did not believe it; that I was there without any passport, and had been travelling in company with a sister of an exile; in short, that he believed me to be a dangerous character. If I was carrying dispatches, why did I not show them? Taking from my pocket a large envelop addressed to the home Government, and bearing the seal of the legation, I handed it over to the official, who made a move to break the seals; but on second thought handed it back to me after merely examining the outside. I was now allowed to depart, though without any apology for the treatment I had received. This unpleasant episode was the only official annoyance that I underwent on the whole journey.

My companion having stopped at Omsk, I was now alone. The country from this point on, and, indeed, the whole region of the Obi river and its tributaries, is much more thickly peopled than eastern Siberia. We were continually passing through villages where the streets were cut out of the deep snow, which had drifted over the roofs of the houses. These Russian villages consist altogether of log houses, generally not more than one story high. As the heavy frosts throw the buildings out of position, the older ones are often so inclined to one side that it is often no easy task to cross a room where the smooth and greasy floor is sometimes at an angle of from fifteen to twenty-five degrees with the horizon. In the waiting-room of the post-houses the walls are generally decorated with one or two coarse prints, either of a religious character or representing the exploits of Yermak; one corner always contains a picture of some saint, gilded in the Byzantine style. In the inscription under one picture of the twelve apostles, the artist had made a slight mistake, by placing the two before the one, thus making it read "The 21 Apostles." A lamp always hangs before these shrines, and no Russian ever enters the room without immediately facing them and making three times the sign of the cross.

It would be difficult to find a country in which the people are more superstitious than in Russia. No Russian maiden will be left alone with her lover in a room where there is a picture of a saint; to meet a priest on leaving a house, is an omen of evil, which can be charmed away only by throwing a pin at him, if you are a woman, or by spitting on his beard, if you are a man. The aversion (which we find in other countries) to beginning any enterprise on Friday, and to making the thirteenth person at table, here assumes an importance unknown elsewhere, and a

Russian will instantly leave a room where three lights happen to be on one table.

At Tiumen I remained over one day. Unfortunately the great fair, which is held here every year in January, was now finished, and the visitors which I had hoped to see from many parts of Asia, had departed. The only consolation I obtained for this loss was a dish of sterlet, a species of sturgeon peculiar to the rivers of western Siberia and to the tributaries of the Caspian. It is certainly the most delicious of all fishes, and is perhaps the greatest delicacy in the markets of St. Petersburg.

Not long after leaving Tiumen the road entered upon the gentle ascent of the eastern flank of the Ural mountains. This range is so low, and its approach, especially from the east, so easy, that I reached Ekaterinburg without appreciating the fact that I was near the summit of one of the most celebrated mountain ranges of the world.

At Ekaterinburg I presented letters of introduction to Colonel Lenartzen, the director of the mint. A cordial reception extended to me by this gentleman induced me to remain for several days, in order to make some interesting excursions in the neighborhood. The first day was passed in visiting the mint, where only copper is coined, and afterward in the stone-cutting establishments belonging to Government and to private individuals. In the imperial establishment are made the greater part of those vases, tables, and columns of malachite, jasper, aventurine quartz, and porphyry, which adorn the palaces of Europe. In the private workshops smaller objects of ornament are made from the many beautiful minerals of Asia; the chief of these are malachite, rhodonite, lapis-lazuli, aqua-marine, topaz, and quartz in all its forms, of agate, chalcedony, jasper, bloodstone, amethyst, and clear and smoky rock crystal.

On the second day, in company with Colonel Lenartzen, I drove out to the nearest gold-washings, about nine wersts from Ekaterinburg. The country is so slightly undulating as to be almost a plain. The placers are in the small swampy depressions occupied by rivulets. Here, under a covering of about ten feet of sand capped with peat, there lies a bed about two feet thick of auriferous sand, which is very clayey, and contains large quantities of fragments of chloritic and greenstone schists, quartz, diorite, etc. This material, after being thawed (in winter), is thrown upon a large circular iron plate, called chashha, perforated with holes one-half inch in diameter, where, in order to clear the gravel and fragments from the auriferous clay and sand, it is submitted to the attrition of heavy iron rakes, moved by a vertical shaft, which rises through the centre of the perforated table. On this table, which had rather more than ten feet diameter, about two thousand puds are worked in ten hours.

This preparatory process, which has for its object merely the separation of coarse gravel and rubble from the pay-dirt, is performed, where this is comparatively free from clay, in revolving perforated cylinders or botchka. From both machines the sand, with its gold, after passing through the holes, is brought upon a kind of graduated inclined plane, something like a German liegeder-herd, consisting of a series of short inclined terraces of boards, upon which the finer gravel and sand, after falling from the previous machine, is manipulated with scrapers for the purpose of concentrating the gold. The success of this second process depends entirely upon the skill of the workmen, whose duty it is to keep the mass from accumulating, and the clay from settling into a stiff bed, over which the gold would escape; for this purpose he uses a broad wooden hoe and a spade. The greater part of the gold remains on the upper terrace. The sediment remaining upon the different terraces is removed three times a day to a small liegeder-herd (the same that is used for trials), and is here washed to its final separation. The yield for the day was about one solothnik of gold per 100 puds of the pay-dirt.

At the placers of Biriasowsk, near Ekaterinburg, the average yield is 23 dolias per 100 puds, an amount which pays when the auriferous deposit is not more than three feet and a half below the surface.

A chashha twelve feet in diameter is said to be capable of working about 7,000 puds in eleven hours. In the Ural they are preferred to the revolving cylinders, because they require much less power to turn them. The latter machine is used chiefly in eastern Siberia, where its capacity is estimated at 20,000 puds of sandy earth daily. The tailings are not allowed to contain more than 12 dolias to the 100 puds.

I have inserted in the Appendix a table showing the statistics of production in the private gold washings during twenty years in Trans-Baikalia. From these returns it will appear that the total product of the district from 1843 to 1863 was about 905 puds of gold dust, which (considering that experience has shown this to have a fineness of .885, and that the value of pure gold is reckoned at 13,500 roubles per pud) would give 10,812,-487 roubles. On this amount the royalty exacted by Government was 1,213,444 roubles, besides a further tax of 233,052 roubles. The average yield for the whole period was 85 dolias per 100 puds, or .00002577. In all there were employed 33,347 men, which, if the returns are correct, would give only 324 roubles per man. The probability is that the amount returned is considerably below the product. The very large royalty exacted by Government upon the gross product is a serious obstacle to the development of the Siberian gold fields, as it renders it impossible to work deposits which will not pay at least 20 per cent. more than the cost of production, in order to cover Government demands and interest on capital. And the number of placers which would pay without these taxes must be many times greater than of those which can bear them.

Certainly immense areas of auriferous sand, which would otherwise be workable with a large profit, are practically shut out from development, keeping withdrawn from circulation large amounts of gold which can be illy spared in the present condition of Russian finances.

During the year 1864 Colonel Buthets produced at his placer, east of Kiachta, seven puds of gold, worth 84,000 roubles, at a cost of 51,000 roubles, leaving a net gain of 31,000 roubles. On this the Government royalty and tax amounted to 9,000 roubles, being nearly eleven per cent. upon the gross product, and nearly thirty upon the net.

On the third day of my stay at Ekaterinburg I started on an excursion to the iron and copper works of Nijni Tagilsk, north of Ekaterinburg, on the eastern flank of the Ural mountains. Here are the extensive mines and smelting works belonging to the Demidoff family. The iron ore is obtained from an immense mass of magnetite, surrounded by greenstone. Containing very generally a small amount of iron pyrites, it has in places copper ores, principally malachite and red oxide, to an extent which renders them useful only as a flux for the siliceous copper ores. The average yield of this ore is about 53 per cent. of iron.

The copper mine is near the iron mountain, and being in limestone, near the contact between this and the greenstone is perhaps a contact deposit. The outcrop contains much magnetic iron associated with the different copper ores, which is a very general phenomenon in copper deposits at the contact between limestone and hornblendic rocks. The ores are here mostly oxidized, though containing some sulphurets, and occur in a siliceous gangue. The average yield is 2.72 per cent. of copper. This mine has furnished the greater part of the malachite for which the Ural mountains have long been famous.

Through the courtesy of Mr. Nietki I was shown through the works, and had an opportunity of seeing the process of manufacture of the celebrated Russian sheet-iron, which has, I believe, never been described.

The magnetic ore is roasted at the mine, in heaps of 10,000 or 15,000 tons, to remove the little sulphur it contains. It is then smelted in charcoal blast furnaces. After being puddled, the iron is rolled into plates about 2½ feet long, 5 inches wide, and ½ inch thick. These, after being heated in a furnace with a very reducing flame, are quickly brushed, to remove any foreign substance that may have fallen upon them, and are then passed between rolls, the upper one of which is unconnected with the lower, rolling only by friction. By the time the sheet is cooled it is about fifteen inches wide. Packages of three sheets are now laid in the furnace, and then rolled again, after the upper sheet has been brushed, and charcoal powder thrown between them to prevent adhesion. If thin iron is desired, the sheets are subjected to a third heating, in packages of four or six, and re-rolled, after which they are trimmed to the proper dimensions. They are now sent to the forge, where they are heated and hammered three times, in packages of from sixty to eighty. After the first hammering each sheet is swabbed with a wet mop to harden the surface; it is said that tar is sometimes used for this purpose.

Two packages, one hot and one cold, are now mixed in alternate sheets, to produce the greenish color in cooling, and the mixed package is then passed backward and forward under a large hammer, and after this is again mixed and re-hammered.

The superiority of the Russian product is due in great part to the cleanliness of the work, and to the carefulness and skill of the workmen. Every sheet that is at all spotted is thrown into the second or third class, and the difference in value between these and the first quality is deducted from the pay of the workmen. The clippings of the sheets are worked up into fine iron, and loss of material by the whole process is reduced to from 12 to 15 per cent.

The fire-proof bricks used in heating-furnaces are made from a fine quartz sand, which is merely sprinkled with lime-water before being moulded and burned, a method of making fire-bricks which might be very useful in many cases to our own metalurgists.

Formerly the large population employed at the Demidoff and adjoining works was in a condition of serfdom. Only a short time had passed since they had been emancipated, and yet the superintendent informed me that the labor had already improved at least 30 per cent.

Formerly the proprietors were obliged by law to maintain the old and infirm, indeed to support all the unproductive part of the population; but now, this duty having devolved upon the freedmen, it forms an incentive to habits of sobriety and economy.

On leaving Ekaterinburg I took in as fellow-passenger a Russian, who was going to Nijni Novgorod. Almost imperceptibly we reached the summit of the Ural mountains, a fact which I should not have known had not my companion called attention to a small monument which marked the boundary between Asia and Europe. The descent on the western side of the range is much more perceptible than that toward Asia, and presents a great number of fine views over the valleys of the small streams which flow toward the Volga.

My companion was a true Russian. Every time that we passed a church or a cross, even though in the midst of conversation, he would suddenly stop and repeat a short prayer, while he crossed himself three times. The fear of missing an opportunity to perform this ceremony kept him constantly employed in spying out the church towers and steeples of towns we were passing through, or of villages lying off the road.

Every time we met a group of exiles he would stop the driver, and, after distributing here and there a few kopeks, he repeated the same ceremony. I did not learn whether this was his habit through life; if it was, he must often have been like the English statesman, who, falling into the habit of touching every post he passed, often imagined that he had missed one, and was then sure to be an unhappy man till he had returned and touched it.

During the whole journey from Irkutsk I had passed at intervals groups of exiles, but near the boundary of Siberia they were both more frequent and numerous. Made up of representatives of every class of society, from prince to peasant, these unhappy people dragged slowly forward on the long journey to the land of their imprisonment. A number of them were gathered around the monument which marks the line between Asia and Europe.

The joy which I felt on seeing this sign of a rapid approach to familiar places, and home, was almost taken away by the thought of the widely-different feelings with which these exiles must regard what was to them an emblem of separation from the world and all that is dear. I afterward learned that an intimate friend, one of my fellow-students, having been implicated in the Polish rebellion, had been exiled to Siberia, and there is every probability that we passed each other on the road.

We were now traversing a country in which the population grew denser, and the cities and towns more frequent, with every day's journey westward till we reached Kazan, in the valley of the Volga. I would willingly have stayed some time in this ancient capital of the Mongol empire in the west; its inhabitants are for the most part descendants of the Mohammedan subjects of the Khans, who still adhere strictly to their ancient faith, and rank as the best elements of the population.

A journey of less than two days from Kazan brought me to Nijni Novgorod, the eastern terminus of the Russian railroads.

Exclusive of stoppages at Ekaterinburg and Tiumen, I had made the journey from Irkutsk to this point in twenty-two days and a half; or, excluding the delays in changing horses and eating, I had travelled 3,112 miles in 352 hours, being an average rate of 8.8 miles per hour. The same journey is often made by officers travelling as couriers in fifteen days.

I had just time to make arrangements to take the train, and in half an hour after my arrival I was being whirled rapidly toward

Moscow. Thence I went by railroad to St. Petersburg and Paris, and through England, and by steamer to New York; thus finishing an eventful journey of five years' duration, around the world in the northern temperate zone. In this journey nearly 17,000 miles of my wanderings were by land, 6,000 of these being accomplished on horseback.

Although the journey described in the foregoing narrative was confined to the northern temperate zone, during it very nearly the greatest possible extremes of climate were met with. On the deserts of the Gulf of California the thermometer ranged for weeks as high as 120 and 126 degrees (F.) in the shade, and nearly 160 degrees in the sun; while in Siberia it fell to 70 degrees below zero—extremes differing by 230 degrees. The maximum occurred in America in Lat. 32 degrees N., and the minimum in Asia 53 degrees N., or at points differing only 21 degrees of latitude.

In this narrative of a comprehensive journey I have endeavored to convey to the reader a general idea of the leading characteristics of countries and peoples which are but little known to us, but with whom the march of events shows we are rapidly coming into a more and more intimate contact.

If we look at a map of the world with reference to the inevitable future of the northern temperate zone, we shall find its greatest cultivable areas divided between two great sections of mankind, the Anglo-Saxon and the Sclavonic. And these also are the areas which admit of a sure increase of population to a point compared with which the present numbers are almost as nothing.

An eminent English geographer has calculated that, considering the rate of increase in the United States, the area of cultivable land in the two Americas, and the capacity of that area for supporting life, it is possible that within a little more than three centuries the population of North and South America will be between two and three thousand millions.

And in view of the relative rates of increase and absorption now ruling among the different races on these continents, it is probable that at some future period its population will be in so far homogeneous that it will speak one language, and have one form of government.

A similar calculation applied to the eastern continent would point to a not less wonderful expansion of the Sclavonic race, from the Baltic sea to the Pacific ocean. Leaving out of consideration all the rest of its territory, European Russia possesses, south of the latitude of Moscow, a region of the most fertile agricultural land, whose extent and productiveness are so great that it is not too much to say that it is capable of supporting a population four times as large as that of China. Until recently the tendency of the political and social organization of Russia has been to prevent a rapid increase of population; but the recent political reform, and the growing network of railroad and steamboat communication, are infusing a new life in the empire, and there is no reason to doubt that facilities for expansion will be followed there, as elsewhere, by a growth in the ratio of increase of population. It will be strange if, within the next ten or twenty years, Russia, which is by nature the granary of Europe, does not come into a competition with our western States, which, perhaps, not even the utmost exertion on our part will enable us to hold out against.

When we consider the immense extent of this empire, and its capacity for population, wealth, and power, and then compare with it the small extent of western Europe, split up into small nationalities, with an overflowing population dependent on the east and west for its supply of food, the belief of the Pan-slavist seems almost prophetic; Russia, more than America, "hangs like a thunder cloud" over its western neighbors.

The expansion from the west and from the east to the opposite shores of the Pacific of two races and a civilization hitherto intimately connected with the Atlantic coasts, is already marking out for the Great ocean a most important part in the early future. Into this future history another element seems destined to enter; I mean the part that will be taken by the Chinese and Japanese peoples.

The immense resources of China in coal and iron and other minerals, in labor and the means of supporting life, and in the conformation of its surface, are elements which in the present and coming age cannot be idle. The utilizing of these resources cannot fail to be followed by the same results there as elsewhere, raising the nation by which they are developed to a position of authority in the world's affairs. There seems to me to be little doubt that this result will be accomplished by the Chinese people. In every direction we see in this race evidences of that vitality which has made of them a great nation, and which has kept them erect through all the vicissitudes of the rest of the world through long ages, which have witnessed the destruction and scattering of races and the rise and fall of great empires. This vitality is becoming apparant in a new and equally important direction: the Chinese are showing themselves to be essentially fitted to be colonizers, and as such they seem already to be resolving a great geographical problem. They are showing themselves capable of peopling and making useful to the world the vast extent of the peninsular and island territory of Further India and Australasia. Here they exhibit the same energy as at home, and that too in climates where neither the native Malay inhabitants will, nor the European laborer can, endure fatigue. Throughout these regions, wherever they obtain a foothold, they absorb both the trade and the industry which supports it.

In a large English machine-shop at Singapore, the owners have substituted entirely Chinese for English workmen, finding the former more sober and enduring, and after instruction even better mechanics. In this same English colony, Chinese capitalists are said to have driven their European rivals almost or quite out of the field. In the Sandwich Islands, of six sugar plantations expected to produce, in 1865, 20,000 tons of sugar, two were owned by Chinese capitalists and worked by Chinese labor. In our own western territories, where they are treated worse than dogs, this race is obtaining a foothold, and is destined to assume a political importance pregnant with great good or great evil. The introduction of this labor upon the Pacific railroad is certain to give the Chinaman the same incentive to emigrate from his over-crowded country as that which impels the Irishman across the Atlantic.

Excepting our ignorance as to the results of amalgamation between the European and the Mongolian races, and the danger of the formation of caste if such a mixture does not take place, I see no reason why such an immigration should be followed by other than the most desirable consequences. There are many parts of Central and South America better adapted to a Chinese population than to any other. And the same remark might apply to the far north, for they show the same energy in the extreme cold on the Siberian frontier. The day of the first meeting of a through train on the Pacific railroad with the Chinese-American steamers was the beginning of a new era in the history of the Pacific world. This line across the continent and across the ocean is surely but the beginning of a great network, which on the new maps of every decade will measure the growing enterprise of our own continent, of the Pacific, and of eastern and northern Asia.

Thus there is being completed a grand cycle in the history of civilization. The compass, printing, gunpowder, the use of coal, and a vague knowledge of some subtle fluid in the air and earth—all these had their origin among a people on the western shores of the Pacific. Long applied in the land of their birth, in their simplest forms, to their simplest uses, these instruments of civilization have travelled westward around the globe during 600 years, becoming perfected, and building up sciences and arts which give command over time and space, over force and matter, until now the only step that remains to complete the circle and the cycle is their engraftment on the stock from which they sprung.

APPENDICES.

APPENDIX I.

EXTRACT FROM REPORT OF CONSUL HARVEY, OF NINGPO, TO SIR F. BRUCE, ON THE REBELLION. 1862.

THREE months have elapsed since Ningpo fell into the hands of the insurgents; and from the hour of its capture to the moment when I am penning these lines, not one single step in the direction of a "good government" has been taken by the Taipings—not any attempt made to organize a political body or commercial institutions—not a vestige, not a trace of anything approaching to order, or regularity of action, or consistency of purpose, can be found in any one of their public acts; the words "governmental machinery," as applied to Taiping, have no possible meaning here; and, in short, desolation is the only end obtained—as it has always been wherever the sway of the marauders has had its full scope, and their power the liberty of unchecked excesses. I feel that this is but a melancholy result to have to report; and this sad account may, probably, not prove satisfactory to, or be concurred in, by those whose minds have been deceived, and their ardent imaginations carried away by exaggerated expectations, such as "regeneration of the. Empire," "redemption of China," "introduction of Christianity," and "salvation of the people." But to those who, like myself, were not influenced by these imaginary hopes, and who judged of Taipingdom in sober sense and dispassionately, the last three months' probation is by no means startling, the experiment having produced exactly what was expected—ruin, desolation, and the annihilation of every vital principle in all that surrounds the presence, or lies under the ban, of the Taipings.

It is palpable that a party which, after ten years' full trial, is found to produce nothing, and to destroy everything, cannot pretend to last, or be admitted, even indirectly, into the comity of nations; and that, on the contrary, it deserves to bring upon itself the well-merited opprobrium of all the enlightened classes of society.

These may appear strong expressions, but it seems to me that the time has at length arrived when, to speak of the Taipings, and to judge of their acts, the utmost freedom of opinion and of expression should be excused by public functionaries in China; on that account, therefore, I consider I am only fulfilling a duty in passing my judgment, such as it is, and whatever may be its worth, upon this extraordinary movement. I repeat, I have no bias one way or the other; and, indeed, I should state that personally I have received every mark of courtesy and proper regard from the Taiping chiefs; and, further, I have found in official dealings with them a rough and blunt sort of honesty quite unexpected and surprising, after years of public intercourse with the imperial mandarins. Nevertheless, the Taipings, with their frank demeanor and bluff energy, have a fume of blood and a look of carnage about them, from which I, for one, recoil with horror.

With these prefatory remarks I shall now reply, as well as I am able, to the several points mooted in your Excellency's dispatch, and respecting which your Excellency is desirous of having my opinion. In doing so, I would respectfully remind your Excellency that the information required has been obtained with difficulty from the naturally suspicious Taipings, who, amongst their peculiarities, possess a power of concealment and general secresy quite wonderful to meet in China. I think, however, I may well rely on the correctness of the following statement.

The first point has reference to the payment of the Taiping troops. The insurgent soldiery do not, as an established rule, receive pay; they live like pirates on whatever they can obtain in the shape of booty, either in kind or specie. If the capture of a city has produced a rich harvest of plunder, the men benefit generally in the prize; if, on the contrary, the town has yielded little profit, the Taipings wait for better days with exemplary patience. The neighboring districts are then (and indeed in almost all instances) made to contribute to the support of the army. The country about Ningpo, for example, was compelled to remit its quota of tribute in the shape of rice, pigs, fowls, vegetables, and the like farm produce, to feed the troops. The peasants, forced to send in these supplies, were seen by me bringing provisions, etc., into the city with chains and ropes round their necks in token of servitude. That the Taiping soldiers live upon what they can get may be inferred clearly from the invariable answer made to me a dozen times, and which, I remember, was likewise given to Mr. Consul Parks in my presence. On questioning decently-dressed Taiping soldiers as to how they liked their profession, the reply has ever been the following: "Why should I not like it? I help myself to everything I choose to lay hands upon; and if interfered with I just cut the man's head off who so interferes"—at the same time making a motion with his hand as if he were sawing off a head. This being an answer often heard, and the motion being a notorious one with the chiefs in the city, I submit both as apt illustrations of Taiping institutions, and of their reckless contempt for human life.

The Taipings possess a regular embodied force, a draft from which forms the nucleus of the body of men sent upon any special service or expedition, such nucleus being composed of old and well-tried rebels of several years' standing; and the remainder of the armed force, in each case, being younger recruits, or peasants pressed into the service. The corps which attacked and captured Ningpo might have had one old rebel in ten in its formation, the veterans serving principally to keep in a proper state of submission the younger volunteers or pressed men, as well as to inspire courage to those who might recoil from their duty, such inspiration being particularly Taiping in its nature. Another peculiarity of the rebels is their habit of drafting from one province to another the inhabitants of conquered districts—the policy of which course being self-evident, I need not enlarge upon it. I should imagine that at the present hour, in the city of Ningpo, more than twenty different dialects are spoken among the rebels—dialects pertaining to distant provinces and districts—in the same manner that, I suppose, the Ningpo dialect is now becoming familiar, hundreds of miles from the port, to ears that were never intended or expected to receive it. What prosperity can the most sanguine expect under such rule, when the men of the soil are driven into exile and misery, leaving behind them their houses in ruins, and their wretched families to die of starvation?

It is notorious that their forces are swelled considerably by all the bad characters of the districts they pass through, and who, being under no possible moral control (except so far as military obedience and a pseudo discipline are concerned), commit every excess known, and, let me add, almost unknown to the human mind. These are delicate matters to allude to in a public dispatch, but my meaning will be sufficiently clear, when I state that the conduct of some of these monsters to women and young girls is such that no pen, however guarded, could convey an idea. In regard, therefore, to your Excellency's query as to their behavior to the young women who fall into their hands, I have too good cause to know that it is horrible beyond belief or description. Your Excellency is doubtless aware that marriage is strictly forbidden amongst the Taipings, and forms, with opium-smoking, a capital offence; and if the latter habit or vice is often winked at, it would be next to impossible for an ordinary rebel to live with a wife or a concubine. The standing orders are, that marriage will only be allowed when the empire has been conquered; until which time the penalty for marrying or cohabiting with a woman is death. As a compensation, however, and, I presume, as a reward for valor, it appears that in captured towns and cities, where the population have not had time to resort to flight, three whole days are given to the Taiping soldiers to do whatever they please—to commit any excess, and to perpetrate every abomination under the sun; after which, not a single woman is permitted to remain in the city. I think these statements will suffice, and I need proceed no further upon this distressing topic.

Their great aim—I should say their chief condition of success—is to strike terror: first by numbers, and secondly by the tawdry harlequin garb worn by them, and which (however incredible it may seem) has such a strange effect on the minds of all classes of people in this country. Your Excellency will perceive in this unaccountable effect another instance of the perversion of thought, and of the opposite mode of analyzing and accounting for causes and effects ruling with the Chinese race in contradistinction to Europeans. With us the burlesque costume, and other ridiculous devices of the Taipings, would only tend to raise a smile; but I firmly believe that this dress, *per se*, has an effect the very reverse on the ignorant and somewhat primitive inhabitants of this country, and is half the battle with the rebels, as they well know. Their long, shaggy, black hair again adds to the wildness of their look; and when this fantastical appearance is accompanied by a certain show of fury and madness, it is really little to be wondered at, if the mild Chinese, constituted as we know them to be, either take to flight or submit tamely.

Able-bodied men, as stated above, are compelled to serve in their ranks, whatever may have been their previous calling in life; for after the loss of their property some of them have no option left but to fight or to starve. Sometimes, also, respectable denizens are under the absolute necessity of joining the Taiping flag, solely because they find that in conquered districts such a compromise is unavoidable, in order to save remnants of property, and very frequently to place their necks out of jeopardy. It is simply, in all instances, a forced subjection. I do not myself believe that the insurgents have had the voluntary allegiance of half-a-dozen respectable Chinese since they first appeared at Nanking in 1853. I will even go further, and express my conviction that not one single respectable Chinaman has ever gone over to the Taipings of his own free will and accord. How could this be possible? The respectable Chinese are an orderly, shrewd race of men, and they must feel, and are convinced, that property, confidence, and a good name can never follow in the footsteps of brigandage, however extensive the scale upon which it may be carried on.

The military tactics of the Taipings are of the simplest, and the most primitive in their action; indeed, I doubt whether the word "tactics" can in any way be applied to their uniform mode of warfare. Numbers, as I have already remarked, is the first consideration with them; and these they pour into any given place, or upon any spot selected as a prize. Before the main bodies appear, however, spies and emissaries are sent secretly to feel the way, and to spread false reports; and in the midst of the panic and alarm caused by these reports and intrigues, the spies set fire, if they are able, to detached buildings, and often to entire streets, in and out of the city. Should these emissaries be seized and beheaded by the mandarins, others are deputed by the rebels to take their place without delay, when similar manœuvres are again commenced, until either the mandarins or the city population take to flight, or, as in the case of Ningpo, such thorough demoralization is created that the place falls an easy prey to the insurgents. Meanwhile, run-away villagers have not failed to rush in, breathless, with exaggerated reports of the numbers and doings of the Taiping forces seen by them. In the confusion, a few rebels appear in the distance, their gaudy multi-colored dress having its usual strange effect, and their melancholy shouts and yells striking terror in the hearts of the timid Chinese. If, then, the game has been so far successfully played out, and the coast appears pretty clear, very little remains to be done; hundreds and thousands of insurgents rush wildly on to the goal, armed with knives, spears, and fowling-pieces, carrying, of course, everything before them. It is then, and then only, that the chiefs, or leaders, or princes, appear for the first time; for these are seldom or never heard of, nor is their immediate action seen, until the highroad has been opened by the skirmishers—called in Shanghae marauders. The late events at that port show, I think, the correctness of the above account. In the repeated attacks upon Shanghae, the supposed marauders were, in accordance with the universal usage of the Taipings, thrown in detachments in advance, burning villages, and creating panic, the chiefs, of course, remaining behind, watching the result of the game, which then, I am happy to say, turned out, as we know, to have been a losing one, thanks to Sir James Hope and our volunteers. I think the Shanghae lesson will have a salutary effect on the Taipings, for they are in painful dread of hard blows, notwithstanding their spiritual origin and pretensions.

APPENDIX II.

RELIGIOUS BEARING OF THE REBELLION. BY REV. W. MUIRHEAD.

HAVING lately resided at Nanking for a month, in the prosecution of my missionary work, and mingled with all classes of the insurgents, the following is a record of my impressions as to the religious bearing of the movement. The whole cast of it is determined by the character and influence of the Chief, who is, therefore, the first object of attention.

The Chief.—His usual name is the Heavenly Prince. He is about fifty years of age, and resides in a palace within the city, which is commonly designated the Heavenly Court. He is never seen beyond its walls. The palace has been built during the last three years, and is still far from being finished. It is divided into two main courts; in the outer of which there are a large number of male attendants, none of whom, however, are admitted inside. Within this latter circle only females are allowed, who perform every kind of manual labor. The Prince is said to have about thirty wives, and at least double that number of concubines, to whom accessions are made from year to year. Over the whole his aged mother presides, while his son, who is now thirteen years of age, has been taken, as a matter of policy, into equal sovereignty with himself. Previous to the Prince's arrival at Nanking, he was on free and intimate terms with many of his immediate adherents; but since that time he has assumed imperial dignity with a high hand, and treats even the next to him in authority in a formal and distant manner. Notwithstanding his seclusion, he is the head and soul of the movement. All fear him, and feel that he is indispensable to its continuance and success. Though much is left to the conduct of his subordinates, the whole takes its inspiration and direction from him. He holds levees of the kings and chief men at stated times; but it is only Kan-Wang, his cousin and Prime Minister, who can go freely into his presence. Of the business done at the public levees, religious worship is a large element, which consists in kneeling and chanting several doxologies to God, combined with the Imperial anthem to himself and his son, who is always seated at his side. The former were composed by different foreign missionaries, with a few alterations; and the latter is an ascription of long life, equivalent to the phrase "May the Heavenly Prince live for ever!" At times also the Prince delivers to them a set discourse of a purely religious nature, exhorting them to piety toward God, faith in Christ, union with each other, and diligence in propagating the gospel. The different kings are at liberty to speak to him on these occasions only through his Prime Minister, and the conversation is generally carried on in his native dialect, which obtains in a small district of Canton. The profession and apparent belief of the Prince is that he is the veritable second son of God, in common with Christ, and in contra-distinction to other men. Christ, in his estimation, is not possessed of Divine nature, but was commissioned, like himself, to accomplish a certain object; and looking at Christ only in this point of view, he claims fraternal personal relationship to him. There is, according to his creed, a true Heavenly Father and Mother, a veritable Heavenly Brother (Christ) and Sister, with all of whom he individually sustains a peculiar family connection, and into that circle his own son has been received in the same absolute and entire sense. This, with many other things, he says he has ascertained by special Divine revelation, with which at various times he has been largely favored. That it is really so is maintained by many zealous adherents, while it is questioned and denied by others, though not in an open and public manner. The Prince announces that he has been appointed to institute a new Heavenly Kingdom, in which idolatry and the Manchus are alike to be destroyed, and the worship of the Heavenly Father and Christ to be observed. His position and that of his son in the matter is, that having an immediate divine commission entrusted to them, they are to be honored and obeyed accordingly. In the proclamations that are used, the authority of the Heavenly Father and Heavenly Brother is always prominently introduced, as forming the rule of action in whatever relates to the order of the court, or to the operations that are being carried on. Sometimes Scripture is referred to in these by direct quotation, and it is held to be no violation of its teachings, when the visions of dreams said to have been accorded to the Chief, his son, and several of his former kings, are brought forward as of equal importance in any matter.

With regard to his personal appearance, he is described as being of a large stature, with a flowing black beard, and having bright, intelligent, and prepossessing features. However absurd many of his doings and sayings seem to be, so as even to suggest the idea of his partial insanity, he impresses those acquainted with him with a sense of surpassing ability, penetrating in his ideas of men and things, and mentally as well as physically persuading every one of his right and title to the place he occupies. His professed, and without doubt, real object, is to introduce a state of things very different from what has hitherto obtained in China. Being thoroughly opposed to all idolatrous systems and practices, he suppresses the whole wheresoever his influence extends. Buddhism and Taouism obtain no place in his creed or in his favor. Confucianism, as now taught, is discouraged and held in abeyance. He has undertaken, personally, to revise the Confucian classics, and to erase alike from the text and commentary whatever is opposed to his views.

Other supervisions of long established customs are in progress, but they want a sufficient field to carry them out, and time to attend to them, from the pressure of public business.

As to the kind of Christianity he proposes to introduce, and his manner of doing it, the Bible will form the basis of instruction; his own religious literature, at present comprising thirty or forty volumes, being also taught as the necessary exponent and complement of the sacred volume. Literary examinations are held during the year at Nanking, attended by about two hundred students. These are trained in the above volumes, and write essays on themes connected with or taken from Scripture. According to their apparent proficiency in Bible knowledge is their position, both in a civil and military point of view, determined.

The essays that have been published betray the erratic influence of the Prince's dreams and visions far more than the result of Bible study. Though they contain much that is good and true, a large part is, like the volumes in question, a tissue of falsehood, designed to promote the Chief's own selfish object, and deserving the severest reprobation.

I asked the Prime Minister, on seeing these things, if he believed them. He replied that he did not; but though the book was issued under his name, he was obliged to let it pass, as it was the determination of the Prince to do so. These things, indeed, are only the transcript of the Prince's sentiments bearing upon his Heavenly pretensions and the elevation of the eastern king to heaven, who was murdered by his orders in cold blood. Those who write such essays have told me that they are no expression of their own private belief, but they are the mere echo of what they have read in the authorized ritual of the dynasty. The successful essayists thus elevated to office are to be called upon to instruct those around them, and so, from the highest to the lowest, an influence is to go forth for the enlightenment or renovation of the mass.

Foreign missionaries are not wanted to do the work of evangelists or pastors: first, because the Chinese are too proud to be taught by foreigners, and it is supposed they are self-sufficient to do it; again, because missionaries are too divided in their opinions and conduct in relation to each other, and also their presence would interfere with the Prince's way of christianizing his people, which, the Premier assured me, was a primary idea with him. As to the desolation and destruction attendant upon the movement, it is alleged that they are by no means an essential element of it; only positive orders are given out as received by the Heavenly Prince to exterminate the powers that be, and therefore all who submit to these and oppose him come in for their share of the punishment. At the same time they aver that much of the evil that takes place is not committed by them, but by local bands ever ready for mischief.

The Kings.—There are ten of these at present, and the number may be increased at pleasure. They are all Canton or Kwang-si men, and consist of those who have long been connected with the movement, who have become distinguished in the course of it, and who may be relied on for the future. They are described as "brethren of the same womb" in relation to each other, in contra-distinction to their chiefs, who are thus one with Christ, and to the people at large, who are so among themselves. Their appointment comes from the Prince, and their principal work is the active conduct of the war. They have each a large number of officers and men under them, whom they augment by impressing country people when out in the field. They proceed on service by direction of the Prince, with whom, through the Prime Minister, they maintain constant correspondence, and contribute to his support from the spoil they have taken in fight. They are just so many generals under him as the head, and their duties and responsibilities are of a corresponding kind. They have not distinct provinces assigned to them to subdue and govern, but, while aggrandizing themselves, are severally and unitedly promoting the imperial interests of their Heavenly Prince. Whether at home or in the field, the religious department is alike attended to by these kings; they each take their part in observing the prescribed ritual with the humblest around them; it consists in "saying grace" at meals, and in chanting the doxologies on Friday night, which forms the commencement of their Sabbath—not that these are scrupulously performed, though enjoined in the regulations of the service; but the matter is attended to so often as to be a well-known thing, through their means, equally at home and in the camp. On conversing with several of the kings on the point, they are always forward in identifying themselves with us. They claim to be Christians in common with ourselves, and when any difference is alluded to in our opinions and practices they generally excuse it by saying that we have been longer acquainted with the subject, or that their customs are required by the nature of the case, at least by the orders of their chiefs. As to the influence of religion on their hearts and lives, that can hardly be expected in the manner we contemplate it. Their previous training, the imperial regime under which they are placed, and their absorbing attention to public affairs, preclude all idea of any genuine Christian experience on their part. At the same time, they may be regarded as being as much under the power of religion, in the form it has assumed among them, as the Chinese generally are under the power of any religion whatever. Their pressing thought—and they say they have no time to think of other things—is the promotion of their political interests. They are for the most part indifferent scholars, and, besides, lack opportunity for learning what practical Christianity is.

In a political point of view, these kings occupy, in relation to the people, a place similar to the high mandarins of the present Government; and there is, undoubtedly, more truth, more life, more reality in the religious faith of the former than in that of the latter.

The Officers and People.—The former are very numerous, and rank in order after a well-established and organized system. Public offices, large and small, exist in connection with every royal palace; and according to the dignity of those who preside over them, have they subordinates and servants in turn. In these offices it is required that the usual religious ceremonies be attended to for the instruction of all parties. Every Friday flags are hung out at different places, intimating that to-morrow is Sunday, and ought to be solemnly kept. It is by no means to be disregarded. About midnight guns are fired to apprise the attendants at each office that the Sabbath is approaching, and calling them to worship. This is done by all in connection with such establishments kneeling in a public hall, and chanting the doxologies; while small squibs are fired off, gongs beaten, candles lighted, and a written prayer is burned on the occasion, expressive of gratitude and praise to God. The whole takes up very little time, and much resembles the ceremonies in use among their heathen countrymen. On asking the Prime Minister as to the reason of all this, he said that such was the idea of the Heavenly Prince, and that rites of this kind were considered necessary to supply the vacancy caused by the overthrow of idolatry. Without any of these things, the people, it is remarked by him, would not know how or what to worship. One consequence of the system of instruction and worship thus pursued is, that there is a widespread knowledge of the fundamental truths of religion, such as the name of God, his overruling providence, the necessity of all men honoring him alone, and obeying his commandments; together with the name of Christ, his relation to the Father, his incarnation and atoning death, resurrection, and ascension; the happiness of heaven, and the miseries of hell, etc.

During my residence at Nanking, and on my way up, I largely engaged in public preaching, and privately talked with numbers on these subjects, and found them more or less familiar themes, in perfect contrast to my previous experience among the heathen Chinese. My chief object was to enforce the legitimate influence of what they already knew, just as has to be done in our native land.

While surrounded by numbers of people listening to what I had to say, I have frequently witnessed officers on horseback passing by, who at first looked rather suspiciously at the unusual spectacle, but having stopped and heard for a time they soon appeared pleased, and said it was the true doctrine that I was preaching. I mention this not to imply any heartfelt appreciation of the truth in their case, but to show they professed a nominal acquaintance with it as a distinctive element of their system. So in regard to their adherents at large: their knowledge of Christianity, and their habit of repeating a few doxologies were only a necessary effect of the circumstances in which they are placed, and it could not be expected to be otherwise. Many of their older adherents, however, appear sincerely to believe in the Chief and his religious system.

With respect to the origin and character of these men and officers, by far the greatest part of them have been kidnapped. Many have long been in the service, and on being talked to about their friends and relatives, some lamented that they could not return to them; others were indifferent, having been for years accustomed to the present state of things, and seeing no prospect of a change for the better.

The lower the scale that my investigations went, as to the circumstances and condition of the people, I found them groaning in deep misery. They had been dragged from home, and knew nothing of their families, whether dead or alive. They were grievously oppressed, in their view, by hard task-masters, and were compelled to labor with no other payment than their food. Many a curse did they utter in secret against their rulers, but they had no means of escape, no means of redress.

The more active part of the community were generally young men, and of the whole there was a large proportion of boys. These are employed as attendants upon the head men in the various offices, and it is expected that they will grow up under the regime better fitted to carry out its objects than those more advanced in life. This principle has already been in operation for several years, and is yielding good fruits to the dynasty. The moral and religious character of all classes is just such as might have been expected in the circumstances. Marriage is allowed in the case of public officers, who may have one or more wives, according to their rank. Whatever abuses may take place on the part of the common soldiers when a town is sacked, prostitution is severely punished at head-quarters, and it is impossible for it to be practised to a large extent, owing to the smallness of the female population in the rebel cities. It is necessary to observe that at such places there is no population whatever, in the proper sense of the term. All are connected with the different public offices. Their names are duly registered. They are under martial law, and require passports on every occasion. Various things strongly prohibited in the rules, such as tobacco and opium-smoking, wine-drinking, etc., are in general use, though perhaps not so publicly or so extensively as elsewhere. It is said that at present they must be connived at. The ruthless manner in which the temples are destroyed, and the idols desecrated, might suggest the idea of something like a Mahommedan spirit of iconoclasm among the insurgents. In the case of the Chief it is acted out on similar grounds to those alleged by the Islamic imposter, namely, dreams or visions, or Divine revelations; and with their adherents it is much the same—either inspired by blind faith in their respective leaders, or simple obedience to orders, while a love for reckless destruction may be considered as more the actuating motive than aught else. Those things which were once held to be sacred having been dishonored on various occasions without harm, the idea is entertained that it may be done with impunity again; but it is not to be supposed that the destruction is caused by a feeling of hatred and opposition to idolatry, or by any intelligent obedience to a Divine command, on the part of the rebels at large. It is enough that the Heavenly Prince has ordered it; and in connection with him the thing must be done—otherwise the disobedient will suffer. As to the destruction of life and property that takes place when a town or city is seized, it is to be accounted for in this way: the soldiers get no pay, and the spoil which then falls into their hands is deemed a lawful equivalent. It is said to be a Chinese statute, that for three days after the capture of a place the soldiers are at liberty to do what they please. A most unreasonable degree of power is given to officers of almost every grade, so that they can kill and destroy in a summary manner. When resistance is shown on the part of the inhabitants, it is retaliated in this way, too often exemplified; and again, all parties in search of spoil hesitate not to use fire and sword, should they meet with disappointment or refusal.

On speaking to the principal men of the cruelty and folly of these proceedings, they say that they cannot altogether help it. They try to prevent these evils, and not unfrequently punish with death those who commit them; yet were they absolutely to put them down, it might injure their cause with their adherents. Besides, they own that it is the judgment of God upon the people for having sided with their enemies and allowed themselves to be deceived by the devil. As to the consequences of these things in the destruction of trade, and the alienation of the people, the former does not much concern them in the meantime; while in regard to the latter they say that they lament it, but if the people will not submit they must die. Altogether, they think themselves to be so much under the protection and guidance of the Heavenly Father that he is directing and prospering them even in the course of desolation they have pursued for years. In all this the common soldiers have little to say—they are mere instruments in the hands of others; it is the career now before them; it is followed out by their commanders, and must be, at their peril, by them also. They are already inured to it, and their worst passions are gratified by a life of plunder, sensuality, and vice. Though without any understanding of, or sympathy with, spiritual Christianity, they find no difficulty in complying with its outward forms, and professing its inward faith, just as in other lands under more favored circumstances.

General Conclusions.—1. In a secular point of view the movement at present is only destructive. It breaks up all domestic and social ties; it annihilates trade, alike native and foreign; it scatters large and flourishing communities, and blasts the peace and prospects of the empire. Its programme as to the future is grand enough. Were it to be carried out, an era of unparalleled and unthought-of progress would commence in the history of China. Every branch of Western industry and civilization would be encouraged and promoted, the resources of the country largely developed, and the social, intellectual, and moral advancement of the people sought after in an attainable form. All this has been proposed by the Prime Minister, a man of moderate ability, who is undoubtedly sincere in his ideas, and has acquired them during a long residence at Hong Kong, in connection with foreigners. The whole has been approved and ordered to be placed on record by the Heavenly Prince as in contemplation when peace is restored.

Meanwhile there is little prospect of this last being the case. Apart from the question whether the insurgents are likely to succeed in the end, there seems to be a long interval between the present and the final issue on either side. They are, in a Chinese aspect, a very formidable power, which the authorities find it difficult to cope with. The reason of this is evident, but it lies more in the scope of political men to enter into it. Then again, even should the rebels eventually succeed, it may well be doubted if they have the energy, enterprise, and intelligence to carry out their plans. Considering that in the outward progress of civilization in China the above improvements must be made, it will only be necessary to interest the people in them by direct foreign influence. The men and means are to be found in the country in abundance, and these rightly employed would work out great results. For this end we do not consider a change of dynasty at all requisite. It is evident that the one now existing is far superior in its ruling qualities to whatever else we see in the field, the rebel administration being at least no improvement upon it.

2. In a religious point of view, the movement at present is no less destructive. Its first aim is the subversion of the old religions, root and branch. To the extent of its influence, this is the case everywhere. The temples are demolished, the idols dishonored, and the worship of heaven and earth, ancestors and sages, proscribed and abandoned. The systems of Bhud and Tao are declared null and void, and only so much of the Confucian doctrine as is consistent with the rebel creed is to be retained for use. In regard to the future, it is proposed to Christianize the empire by a process truly Chinese, and perhaps effectual in a mere nominal light. The means in operation for the purpose will, we fear, be productive of vast mischief, and only serve to introduce a spurious kind of Christianity. The designs of the Chief, at best, are to make the profession of the Christian religion as general as any of the present forms of religion. Having little idea of a spiritual character and requirements, the change he would inaugurate would be superficial in the extreme, and, as in the political regime, while outwardly there might be a difference in the state of things, there would be little radical alteration. Still, in view of all, we look with anxiety upon the movement, lamenting its errors and abominations, yet disposed to think that Providence has a wise and gracious end to serve by it."

APPENDIX III.

THE FOLLOWING NOTES ON THE AGRICULTURAL PRODUCTIONS OF CHIHLI ARE EXTRACTED FROM THE VALUABLE REPORT OF MR. CONSUL GIBSON TO THE BRITISH GOVERNMENT. BLUE BOOK, CHINA, NO. 4. 1864.

AGRICULTURE.

Nature and Yield of Crops.—The agricultural productions of this province are very inferior, both in quantity and quality, to the produce of the central and southern provinces of the Empire. The following sorts of grain are generally cultivated in the Tien-tsin district, viz., wheat, millet, barley, peas, Indian corn, and rice. The price of rice, most of which is imported from the south, regulates the grain market. Wheat, which regulates the market at home, is here of comparatively little importance.

The table annexed will show the value of the various sorts of grain most common in this district.

TABLE SHOWING THE MARKET PRICES OF THE DIFFERENT KINDS OF GRAIN CULTIVATED IN THE TIEN-TSIN DISTRICT.

DESCRIPTION OF GRAIN.	PRICE IN MEXICAN DOLLARS.
Winter Wheat	3.50 per 133⅓ lbs.
Spring "	3.40 " " "
Buck "	2.25 " " "
Bearded "	1.30 " " "
Barley	1.12 " " "
White Millet	1.50 " " "
Yellow "	1.50 " " "
Red Barbadoes Millet	2.00 " " "
White " "	2.00 " " "
White Millet, (large)	1.75 " " "
Yellow " "	1.75 " " "
Green Peas, (large)	2.40 " " "
Black " "	1.80 " " "
Green " (small)	2.00 " " "
Hempseed	3.50 " " "
Indian Corn	1.50 " " "
Rice	5.50 " " "

Wheat.—Wheat is not extensively grown in this district. The two varieties most common, however, are winter wheat (T. hybernum) and branded wheat (T. turgidum); spring wheat (T. aestivum) is scarce. The soil, in most places, is too light for wheat. An acre of land yields from twenty-five to fifty quarters of wheat, according to quality.

Millet.—Millet is very extensively cultivated in this district. There are numerous varieties; but the Kao-liang or Barbadoes millet is the most common. The light sandy soil seems to agree well with this grain. The yield on an acre of average land is about 1,200 lbs. The poor people live on millet to a very large extent. A highly-intoxicating wine is extracted from fermented millet, and extensively used in this and other districts. The stalks of the Barbadoes millet contain a great deal of woody matter, and are much used for fuel. Fences are often constructed of them.

Barley.—Barley is not uncommon. The yield of barley on an acre of average land is about 1,400 lbs. or 50 quarters.

Peas.—Peas are cultivated largely in this district. An acre of land produces about 1,600 lbs. of peas. A small quantity of peas was exported in 1862, and there is a large local traffic in this produce.

Indian Corn.—Indian corn is extensively grown in this neighborhood. The grain is generally ground into flour, and largely consumed by the poorer classes. An acre of indifferent land will yield about 800 lbs. of Indian corn ; an acre of good land double that quantity.

Rice.—This district is not suitable for rice cultivation; nevertheless, in certain localities rice is grown. It is, however, very inferior, both in size and color to the rice imported from the south. An acre of ground yields about 1,200 lbs. of rice.

Vegetables.—Vegetables are largely cultivated. The "pai-tsai" (called by foreigners the Shan-tung cabbage) excels in flavor, though not in size, any English vegetable of the same class. Its price in the market is about ¾d. per lb. Parsley and turnips are spoiled in the cultivation. The carrots and sweet potatoes are uniformly good. The arrow-root plant (Maranta arundinacea) is cultivated in the southwest part of this province. The arrowroot made from its tubers is palatable, but coarse and dark colored. The potato of Europe is grown successfully in this district; it exhibits no symptoms of disease, and sells at the rate of five shillings per 133⅓ lbs. Many other sorts of vegetables abound, but those enumerated are the most common; all, however, are equally cheap.

Mustard.—Mustard is cultivated largely. Native mustard is very strong and pungent, but very coarse and dark colored.

Rhubarb.—Rhubarb is also grown; it is used medicinally. A small quantity was exported last season.

Castor Oil Plant.—The castor oil plant is also cultivated, but sparingly. The berries are used as medicine.

Fruit.—Fruit of all kinds to be met with in a temperate climate is plentiful and cheap, but is sadly defective in flavor as compared with English fruit. The apples and pears are flavorless. The peaches are bitter, but the natives generally pull them before they are ripe. Walnuts, chestnuts, and dates [jujubes] abound. The grapes are remarkably good. Three varieties are common in the market, viz: 1st, a very small round grape; 2d, a very large grape, rather sweet to the taste; and 3d, a full round grape which tastes a little tart. In autumn all the three sorts are very cheap.

Hay.—Hay can be bought in the market, but it is very inferior stuff. The food of horses consists generally of hard unnutritious chopped straw mixed with millet, Indian corn crushed, or barley.

Horses.—The native horses are small and ugly, but remarkable for their quality of endurance. Their height is about twelve hands, head disproportionately large, ears long, neck short and massive, chest broad and ample, body short, legs strong and sinewy. The native horse requires no attention, or rather receives none. He eats anything, and lives anywhere. A good native horse costs about five pounds at Tien-tsin, but in the so-called desert of Gobi, where he is reared, only about one pound ten shillings.

Black Cattle.—The cattle, in common with the horses, come from the Gobi. There are two breeds: the one large and somewhat coarse, the other small and fine. The large breed resembles much at a little distance the Highland bullock; the small breed are generally spotted red and white, and are not unlike the Ayrshire breed.

The beef exposed for sale in the market is good. Its quality might, however, be improved by better feeding and treatment, but the Chinese understand nothing about the rearing of stock. Beef costs in the market about 2d. per lb.

Sheep.—The sheep also came from the desert of Gobi. The breed sent down from Mongolia is almost always the large long-eared, broad-tailed sort. The Mongolians have another much finer breed, but they do not find their way down to Tien-tsin. The quality of the mutton is good, but equally with the beef might be improved. It costs in the market about 2¼d. per lb.

Pigs.—The breed of pigs in this district is exceedingly inferior. Pork is abundant, but of bad quality. This is entirely owing to the fact that the pigs are not properly fed. There is no attention paid to them whatever. Their food consists of anything they can pick up.

Poultry.—The breed of poultry is good. The fowls are large, abundant, and cheap. Ducks and geese are reared in great numbers, and the market is well supplied with them at a cheap rate. In winter, hares, partridges, pheasants, land grouse, wild duck and teal abound in the market; and in their season, quail, and a most diminutive though highly delicate little bird, called by the natives the "iron bird," from the color of its plumage.

Together, the agricultural productions of this district are numerous and important. The population is large, but the means of living are abundant and cheap, and there is much less destitution in this than in many other far richer districts of the Empire.

APPENDIX IV.

ANALYSES OF CHINESE AND JAPANESE COALS, MADE FOR R. PUMPELLY BY MR. JAMES A. MACDONALD, M.A., OF THE SHEFFIELD LABORATORY, YALE COLLEGE.

In the following analyses, each determination is the mean of two closely agreeing ones. For the water determination, the coal was pulverized and heated in an air-bath at 110 deg. C. until it gave a constant weight. A portion was then ignited in fragments, in a closed crucible, to determine the "volatile matter." The ash was estimated in the usual manner by incineration.

I. Tatsau mine (43 feet seam), near Chaitang. Hard anthracite. Decrepitates very slightly, and yields a little HO in a closed tube. Specific gravity, 1.57.

Carbon	89.81
Volatile matter	3.08
Water	2.67
Ash	4.44
	100.00

II. Futau mine, Chaitang (west of Peking). Bright, bituminous, coking coal, yielding a little HO in the closed tube. Specific gravity, 1.30.

Carbon	85.77
Volatile matter	11.94
Water	0.35
Ash	1.94
	100.00

III. Chingshui (near Chaitang, west of Peking). Soft bituminous coal, coking in a tube, and giving some HO. Specific gravity, 1.37.

Carbon	81.32
Volatile matter	5.62
Water	0.36
Ash	12.70
	100.00

IV. Teyih mine (near Muntakau, west of Peking). Soft, crumbling anthracite. Gives some HO in a closed tube. Specific gravity, 1.74.

Carbon	80.75
Volatile matter	5.43
Water	2.42
Ash	11.40
	100.00

V. Tashitung mine (Fangshan, southwest of Peking). Hard anthracite, coated with some carbonate. Decrepitates, and gives off some HO in a closed tube. Specific gravity, 1.84.

Carbon	86.62
Volatile matter	4.64
Water	2.64
Ash	6.10
	100.00

VI. Kwei (first mine above Kwei, on the upper Yangtz' in Hupeh). Rather a soft coal. When heated in a closed tube gives off HO, and a slightly bituminous odor, without decrepitating. Specific gravity, 1.44.

Carbon	85.63
Volatile matter	4.10
Water	0.38
Ash	9.89
	100.00

VII. Mine of Siangtung (in Hunan). Hard, fine-grained anthracite. Gives off HO, and decrepitates violently in a closed tube. Specific gravity, 1.65.

Carbon	96.21
Volatile matter	0.65
Water	1.45
Ash	1.69
	100.00

VIII. Another coal from Siangtung. Hard anthracite. Gives HO in a closed tube, and decrepitates but slightly. Specific gravity, 1.61.

Carbon	94.59
Volatile matter	1.18
Water	1.65
Ash	2.58
	100.00

IX. Laicha Ho (Southern Hunan). Hard anthracite. Yields HO and considerable sulphur on heating in a closed tube. Specific gravity, 1.47.

Carbon	88.27
Volatile matter	2.92
Water	0.80
Ash	8.01
	100.00

X. Hangchau (Southern Hunan). Rather soft, bituminous coal, coking in a closed tube. Specific gravity, 1.68.

Carbon	71.80
Volatile matter	15.89
Water	0.65
Ash	11.66
	100.00

XI. Mine near Fangshan (southwest of Peking). Hard anthracite. Yields HO, and decrepitates in a closed tube. Specific gravity, 1.83.

Carbon	90.02
Volatile matter	2.68
Water	2.20
Ash	5.10
	100.00

XII. Coal from Tatung, in Shansi. Clean black, moderately hard, bituminous, coking coal. Decrepitates slightly. Specific gravity, 1.30.

Carbon	65.30
Volatile matter	28.69
Water	1.47
Ash	4.54
	100.00

XIII. Coal from Douy (island of Sagalien). Clear black, bituminous, coking coal. Specific gravity, 1.31.

Carbon	67.51
Volatile matter	22.98
Water	3.51
Ash	6.00
	100.00

XIV. Coal from Iwanai (island of Yesso). Clear, smooth, black or brownish coal. Gives off HO, and cokes in a closed tube. Specific gravity, 1.26.

Carbon	60.26
Volatile matter	29.72
Water	2.30
Ash	7.72
	100.00

XV. Yingwo mine (Fangshan, southwest of Peking). Soft, crumbling anthracite. Yields considerable HO, in a closed tube. Specific gravity.

Carbon	77.58
Volatile matter	3.63
Water	2.50
Ash	16.29
	100.00

APPENDIX V.

Statistics of the Private Gold Placers of the Province of Trans-Baikal—1843-1863.

Years of Working	Amount of Auriferous Sands Washed in Cubic "Sashens." 1 cubic sashen—12·67 cubic yards.	Amount of Sands Washed in "Poudes." 1 Poude—36·10 lbs. avoirdupois.	Quantity of Gold Dust Extracted.				Average Amount of Gold Dust per 100 Poudes of Auriferous Sands.		Number of Men Employed.	Number and Kind of Washing Machines.					Royalty Claimed by Government.		Additional Tax for covering the Expenses of the Government Mining Administration.	
			Poudes.	Funds.	Solothniks.	Dolias.	Solothniks.	Dolias.		Botchka.	Butara.	Chasha.	Broza.	Amerikanka.	Rubles.	Kopeks.	Rubles.	Kop.
1843.	⅓	485	..	.	1	36½	..	27⅜	..	..	..	..	..	..	.	..	..	..
1844.	33½	40,321	..	1	95	78	..	91⅜	..	..	..	..	..	..	361	92¼	15	81
1845.	283¼	339,911	..	25	65	58	..	72¼	390	3	2	..	..	..	2,415	50½	106	73
1846.	1,838¾	2,206,564	4	35	94	27	..	82¼	721	6	7	..	..	..	17,831	76½	916	76
1847.	5,854⅙	7,024,983	16	37	1	79½	..	88¾	1,711	18	13	..	..	..	61,287	14¾	2,174	6¾
1848.	7,366	8,839,310	23	36	45	76	1	3⅝	1,147	20	5	1	..	..	86,244	26	5,785	99
1849.	8,953⅓	10,744,277½	26	4	23	18	..	89½	1,285	19	9	3	..	..	38,775	60	5,342	60
1850.	11,869¾	14,243,760½	32	9	50	76¾	..	83½	1,586	15	6	4	4	..	47,454	72	6,665	30
1851.	10,250⅝	12,305,761	23	35	60	72½	..	71¼	974	8	3	3	2	..	25,955	28	4,080	30
1852.	11,036½	13,243,838	23	8	32	54¾	..	66½	1,276	12	5	5	3	..	30,301	58½	4,641	52
1853.	10,081⅜	12,097,867	23	17	59	67¼	..	71½	1,091	4	4	7	4	..	35,869	87½	4,902	80½
1854.	9,571¼	11,485,420	18	29	45	30	..	60¾	685	5	2	6	4	..	24,820	69¾	3,651	48¼
1855.	9,440	11,328,054	17	..	34	75¾	..	55½	632	7	..	3	..	..	24,859	55	4,726	74½
1856.	8,811¼	10,573,568	8	25	20	7	..	30	815	8	2	3	1	..	9,046	72	2,191	64
1857.	6,102⅜	7,322,821	12	38	30	14½	..	65¼	813	5	..	4	1	..	11,272	97	2,529	56
1858.	17,705	21,246,052	31	31	61	6	..	55⅛	1,510	8	8	5	3	..	25,759	11½	7,131	75½
1859.	25,810¼	30,974,842	59	8	31	24	..	70½	2,224	9	..	5	9	..	62,540	95¾	15,817	97¼
1860.	28,622¼	34,347,594	101	18	40	86½	1	15⅜	2,776	15	3	2	7	1	132,480	97¼	28,742	45
1861.	34,713¼	41,655,986	118	8	30	89½	1	8½	3,006	19	7	3	3	..	151,395	29½	34,614	80
1862.	40,232⅓	48,278,618	147	29	78	79	1	16¾	3,382	26	2	..	5	..	200,817	..	43,819	3½
Total from 1843 to 1863 (exclusive).	327,015¼ = 4,143,280 cub. yds.	392,191,342 = 7,079,053 tons.	905	1	32	42½ = 39,703·7772 lbs. Troy.	..	85 — 323 grains per ton — 551 gr. per cub. yd.	33,347	244	89	70	66	1	1,213,444	95¼	233,052	6¼

Remarks.

The royalty and additional tax are only very approximate.

Experience has shown that the mean fineness of the Gold of this district is 85·96ths.

1 Poude=40 Funds.

1 Fund=96 Solothniks.

1 Solothnik=96 Dolias.

A Botchka is a revolving perforated cylinder.

A Butara is an inclined trough with a perforated iron plate at its upper end much like a *fixed* "rocker."

A Chasha is a basin with a flat iron bottom, round and about 10 feet diameter, in which the gravel and stones are separated from the clay by revolving arms that radiate horizontally from a vertical shaft in the centre of the basin.

Botchka is used for very sandy pay dirt, and the Chasha for clayey material.

The tailings must not contain more than 12 Dolias, average per 100 Poudes of tailings.

INDEX.

D

L

M

N

O

T